# Language and the Joint Creation of Knowledge

In the **World Library of Educationalists series**, international experts themselves compile career-long collections of what they judge to be their finest pieces – extracts from books, key articles, salient research findings, major theoretical and practical contributions – so the world can read them in a single manageable volume. Readers will be able to follow the themes and strands and see how their work contributes to the development of the field.

*Language and the Joint Creation of Knowledge* draws on the most prominent writing of Neil Mercer, covering his ground-breaking and critically acclaimed work on the role of talk in education, and on the relationship between spoken language and cognition.

The text explores key themes, relating theoretical ideas to research evidence and to practical educational situations that improve children's lives. Offering students and researchers a clear, accessible and up-to-date account of a sociocultural perspective on the relationship between spoken language and cognition, it explains one of the key themes in Neil Mercer's work – that humans have uniquely evolved the capacity to think together, or 'interthink'.

Offering a crucial insight into the work of Neil Mercer, this selection showcases why his approach has become the dominant paradigm in educational research, and why it is increasingly influential in the psychology of teaching and learning. This unique collection of published articles and chapters, which represent the key themes and range of his research over the last 40 years, will be of interest to all followers of his work and any reader interested in the role of language in education.

**Neil Mercer** is Emeritus Professor of Education at the University of Cambridge, where he is also the Director of Oracy Cambridge: the Hughes Hall Centre for Effective Spoken Communication and a Life Fellow of the college Hughes Hall. He is a psychologist with particular interests in the use of talk for thinking collectively, the development of children's spoken language abilities, and the role of teachers in that development. He has worked extensively and internationally with teachers, researchers and educational policy makers.

# World Library of Educationalists series

**Education, Ethnicity, Society and Global Change in Asia**
The Selected Works of Gerard A. Postiglione
*Gerard A. Postiglione*

**Leading Learning/Learning Leading: A Retrospective on a Life's Work**
The Selected Works of Robert J. Starratt
*Robert J. Starratt*

**Communicative Competence, Classroom Interaction, and Educational Equity**
The Selected Works of Courtney B. Cazden
*Courtney B. Cazden*

**Ideological, Cultural, and Linguistic Roots of Educational Reforms to Address the Ecological Crisis**
The Selected Works of C. A. (Chet) Bowers
*C. A. Bowers*

**Religious Education in Plural Societies**
The Selected Works of Robert Jackson
*Robert Jackson*

**Thinking Philosophically About Education**
The Selected Works of Richard Pring
*Richard Pring*

**Language and the Joint Creation of Knowledge**
The Selected Works of Neil Mercer
*Neil Mercer*

For more information on this series, visit: www.routledge.com/World-Library-of-Educationalists/book-series/WORLDLIBEDU

# Language and the Joint Creation of Knowledge
## The Selected Works of Neil Mercer

Neil Mercer

Routledge
Taylor & Francis Group

LONDON AND NEW YORK

First published 2019 by Routledge

2 Park Square, Milton Park, Abingdon, Oxfordshire OX14 4RN
52 Vanderbilt Avenue, New York, NY 10017

*Routledge is an imprint of the Taylor & Francis Group, an informa business*

First issued in paperback 2019

*British Library Cataloguing-in-Publication Data*
A catalogue record for this book is available from the British Library

*Library of Congress Cataloging-in-Publication Data*
Names: Mercer, Neil, author.
Title: Language and the joint creation of knowledge : the selected
   works of Neil Mercer / Neil Mercer.
Description: Abingdon, Oxon ; New York, NY : Routledge, 2019. |
   Includes bibliographical references.
Identifiers: LCCN 2018054750 | ISBN 9780367002077 (hbk) |
   ISBN 9780429400759 (ebk)
Subjects: LCSH: Communication in education. | Interaction
   analysis in education. | Learning, Psychology of. | Teacher-student
   relationships.
Classification: LCC LB1033.5 .M3825 2019 | DDC 371.102/2—dc23
LC record available at https://lccn.loc.gov/2018054750

ISBN: 978-0-367-36748-0

Typeset in Sabon
by Apex CoVantage, LLC

# Contents

# Acknowledgements

Chapter 1, 'Community language and education', by N. Mercer and J. Maybin, originally appeared in N. Mercer (ed.), *Language in School and Community*, London: Edward Arnold, 1981, pp. 77–95.

Chapter 2, 'Researching Common Knowledge: investigating the development of shared understanding in the classroom', by N. Mercer, originally appeared in G. Walford (ed.), *Doing Educational Research*, London: Routledge, 1991, pp. 41–58.

Chapter 3, 'The quality of talk in children's collaborative activity in the classroom', by N. Mercer, originally appeared in the special issue 'Co-operation and social context in adult-child interaction', *Learning and Instruction* (Elsevier), 6, 4 (1996), 359–378.

Chapter 4, 'Laying the foundations', originally appeared as Chapter 2 in N. Mercer, *Words and Minds: How we Use Language to Think Together*, London: Routledge, 2000, pp. 16–45.

Chapter 5, 'Language for teaching a language', by N. Mercer, originally appeared in C.N. Candlin and N. Mercer (eds), *English Language Teaching in its Social Context*, London: Routledge, 2001, pp. 244–257.

Chapter 6, 'Developing dialogues', by N. Mercer, originally appeared in G. Wells and G. Claxton (eds), *Learning for Life in the 21st Century: Sociocultural Perspectives on the Future of Education*, Oxford: Blackwell, 2002, pp. 141–153.

Chapter 7, 'Reasoning as a scientist: ways of helping children to use language to learn science', by N. Mercer, R. Dawes, R. Wegerif and C. Sams, originally appeared in *British Educational Research Journal* (Carfax Publishing), 30, 3 (2004), 367–385.

Chapter 8, 'Sociocultural discourse analysis: analysing classroom talk as a social mode of thinking', by N. Mercer, originally appeared in *Journal of Applied Linguistics* (Equinox Publishing), 1, 2 (2005), 137–168.

Chapter 9, 'The seeds of time: why classroom dialogue needs a temporal analysis', by N. Mercer, originally appeared in *Journal of the Learning Sciences* (Routledge), 17, 1 (2008), 33–59.

Chapter 10, 'The analysis of classroom talk: methods and methodologies', by N. Mercer, originally appeared in *British Journal of Educational Psychology* (Wiley), 80 (2009), 1–14.

Chapter 11, 'Dialogic teaching in the primary science classroom', by N. Mercer, L. Dawes and J. Kleine Staarman, originally appeared in *Language and Education* (Taylor and Francis), *23*, 4 (2009), 1–17.

Chapter 12, 'Using interactive whiteboards to orchestrate classroom dialogue', by N. Mercer, S. Hennessy and P. Warwick, originally appeared in *Technology, Pedagogy and Education* (Taylor and Francis), *19*, 2 (2010), 195–209.

Chapter 13, 'The social brain, language, and goal-directed collective thinking: a social conception of cognition and its implications for understanding how we think, teach, and learn', by N. Mercer, originally appeared in *Educational Psychologist* (Routledge), *48*, 3 (2013), 148–168.

Chapter 14, 'Classroom talk and the development of self-regulation and metacognition', by N. Mercer, originally appeared in D. Whitebread, N. Mercer, C. Howe and A. Tolmie (eds), *Self-Regulation and Dialogue in Primary Classrooms* (Leicester: British Psychological Society), BJEP Monograph Series II, *10* (2013), 1–24.

Chapter 15, 'The study of talk between teachers and students, from the 1970s until the 2010s', by N. Mercer and L. Dawes, originally appeared in *Oxford Review of Education* (Routledge), *40*, 4 (2014), 430–445.

Chapter 16, 'Dialogue, thinking together and digital technology in the classroom: some educational implications of a continuing line of inquiry', by N. Mercer, S. Hennessy and P. Warwick, originally appeared in *International Journal of Educational Research* (2017). http://dx.doi.org/10.1016/j.ijer.2017.08.007.

Chapter 17, 'An oracy assessment toolkit: Linking research and development in the assessment of students' spoken language skills at age 11-12', by N. Mercer, P. Warwick, and A. Ahmed, originally appeared in Learning and Instruction (*Elsevier*), 48, 51–60.

# Introduction

## The organisation of the book

The pieces of writing that make up this book have been arranged chronologically. Their sequence therefore represents, in many ways, the development of my thinking about the topics they deal with, as well as the historical sequence of the various projects which generated them. Most of my research has been on talk in classrooms, and that includes the talk of both teachers and their students. One of my main aims has been to understand how we use spoken language as a tool for carrying out teaching-and-learning; the complex, interactive process for which we lack a precise and accurate term in English. I have also tried to understand how schools can develop children's skills in using spoken language for communicating and reasoning. That has included an interest in educational uses of information technology. I see myself as an applied researcher who wants to provide insights and evidence which can inform educational practice and policy. In that pursuit, I have inevitably also become concerned with how such applied research is best pursued: that is, with research methodology. Underpinning all those topics, as a psychologist I have a general interest in the relationship between language and cognition, and specifically in how people use language to think collectively, creatively and productively. All of this is represented in the chapters which follow.

## A personal history

I have been interested in the relationship between talk and thinking for almost as long as I can remember. When I was a child, my family moved to live about 100 miles north in England, from southern Lancashire to northwestern Cumbria. Not far, one might think, but Lancashire and Cumbria were (and still are, to some extent) very different places with distinctive histories, dialects and accents. I found my new schoolmates often used other words and expressions from those I had learned, and they sometimes found the way I spoke hilarious. In Lancashire it rained 'hard', but in Cumbria it rained 'fast' – a different way of thinking about it. Lancastrian children went 'wom' (home) after school, while Cumbrians went 'yam'. School life also made me realise that spoken language had distinct social domains, with their boundaries policed quite strongly by adults. Dialect and slang were fine in the playground, but not to be used in the classroom. In class, all communications had to go via the teacher; you didn't ask other pupils questions. The legacy of my early interests can be seen in Chapter 1, 'Community language and education', which I wrote with an Open University colleague, the social anthropologist Janet Maybin. My grammar school education was thought provoking, and discomforting, in other ways too. Sometimes I succeeded very well academically, but other times I did not, though I could not always understand why: teachers at that time rarely provided targeted feedback. That experience gave me a personal interest in the ways and extent that teachers and students develop a shared understanding of the educational process.

I had to re-sit my A levels, having spent too many late nights out playing the guitar and mandolin. Looking around then for a subject to study at university, I discovered psychology through the popular books of Hans Eysenck (who I met once, though I was too overawed to say anything much). I have never regretted choosing to study it, despite my school physics teacher warning me that it sounded 'a bit airy-fairy!' In my final year as an undergraduate student at Manchester I began research on spontaneous speech and continued do so through a PhD in psycholinguistics at Leicester. Although I enjoyed that work, when I completed my doctorate I knew that I did not want to continue as a laboratory-bound researcher. A key influence was a book called *The Psychology of Language and Instruction* (de Cecco, 1967) – still within reach on a shelf behind me – a wonderful compilation of works by such eminent figures as Lev Vygotsky, Jean Piaget, Benjamin Whorf, Noam Chomsky, Susan Ervin-Tripp, Dell Hymes, Roger Brown and Jean Berko. But it was probably the work of Douglas Barnes (1971), Basil Bernstein (1971) and Jerome Bruner (1971) which convinced me that the most interesting and useful research might be done in the real world of the classroom. As both a teacher and learner, I felt that I still knew very little about the process of teaching-and-learning, and why it sometimes went well or badly – even if those involved were quite motivated. I also became interested in the broader issue of how spoken language is used to create shared knowledge and understanding. In the everyday talk of classrooms, knowledge gets constructed, presented, received, rejected, evaluated, understood and misunderstood. People's life chances may be affected by the outcomes. A careful examination of how this is done should tell us something of psychological interest and practical educational value.

By 1980 I was working at the Open University (OU), where I gained my first major educational research grant with Derek Edwards, a social psychologist at Loughborough University who has had a big influence on my conception of the relationship between language and cognition (see Edwards, 1997). That work, which also involved Janet Maybin, is described in Chapter 2 of this book, 'Researching Common Knowledge'. I worked with enjoyment for many years at the OU, where I was the only psychologist in the Centre for Language and Communications; my colleagues, such as Joan Swann and Barbara Mayor, were mainly linguists. Linguistics has therefore had quite a profound impact on how I think about language and do research, not least in the realisation that while forms of language are related to language functions, they do not define them. I also became involved in researching the teaching and learning of second languages, as described in Chapter 5, 'Language for teaching a language'. But I retained a general interest in the special, social nature of human cognition, as represented in the early part of the book by Chapter 4, 'Laying the foundations', and by the work I carried out with another OU psychologist, Karen Littleton.

The relationship between language use and the development of reasoning was an important strand of the rationale for the *Thinking Together* research and pedagogy which Rupert Wegerif (who was then a PhD student), Lyn Dawes (my wife, then a primary school teacher) and I developed in the late 1980s (Dawes, Mercer and Wegerif, 2000). Internationally, I worked closely with Sylvia Rojas-Drummond and her colleagues at the National Autonomous University of Mexico (Rojas-Drummond and Mercer, 2004). Our work focused on developing children's use of talk as a tool for reasoning together; a topic which seemed to have been given surprisingly little direct attention. It figures in Chapters 6 'Developing dialogues', and 7, 'Reasoning as a scientist'.

## Language and cognition

When I moved to Cambridge in 2005, I found myself in a research group of psychologists, some of whom (such as David Whitebread) were studying cognitive development in the early years and others (such as Christine Howe and Linda Hargreaves) who had done important work on collaborative learning. This reignited my interest in the relationship between language and cognitive development, and the results are Chapters 13, 'The social brain, language, and goal-directed collective thinking' and 14, 'Classroom talk and the development of self-regulation and metacognition'.

## Computers and talk in school

Another theme which has intermittently figured in my research is the use of computers to stimulate and resource children's collaborative discussions. This really began in the late 1980s with a project called Spoken Language and New Technology (SLANT). Our team included researchers from the University of East Anglia (Maggie McLure, Terry Phillips and John Elliot), as well as Peter Scrimshaw and Eunice Fisher from the OU. That research is described in Chapter 3, 'The quality of talk in children's collaborative activity in the classroom'. Working with Rupert Wegerif and Lyn Dawes (both more technologically able than me) drew me further into research on the use of computers in the classroom, as described in Chapter 7; and I became involved in similar research again at Cambridge, with Sara Hennessy, Paul Warwick and Ruth Kershner. Our joint work is represented by Chapter 16, 'Dialogue, thinking together and digital technology in the classroom'.

## Research methods

Chapters 2, 8, 9 and 10 deal with research methodology. My PhD used both qualitative and quantitative research methods, and I have generally favoured a 'mixed methods' approach. Whilst wanting to maintain a close focus on the ways talk was used in classroom interactions, I became convinced – mainly by Rupert Wegerif – that if we wanted to have an impact on educational policy makers, we would need to show how certain ways of using talk were related, statistically, to positive educational outcomes. This meant demonstrating that children's scores improved on some formal assessment of subject learning and/or some more general capacity such as reasoning (as described in Chapter 7). Such a methodological approach figures in some way in many chapters, but is described most explicitly in Chapter 8, 'Socio-cultural discourse analysis', and Chapter 10, 'The analysis of classroom talk'. Chapter 9, 'The seeds of time', focuses on one of my special interests, the temporal nature of the process of teaching and learning.

## Dialogic teaching

Two educational aspects of talk are dealt with in this book. One aspect is the use of talk for classroom teaching. The other is the development of children's skills in using spoken language. These educational aspects of talk are like two sides of a coin, in that they can be considered separately but are essentially inseparable. I will discuss each in turn, because confusion between them has created problems, not least in discussions between researchers and policy makers. The importance of distinguishing them has only become apparent to me quite recently, and so it is not made explicit in some of my work included here.

The first aspect concerns teachers' use of talk as the main 'tool of their trade'. There is quite a long history of observational research on teachers' use of talk, as Lyn Dawes and I describe in Chapter 15, 'The study of talk between teachers and students'. In recent years this has crystallised in the promotion of a pedagogic approach called 'dialogic teaching'. Strongly associated with the work of researchers such as Phil Scott (2008), Robin Alexander (2008), Martin Nystrand (1997), Lauren Resnick (Resnick, Asterhan and Clarke, 2015) and Gordon Wells (1999), dialogic teaching is concerned with ensuring that talk is used effectively for educational purposes. My involvement with research on that topic is represented most explicitly by Chapter 11, 'Dialogic teaching in the primary science classroom', which emerged from a research project I co-directed with Phil Scott. Proponents of a dialogic approach to classroom education argue that students, as well as teachers, need to be actively using talk to construct an understanding of curriculum content. That contrasts with a view of classroom education as a process in which curriculum content should be transmitted by a teacher talking to an attentive, but generally silent, class of students. The latter view underpins the considerable resistance to dialogic teaching by those attached to more traditional pedagogies, who use the apparent effectiveness of teaching methods employed in other countries such as China to support their opposition. Those 'traditionalists' may also claim that dialogic proponents are arguing for a 'progressive' pedagogy in which pupils are allowed to talk as much as they like, while teachers avoid direct instruction and instead 'facilitate' children's self-directed learning. That is simply not the case.

It is unfortunate that discussions about teacher talk in the press and social media often portray the field of pedagogy as a battle between 'traditional' and 'progressive' approaches. Journalists like simple dichotomies, but as researchers – and educators – we should be wary of them. It is worth noting that there have been no systematic studies of teaching, either small or large scale, which support the view that maintaining a traditional, 'monologic', instructional approach helps students achieve the best results, or that pursuing a highly progressive, non-instructional, student-led approach does so either. In fact, the reasonable conclusion to draw from the available research evidence is that the most beneficial outcomes occur when practitioners achieve a strategic balance in their teaching between authoritative instruction and more equitable dialogue. That balance, in my view, is what 'dialogic teaching' should be seen to represent.

It is certainly the case, however, that research support for dialogic teaching has relied on accumulated evidence from many relatively small-scale studies. But at the time of writing two large-scale projects have just been completed. One was carried out by Robin Alexander and Frank and Jan Hardman at the University of York (Alexander, 2018),[1] and the other by Christine Howe, Sara Hennessy and myself with other colleagues at Cambridge (Howe, Hennessy, Mercer, Vrikki, & Wheatley, 2019).[2] These have provided evidence from the analysis of substantial sets of classroom data, with each involving more than 70 British primary teachers. The results of both projects support the view that what teachers do with talk makes a difference to students' learning. For example, in our research we found that children in Year 6 (aged about 11) whose teachers frequently involved many members of their class in dialogue and also encouraged them to elaborate their ideas gained better results in mathematics and English than those of teachers who did not. High levels of elaboration were also linked to children's more positive attitudes to education. The York study showed similar and other benefits for children's attainment in Year 5 when their teachers were trained to be more 'dialogic', compared with teachers who followed their usual practices. We therefore now have substantial research evidence in support of a dialogic approach to teaching.

## Oracy education

In the late 1980s, while at the OU, I became involved with the National Oracy Project – a government funded scheme which encouraged schools throughout the UK to recognise and celebrate the spoken language of children, in all its richness and diversity. If that had been its sole aim, it could certainly be judged successful. But it also had the aim of giving the study of spoken language more pride of place in the school curriculum. That aim, regretfully, was stymied in the UK in the early 1990s by a 'back to basics' government agenda. Even the word 'oracy', coined by the educational researcher Andrew Wilkinson in the 1960s with the aim of giving spoken language skills some parity with literacy skills, fell into disuse.

'Oracy' came alive again for me in 2011 when Lyn Dawes and I were invited to meet representatives of *School 21* – Peter Hyman, Oli de Botton and, later, Ed Fidoe – whose new school in the east end of London was going to develop an 'oracy-led curriculum'. To their immense credit, they did just that. Working with them and other organisations, such as the English Speaking Union, and through the establishment of the study centre *Oracy Cambridge*[3] at the Cambridge college Hughes Hall, my colleagues and I have since made a collective effort to put oracy back on the mainstream educational agenda (see, for example, ESU, 2016). At the time of writing, it seems that the teaching of spoken language skills is becoming recognised as a curriculum subject in its own right, on a par with literacy and numeracy. There is a growing interest amongst teachers (and occupational trainers) in how oracy can be taught and learned most effectively. There is also a gradually increasing recognition by politicians and policy makers, internationally, that oracy must be included in the '21st century skills' that young people need and which education systems should promote.

Discussions of oracy often focus on presentational, public speaking skills as used in making speeches and taking part in debates; but using talk to work effectively with others in a group is also a key aspect of oracy. Listening skills are an important aspect of spoken communication too, though they are often overlooked. For example, the *Oxford English Dictionary* defines oracy simply as 'the ability to express oneself fluently and grammatically in speech'; but the ability to listen attentively to an interlocutor or presenter, or to consider the needs of an audience, is also an important feature of effective spoken communication. A concern with developing children's spoken language awareness and their ability to use talk to work well in groups figures in several of the chapters of this book, but especially in the work I have done with Rupert Wegerif, Lyn Dawes, Karen Littleton, Christine Howe and others including Sylvia Rojas-Drummond, Claire Sams and Judith Kleine Staarman. Reports of this work can be found in Chapters 7 and 11. Chapter 17, 'An Oracy Assessment Toolkit', describes some of the recent work I have carried out with my Cambridge colleagues Ayesha Ahmed and Paul Warwick.

## An important distinction

Though both concepts are important, I feel that conflating dialogic teaching and oracy education may be hindering some potentially valuable educational reforms, as I can explain from my own experience from a few years ago. In the early 2000s, I was one of several researchers trying to influence the outcomes of the reform of the National Curriculum for primary schools in England (the statutory guidance on what children should be taught). We met with significant opposition from some politicians in our attempts to maintain and enhance what was then called 'Speaking and Listening' in the English curriculum. We were arguing that oracy skills should be directly taught, as was already the case for reading and writing skills. Although in the end we achieved some success, it was only with hindsight that I realised that a substantial aspect of the opposition arose from the misconception that we were arguing for dialogic teaching rather than oracy education. Our opponents had claimed that we were talking about pedagogy rather than curriculum content. They thought we were arguing for certain ways of using talk for teaching, not for what children should be taught; and pedagogy (as opposed to curriculum content) fell outside the remit of the National Curriculum. That alone obstructed our efforts; but because they took a 'traditional' perspective on teaching, our opponents were also wary of anything that seemed like 'progressive education', which is how they saw dialogic teaching. Their confusion was understandable, perhaps, given that some oracy advocates also argue in support of dialogic teaching – but the distinction is important. *Oracy education* is the direct, explicit teaching of speaking and listening skills as part of the curriculum, comparable to, say, the direct, explicit teaching of algebraic skills as part of mathematics. *Dialogic teaching* is the use of the best, evidence-based talk strategies for teaching any subject, whether it be maths, history, English, a second language, sport, oracy or whatever. Of course, the case for each gives a special emphasis to the educational importance of talk which is lacking in both traditional curricula and traditional pedagogies; and dialogic teaching certainly requires teachers to have good oracy skills. But the case for each depends on a different evidence base and involves different changes in policy and practice. Confusion may make the promoting and uptake of either, or both, more difficult.

## Language and collective thinking outside the classroom

I have a strong interest in how people use talk for thinking together, not just in school but in life in general – for example, in the world of work, in the arts and in higher education. At one level, my motivation is theoretical: to generate a better understanding of the essentially social nature of human cognition, and of the role of language in its evolutionary development and functioning. At another level, it is practical; to help us to use language most effectively to share information, guide learning, develop joint understanding, critically evaluate ideas and find creative solutions to life's burning issues. My strong belief, based on the available evidence, is that the most successful, creative human endeavours depend on the collaboration of two or more people. The idea that the highest achievements in science, art and other pursuits arise from the efforts of lone geniuses who transcend the constraints of collective thinking is a myth – and a dangerously misleading one, if we want to understand and encourage creativity. This has been well argued by Vera John-Steiner (2006) and Keith Sawyer (2012); and my daughter Anna Mercer (2016, in press) has demonstrated it through her research on the writers Mary Shelley and Percy Bysshe Shelley. I discuss such ideas in Chapter 4, 'Laying the foundations', and Chapter 13, 'The social brain . . .'. Collective creativity was a major theme in the book *Interthinking*, which I wrote with Karen Littleton (Littleton and Mercer, 2013); it has also figured significantly in my work in another way. The applied aspect of my research, and especially its dissemination to teachers, has depended enormously on my collaboration with my wife, Lyn Dawes (with whom I have presented hundreds of professional development sessions). Several of the chapters of this book have been written with co-authors; and, indeed, the whole of my research career since my PhD has been a journey of joint endeavour. Institutional culture has helped: the OU was based on the concept of the 'course team', and Cambridge is a marvellously collaborative place to work. Much of what I have learned about the relationship between language and collective thinking has arisen through the contributions of the co-authors represented here, and of many other colleagues as well. The Doctoral and Masters students I have supervised have been a strong influence, often drawing me in to considering topics and methods I would probably not have engaged with otherwise. Many of my students have been schoolteachers, members of a profession for which I have the greatest respect and admiration; and working with teachers in research projects and professional development courses has constantly reminded me of the importance of pursuing practical, useful outcomes in educational research.

## Notes

1   https://educationendowmentfoundation.org.uk/projects-and-evaluation/projects/dialogic-teaching
2   www.educ.cam.ac.uk/research/projects/classroomdialogue
3   https://oracycambridge.org

## References

Alexander, R. (2008). *Towards Dialogic Teaching: Rethinking Classroom Talk*. Cambridge: Dialogos.
Alexander, R. (2018). Developing dialogic teaching: Genesis, process, trial. *Research Papers in Education*. https://doi.org/10.1080/02671522.2018.1481140

Barnes, D. (1971). Language in the Secondary Classroom. In D. Barnes, J. Britton and H. Rosen (Eds.), *Language, the Learner and the School*. Harmondsworth: Penguin.

Bernstein, B. (1971). *Class, Codes and Control*, Vol. 1. London: Routledge & Kegan Paul.

Bruner, J. (1971). *The Relevance of Education*. Harmondsworth: Penguin.

Dawes, L., Mercer, N. and Wegerif, R. (2000). *Thinking Together: Activities for Teachers and Children at Key Stage 2*. Birmingham: Questions Publishing Co.

De Cecco, J. P. (Ed.). (1967). *The Psychology of Language, Thought, and Instruction: Readings*. New York: Holt, Rinehart & Winston.

Edwards, D. (1997). *Discourse and Cognition*. London: Sage.

ESU. (2016). *Speaking Frankly: The Case for Oracy in the Curriculum*. London: English-Speaking Union.

Howe, C., Hennessy, S., Mercer, N., Vrikki, M., & Wheatley, L. (2019) Teacher-student dialogue during classroom teaching: Does it really impact upon student outcomes? *The Journal of the Learning Sciences*. doi:10.1080/10508406.2019.1573730

John-Steiner, V. (2006). *Creative Collaboration*, 2nd edn. New York: Oxford University Press.

Littleton, K., & Mercer, N. (2013). *Interthinking: Putting Talk to Work*. Abingdon: Routledge.

Mercer, A. (2016). Beyond *Frankenstein*: The Collaborative Literary Relationship of Percy Bysshe and Mary Shelley. *The Keats-Shelley Review*, *30*, 1, 80–85.

Mercer, A. (in press). *The Collaborative Literary Relationship of Percy Bysshe Shelley and Mary Wollstonecraft Shelley*. Abingdon: Routledge.

Nystrand, M. (1997). *Opening Dialogue: Understanding the Dynamics of Language and Learning in the English Classroom*. New York: Teachers College Press.

Resnick, L. B., Asterhan, C. S. C., & Clarke, S. N. (2015). Talk, Learning and Teaching. In L. B. Resnick, C. S. C. Asterhan & S. N. Clarke (Eds.), *Socializing Intelligence Through Academic Talk and Dialogue*. Washington, DC: American Educational Research Association.

Rojas-Drummond, S., & Mercer, N. (2004). Scaffolding the development of effective collaboration and learning. *International Journal of Educational Research*, *39*, 99–111.

Sawyer, R. K. (2012). *Explaining Creativity: The Science of Human Innovation*, 2nd edn. New York: Oxford University Press.

Scott, P. (2008). Talking a Way to Understanding in Science Classrooms. In N. Mercer & S. Hodgkinson (Eds.), *Exploring Talk in School*. London: Sage.

Wells, G. (1999). *Dialogic Inquiry: Towards a Sociocultural Practice and Theory of Education*. Cambridge: Cambridge University Press.

*As I explain in the Introduction to this book, I was drawn into the study of language in school through my experiences as a child; and this is reflected in the contents of this piece, which I wrote with Janet Maybin not very long after I had joined her at the Open University. Despite it being written almost three decades ago, I am sorry to say that misconceptions and prejudices about the relationship between the languages of school and community, as discussed in this article, are still rife (in the UK at least). Just a month before writing this, I read in the national British press that some teachers with northern accents (like my own) were being told by their managers that they ought to 'lose' them in the interests of professional development.*

# 1 Community language and education

*Mercer, N. & Maybin, J. (1981). Community language and education. In N. Mercer (ed.),* Language in School and Community. *London: Edward Arnold, pp. 77–95.*

## Introduction

Children have already begun to communicate with the people around them before they learn their first word. And when they do begin to speak and listen, they do so in the context of existing social relationships which are vital for their developing self-identity. Learning to use language means using it to relate to the people who matter, and this means being sensitive not only to what is said, but how it is expressed and the effect it has on the people who hear it. In the earliest years of life, of course, relationships with parents and immediate family are the strongest influences on language behaviour; later on, relationships with others, like friends and teachers, may become important.

The acquisition of a first language is the acquisition of a particular kind of social experience. And even within one small nation like Britain this experience is open to enormous variety. Factors such as the family's geographical and social background and the strength of different social relationships which are formed in the community determine the kind of English (or other mother-tongue) that we acquire and the ways we will use it. What is more, such social factors not only determine the ways we speak, they influence our attitudes to the ways other people use language and inevitably our feelings about the speakers themselves.

There is nothing new in pointing out that English is spoken in many different ways, or that 'it is impossible for an Englishman to open his mouth without making some other Englishman despise him' (G. B. Shaw). What is relatively new, however, is the realization that attitudes to language variation are a controversial educational issue.

If in the past there was very little educational debate about language variation, this was because interest in regional accents and dialects of English in schools was almost entirely concerned with how to eliminate them and assert the supremacy of the 'Queen's English', which was assumed to be the only language appropriate for educational endeavours. As this assumption, like many other conventional wisdoms, has been questioned now by many people involved in education, those concerned with classroom practice have had to ask themselves: if what was going on wasn't right, what should be done instead? Faced with this problem, the classroom teacher will find few ready answers. The less value-laden accounts of language variation offered in recent years by linguists like William Labov (1972) do not, in themselves, generate a school language policy.

In the gap between theory and practice which quite clearly exists in this area, enormous confusion has arisen. This reveals itself in many ways; in misconceptions about the nature of language variation, what it means in terms of children's experience in their school and elsewhere in their community, how it affects teachers' attitudes and how it relates to justifiable educational aims and ideals. One of our concerns in recent years has been to collaborate with teachers in exploring and classifying the practical classroom implications of language variation (see, in particular, Mercer and Edwards, 1979). Our intention in this chapter is to set out some kind of conceptual framework for handling the issues involved.[1]

Our discussion in this chapter rests on the truth of certain statements about language and education which we feel have now been sufficiently well established to be taken as given. One is that there are no 'primitive' or 'inadequate' languages or language varieties; if the speech of any social group is regarded as 'inferior', this is understandable in terms of the social status of that group and the social values of society, not through linguistic analysis. The other is that educational values, and not least those implicit in the 'hidden curriculum' of daily classroom life, inevitably reflect the broader social values and established interests of the dominant social groups or classes of society. This does not mean that we think that education cannot be a force for social change, as we believe it can and should generate a basis for constructive social criticism. Any useful discussion of language variation and education, however, must take account of the real constraints within which teachers and schoolchildren operate. What we intended to do here, working from these basic assumptions, is to look at the nature of language variation itself, to consider its implications for social life in and out of school, and to try to interpret these implications in terms of classroom practice.

## The nature of language variation

The kinds of language variation which concern us most here are four: *language*, *accent*, *dialect* and *register*. Variation in terms of different *languages* is, of course, the most obvious of these to appear to present educational problems. If a child at home speaks a mother-tongue very different from the language at school, then a teacher might well expect this to create communication problems of a different order than for children speaking the same language in and out of school. The problems of bilingual children are, however, relevant to us here in that these problems will not be entirely, or even predominantly, linguistic. The language of their home, and the culture of the ethnic group of which they are members, will itself have a status or value in society, and they will be aware of this. Although our discussion will mainly focus on variation within the English language, many of the points we raise will have equal relevance to bilingual children in British schools.

*Accent* refers to the different ways people pronounce the same language. (This may involve differences in intonation patterns and rate of speech, as well as the pronunciation of specific words.) Everyone has an accent of some kind; if we say that someone from Durham has 'lost his Geordie accent' we really mean that he has found another one – probably the non-regional 'BBC' accent known as RP (Received Pronunciation).

The term *dialect* refers to the natural variation in grammar and vocabulary that exists between local forms of the same language in different regions, or as spoken by different social groups. Of course, different accents and dialects do 'go together', but they are not inevitably and inseparably combined. The whole of a BBC news bulletin could be read out in a broad Geordie, Belfast or Cockney accent, while remaining in the same Standard English dialect in which it was written. Likewise, one could, in the pursuit of eccentric art, read out the dialect poems of Robert Burns or Linton Kwesi Johnson in an RP accent – they would still contain lowland Scots or Creole words and constructions.

The fourth kind of variation is that in terms of *register*. By this we mean the different kinds of language which are conventionally used in different kinds of social situations.[2] The relative formality of an occasion, for example, usually influences the kind of language used. In formal public meetings it is normal to hear people saying things like: 'With all due respect, Mr Chairman, I feel it is necessary to point out that this is not the case . . .' In a discussion amongst friends in a pub, that kind of language would, to say the least, seem odd. You might, however, hear someone say: 'What? You must be nuts if you believe that. Shut up and listen for a change . . .'

Both of the above examples are, of course, Standard English. They might well be both uttered by the same speaker in the same day, as we all vary our style of speech quite dramatically depending on where we are, who we are talking to, and our purpose in doing so. The examples represent different registers, and all speakers possess a repertoire of such registers or styles. This is really a kind of language variation that occurs within any one dialect. (Speakers may, of course, feel it appropriate to change dialects, too, according to social circumstances, but if they do they are making a rather different kind of linguistic choice – one more akin to choosing which language to use in bilingual company.)

We have tried to distinguish accent, dialect and register variation not for the sake of pedantry, but because the definition of educational policy on language variation has been beset by confusion about these kinds of variation. A teacher, concerned about 'language standards', might object if a pupil responded to the question 'What's wrong with you today, Mary?' with the statement: 'I'm bloody knackered, Miss!' If she did object, however, this would be an objection to the pupil's choice of register (one suited to informal conversations amongst familiar people of equal status), not to her dialect (which in this case, as Peter Trudgill has pointed out, is perfectly consistent with the rules of Standard English). If, on the other hand, a Cumbrian pupil replied: 'I's badly today, Miss', then the teacher's response would depend on whether or not she wanted to hear Cumbrian dialect spoken in her classroom.

Of course, register, accent and dialect changes may co-vary in practice to a large extent. For many children, the speech of their playground and community will not only be a regional dialect, it will involve registers in which language is less formal, less explicit and no doubt more profane than in the classroom. And although it complicates matters somewhat, we have to recognize that children may choose to use a 'non-standard' dialect in class for the same reasons that they might deliberately choose an inappropriately informal register – to put 'social distance' between them and their teacher, to appeal to the solidarity of their classmates and to show disrespect for the formality of school. Speech in any dialect can, of course, be as explicit or formal as the occasion demands, as demonstrated by dialect poetry and by examples like the Northamptonshire teacher who gives complete lessons in the local dialect.[3] Children whose native dialect is Standard English all acquire informal registers, and even BBC newsreaders are reputed to be both casual and profane conversationalists on occasion!

Confusion about accent, dialect and register variation is common. The earlier writings of Basil Bernstein reveal that he wasn't sure which kind of variation he was concerned with, and the same applies to some of his critics. Eventually, however, it seems he decided he was definitely not talking about dialect variation and was perhaps talking about register.[4] Although only recently published, the HMI Secondary Survey (DES, 1980) unfortunately seems to add to the chaos in this area. Consider the following paragraph from the survey report, headed 'Some general observations', on spoken language in the classroom.

> On the whole, there was a gap between the language of the teacher and that of the pupil, and this is not a new phenomenon. Most of the language of classroom talk and of textbooks was in standard English, and it was a part of the concern of teachers to help pupils to acquire this form of English through talking as well as through the related activities of reading and writing. The best teachers were sensitive to differences in language and led their pupils discreetly and by a variety of means towards a wider range of language use and a surer command of language itself. Very occasionally, a teacher adopted features of the language of pupils,

and superficially this enhanced social relations. But there was ample evidence of pupils making it quite clear that they recognized this as a device, and that the cost of it in terms of setting a positive language example was high. Perhaps the most encouraging example to any teacher who was anxious to maintain linguistic standards came from a young teacher who intimated that her colleagues regarded her way of talking as 'posh'. Yet she conducted one of the most successful discussion lessons seen in that school, with a group of pupils generally regarded as difficult and uncooperative. She did so without abandoning her normal manner of speech, and the class was not in any way alienated.

(Chapter 6, p. 99)

In these comments the inspectors confuse two entirely different propositions – that RP accented standard English should be promoted in schools at the expense of other dialects, and that a basic aim of education should be to develop 'a surer command of language itself'. But there is also a much more worrying hidden message here, which to expose fully we must consider the research of social psychologists Giles and Powesland (1975). They have commented on the fact that people's accents and dialect (which together Giles and Powesland term *speech style*) are not entirely static; we may vary our accent depending on who we are speaking to and the kind of relationship we wish to establish with them. When two conversationalists are mutually concerned to establish a good social relationship, they often modify their speech style towards that of the other to some extent; this is called *convergence* and can be seen as a dynamic paralinguistic method of expressing mutual respect. To avoid doing this, or to actually diverge from the speech style of a fellow conversationalist (i.e. make one's accent less like his than would otherwise be the case), is often used as a way of putting 'social distance' between one speaker and the other – perhaps because the latter, and his speech style, is perceived as unattractive or as having lower social status by the 'diverging' speaker.

The inspectors are clearly implying that teachers should avoid speech style convergence, but that pupils should be encouraged to converge on the style of their teacher. Look at the value-laden terms they use to describe this perfectly normal feature of conversational interaction; it only happens 'very occasionally', and it only 'superficially' enhances social relations. Moreover, pupils recognize it as 'a device', and it exacts a high cost 'in terms of setting a positive language example'. (One would be interested to see the 'ample evidence' for the pupils' dismissal of this in the way that the inspectors claim, as evidence of that kind is notoriously hard for social psychologists to gather, even under controlled research conditions.)

On the other hand, the teacher who steadfastly maintains her RP accent ('posh' even to her teaching colleagues) is applauded *simply for doing* so and is singled out as 'the most encouraging example to any teacher'! We are not suggesting that this teacher should self-consciously change her natural accent towards the regional variety of her pupils (accent convergence is not, normally, a self-conscious act); patronizing histrionics of that kind would help nobody. The distressing implication of the inspectors' comments is, however, that teachers should by their own speech behaviour, and by their response to pupils' speech, seek to make their pupils feel they and the speech style of their community are of lower status and generally inferior to the teacher's own self and speech style as an 'educated person'.

In order to conclude this part of the discussion, and to prepare for a consideration of other, policy-related issues, we will try to make clear our own position on language variation and language development in school. If a teacher who wishes to 'set a positive language example' and 'promote language development' means by this helping children to learn how to convey ideas, concepts, facts and feelings in language which is clear and elegant as the occasion demands, then he or she is quite properly doing his or her job. This means making children more aware of the existing and potential range of their language skills and must also involve some consideration of the attitudes and assumptions which different speech styles embody. If a teacher also feels that the business of the classroom is generally best conducted through language which is relatively formal, then this reflects a personal approach to teaching which can be justified perfectly well – though not in terms of language development *per se* (it may, for example, be part of a teacher's toolkit for maintaining classroom order, for ensuring that quieter, more hesitant children are not shouted down by others, and so on). However, promoting language development, 'maintaining language standards' and similar catch-phrases cannot, in our opinion, be used with any educational justification for trying to eliminate 'non-standard' accents and dialects from children's speech, in or out of the classroom.[5] Neither is there any educational justification for trying to eliminate certain registers or ways of speaking (e.g. the 'catch-phrases' of peer group language) from a child's repertoire, as opposed to broadening that repertoire. Any teacher who tries to do this is not only wasting his own time and that of his pupils, he is arguably wasting a potential resource for language development present in the classroom. We will explain why we believe this, and what alternative courses of action exist, in the following sections.

## The social significance of 'non-standard' speech varieties

In a recent article, Ellen Ryan (1979) asks 'why do low-prestige language varieties persist?' By 'low-prestige' varieties, she is referring to the fact that, in many languages besides English, one particular dialect has become the 'standard' form of the language, the one which is used to determine 'correct' usage in writing and formal speech. This standard dialect is typically based on the language habits of the social group who have historically accumulated the most power, wealth and hence prestige in a society; in the British case, the upper and middle classes of south eastern England. Other language varieties, used by less prestigious groups, become defined as 'non-standard' and carry less prestige than the standard. In some countries of course, entirely different languages occupy these different status positions – e.g. the American Indian languages have lower status than Spanish in Latin America, while Spanish generally has lower status than English in bilingual regions of the USA.

Generally, research findings show that speakers of non-standard varieties recognize as well as anyone else in their society that their language is not well regarded (see Giles and Powesland, 1975). They know it is considered 'common' and 'broad', and that it may influence the way they are evaluated as individuals. As one Cockney speaker in the BBC series 'Word of Mouth' said, 'you won't get on the Board of Directors with a voice like that!' Yet, as Ryan says, these 'low-prestige' varieties do not die out. So well do they continue to thrive that . . .

> . . . the stubborn persistence of diverse language varieties within many societies demands an explanation. For example, despite the lure of social mobility and years of educational (and frequently political) efforts, there is no apparent move towards universal adoption of RP English in Britain, or of Standard English in the United States, of Castilian in Spain, or of European French in French Canada.
>
> (Ryan, 1979, p. 147)

The resolution of this paradox, of course, lies in the fact that 'prestige' is a relative term. It refers to the social standing that someone or something has *within a particular social group*. And for many people, the most important group as a source of prestige is not the whole of British society, or the middle class of southeast England, but their family and friends and the rest of their home community. Speaking 'posh' may impress some teachers, or the prospective employer glimpsed on some distant horizon, but it doesn't cut much ice in the playground and streets, in the club or on the factory floor. To be more precise it might well impress your mates, but it certainly won't endear you to them.

A further point worth noting here comes from Howard Giles's 'matched guise' experiments on attitudes to regional accents (Giles and Powesland, 1975). As one might expect, he found that speakers were rated as being more intelligent, more reliable and more educated when they used RP than when they used regional accents. He also found, however, that regional speakers were often rated *higher* than RP speakers in terms of personal integrity and attractiveness (e.g. good naturedness and sincerity), thus indicating that a regional accent may convey positive social connotations even outside the speaker's immediate community.

## In support of a bidialectal language policy in school

Trudgill (1975) distinguished three policy approaches to language variation in school – the 'elimination of non-standard dialects', the 'bidialectal', and the 'appreciation of dialect differences' approach. In accord with the present writers, he considers the 'elimination' approach both impractical and educationally dangerous; we offer our own criticism of this approach below. He puts his weight mainly behind the 'appreciation of differences' approach – i.e. that schools should concentrate on changing pupils' attitudes to their own and other dialects, rather than teaching them to use a second (standard) dialect. His support of the 'bidialectal' approach is limited; he sees the advantages of teaching children to write in Standard English as merely being those of placating prejudiced attitudes of examiners and employers and does not accept that the use of Standard English for writing is necessary to ensure readers' comprehension. As teachers are often quick to point out, however, he is very vague about the extent to which variations from standardized vocabulary, spelling and grammar could be permitted on all occasions without creating comprehension problems. While not disagreeing with Trudgill to any great extent, we would argue more strongly than he does for the value of developing children's awareness of the linguistic and social nature of their own and other dialects of English, for such increased awareness can assist the development of more liberal attitudes towards language variation. We also believe that the pursuit of bidialectalism (being able to speak and write in two dialects) is not so unrealistic as Trudgill insists. He writes:

> The point is that . . . with a new dialect you have to retain some aspects of your native variety while rejecting others – and the big problem is to learn which is which. The two linguistic varieties are so similar that it is difficult to keep them apart. The motivation to learn, moreover, is much smaller. If an English-speaking person learns French, then at least he can communicate with French people and read French books and newspapers. But no new communication advantages of this sort arise from learning a new dialect.
>
> (p. 78)

We would agree with Trudgill that if a pupil is not motivated to learn Standard English, then a teacher will not succeed in teaching it. The same problem, however, applies to the acquisition of foreign languages like French – as many a modern languages teacher will testify! Whether or not there are 'communication advantages' to be gained from acquiring a use of Standard English for formal writing, or for certain social encounters, depends on how narrowly one wishes to define 'communication advantage'. As for the difficulty an individual might have in distinguishing between two dialects, we feel that here Trudgill is, surprisingly, perpetuating a traditional and peculiarly British attitude towards language learning which has no real educational or psychological basis. His position here reflects an un-necessary concession to the 'elimination' approach, as we hope to demonstrate below.

As mentioned earlier, the policy on language variation historically favoured in British schools has been that of attempting to eliminate all other than Standard English usages. Besides its demonstrable and inevitable failure, this policy is unfortunate because it may serve to alienate children from education itself. Referring back to our discussion of the social significance of 'non-standard' speech varieties, it can be seen that this policy offers many children an unfortunate and un-necessary choice; between retaining the loyalty and self-identity offered by their social group and becoming an 'educated' person. They may well accept the validity of this choice, and decide that education, part and parcel, is not for them. The reality of this decision is well illustrated in Paul Willis's book, *Learning to Labour* (1977). Amongst the 'low-achieving' adolescents he interviewed, the choice was very clearly perceived as being either 'one of the lads' or an 'earhole' (a swot), and this was often symbolized in speech styles.

William Labov (1972) has, of course, forcibly argued that the 'elimination' approach has contributed to the alienation of Black American adolescents from the school system, because children are more likely to reject school if their mother-tongue is treated as educationally worthless. This is all the more unfortunate and unnecessary because the 'elimination' approach rests on a conception of language learning which is fundamentally incorrect. This view is essentially that the development of productive skills in a second dialect is assisted by, or even entails, the suppression of the first-acquired dialect. That is, for children to be able to write in such a way as to satisfy examiners, or to present themselves formally and favourably when they wish to do so in writing or in interviews, they must first be made to forget their original native speech style. This is a strange notion – rather as if learning French entailed forgetting English, or learning to play rugby entailed forgetting football. There is no psycholinguistic or sociolinguistic evidence to support this view (see Mitchell, 1978), and in fact in many parts of the world being fluent in two or more dialects is common. The associated notion of bilingual or bidialectal 'overload' – whereby acquiring a second language or dialect is seen to place some kind of cognitive strain on the language learner, who will thus be educationally inhibited – is likewise unsubstantiated. Bilingual or bidialectal children do not suffer in educational attainment because of their additional skill (again, see Mitchell, 1978). We believe, therefore, that the pursuit of some form of bidialectal language policy which incorporates an 'appreciation of dialect differences' is a practical and acceptable teaching aim.

## Using children's own language resources

We pointed out at the beginning of this chapter that children, from their earliest years, learn language within the context of social relationships. We would argue that it is essential to build on this out-of-school experience of language rather than to deny it and to help children to develop not just fluent Standard English, but a whole range of language skills and resources through their work in school. We would argue further that this approach will not only give children a much surer command of Standard English, but it will strike at the base of those attitudes which suggested that this language variety was not theirs to start with.

How then, within the confines of one social situation – the classroom – and within the limits of one relationship – that between teachers and pupils – can children be helped to develop competence in all the language varieties they will want to use, and the experience to make appropriate language choices? Probably the richest resource teachers have at their disposal – and it is often an under-exploited one – is the children's own language, and their knowledge about how it works. There is evidence to show that children are sophisticated code-switchers from their earliest years (Shatz and Gelman, 1973). The following three examples of children talking about their language show clear understanding of the difference between talking to your peers and talking to your elders, of the social embarrassment that can arise from even a slightly inappropriate choice of register, and of the way language use in the classroom will vary according to subject area, and level of schooling:

> I'd speak freely to my friends, right, and when I go home I'd have more respect in my voice. I would speak to my parents the same as the senior staff you know.
>
> (14 years)

> I was talking really nice and saying 'Do you like jam?' and all this lot and she's going 'Yea, 'course I do', so I felt really shamed up . . . she was talking naturally and I was talking poshly to her.
>
> (14 years)

> Miss tries every time we come across a new Maths problem, if you say just an ordinary word like 'add' or 'take away', she'd say 'subtract', she wants us to know the language for when we get to secondary school, not just 'adding' and 'taking away'.
>
> (10 years)

Children will compare the relative merits of using different language varieties in a particular context; one West Indian Londoner commented that 'A fel like a could lick yu, go 'weh!' was a much more effective way of telling someone she was angry with them than 'I feel like I could hit you, go away!' And two 12-year-olds, talking about the kinds of books they liked, had this to say:

QUESTION: *So what makes a book really interesting for you?*
DIANE: That's got kids in . . .
JACKIE: Kids in it our age and crimes and everything
DIANE: And language like – and bad language, slang language
QUESTION: *Why does that make it more interesting?*
DIANE: Makes it more funnier
JACKIE: Makes it more realistic

DIANE: Yea 'cos you don't see people going up (*assumes posh accent*) 'Hey you, do you want a sweet?', something like that, you say 'Oi, you, d'yer wan a sweet 'ere?' You just have ordinary play language.

We might question the girls' labelling of informal dialogue as 'bad language', but we would support their enthusiasm for children's books where the characters speak in a language which is realistic in the context of the story.

In their written English, children will also, given the chance, show a sure command of different registers and dialects. The 11-year-old boy who started his film review 'I suppose you think this film is all that usual sort of war rubbish, but fear not . . .' knew exactly who his audience was going to be, while another 11-year-old's use of dialect gives an added vitality to the beginning of his account of 'The Fight':

> I was playing cricket with our Darren, I hit a wacker and it caught him in the gut. He started walking towards me with a rage on his face . . .

To look at a more extended use of dialect, who could fail to be drawn into this girl's account of a visit to her boyfriend in Brixton gaol?

HIM: How come yuh worry bout me an me nuh worry bout you?
ME: Me never tell yuh fe worry bout me! I knew he was only trying to get me vex jus so he would know I care. Bm me nah gan get vex me can tek de insults just for now.

(Example supplied by John Richmond)

Children can often achieve a power through writing in the language variety most comfortable to them that they would otherwise lack. Some may also, incidentally, show a command of Standard English which they hadn't been motivated to draw on before. The children quoted above were able to make clear and confident choices of language style in their written work. The next example (Figure 1.1) is from the writing of a less fortunate pupil.

Valerie was also classed as 'difficult', and in fact her English teacher had more or less given up any hope of her managing to get formal qualifications. She was 15. The direct, informal style of this piece is not sustained through the rest of the story, which drifts into a more formal narrative. The teacher's comments at the end include criticisms of the 'terrible presentation' of the piece. More specifically, her marking shows rejection of three different aspects of the pupil's use of language. Her corrections in the first line suggest that a conversational style like this is inappropriate to written work. Secondly, she rejects the use of dialect; 'the stewardess say' is changed to 'the stewardess speaks', and 'it gives my belly a wave' 'corrected' to the rather less colourful 'there is a sinking feeling in my stomach'. Thirdly, she corrects spellings and other written conventions. We can sense a feeling of despair in the teacher's marking and comments.

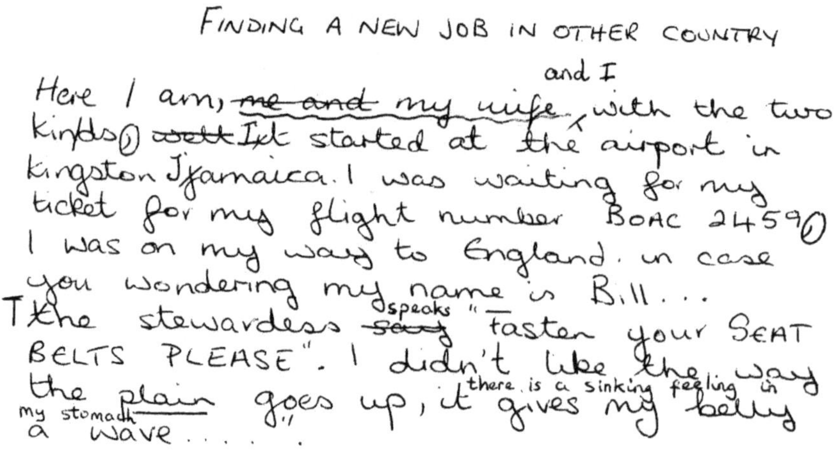
FINDING A NEW JOB IN OTHER COUNTRY

Here I am, ~~me and~~ my wife, and I with the two kids ~~with~~ It started at the airport in Kingston Jamaica. I was waiting for my ticket for my flight number BOAC 2459 I was on my way to England. in case you wondering my name is Bill . . . The stewardess ~~say~~ speaks "fasten your SEAT BELTS PLEASE". I didn't like the way the ~~plain~~ goes up, it gives my belly a wave . . . . .

there is a sinking feeling in my stomach

*Figure 1.1* Valerie's writing

Many of the problems in this piece of work may have arisen from Valerie's lack of a sense of specific purpose or audience for her writing. She may be producing (with diminishing conviction) what she thinks is expected in response to a school task. Yet within these constraints, she still displays certain strengths, which might have been seen as providing some starting points for development.[6] The fact that Valerie is attempting a dialogue with the reader, which involves her in a skilled combination of present, past progressive and past perfect tenses in the first few sentences, is probably not even noticed. The teacher's treatment of the use of dialect and informal register as 'errors' which are marked in the same way as spelling mistakes denies the long-established tradition in the English novel of addressing the reader directly, and the more recent examples of literature written by Londoners with West Indian backgrounds, for example Samuel Selvon. This kind of response to a child's writing does, however, reflect the confusion which is present in many official educational statements about language variation.

Further examples are easily found. The Assessment of Performance Unit, set up by the government to assess school children's language on an unprecedented scale, and in a way that may exert a powerful influence on practice in schools, emphasizes that the 'style' of a writing task should be appropriate to 'subject matter, audience and intention', but states that 'he done it' should be treated as a 'morphological error' (APU, 1978). It may be a matter of dialect choice which a teacher should explore with a pupil, but to treat 'he done it' without qualification as a morphological error is to assert the existence of Standard English as an uncontroversial base-line for correctness rather than letting a sensitivity to subject matter, audience and intention determine the choice of appropriate language. This inconsistency is perpetuated in the differences between the contemporary approaches to language in inservice teacher training courses, and the 'Advice to the Examiner' of most English '0' level and CSE boards. Children who sense the confusion and contradictions in educators' approaches to language work will not have the confidence to develop those language skills and resources they already have, which are too often regarded by the school as not really relevant to the English curriculum.

## Language variation – classroom activities

In the last 15 years there has been a slow but significant increase in language activities which draw on children's own resources to develop their skills. In the early 1970s, the Schools Council Oracy Project constructed listening tests designed to take account of 'addressor, addressee and situation' (Wilkinson, 1974). They also produced their Language in Use materials, the aim of which was to develop 'an awareness of what language is and how it is used and, at the same time, to extend competence in handling language' (Doughty et al., 1971, pp. 8–9). These materials treat language as behaviour rather than as an abstract system; for example:

> Explore, in discussion, whether people need to change their way of speaking when they take up different roles. Consider likely pairs of situations in which an individual would have to use different ways of speaking. Divide the class into groups and ask each to prepare a pair of sketches, which will show the difference.
>
> (Doughty et al., 1971, p. 207)

Suggestions for possible contrasting situations include an employee explaining an accident to (a) the workmate's wife, (b) the foreman and (c) the manager. These attempts to examine a wide range of examples of language use in an environment as restricted as the classroom tend to rely heavily on either role play and improvisation, or the importing of video and audio tape recordings. Most English teachers are now familiar with ideas for activities like these:

> Collect examples of recorded speech from radio or TV. Compare the different registers employed and identify audience, purpose and subject matter.
>
> (BBC, 1980a, p. 3)

or

> Can you guess what the following bits of writing are about and who they are meant for? It might help if you can think of where you might see these bits of writing.
>
> (ILEA, 1979b, pp. 54–55) (Eighteen examples follow.)

Most English teachers have also seen suggestions for examining the way English has changed over the years through looking at studies of place names, versions of old English or the origins of words that English has 'borrowed' from other languages. Although the very fact that these sorts of activities are even considered within a classroom may indicate the beginning of a change in attitude, it may be much more significant to look at whether they are taken seriously enough to question and inform the class syllabus in Standard English. If these activities are introduced to pupils as an 'extra' in an otherwise inflexible English curriculum, the work will obviously not have the same effect on their knowledge and attitudes as it would when carried out as an integral part of language work based on a bidialectal model. Many language activities on accent and dialect, for example, can quite easily be reduced to 'butterfly collecting'. In the Pupil's Notes for a current radio series for 10- to 12-year-olds, the children are asked:

> And have you ever ridden on a dicky? No, not a bird but a donkey – that's the old name for it in parts of Norfolk and Suffolk. Try asking around, especially amongst older people. You may be surprised at what a lot of dialect words there still are to be found.

> (BBC, 1980b, p. 9)

Children are asked later to discuss arguments for and against 'preserving dialects'. Dialect could be treated here as merely a miscellaneous collection of picturesque words and expressions, to be 'collected' from old people before it finally disappears with them into the grave. In some ways, an anthropological approach towards varieties of language that children may not be familiar with is healthy. But any implication that the languages 'out there', beyond the school gates, are of no more than peripheral importance to the children in the classroom is a denial of the linguistic diversity of Britain today, and, often, of the child's own language. Activities like making a slang dictionary, or examining a disc jockey's patter, can lead, in some classrooms, to real insights about the nature of language; in other classrooms, a teacher's treatment can reduce them to token gestures which do nothing to challenge the notion of there being one unchanging, correct form of English.

If a teacher's model of language is a rigid one, then that teacher's handling of these kinds of activities could render them ineffective, or confusing to his or her pupils. The model of language underlying classroom activities determines their validity to the pupils, and their relevance to work in school. It is not enough to start with children's own language experience if the model is not genuinely bidialectal. The materials in 'Dialect and Language Variety' produced by the Ebury Teachers' Centre in London (ILEA, 1979a) argue convincingly for the worth and legitimacy of London children's own language; but rather than emphasizing the dynamic nature of language use they tend to use an 'us and them' approach, thus resurrecting the choice between in-group loyalty and educational participation, which was a product of the 'elimination approach' (see p. 85). For instance:

> The London Cockney accent is especially looked down on, sometimes by Cockney speakers themselves, but mostly by people who hold power; teachers, lawyers, employers etc. . . . Employers of non-manual labour would prefer it if working-class children tried to cover up their background so that they merged in with everyone else.
>
> (ILEA, 1979a, p. 15)

The whole issue about the relationship of language use to power is not one that should be dodged, but whether it should be approached in this sort of way is another question. Activities such as 'Write a short play about two London children in which one accuses the other of stealing a pen. Now rewrite it as though the two characters were upper-class characters from a public school' must inevitably produce a very stereotyped version of upper-class language, the language of 'people who usually speak "posh"; and don't let outsiders in who speak differently'. Many of the activities suggested are admirable in that they encourage children to look not just at language, but at the social context in which it is used, and how context and language interrelate. The setting of this discussion of language variation within a simplistic class conflict model, however, reflects an attitude to language variation which is in some ways as rigid as that which sees only Standard English as acceptable.

## The way forward

Classroom activities on language variation should raise questions about the nature and value of a lot of other language work that goes on in school; but the questions generated often do not seem to spread beyond the confines of that particular lesson, and 'today we're doing dialects' too frequently becomes just another self-contained exercise in the segmented secondary school curriculum. There seem to be two main reasons for this. Firstly, activities which ask children (and teachers) to analyse and discuss the ways in which language varies are calling on linguistic skills which most teachers have not been equipped with in their preservice training, and without which the discussion cannot go beyond a fairly superficial level. An exploration of anecdotal examples cannot on its own provide the analytical framework needed for real advances in understanding, which will produce an informed reassessment of classroom language work.

A respect for, and confidence in, a bidialectal approach in school must depend on linguistic and sociolinguistic knowledge. The second reason for the limited effect of many language activities is the relative impotence of any changes of attitude in one area of school work unless they are supported by changes in other areas. With the increasing emphasis on 'basic skills', language work is marked as one of the most crucial areas of the curriculum. At the level of the whole school language policy there needs to be a commitment to the principles of helping children develop these skills through language work which builds on the competence and resources they already have, and which takes into account the complex language choices they will need to make in the adult world. This official acknowledgement by the school of the worth of children's own language must be reflected in a reappraisal, at classroom level, of the ground-rules for language work. If discussion can be opened up about the criteria for evaluating work, and a real negotiation of ideas occurs between teachers and pupils, then the activities described earlier have a much better chance of being something more than a one-off exercise. Many children's lack of confidence in their own language skills, and limited competence in Standard English (even after 15,000 hours' exposure to school), is the result of cultural barriers; if children can see their language work in school as valuable, and building on resources they already have, we may start to break those barriers down.

## Notes

1   The authors wish to acknowledge the valuable work in this area performed by previous writers, and upon which the present discussion draws extensively. Interested readers are referred in particular to Trudgill (1975) and J. R. Edwards (1979).
2   We are using 'register' here to refer to what some writers have called 'style' (e.g. Trudgill, 1975; J. R. Edwards, 1979). We have avoided the latter term because of its individualistic connotations, i.e. the 'style' of a particular author or speaker.
3   The prevailing climate of attitudes is still such, however, that this particular teacher wishes to remain unidentified.
4   This does not seem an appropriate point to delve into the complexities of Bernstein's theory and related research. The interested reader is referred to McKinnon (1977) and J. R. Edwards (1979) for clarification on these matters.
5   As the Bullock Committee (DES, 1975) put it, 'The aim (of education) is not to alienate the child from a form of language with which he has grown up and which serves him efficiently in the speech community of his neighbourhood.'
6   For a more detailed discussion of working on pupils' strengths rather than their weaknesses to improve their written work, see Keen (1978).

## References

APU. 1978. Assessment of Performance Unit: *Criteria for Assessing Writing.* London: Department of Education and Science.
BBC. 1980a: *Resource Units 11–13 – English, Teachers' Notes.* London: BBC Publications.
BBC. 1980b: *Web of Language, Teachers' Notes.* London: BBC Publications.
DES. 1975: *A Language for Life (The Bullock Report).* London: HMSO.
DES. 1980: *Aspects of Secondary Education in England: A Survey by HM Inspectors of Schools.* London: HMSO.
Doughty, P., Pierce, J. and Thornton, G. 1971: *Language in Use.* London: Edward Arnold (for Schools Council).
Edwards, J. R. 1979: *Language and Disadvantage.* London: Edward Arnold.

Giles, H. and Powesland, P. 1975: *Speech Style and Social Evaluation*. London: Academic Press.

ILEA English Centre. 1979a: *Dialect and Language Variety*. London: Ebury Teachers' Centre.

ILEA English Centre. 1979b: *Languages*. London: Ebury Teachers' Centre.

Keen, J. 1978: *Teaching English: A Linguistic Approach*. London: Methuen.

Labov, W. 1972: *Language in the Inner City*. Philadelphia: University of Philadelphia Press.

McKinnon, D. 1977: *Language and Social Class (Unit 23 E202 Schooling and Society)*. Milton Keynes: Open University.

Mercer, N. and Edwards, D. 1979: *Communication and Context (Block 4, PE232 Language Development)*. Milton Keynes: Open University.

Mitchell, R. 1978: Bilingual Education of Minority Language Groups in the English-speaking World. *Seminar Papers 4*. University of Stirling Department of Education.

Ryan, E. B. 1979: Why Do Low-prestige Language Varieties Persist? In H. Giles and R. St Clair (Eds.), *Language and Social Psychology*. Oxford: Basil Blackwell.

Shatz, M. and Gelman, R. 1973: The Development of Communication Skills: Modifications in the Speech of Young Children as a Function of Listener. *Monographs of the Society for Research in Child Development 38*, No. 152.

Trudgill, P. 1975: *Accent, Dialect and the School*. London: Edward Arnold.

Wilkinson, A. 1974: *The Quality of Listening: The Report of the Schools Council Oracy Project*. London: Macmillan.

Willis, P. 1977: *Learning to Labour*. London: Saxon House.

*I wrote this chapter in response to an invitation by Geoffrey Walford of Oxford University, who was editing a collection of educational research-ers' reflections on work which had a special significance for them. This chapter consists of my reflective account of the first substantial classroom-based research project I was involved in, carried out with Derek Edwards and Janet Maybin, which was the basis of the book* Common Knowledge *(Edwards & Mercer, Routledge, 1987; second edition 2013).*

# 2   Researching *Common Knowledge*

## Studying the content and context of educational discourse

*Mercer, N. (1991). Researching* Common Knowledge: *studying the content and context of educational discourse. In G. Walford (ed.),* Doing Educational Research. *London: Routledge, pp. 41–58.*

## Introduction

The research I will describe in this chapter was carried out by Derek Edwards, Janet Maybin and myself in 1984–6 as a project funded by the Economic and Social Research Council (Edwards, Mercer and Maybin, 1987). As part of a line of research begun in 1979, it has generated one book (Edwards and Mercer, 1987/2013) and the other publications listed in the References at the end of this chapter. My intention here is to describe what kind of research we did, why we did it, how we did it and some of the problems we had in doing it.

### What was the research meant to find out?

My first real job was teaching psychology in the sociology department of Leicester University. At the regular departmental research seminars, one of the professors of sociology would often stop those presenting the research – postgraduates, lecturers, visiting academics – in their tracks by posing a single question. As they described in detail their rich data, their theoretical framework, their methodological complexities, he would interrupt and ask, irritably, 'Yes, yes, but what is your *problem?*' By this he meant (I think): what was your research really meant to achieve? What questions were you trying to answer? What, in a nutshell, did you want to know, and why did you want to know it?

My best attempt at an answer to his question here is this. We wanted to understand how people did teaching and learning together. As participants (teachers and learners) in that process, as well as researchers, we felt that we knew very little about how it worked, how it went right or wrong. In particular, we were interested in knowledge, and how it was shared. Whatever else education is about, it is about knowledge. Every day in classrooms, knowledge gets constructed, presented, received, rejected, evaluated, understood and misunderstood. A careful examination of this process might well tell us something of psychological interest and practical educational value.

### What kind of research did we do?

We knew from the earliest stages of planning the research that we would use observational rather than experimental methods. We had begun this whole line of research in a state of disenchantment with experimental approaches to the study of cognitive development and reasoning (see for example Mercer and Edwards, 1981). Margaret Donaldson (1978) in particular had convinced us that psychological laboratories were very good at constructing experimental artefacts, and we had no desire to create more. It was our view that too many experimenters began by 'modelling' real-life situations which they knew very little about. And (as Desforges, 1985, has pointed out) too many psychologists have pontificated about teaching-and-learning without studying what actually goes on in classrooms. We wanted to know more about what people did when they went about their normal business.

We also knew that we would be making a qualitative, rather than a quantitative, analysis of our observations. We could not pursue our interests by conducting a large-scale, statistical analysis of classroom interactions in which only a relatively superficial consideration of the exchange of meanings would be possible. It was the qualitative nature of classroom talk and its content that interested us most.

### Theory

One function of theories is to set agendas for research – to generate certain kinds of questions which the research will attempt to answer. Another function is to provide a 'universe of discourse' within which the discussion and explanation of research findings can take place. The framework within which our 'problem' was defined was strongly influenced by our reading of Vygotsky (e.g. 1978; see also Wertsch, 1985) and Bruner (e.g. 1986), but also very relevant was psychological research which had explored aspects of the cultural basis of the development of knowledge (though not necessarily in school settings) such as Neisser (1976) and Cole and Scribner (1974). The work of some educational researchers (particularly Barnes, 1976) who had studied communication in the classroom also helped define our universe and shape our methodology. There were other psychological and sociological influences (e.g. Walkerdine, 1982; Mehan, 1979): but this is not the place to go into theory in any depth or detail. However, one respect of the relationship between theory and research practice is, I think, relevant and interesting here. It is the influence of previous researchers whose ideas, while dealing with relevant aspects of the phenomena under investigation and being accorded high status in the field of study, are nevertheless rejected as a basis for the theoretical framework. Sometimes the work of such research-ers can be at least as significant an influence as more 'positive' sources, not least because it motivates: dissatisfaction may generate curiosity. An example might make this point clearer. It concerns our conception of the role of language in thinking and learning, and our model of the process of teaching and learning. We were familiar with the work of Piaget (e.g. 1971), and recognized its influence on both research into cognitive development and modern 'child-centred' educational practice. However, we had become increasingly dissatisfied by the way that language was marginalized in the Piagetian model of cognitive development, and also by the way that the role of the teacher was represented as that of a provider of learning environ-ments, rather than as an active participant or collaborator in the process whereby a child constructs knowledge. In a way that might seem ridiculous to an outsider, our discussion sometimes led us to get *angry* with Piaget and his followers: couldn't they see that there was so much more, a communica-tive aspect to teaching-and-learning, which they had largely ignored? One of our motives in doing the research, then, was quite simply to try to prove them wrong (see Edwards and Mercer, 1987, Chapters 2 and 8 for more on this).

## Collecting data

In planning our observations, we had a number of considerations to take into account. We needed to collect very detailed data on classroom discourse because of the kinds of issues we wished to investigate, and there was obvi-ously a limit to the amount of such data we could handle. It seemed clear that our interests would be best served by subjecting relatively small samples of classroom discourse and activity (in terms of numbers of teachers and classes) to close, intensive analysis, in the hope of discovering how knowl-edge is actually built and shared between teacher and particular groups of pupils. We wanted to look at how teachers introduced new topics, and how they followed this up by setting children tasks, checking on their under-standing, and helping them draw conclusions from what they had done. We also wanted the classroom activities we observed to be as similar as possible to what teachers would normally do with those pupils in their classrooms, while avoiding the technical difficulties of observing and analysing conver-sations and interactions between teachers and all the children in a class of more than 25 children (in which, additionally, much time is taken up by organizational and control aspects). From an earlier phase of research (Mercer and Edwards, 1981), we already had videotaped recording of teach-ers working with whole classes and small groups in four London primary schools. To provide the main source of data for the present (second) phase, we arranged to make video recordings in three local primary schools. As the primary school teachers in these schools followed the usual English practice of organizing children into small groups around communal tables, working together or in parallel on the same task, we decided to set up conditions which would enable us to observe the activities of three such groups of five to six pupils aged between 8 and 11, each working with their usual teacher on one specific topic over three consecutive 'lessons' of 40–60 minutes' duration.

All three schools were state primary schools. Initial contact with the schools was made through the headteachers, with whose agreement and assistance we then met teachers who were working with the appropriate age group who were willing to consider participating in the study (see Maybin, 1987, for a more detailed account of how this fieldwork was organized). The research team's project officer then visited each school, and with each teacher negotiated a suitable plan of activity for the three sessions from within the teacher's existing plan of work. The rationale and general purpose of the research was explained to the teachers. A second visit to each school was made one week before the recording of the first session, to check on final arrangements. By this time, each teacher had identified the group of children that they would be working with for the recording and had also selected the topic which would provide the main theme for the three sessions (see Table 2.1). Teachers were asked about their aims and expectations for these sessions, and their responses were recorded by the project officer.

Video recordings were made by one cameraman, assisted by a sound engineer for some sessions. One member of the research team was also present for each recording and visited the school again one week after the recording sessions, by which time the research team had viewed the recorded material and drawn up questions to use in interviewing the teacher and pupil involved. We had decided that it was important that one of us was present throughout the related sessions so that a researcher would have had direct experience as an observer of the recorded events and would also be aware of any incidents which immediately preceded or followed the recorded sessions. That person would also conduct the relevant interviews with teachers and pupils.

Each pupil was withdrawn from class for an individual 10–20 minute interview. Interviews with teachers were carried out separately outside school hours. All interviews were tape-recorded and transcribed. These interviews focused on such matters as (a) participants' understanding of the substantive content of the session, (b) participants' perceptions of the purpose or aims of the activities they had engaged in and (c) specific enquiries to teachers (and occasionally pupils) about why they had said or done certain things during the sessions. This included discussions with the teachers about the teaching methods they used, as well as some general enquiries about their general teaching style and educational philosophy. All teachers were questioned on certain general issues, of which the following are examples:

> How much work had the pupils done on this topic in previous sessions?
> Had the teacher assumed any knowledge or experience of the topic from outside the recorded sessions?

*Table 2.1* Phase 2 schools: classroom topics

|  | Lesson 1 | Lesson 2 | Lesson 3 |
|---|---|---|---|
| Pendulums | The teacher talked to the group about what a pendulum was, then split the six pupils into three pairs to investigate whether the angle of swing, the weight of the bob or the length of the string, respectively, made any difference to the speed of the pendulum Results were put into matrices, and their significance discussed. | The pupils had plotted the results of their investigations on graphs, using acetate paper. Teacher and pupils discussed these findings, using an overhead projector to study the graphs together. | In the class PE session, their teacher helped the pupils to test out the properties of a 'human pendulum', using the ropes and bars. |
| Clay pots | Pupils learned how to make a clay thumbpot, modelling their own pots under the teacher's guidance and demonstration. | Children made a clay hedgehog or pig, with the teacher's guidance. | Children studied pictures of animals, and then made one of them in clay. |
| Computer graphics | Using the school's new microcomputer, the teacher showed four pupils how to instruct it to draw an F shape. Pupils then tried to write a program for a T shape, using forwards, backwards and angle-turning commands. They tried out and discussed these programs with the teacher, who then helped them write one for an equilateral triangle. | Pupils tried out and modified the programs for octagons, isosceles and equilateral triangles which they had written for homework. The teacher helped them write a program to draw a hexagon, and showed them how to use the 'pen off' and 'pen on' commands, and how to store a program. | The four children with their teacher introduced the work they had been doing to two other pupils from the class, and helped them to write and try out (run) programs for various shapes. |

Source: Reproduced with permission from Maybin (1987, p 177)

What did the teacher want each session to achieve?
How much did the teacher think the pupils had actually learned?
What did the teacher think was the essence of good teaching? Did she try in her teaching to put into practice any particular pedagogic principles?

These questions were adapted to suit the specific content of particular sessions and sequences. The children were also asked a set of basic questions, supplemented or adapted to cover aspects of the contents of the lessons in which they had engaged. These basic questions covered such things as:

> What did they think were the main things they had learned?
> What did they think the teacher wanted them to learn in the session?
> Did they know anything about what they had done prior to the session, from other lessons or from outside school?
> Had they found anything in the session confusing?

More specific questions dealt with particular concepts, procedures and problems encountered in particular sessions. Children obviously differed in the way they responded to these questions. Notably, some seemed more willing or able than others to reflect on what they had said and done. But we found the content of their responses valuable, especially when set against the teacher's interview responses, and I certainly feel that any researcher with preliminary doubts about the feasibility of interviewing children of this age should be reassured by our experience.

The outcome of our visits to the schools was about 450 minutes of video-taped classroom activity and about 270 minutes of audiotaped interviews.

### Some observations on our observations

I would expect the critical reader to ask how far our methods for gathering data were compatible with our aim, stated earlier, of finding out more about what people did when they went about their normal business. We disrupted proceedings by entering classrooms with a video camera, and once there we focused our attention entirely on how the teacher taught one small group of children. There is little doubt that teachers who know that their teaching is going to be recorded and analysed will be more nervous and self-conscious than usual. They may well have spent more time than usual preparing what to teach. Children, too, are not immune to the presence of the camera, and two or three extra adults. In attending to how a teacher dealt with just one group of children, we may have gained an inaccurate impression of the amount of time and attention that the teacher would normally give to such a group. (Primary teachers who have watched the videos we made are sometimes particularly scathing on this matter, with comments to the effect that most other children in the class must have been sedated or bribed into silence.)

I do not, however, believe that any of this creates serious problems for the validity of our research. There was no reason to believe that the children were more than temporarily and superficially affected by the presence of the camera and its operator. The video recordings show that early in the initial sessions, some children are distracted by the camera, but such signs of interest soon diminish and are not apparent at all in the recordings of later sessions. We were not researching classroom management strategies, or quantifying teacher-pupil contact time, so the balance of the teacher's time spent with the target group against that spent with the rest of the class was not a significant consideration. And if the conditions encouraged teachers to do their best and gave them the opportunity to work in a more intensive manner on one topic with one group of children than would usually be possible, that is a positive feature of our design, not a problem. We wanted to be able to sample teaching-and-learning in a relatively intense form, and so we created conditions under which this was possible.

Only the most naive of researchers would not expect their visible presence as an observer to affect the behaviour of those being observed. Any observation of social interactions which is carried out with the knowledge of the participants may affect what is said and done. The crucial issue is whether or not the observation causes serious distortion of phenomena or creates artefacts. All one can do is (a) try to employ observational techniques which will obtain suitable data with the least possible disruption of the processes under observation, and (b) use participants' own views and those of other informed sources (in this case, other teachers) to help judge the representative quality of what has been observed and recorded. Although the teachers involved were sometimes self-critical about their activities in the recorded sessions, neither they nor any other teachers who have since watched the recordings raised issues of 'reality' beyond those of classroom management as mentioned above.

## Analysis

### Observational analysis

If you are a researcher using videotaped data, one danger is that making recordings can delude you into feeling that the observation has somehow been accomplished, when in fact all you have done is laid in some serious observational work for the days, weeks or even months ahead. An experienced ethnographic researcher has estimated that the analysis of 1 hour of classroom interaction on tape will on average take an ethnographer 10 hours (Martyn Hammersley, personal communication: but see Hammersley, 1983, for a discussion of relevant methodological issues). The analytic methods we employed were similar to those of ethnography, in that we were similarly concerned with the minutiae of what was said and done; and we were interested in participants' accounts and interpretations of what they said and did. We differed from most classroom ethnographers, I believe, in being less concerned with the sociological themes of 'social order' and 'control' (cf. Young, 1971; Edwards, 1980) and more with the psychological ones of 'knowledge' and 'communication'.

Through preliminary work we had come to realize that other existing methods for analysing classroom discourse were not suitable for our needs.

For example, the commonly employed method known as 'interaction analysis' (Flanders, 1970) or 'systematic observation' (Galton, Simon and Croll, 1980) involves all events being assigned by observers to previously defined categories, with the coded results thus obtained providing the data for the next stage of analysis. That is, the discourse itself does not remain accessible to analysts after the observed classroom activity is over, and so the analysis is wholly dependent on the *a priori* adequacy of the category scheme and on the observers' skills in applying it. As our interest lay in the continuous, cumulative processes by which a common knowledge is developed in classrooms, and as we were making full records of all that was said and done, it was clear that our needs would not be served by reducing our data to numerical frequency codings.

On the other hand, the 'discourse analysis' methods which have been used by some linguists to study classroom talk (e.g. Sinclair and Coulthard, 1975; Stubbs, 1981), while not involving the early loss of actual discourse during analysis, were no more suited to our purposes because they had been designed to deal only with the *structure* of discourse, not the *content* of what is said and done. (A critical comparison and evaluation of these, and other, methods of analysing classroom talk can be found in Edwards and Mercer, 1986, pp. 176–179 and Edwards and Mercer, 1987, ch. 2.)

The method we employed involved the complete transcription of all the discourse recorded on videotape. Fortunately, the ESRC provided us with a project secretary who transcribed all the tapes. Having checked the accuracy of the typed transcripts against the recordings, one of the researchers then watched the recordings of each of the three-session sequences, writing on the transcripts any information about physical context and non-verbal communication which was necessary to make sense of what was said and done. An example of a transcript at the end of this stage is provided below. It is taken from one of the 'pendulums' sessions described in Table 2.1. (Figure 1) (Note: pauses of less than 2 seconds are represented thus /, those of more than 2 seconds //. **Bold type** indicates emphatic speech.)

Next, the researchers (together) reviewed the video recordings, armed with the transcripts which now included the 'context notes' as a right-hand column of typescript. This was undoubtedly the most important part of the process of analysis; but it is also the one I find the most difficult to describe programmatically. Basically, it involved watching and discussing the video recordings, stopping and reviewing sequences whenever necessary, and making notes on what took place. One of our aims was to track themes or elements of knowledge – such diverse things as given information, technical terms, ways of doing things, criteria for success, past events and shared experiences invoked by participants – through the lessons, watching for them to emerge, surfacing like dolphins, in the discourse. We wanted to see how participants took them up (if at all) and carried them along, how they were used, how they changed, how they related to each other, and what significance was attached to them. We noticed how *continuity* of experience was established through discourse.

| | |
|---|---|
| T: Now he didn't have a watch/but he **had** on **him** something that was a very good timekeeper that he could use to hand straight away/ | *T snaps fingers on 'straight away', and looks invitingly at pupils as if posing a question or inviting a response.* |
| You've got it. I've got it. What is it?// What could we use to count beats? What have **you** got?// You can feel it **here**. | *T points on 'You've' and 'I've'. T beats hand on table slowly, looks around group of pupils, who smile and shrug. T puts fingers on T's wrist pulse.* |
| PUPILS: Pulse. | *(In near unison.)* |
| T: A pulse. Everybody see if you can find it. | *All copy T, feeling for wrist pulses.* |

*Figure 2.1* Pendulums

## Content, continuity and context

As well as the *content* of discourse, we were concerned with its *context*. Our consistent view has been that educational discourse is never 'context free': the intelligibility of its meanings always depends on the invocation (explicitly or implicitly) by speakers of an educational 'universe of discourse' (see Edwards and Mercer, 1986; Mercer, Edwards and Maybin, 1988; Edwards and Mercer, 1989). At the most obvious level, our concern with context meant that we noticed how the physical 'props' of the classroom – equipment, drawings, texts, computer screen representations – were invoked by speakers to support the discourse. At a more subtle level, we tried to see how certain events and items of knowledge were used to contextualize others: a piece of corrective advice offered by the teacher might, for example, be contextualized by a reference to some past, shared event ('Remember how we did it yesterday'): a child's re-formulation of an answer might reflect a model offered earlier by the teacher. At the deepest – and most uncertain – level of analysis, we were looking for evidence of those 'taken-for-granted' assumptions which, although rarely or never explicitly invoked or discussed by participants, nevertheless define the process of 'doing education'. We have called these kinds of assumptions 'educational ground-rules' (Mercer and Edwards, 1981; Edwards and Mercer, 1987).

To make these analytic procedures clearer and less abstract, I include here an example of the products of this process. It is an extract from one of our research publications (Edwards and Mercer, 1989). In it, we draw on the analysis of two of the three recorded topics, 'computer graphics' and 'clay pottery' (see Table 2.1, above), to exemplify matters of discourse content, continuity and context as discussed above.

The teacher began the lesson by introducing the pupils to their new computer and immediately established a context for it in terms of their previous experience with computers in the classroom (Sequence 1, below). Lessons typically began in this manner, with introductions to the work to be done and continuity links established with what had been done previously. Thus Lesson 2, recorded a week later, began with a back reference to where the previous lesson had left off (Sequence 2, below).

Besides these opening links, explicit references were also made during lessons to what had been done and said earlier. Sequence 3 lists the teacher's back references from the last three lessons of making clay pottery. (This is a different teacher, pupils and school.)

In Sequence 3, the teacher's remarks to John and Lorraine reflect the fact that constructing a continuity of shared knowledge can be a problematic process. Indeed, all of the cases listed in Sequence 3 occurred in the context of some difficulty arising with regard to the understanding that teacher and pupils had established up to that point in the lesson. That is, the teacher was most likely to point out that knowledge was, in her opinion, shared when pupils were acting as though it were not. When the pupils seemed not to have grasped some significant principle, procedure or instruction, the teacher would remind them that this matter had, in fact, been dealt with previously.

SEQUENCE 1: Introducing the lesson.

T: Right/this our new computer/the four eighty zed. You haven't seen this one before. Erm when you've used computer programs before/ what's happened is that the words have come up on the screen/or the instructions/for you/have come up on the screen/and you've just answered the questions/and/typed in/what the/ computer wanted you to do. This program is different. In this program the computer doesn't know what to do. You've got to tell it what to do/so you have got to instruct the computer.

*(An RML 480Z micro)*

*Teacher gestures with arm toward screen.*

SEQUENCE 2: Building upon the previous lesson.

T: Now you've got your programs from last
   week have you/to show me what you're
PUPILS: Yes
T: (continuing) going to do/with angles not ninety
   degrees./We had to try something else didn't
   we. What did you find most difficult Susan?
   What's yours?

*T reminding pupils of instructions she gave last week.*

SEQUENCE 3: Back references to shared experience and talk.

– What did I tell you about thin bits? What happens when they dry?
– What did I tell you about eyes?
– Can you remember what you forgot to do Patricia/ when you put that
   little belt thing around?
– Look when you put its eyes in./ I did tell you this before Lorraine.
– John/you seem to have forgotten everything you've learned don't you?
– Don't forget/if it's too wide chop it off.


Sequence 4: Continuity: What have you been doing all along?

| | |
|---|---|
| T: Now/how are you fixing them on Katie? | |
| Katie: Putting them/well its ( ... ) | *Katie mutters* |
| T: Now/what do you think you should do what | *hesitantly.* |
|   have you been doing all along every time | |
|   you've joined anything? | |
| Katie: Putting grooves in it. | |
| T: Putting grooves in it/haven't you and water/ | |
|   grooves and water/the water to fill up the | |
|   grooves/on both bits of clay./You must do it/ | |
|   otherwise it will dry/and when it's dry like | |
|   those are dry/those ears will just be lying on | |
|   the floor/or on the table. Take them off/otherwise | *Katie refits the* |
|   you'll be very sad./You've got to do | *ears.* |
|   things the right way round with clay or they | |
|   just don't work. | |

(Edwards and Mercer, 1989, pp.94–6, reprinted with
the permission of Ablex Publishing Corporation)

*Figure 2.2* Four sequences of classroom talk


It has been suggested that this association of explicit references to past shared experience, including previous discourse, with occasions on which the commonality of knowledge appears to be in doubt is a general feature of conversation, not something peculiar to school classrooms. It has been observed in adult conversation in educational and noneducational settings (Edwards and Middleton, 1986; Mercer and Edwards, 1987) and in parent-child conversation during early language learning (Edwards and Goodwin, 1986). In the classroom, however, such explicit appeals to significant aspects of past shared experience might have an important pedagogic function. As transactions between child and adult, they occur in Vygotsky's 'zone of proximal development', at precisely the points at which common knowledge is being created. It is the teacher's role to draw children's attention to such matters, and so establish knowledge that is both common and communicable. The next sequence illustrates this very clearly.

## *Interviews*

As mentioned earlier, we felt that the interviews with both teachers and children were useful and informative. It may be relevant here to define the status of the interview data in our analysis. The interviews with teachers before the observed sessions were intended to inform us about what would be going on, and what the teacher's pedagogic aims and expectations were for the children involved. The interviews with teachers and pupils which followed the video-taped sessions were simply an additional source of information about what was said and done. In the research of some ethnomethodologists, conversation analysts or discourse analysts (see, for examples and discussion of such research, Potter and Wetherell, 1987), interview data may be the prime data: the interviews themselves provide the discourse or conversations which are then analysed to explain actions, 'interpretative practices', attitudes or beliefs. In our analysis, however, the interview data had a *supplementary* status: we talked to participants in order to elicit their ideas about the content and purpose of the activities in which they had been observed to engage, and to help us resolve any ambiguities in what had been said during the recorded sessions.

## Presentation and dissemination

Matters of dissemination – how to write up the research, where to get it published, and so on – usually become a matter for consideration by researchers well before the completion of a project. There are two common problems to be faced. One is identifying the audiences to whom the research is to be disseminated. The second is deciding how best to communicate the findings of the research to those audiences.

In the case of our research we identified two main audiences. The first was the academic community – other researchers, teachers in higher education, students. To this audience, we wished to describe a piece of research which could be seen as contributing to the fields of study of psychology, discourse analysis and educational research. For this audience we wrote journal articles and a book and presented papers at conferences. The other main audience was the professional educational community – teachers, educational policy makers, teacher-trainers – who we hoped would appreciate the benefits of an 'applied' piece of research. For this audience, we wrote articles in the educational press (e.g. Mercer and Edwards, 1988), wrote material for Open University INSET courses for teachers and ran INSET sessions for local educational authorities. We hoped the book (Edwards and Mercer, 1987) would reach this audience also.

Communicating with these audiences was, initially, no easy matter. By the very nature of our involvement in the project, our immersion in the analytic procedures described earlier, we had developed a highly contextualized discourse for discussing, among ourselves, the data, analysis and theory with which we worked. Somewhat to our surprise, we often found that it was difficult to talk about the research to people outside the project, even if they were social scientists or educational researchers. We felt it was necessary to identify and 'highlight' distinctive qualities of what we had done and found.

In attempting to overcome these difficulties, we came to realize that what initially appeared to be a part of the communication problem was in fact a resource for its solution. This was our own vocabulary of 'key terms' which had emerged through the analytic process and through our discussions of other relevant research. We had developed a set of terms and concepts in order to talk to each other about the research: we began now to consider how useful they would be for communicating our findings to others. This phase of research had begun with one such term (mentioned earlier) well established: *educational ground rules*. It was not really an original usage on our part (Neisser, 1976; Bernstein, 1981 both use 'ground rules' to refer to implicit understandings about how educational activities should be carried out), but we had used it in a particular way, to explain particular phenomena we had studied. We also used *context* and *continuity* with specific meanings. In describing teacher-talk we introduced terms like *cued elicitation* (whereby a teacher encourages a particular response from pupils through intonation, gesture or other physical activity). In discussing qualities and kinds of educational knowledge we distinguished between *principled* and *ritual* understanding. The precise meaning of any of these terms is not important here (see Chapter 8 of Edwards and Mercer, 1987); I include them because they figured in our attempts to move from the 'closed', highly contextualized discourse of researchers engaged in doing the research (within which some of these terms had emerged) into a more 'open', explicit form of discourse suitable for communicating with wider audiences. Contrary to some opinions, the introduction of new technical terms does not necessarily hinder communication with wider audiences. If well chosen, and properly explained, key terms can help people perceive the distinctive qualities of a piece of research and help them take on new perspectives and ideas which the researchers have developed. Readers may judge the success of our efforts by looking at any of our publications listed below.

We spent a lot of time and effort planning our dissemination and writing up the research. Nevertheless, our dissemination plans encountered some hitches. For instance, we hoped for a simultaneous launch of *Common Knowledge* in Britain and the USA, but the combined effects of our publisher's involvement in a corporate merger and the loss of a book manuscript in the international post prevented this: the book first appeared in the USA only as an inaccessibly priced hardback. Reviews of the book seemed slow to appear. It emerged that some of the people we most hoped would read and review the book had never even received a review copy. Persistent pressure from us eventually sorted out some of these problems, and the book has now appeared in an American paperback and in a Spanish language edition (Edwards and Mercer, 1988). So although fame and fortune on the grand scale still skilfully evade us, we seem to have been reasonably successful so far in reaching the audiences we aimed for. Our papers have been accepted for publication by referenced journals. Our research has been cited in government policy documents (The Kingman Report, 1988), and *Common Knowledge* has been adopted as a set book for postgraduates and is used on in-service courses for teachers. BBC Radio 4's general interest programme *Science Now* even included an item on our research and its implications for teaching and learning (October, 1989). It is of course particularly reassuring to have now met or read of teachers who have found our ideas interesting and useful (e.g. National Oracy Project, 1989a, b) and to find that some of the researchers who we most respect see value in our work too (e.g. Barnes, 1987; Cazden and Mehan, 1989).

## References

Barnes, D. (1976) *From Communication to Curriculum*, Harmondsworth, Penguin.

Barnes, D. (1987) 'The nature of signals: An interview with Douglas Barnes', *The English Magazine* 19, Autumn, 4–10.

Bernstein, B. (1981) 'Codes, modalities and the process of reproduction: A model', *Language in Society* 10, 327–363.

Bruner, J.S. (1986) *Actual Minds, Possible Worlds*, London, Harvard University Press.

Cazden, C.B. and Mehan, H. (1989) 'Principles of sociology and anthropology: Context, code, classroom and culture', in Reynolds, M.C. (ed.) *Knowledge Base for the Beginning Teacher*, New York, Pergamon.

Cole, M. and Scribner, S. (1974) *Culture and Thought*, New York, Wiley.

Desforges, C. (1985) 'Training for the management of learning in the primary school', in Francis, H. (ed.) *Learning to Teach: Psychology in Teacher Training*, Lewis, Falmer Press.

Donaldson, M. (1978) *Children's Minds*, London, Fontana.

Edwards, A.D. (1980) 'Patterns of power and authority in classroom talk', in Woods, P. (ed.) *Teacher Strategies: Explorations in the Sociology of the School*, London, Groom Helm.

Edwards, D. and Goodwin, R.Q. (1986) 'The language of shared attention and visual experience: A functional study of early nomination', *Journal of Pragmatics* 9, 475–493.

Edwards, D. and Mercer, N. (1986) 'Context and continuity: Classroom discourse and the development of shared knowledge', in Durkin, K. (ed.) *Language Development in the School Years*, London, Groom Helm.

Edwards, D. and Mercer, N. (1987) *Common Knowledge: The Development of Understanding in the Classroom*, London, Routledge.

Edwards, D. and Mercer, N. (1988) *El conocimiento Compartido: el desarrollo de la comprensión en elaula*, Barcelona: Ediciones Paidós.

Edwards, D. and Mercer, N. (1989) 'Reconstructing context: The conventionalization of classroom knowledge', *Discourse Processes* 12, 91–104.

Edwards, D., Mercer, N. and Maybin, J. (1987) 'The development of joint understanding in the classroom', *ESRC End of Awards Report*, Award no. C00232236.

Edwards, D. and Middleton, D. (1986) 'Conversation and remembering: Constructing an account of shared experience through conversational discourse', *Discourse Processes* 9, 423–459.

Flanders, N.A. (1970) *Analysing Teacher Behaviour*, Reading, MA, Addison-Wesley.

Galton, M., Simon, B. and Croll, P. (1980) *Inside the Primary Classroom* (the Oracle project), London, Routledge & Kegan Paul.

Hammersley, M. (ed.) (1983) *The Ethnography of Schooling*, Driffield, Nafferton.

The Kingman Report. (1988) *Report of the Committee of Inquiry into the Teaching of English Language*, Chairman: Sir John Kingman, London, HMSO.

Maybin, J. (1987) 'Appendix: Outline of the research project', in Edwards, D. and Mercer, N. (eds.) *Common Knowledge: The Development of Understanding in the Classroom*, London, Routledge.

Mehan, H. (1979) *Learning Lessons: Social Organization in the Classroom*, Cambridge, MA, Harvard University Press.

Mercer, N. and Edwards, D. (1981) 'Ground-rules for mutual understanding: A social psychological approach to classroom knowledge', in Mercer, N. (ed.) *Language in School and Community*, London, Edward Arnold.

Mercer, N. and Edwards, D. (1987) 'Knowledge development in adult learning groups', *Open Learning* 2, 22–28.

Mercer, N. and Edwards, D. (1988) 'Re-potting primary science', *Times Educational Supplement* 1, January.

Mercer, N., Edwards, D. and Maybin, J. (1988) 'Putting context into oracy: The construction of shared knowledge through classroom discourse', in MacLure, M., Phillips, T. and Wilkinson, A. (eds.) *Oracy Matters*, Milton Keynes, Open University Press.

National Oracy Project (1989a) *Oracy Issues* 3, Summer, p. 6.

National Oracy Project (1989b) *Talk* 1, Spring, pp. 34–36.

Neisser, U. (1976) 'General academic and artificial intelligence', in Resnick, L.B. (ed.) *The Nature of Intelligence*, New York, Lawrence Erlbaum.

Piaget, J. (1971) *Science as Education and the Psychology of the Child*, London, Longman.

Potter, J. and Wetherell, M. (1987) *Discourse and Social Psychology: Beyond Attitudes and Behaviour*, London, Sage.

Sinclair, J.M. and Coulthard, R.M. (1975) *Towards an Analysis of Discourse: The English Used by Teachers and Pupils*, Oxford, Oxford University Press.

Stubbs, M. (1981) 'Scratching the surface: Linguistic data in educational research', in Adelman, C. (ed.) *Uttering, Muttering: Collecting, Using and Reporting Talk for Social and Educational Research*, London, Grant McIntyre.

Vygotsky, L.S. (1978) *Mind in Society: The Development of Higher Psychological Processes*, London, Harvard University Press.

Walkerdine, V. (1982) 'From context to text: A psychosemiotic approach to abstract thought', in Beveridge, M. (ed.) *Children Thinking Through Language*, London, Edward Arnold.

Wertsch, J.V. (ed.) (1985) *Culture, Communication and Cognition: Vygotskian Perspectives*, Cambridge, Cambridge University Press.

Young, M.F.D. (1971) *Knowledge and Control: New Directions for the Sociology of Education*, London, Collier-Macmillan.

*This chapter is based on an early research project on the use of computers for resourcing group-based activities in the classroom. The project's title, "Spoken Language and New Technology" (SLANT), shows its age! The research team included Open University colleagues Peter Scrimshaw and Eunice Fisher, with John Elliot, Terry Phillips and Maggie Maclure of the University of East Anglia. Rupert Wegerif participated as a PhD student and Lyn Dawes as a classroom teacher. It was during this project, in 1992, that we first identified three types of talk in groups: disputational, cumulative and exploratory*

# 3 The quality of talk in children's collaborative activity in the classroom

*Mercer, N. (1996). The quality of talk in children's collaborative activity in the classroom. Special issue, 'Co-operation and social context in adult-child interaction'*, Learning and Instruction *(Elsevier), 6, 4, 359–378.*

## Abstract

This paper describes research based on observational data of the talk of children working together on educational activities in primary school class-rooms. It offers an analysis of the quality of observed talk, an analysis which emerges from a sociocultural perspective on the process of teaching and learning. The paper is organized around four main themes: (a) the role of oral language and joint activity in the construction of knowledge; (b) education in schools as a cultural and linguistic activity; (c) the role of a teacher in fostering certain kinds of discourse; and (d) the need for applied educational research to be based on close working relationships between teachers and researchers. **Copyright© 1996 Elsevier Science Ltd**

## Introduction

In this paper I will discuss ways that the talk of children working together on educational activities in primary school classrooms can be analysed in terms of its quality as a social mode of thinking. I will draw mainly on findings from the SLANT (Spoken Language and New Technology) research project, recently completed, which studied children aged 5–12 working in pairs or small groups on computer-based activities. The paper has four main themes: (a) the role of oral language and joint activity in the construction of knowledge; (b) education in schools as a cultural and linguistic activity; (c) the role of a teacher in fostering certain kinds of dis-course; and (d) the need for applied educational research to be based on close working relationships between teachers and researchers. I will begin by discussing some prior research into children's collaborative problem-solving activity and talk.

## Prior research on collaboration in learning

Communication between learners has not figured prominently in theories of the development of knowledge and understanding. Piaget, in his early work, did sketch out a role for the significance of interaction between peers – it helped children to decentre, to become sensitive to other perspectives on the world than their own. (See Light & Littleton, 1994, for a discussion of this aspect of Piaget's research.) In his later work, however, with its focus on the activities of individuals, he did not give the topic much attention. But there have been some interesting recent developments in the Piagetian tradition. Followers of Piaget such as Willem Doise, Anne-Nelly Perret-Clermont and Gabriel Mugny have used the concept of *socio-cognitive conflict* to take account of how a child's understanding may be shifted by interacting with another child who has a rather different understanding of events (see, e.g., Bell, Grossen, & Perret-Clermont, 1985; Doise & Mugny, 1984). The basic idea is that when two contrasting world-views are brought into contact, and the resulting conflict has to be resolved to solve some problem, this is likely to stimulate some cognitive restructuring – some learning and improved understanding. The concept of socio-cognitive conflict has some interesting potential for the study of joint activity in the classroom. But neo-Piagetians have not studied the actual talk involved in such conflicts of ideas – perhaps because language still occupies a relatively marginal role in their theory. The main aim in most of their research has also been to determine whether interaction improved later *individual* performance (rather than being interested in the joint construction of knowledge).

Vygotsky's theory, on the other hand, is essentially concerned with teaching-and-learning, rather than joint learning. Some neo-Vygotskians have researched learners' joint activity, but as Wells (1992) suggests, they differ from the Piagetians by stressing co-operation rather than conflict. Most of this research involves adapting ideas from the study of asymmetrical (i.e. teacher–learner) relationships to the study of more symmetrical ones (i.e. learner–learner). Thus Bruner (1985) talks of how a "more competent peer" can provide the "scaffolding" support for a learner. Others have since suggested that learners having to explain ideas to each other, whatever the relative ability of those involved, is useful because this encourages the development of a more explicit, organized, distanced kind of understanding (Fletcher, 1985). But we still lack suitable concepts for dealing with this process.

Although theory may not have kept pace, there has been a great deal of research interest in collaborative learning in recent years. It has been investigated in various ways, which can be loosely categorized as either (a) experimental studies in which pairs of subjects carry out specially designed problem-solving tasks, and (b) observational analyses of the talk of children working together on curriculum-based tasks in school. This diversity of methodology may prove one of the strengths of such research on talk and learning, rather than a problem. I will briefly and very selectively review each of these lines of enquiry and draw out some points which are relevant.

### Experimental research

In Europe and the U.S.A. in recent years there have been many experimental comparisons of children working in pairs and groups (see, for example, Howe, 1993; Light & Littleton, 1994). Typically, this research has shown its neo-Piagetian influence by focusing on individual learning outcomes rather than on the *process* of learning together. Some of the findings of this research support the value of collaborative learning: but others have shown how under some conditions working with a partner is *less* effective than working on your own. Some experiments have been designed to determine what makes the crucial difference. One factor that does seem important is whether or not the experimental conditions are such that the children *have* to communicate and collaborate to solve a problem, rather than simply being allowed to do so (Light & Glachan, 1985). On the basis of a range of studies of children working in pairs on computer-based problems, Light 1993) suggests that having to use language to make plans explicit, to make decisions and to interpret feedback seems to facilitate problem-solving and promote understanding. One of the tasks used by Light and his fellow researchers was a kind of adventure game, in which the quest was to find and rescue a king's crown, hidden on an island (shown on a map on the computer screen). Choosing from a range of possible strategies, the children could manipulate several characters and means of transport to avoid the pirates who blocked their way. The analysis of children's talk showed that those pairs who did most verbal planning, negotiation and discussion of feedback were the most successful in solving the problems. Using talk to reconcile conflicting suggestions for action seemed particularly important, and successful pairs also seemed to be those in which decision-making was most evenly shared between partners (Barbieri & Light, 1992; Blaye, Light, Joiner, & Sheldon, 1991). Under such conditions, both children of a pair often learned better than when working alone. On the other hand, this research does not support the idea that working with a more competent peer is necessarily helpful for learning, as children who were considered to be of similar ability seemed to learn better than those in more asymmetrical pairs. Working with a more knowledgeable and capable partner who dominates decision-making and insists on the use of their own problem-solving strategies may hinder rather than help the less able (Hoyles, Healy, & Pozzi, 1992; Messer, Joiner, Light, & Littleton, 1993; Light, Littleton, Messer, & Joiner, 1994).

There has also been some recent interest in how collaborative activity may facilitate certain kinds of cognitive operations. For example, some experimental research has considered whether discussion helps children to *generalize* what they have learned (i.e. the extent to which they are able to use what they have learned in one situation or through solving one specific kind of problem, when dealing with other related situations and problems). This interest partly arose because previous research had indicated that children do not find it easy to generalize their understanding from one kind of problem or one area of the curriculum to another (see, e.g., Lave, 1992). To some extent, this seems to be because their understanding is often procedural rather than principled – they learn to follow some practical procedures (e.g. learning a particular method for doing long divisions, or for doing science experiments and writing them up) without ever coming to understand the underlying principles involved (Edwards & Mercer, 1987). There is now support for the idea that through sharing ideas, children can achieve more generalizable kinds of understanding if they are actively helped and encouraged to do so. For example, Hatano and Inagaki (1992) investigated how Japanese 6-year-olds used their experience of raising one kind of pet animal (e.g. a goldfish) to make sense of the life processes and care needs of other living things. One of their findings, which is particularly relevant here, was that when children had to share ideas about caring for animals – to explain, discuss and sometimes justify the opinions they held – this led to a better, more generalizable and principled understanding.

### Observational research

In their wide review of studies of group work in primary classrooms (and some experimental studies) Galton and Williamson (1992, p. 43) conclude: "For successful collaboration to take place pupils need to be taught how to collaborate so that they have a clear idea of what is expected of them." However, hardly any of the research reviewed by Galton and Williamson made a close analysis of pupils' talk, and so cannot add much to our understanding of how knowledge is constructed through particular language practices in actual language events. It is therefore interesting to also consider the findings of a style of observational research not included in Galton and Williamson's review, in which researchers have concentrated on the detailed analysis of recorded talk and on the process of discussion in classrooms rather than on its outcomes.

Two pioneers of this kind of research were Barnes and Todd (1978). They show how knowledge is treated by pupils or students as a *negotiable* commodity when they are enthusiastically engaged in joint tasks. They suggest that pupils are more likely to engage in open, extended discussion and argument when they are talking with peers outside the visible control of their teacher, and that this kind of talk enables them to take a more active and independent ownership of knowledge. As Barnes and Todd put it:

> Our point is that to place the responsibility in the learners' hands changes the nature of that learning by requiring them to negotiate their own criteria of relevance and truth. If schooling is to prepare young people for responsible adult life, such learning has an important place in the repertoire of social relationships which teachers have at their disposal.
> (Barnes & Todd, 1978, p. 127)

They also suggest that classroom discussion has to meet certain requirements for explicitness which would not normally be required in everyday discourse. Relevant information should be shared effectively, opinions should be clearly explained and explanations examined critically: that knowledge should be made publicly *accountable*. Barnes and Todd argue that the successful pursuit of educational activity through group work depends on learners (a) sharing the same ideas about what is relevant to the discussion, and (b) having a joint conception of what they are trying to achieve by it. These conclusions are in accord with those drawn by Galton and Williamson (1992; see also Hoyles, Sutherland, & Healy, 1990).

## Evaluating talk

The diverse field of research which I have briefly reviewed does not provide a neat set of findings which can easily be integrated or reconciled. However, it does support the conclusion that talk between learners has been shown to be valuable for the construction of knowledge. Joint activity provides opportunities for practising and developing ways of reasoning with language, and the same kinds of opportunities are unlikely to arise in teacher-led discussions. This conclusion can be used to justify group work and other forms of collaborative activity in the classroom. But the research also shows that while encouraging talk between learners may help the development of understanding, not all kinds of talk and collaboration are of equal educational value.

It is possible to distil from the findings of the research I have received a description of a kind of talk which is good for solving intellectual problems and advancing understanding. First, it is talk in which partners present ideas as clearly and as explicitly as necessary for them to become shared and jointly evaluated. Second, it is talk in which partners *reason* together – problems are jointly analysed, possible explanations are compared, joint decisions are reached. From an observer's point of view, their reasoning is *visible* in the talk.

The research also helps us describe some favourable *conditions* for the emergence of this kind of talk. First, partners must have to talk to do the task, so their conversation is not merely an incidental accompaniment. Second, the activity should be designed to encourage co-operation, rather than competition, between partners. Third, participants have a good, shared understanding of the point and purpose of the activity. In satisfying these three conditions one would be aiming to create a working environment which encourages a free exchange of relevant ideas and the active participation of all involved.

## "Ground rules" for classroom talk

There has been a good deal of educational research on classroom talk as a medium for social control (see Edwards & Westgate, 1994, for a review). But only quite recently has there been much research into its function as a medium for sharing knowledge and one through which adults influence the representations of reality, the interpretations of experience, which children eventually adopt. Moreover, most of the recent, neo-Vygotskian research which has developed this theme (e.g. that discussed by Wood, 1988; and Rogoff, 1990) has focused on one-to-one relationships and has been located in homes and nurseries rather than classrooms, where quite different *ground rules* operate, and the process of teaching and learning is embedded in different kinds of cultural settings and adult–child relationships.

One important and problematic aspect of classroom education is learners' appreciation of *educational* ground rules (Mercer & Edwards, 1981; Edwards & Mercer, 1987; Sheeran & Barnes, 1991). These are the implicit norms and expectations that it is necessary to take account of to participate successfully in educational discourse. Becoming educated means becoming able to follow the ground rules: but having acquired these rules, people then tend to assume that what is involved is no more than common sense. As Sheeran and Barnes say: "In spite of their importance, these tacit expectations or ground rules are seldom discussed with pupils, because the teachers themselves are largely unaware of them" (1991, p. 2). They go on to show how many of the requirements for providing satisfactory essays and other written work in different school subjects are never made explicit to pupils. And even when some of those requirements are made clear, teachers hardly ever provide justifications which will help children understand *why* they should write in particular ways. Classroom research has provided many examples of how children's interpretations of the ground rules may differ in important ways from those of their classmates and/or their teachers. For example, while some children may see discussion group activities as an opportunity for airing problems and misunderstandings, others in the same group may see them only as occasions on which you must try to demonstrate that you know the right answers. Yet other children may think that the real imperative is to talk fluently and copiously (Mercer, Edwards, & Maybin, 1988). Research on GCSE oral English examinations has suggested that children sometimes graft the ground rules of TV chat shows on to their discussions (Hewitt, 1989). There is evidence that when teachers bring ground rules for discussion out into the open for consideration with their classes, this can lead to improved motivation and levels of performance amongst the children (Brown & Palincsar, 1989; Prentice, 1991; Steel, 1991; Dawes, Fisher, & Mercer, 1992).

## The SLANT project

I will next present and discuss some examples of children talking together in classrooms, which were recorded for the SLANT (Spoken Language and New Technology) project on talk at the computer in primary schools. This project is described in more detail elsewhere (e.g. Mercer, 1994; see also Mercer & Fisher, 1992). The main aims in the project were to see how computer-based activities stimulated talk amongst children, and to understand the role of the teacher in organizing and supporting joint activity at the computer. Here, however, I will use the SLANT data and analysis to discuss some general features of the quality of talk of children working together and the teacher's role in supporting it.

The design of the project was based on a notion of close partnership between the researchers in the central team and the primary teachers in whose classrooms the research was to be carried out. In part, this reflected the influence of the *educational action research* paradigm developed by SLANT team member John Elliot (1991) and others, though such action research typically accords greater priority to the maintenance of control by teachers of the research agenda. SLANT may well be more appropriately described as *interactive* research, to use the term coined by Judith Green (pers. comm.) for such applied, joint researcher–practitioner enterprises. The teachers developed activities (usually in discussion with a researcher) in accord with their normal curriculum goals. After spending some time in more general observation in the classrooms, the researchers made video recordings of one or more groups of children doing the activities, usually over a series of lessons. In this way, SLANT researchers recorded approximately 60 hours of classroom talk in 10 English primary schools, with 50 children aged between 5 and 13 being video-recorded working at the computer on a range of activities based on software which included word-processing packages, adventure games, simulations, databases and mathematics programs. Once the research was under way, regular meetings between teachers and researchers (which usually involved viewing of recently recorded data) often led to new ideas for activities and to further recording. Researchers and teachers also talked about the activities with the children involved.

As the project progressed, we realized that we needed to develop two main aspects of our analytic framework: (1) a clearer notion of the boundaries of an activity; and (2) some ways of describing, distinguishing between and evaluating the different kinds of talk that we observed.

### Activities in context

The analytic perspective of the SLANT project on the process of teaching and learning can be described as sociocultural, strongly influenced by neo-Vygotskian psychological research, by sociolinguistics and cultural anthropology (as exemplified by Wertsch, 1985; Barnes & Todd, 1978, 1995; Heath, 1982). This perspective encourages a revision of the traditional, common-sense conception of the boundaries of a problem-solving or learning task. When children begin any collaborative activity in the classroom, they bring to it their past experience of doing other kinds of joint activities and other kinds of school work. Such past experience, as well as their personal relationship with the other children and with their teacher, will influence what sense they make of the activity. We felt that to understand the quality of talk and collaboration that we saw going on in our video recordings of children engaged in computer-based activities, we needed to take into account much more than just the tasks children faced on the screen. We needed to look at the ways activities were set up by teachers, and what the teacher expected the children to achieve from doing the work. Also crucially important was how children made sense of any activity in practice. For example, sometimes children seemed to treat a computer-based task as a competitive game, rather than a collective endeavour. All these *contextualizing factors* were potentially strong influences on the ways children talked and acted in collaboration (Mercer & Fisher, 1992). Of course, the quality of software is one other important factor, and certainly some kinds of programs tend to constrain talk more than others (Fisher, 1993); but software is not always the factor of overwhelming importance, as one might think from reading most research on IT in education (as discussed by Crook, 1991; Jones & Mercer, 1993). The same kind of program, used by different teachers and children, can generate activities which are quite different in terms of the kind and quality of talk and collaboration that emerge. Our conception of context as consisting of both historical and contemporary factors influencing the construction of meaning (Mercer, 1992) also led us to reject the idea that the start of the activity was necessarily marked by the point at which the children started to operate the computer, or ended at the point when they stopped.

### Observational data

Presented below are three sequences of collaborative talk from sessions which varied in length from about 35 to 90 minutes (the varying length of sessions reflected differences in the kinds of activities that the children were engaged in). I have made this particular selection in order to illustrate and typify some interesting variations in the ways that we observed children to talk as they worked at the computer. The sessions that provided these sequences were recorded over a period of 14 months in the same school – a modern primary with a mixed catchment. It is situated on a city housing estate with more than its share of social and economic problems. The children in these sessions were all aged 9–10 years. Each of the pairs or groups involved were recorded working in sets of related sessions, all in their normal classroom (with other activity going on around them), spread over days or weeks. The video data was obtained by situating a camera to one side of the computer, at such an angle that the screen display was visible and the faces of both children were partially so. Talk was recorded on a remote directional microphone attached to the front of the computer, and all talk recorded was transcribed. I have kept the transcription format as simple as possible, in that I have only included information about such things as pauses, overlapping speech or non-verbal aspects of communication (*in italics*) where I felt these were essential to the comprehensibility of the speech and the presentation of an analysis. I have also punctuated the transcribed speech, in accord with my own intuitions, to make it easier to read.

In all three of the selected sequences, the children can be observed to be solving some kind of problem and talking as they do so. And in all of them, the children can be seen to be well on task in that they are dealing enthusiastically with legitimate aspects of the work they have been set by their teacher. After presenting each sequence, I will comment on the talk and joint learning activity which is taking place.

### Sequence 1: finding the elephant

In this sequence two 10-year-old boys, Sean and Lester, are using an educational software package called *Smile*, which provides a series of mathematics-related puzzles. The puzzle that they are doing involves finding an elephant lost in New York (its streets being represented by a grid on the screen) by keying in co-ordinates and reacting to computer feedback on how close they get to their hidden target. Following their teacher's instructions, they take consecutive turns to key in pairs of co-ordinates. They have been doing the puzzle for about 5 minutes.

LESTER:  1, 2, 3, 4, 5 (*counting grid squares on the screen with his finger, before he takes his turn*)

SEAN:  1. It's there.

LESTER:  So it has got to be . . .

SEAN:  5, 4 (*suggesting a set of co-ordinates*)

LESTER:  (*ignoring Sean*) . . . 4, 3. No, we have had 4, 3.

SEAN:  4, 5. No, 4, 4.

LESTER:  4, 3 (*presses keys for his turn*). What! (*he fails to find the elephant*). That's easy, I know where it is, opposite.

SEAN:  (*sits silently for a while, looking at the screen.*)

LESTER:  I can do it.

SEAN:  (*still staring at the screen*) No, not up, down.

LESTER:  It can't be.

SEAN:  It can.

LESTER:  I know where it is.

SEAN:  (*eventually takes his turn, but fails to find the elephant.*)

LESTER:  I told you it weren't over there. (*he then takes his turn, without success*)

SEAN:  Eh heh heh heh. (*laughing gleefully*)

In this sequence, we see two boys actively and enthusiastically engaged in their task. They argue about who knows best, sometimes trying to justify their claims by recourse to the evidence on the screen. They offer suggestions, comments and advice on each other's actions, and ask each other a few questions. In the session as a whole, there was a lot of talk, and it was all on task. But consider the sequence as a piece of joint constructive problem-solving, and especially as one which would help the boys develop their ability to deal with problems in an educated way, and its quality is doubtful. The talk nearly all consists of short assertions, rebuttals or comments which are not constructive. Sequence 1 was typical of the talk in this session. The amount of real collaboration – in the sense of sharing of ideas, joint evaluation of information, hypothesizing and decision-making, or even taking any advice offered – was minimal. The boys effectively redefined this supposedly collaborative activity as a *competitive* one. They took alternate turns: but then so do opponents in tennis. In the session as a whole, each time they did the puzzle, whoever happened to key in the last pair of co-ordinates before the elephant was found claimed this vociferously as a personal victory. It was difficult to see what either boy was learning about learning through talk, or about maths, from doing this activity. They both seemed to understand the concept of co-ordinates already, and their strategies did not seem to change or develop as they played.

### Sequence 2: fantabuloso

This is from a session in which two 10-year-old girls, Katie and Anne, were working on the production of their own class newspaper, using some desk-top publishing software for schools called *Front Page Extra*. They were friends, who had successfully worked together before. Their teacher had helped them load the program and set up the screen for their immediate task, which was to design and write their front page. At the point the sequence begins, they have been engaged in the task for about an hour and a quarter and are trying to compose some text for their front page.

KATIE:   Okay, so right then. What shall we write?
ANNE:   We can have something like those autograph columns and things like that and items, messages
KATIE:   Inside these covers (*pause 3+ secs*). Our fun-filled
ANNE:   That's it!
KATIE:   Something
ANNE:   Something like that!
KATIE:   Yeah
ANNE:   Inside this fabulous fun-filled covers are – how can we have a fun-filled cover? Let me try
KATIE:   Inside these (*pause 3+ secs*)
ANNE:   Hah huh (*laughs*)
ANNE:   You sound happy on this. Fantabuloso (*laughs*)
KATIE:   Inside these inside these fant, inside these fun-filled, no inside these covers these fantastic these brilliant
ANNE:   Brilliant
KATIE:   Is it brilliant?
ANNE:   No
KATIE:   No Fantast fantabuloso shall we put that ?
ANNE:   Yeah (*inaudible*) fantabluloso
KATIE:   Fan-tab-u-lo-so
ANNE:   Loso. Fantabuloso.
KATIE:   Fantabuloso oso
ANNE:   Fantabuloso ho!

In this sequence, we see Katie and Anne talking through their text. They ask each other questions (though Anne's question "how can we have a fun-filled cover?" seems more the expression of a problem rather than a request for information from her partner), they make suggestions and offer some reasons for the decisions they take. They confirm and validate each other's statements, explicitly ("That's it") or implicitly by repeating them ("Inside these . . ."). They are not only constructing their text together, they are constructing a joint understanding of what the text should be like. They clearly enjoy working together, perhaps reflecting a past shared history of successful collaboration. There is no real disagreement: they do not challenge each other's suggestions, and do not seem to feel the need to justify opinions or explain their reasons.

### Sequence 3: planning a raid

The next sequence shows a group of three children aged 9 and 10 (two boys and a girl) using a program called *Viking England*, a kind of historical simulation package which allows children to take on the active roles of Viking raiders planning an invasion of the English coast. They had all recently been working in different groups, but two of them had worked together before. In response to events and to questions which appear on the screen, members of the raiding party had to decide what resources are required for the raid, how to overcome the opposition through strategy, and so on. In this sequence they are trying to decide which of four possible sites they should raid (a monastery, a village of huts, a castle or a harbour).

DIANA: Let's discuss it. Which one shall we go for?

ALL: (*inaudible – reading from instructions*)

PETER: 1 2 3 or 4 (*reading out the number of options available*). Well we've got no other chance of getting more money because

ADRIAN: And there's a monastery

DIANA: And if we take number 2 there's that (*inaudible*)

PETER: Yeh but because the huts will be guarded

ALL: Yeh

ADRIAN: And that will probably be guarded

DIANA: It's surrounded by trees

PETER: Yeh

ADRIAN: And there's a rock guarding us there

PETER: Yes there's some rocks there. So I think, I think it should be 1

ADRIAN: Because the monastery might be unguarded

DIANA: Yes 1

ADRIAN: 1 yeh

PETER: Yeh but what about 2? That, it might be not guarded. Just because there's huts there, it doesn't mean it's not guarded, does it? What do you think?

DIANA: Yes it doesn't mean it's not. It doesn't mean to say it's *not* guarded, does it? It may well be guarded. I think we should go for number 1 because I'm pretty sure it's not guarded

ADRIAN:   Yeh

PETER:   OK, yes number 1 (*he keys in 1 on keyboard*). No (*computer responds inappropriately*)

ADRIAN:   You have to use them numbers (*he points to the number keys on right of board, and Peter uses them to obtain the right result. Adrian begins to read from screen display*) "You have chosen to raid area 1."

In Sequence 3 we again see some children on task, asking each other questions, commenting and making suggestions. They discuss the various options, and also remind each other of relevant information. They are using talk to share information and plan together. They discuss and evaluate possible courses of action and make joint decisions. There is a lot of explicit reasoning in the talk. What is more, this reasoning is essentially *interactive* – not really reducible to the form and content of individual statements, but more to do with how the discourse as a whole represents a social, shared thought process. There was a lot of this kind of talk in the *Viking England* activity, in which the children seemed to be reasoning together and building up shared knowledge and understanding to a new level through their talk.

## Three ways of talking and thinking

Sequences 1–3 can be used to illustrate and typify three distinctive ways of talking and thinking.

(1) The first way of talking is *disputational talk*, which is characterized by disagreement and individualized decision-making. There are few attempts to pool resources, or to offer constructive criticism of suggestions. This is how Sean and Lester talk in Sequence 1. Disputational talk also has some characteristic discourse features, notably short exchanges consisting of assertions and counter-assertions.

(2) Next there is *cumulative talk*, in which speakers build positively but uncritically on what the other has said. Partners use talk to construct a "common knowledge" by accumulation. Cumulative talk is characterized by repetitions, confirmations and elaborations. We can see Katie and Anne talking like this in Sequence 2.

(3) *Exploratory talk* occurs when partners engage critically but constructively with each other's ideas. Diana, Peter and Adrian talk like this in Sequence 3. Statements and suggestions are offered for joint consideration. These may be challenged and counter-challenged, but challenges are justified and alternative hypotheses are offered. Compared with the other two types, in exploratory talk *knowledge is made more publicly accountable and reasoning is more visible in the talk*. Progress then emerges from the eventual joint agreement reached.

*Disputational, cumulative* and *exploratory* are not meant to be descriptive categories into which all observed speech can be neatly and separately coded (as might be done in systematic observation research, c.f. Croll, 1986). They are analytic categories, typifications of ways that children in the SLANT project talked together. The concepts of disputational talk, cumulative talk and exploratory talk are embryonic models of three *distinctive social modes of thinking*, models which could help us understand how actual talk (which is inevitably resistant to neat categorization) is used by people to think together. My theoretical argument here has three interwoven parts. First, I am arguing that particular ways of talking permit certain social modes of thinking. Second, particular social modes of thinking are developed in particular kinds of collaborative relationships. And third, collaborative relationships are shaped by participants' culturally based definitions of the situation. (A more elaborated discussion of this can be found in Mercer, 1995.)

### Three levels of analysis

To describe and evaluate the actual talk which goes on in any collaborative educational activity, we need to incorporate the models of talk into an analysis which operates at three levels (I am using *level* here to mean something like depth of focus). The first level is *linguistic*: we examine the talk as spoken text. What kinds of "speech acts" do the students perform? (Do they assert, challenge, explain, request . . .?) What kinds of exchanges take place? (That is, how do speakers build their conversations, how do they respond and react to each other's talk?) What topics are discussed? It is at this level that we can see that disputational talk typifies talk dominated by assertions and counter-assertions, with few of the repetitions and elaborations which characterize cumulative talk. Exploratory talk, in comparison, typifies talk which combines challenges and requests for clarification with responses which provide explanations and justifications. This linguistic level of analysis is thus intended to deal with the content and function of talk, and while this means that attention is necessarily to some of its structural features, the purpose is not to describe how spoken language is constructed as cohesive text (as might be the case in research in systemic linguistics: c.f. Hasan, 1994).

The second level is *psychological*: an analysis of the talk as thought and action. What kinds of ground rules do the speakers seem to be following? How do the ways the speakers interact, the topics they discuss and the issues they raise reflect their interests and concerns? To what extent is reasoning visibly being pursued through the talk? We may be able to use the models of talk to typify the kind of communicative relationship that the speakers are acting out, and the ground rules that they use to do so. So, for example, in disputational talk the relationship is competitive; information is flaunted rather than shared, differences of opinion are opposed rather than resolved, and the general orientation is defensive. Cumulative talk seems to operate more on implicit concerns with solidarity and trust, and the ground rules seem to require the constant repetition and confirmation of partners' ideas and opinions. Exploratory talk foregrounds reasoning. Its ground rules require that the views of all participants are sought and considered, that proposals are explicitly stated and evaluated, and that explicit agreement precedes decisions and actions. Both cumulative and exploratory talk seem to be aimed at the achievement of consensus while disputational talk does not. In disputational talk, although a lot of interaction may be going on, the reasoning involved is very individualized and tacit. In cumulative talk, by comparison, ideas and information are certainly shared and joint decisions may be reached; but there is little in the way of challenge or constructive conflict in the process of constructing knowledge. Exploratory talk, by incorporating both conflict and the open sharing of ideas, represents the more visible pursuit of rational consensus through conversation. More than the other two types, it is like the kind of talk which has been found to be most effective for solving problems through collaborative activity (as discussed earlier in this paper).

To make judgements about the educational value of any observed talk, an additional level of analysis is required. This could be called the *cultural* level, because it inevitably involves some consideration of the nature of educated discourse and of the kinds of reasoning that are valued and encouraged in the cultural institutions of formal education. And here, the analytic category of exploratory talk has a special educational significance. It typifies language which embodies certain principles – of accountability, of clarity, of constructive criticism and receptiveness to well-argued proposals – which are valued highly in many societies. In many of our key social institutions – for example, the law, government administration, research in the sciences and arts, and the negotiation of business – people have to use language to critically interrogate the quality of the claims, hypotheses and proposals made by other people, to express clearly their own understandings, to reach consensual agreement and make joint decisions. The ideal of a speech situation in which everyone is free to express their views and in which the most reasonable views gain general acceptance is implicit in many areas of social life (Habermas, 1979, 1984; Wegerif, 1994). Even if people often violate the principles involved, those principles are still invoked as ideals.

## The role of the teacher

I now turn to the third and fourth of my main topics, the role of a teacher in fostering certain kinds of discourse, and the partnership between teachers and researchers. The existence of a great deal of exploratory talk in the session which provided Sequence 3 *Planning a Raid* was not accidental. By the time that the SLANT project had been running for about a year, it had become clear that for many of the recorded sessions both teachers and researchers (who had reviewed the recordings) were disappointed with the quality of talk which had taken place. The children rarely seemed to spend much time considering and evaluating information, ideas were often only partially expressed, and in some pairs and groups partners seemed to ignore each other's views, or the talk and decision-making was dominated by a few of the group members. The children involved seemed to be operating on disparate sets of ground rules for talking and collaborating at the computer. These matters were discussed at length by teachers and researchers, and in accord with the "action research" philosophy which informed the project, this led to some of the teachers designing new, different kinds of activities.

In the school in which Sequences 1–3 were recorded, this discussion resulted in the following plan for action. First, researchers and the teacher selected one educational computer program (from those in use in the school) which seemed to provide a good basis for a collaborative activity which would *require* the children to share information and make joint decisions. This was *Viking England*, as described at the beginning of Sequence 3. Teacher and researchers then discussed what ground rules the children might be encouraged to follow, though the final decision about what these would be and how they would be presented was left with the teacher. It was eventually agreed that she would stress the importance of:

- sharing all relevant information and suggestions
- having to provide reasons to back up assertions and opinions and suggestions
- asking for reasons when appropriate
- reaching agreement about what action to take, if at all possible
- accepting that the group (rather than any individual member) was responsible for decisions and actions and for any successes and failures which ensued.

The teacher then planned for her class some awareness-raising activities on talk and collaborative activity, away from the computer. Eight three-person groups were set up by the teacher. Each group included at least one child with special needs in literacy, and another who was an able and fluent reader, and consideration was taken of how children's personal styles and relationships in the class might affect who would work best together. In their groups, the children then did some activities intended to raise their awareness of the nature and quality of classroom discussion. These were taken and adapted from some published material on oracy for teachers (Brooks, Latham, & Rex, 1986; Open University, 1991), and included such activities as:

(a) Listening to a tape of sound effects. The group had to try to decide together what they thought each was, nominate a writer to record their ideas and then report back to the class.
(b) Each child had to describe to their group an event that had happened to them during their Christmas holiday. One of the listeners then re-told the story to the class.

(c) Two of the group sat back to back, and one of them had a minute to draw a shape or pattern. That person then described the shape, and the other had to draw it from this description (with other group members as an attentive audience).

The teacher also led some group and class discussions about arguments, taking turns and other topics related to taking part in conversations. Through picking up ideas and opinions offered by the children, the teacher was able to gain some insights into the children's current understanding of how discussions should be conducted. She was also able to make clear some of her own ideas on how groups should operate, to which the children seemed quite receptive. She continued to stress the need for all relevant views to be heard, for agreement to be sought if possible, and for groups rather than individuals to feel responsible for decisions reached and actions pursued. (For the teacher's own account of this see Dawes, 1993; Dawes et al., 1992.)

The children then went on to do collaborative activities at the computer, in pairs or groups of three. But before each group began this activity, the teacher reminded them of the earlier activities and encouraged each of these new sets of children to explicitly rehearse the ground rules for discussion that they would follow. The result was a dramatic increase in the amount of exploratory talk in these groups, in comparison with earlier recorded activities. It also seemed to the teacher and researchers that the enthusiasm and involvement of the children was improved, although we have no objective measures of this and any such change may at least in part be due to the novelty effect of this series of talk activities.

I have concentrated here on the apparent effects of the teacher's preparatory work (the talk awareness activities and the ways she set up the groups) rather than the contribution made by the *Viking England* computer software. The choice of that software, or at least that kind of software, was probably important for the success of the initial activity. But the ground rules that were established in this way were not just used for *Viking England*, and were successfully applied by the children in other, non-computer-based activities. That is, it appeared that the children had become aware of how the exploratory way of talking could be appropriately applied (as a social mode of thinking) in other classroom activities. One can therefore conclude that the teacher had enabled the children to revise and extend their culturally based assumptions, their interpretations of educational ground rules about how language can be used to mediate collaborative relationships in school.

The next sequence was recorded some months later, when the same teacher was rehearsing the ground rules with a group of 10-year-olds who were about to begin an activity (not computer-based) in which they had to identify various animals of the Brazilian rain forest. She has just established that they have all the pictures of animals that they require (I have marked words she stresses **in bold type**).

*Sequence 4: rehearsing the ground rules*

TEACHER:   The next thing you've got to do is to decide **between** you which is which. So if you have a reason for thinking that's (*holding up a picture of a manatee*) a scarlet macaw you say "I think it is because it has flippers" (*children laugh*). So then you would have to accept someone else's opinion if it was different from yours, so you would say something like "Do you you agree?" (*one boy says "no"*) or "I think that's wrong" (*boy says "yes"*). And the person who was going to disagree with you wouldn't just say "no", you would have to have a **reason** for disagreeing. What (*addressing the boy who spoke*) would be your **reason** for disagreeing with that (*she shows him the picture*) being a scarlet macaw?

PAUL:   Because macaws don't have flippers.

OLIVER:   Because the macaw is a parrot! (*laughing*)

TEACHER:   Right. What ever point of view you want to put over, you will have to try to think of your reason for giving it.

The children then went on to do the activity, and the next sequence is an extract from a late stage when they were trying to classify all the animals as either herbivores or carnivores.

*Sequence 5: classifying animals*

EMMELINE:   Now we've got a fish – uh – the

OLIVER:   What sort, the piranha.

EMMELINE:   No, the little, not the scaly one.

MADDY:   Lun, lungf . . . (*hesitating*)

OLIVER:   Lungfish

MADDY:   It probably feeds on things in the river, because it's not going to go out and catch a monkey or something, is it? (*all laugh*)

EMMELINE:   Yeah. Could bri.

OLIVER:   (*interrupting*) There is of course river plants, some of them do feed on river plants, and leaves that fall in the river.

MADDY:   Yeah, it's probably a herbivore.

BEN:   We haven't got anything to tell.

EMMELINE:   What do you think it should be?

OLIVER:   No, actually I think we should put it in "carnivore", most fish are.

EMMELINE:   No, because, ma.

OLIVER:   (*interrupting*) It's our best and most fish are.

EMMELINE:   (*interrupting*) Yeah, but we've got this one here, and this one here.
       (*She indicates some fish cards in both "carnivore" and "herbivore" piles on the table. The discussion continues, unresolved. until Ben says . . .*)

| BEN: | Let's have a vote, have a vote. |
|---|---|
| EMMELINE: | Yeah, let's have a vote. |
| BEN: | (*to Oliver*) What do you think? |
| OLIVER: | I think "carnivore". |
| BEN: | (*to Maddy*) What do you reckon? |
| MADDY: | I think "herbivore". |
| BEN: | (*to Emmeline*) What do you reckon? |
| EMMELINE: | "Herbivore". |
| OLIVER: | (*to Ben*) What do you reckon? |
| BEN: | (*laughing, looking sheepish and uncertain, doesn't answer*) |
| OLIVER: | Come on, this isn't worth it, it's a lungf . . . |
| BEN: | Carnivore |
| OLIVER: | Carnivore, that's two each. |
| BEN: | Let's, OK (*he prepares to toss a coin*) |
| OLIVER: | No, don't both flipping a coin, it's meant to be |
| BEN: | (*interrupts, tosses coin*) Flip |
| OLIVER: | . . . thinking! |
| BEN: | Heads or tails? |
| OLIVER: | Lung, no shush! |
| EMMELINE: | It's heads. Well, you win. |
| OLIVER: | (*picks up the "lungfish" card and reads*) "The lungfish has a pair or lungs and small gills and burrows in the mud and breathes air". It can't be a herbivore because what would it eat when it's on its own in the sand? There's nothing to eat. |

The children then resumed their debate about the lungfish, and eventually decided that they had insufficient information and would leave the lungfish card to one side and deal with it later when the teacher returned. The session which provided Sequence 5 was not a perfect model of equitable, rational discussion: in their excitement the children sometimes interrupt each other, one of the boys sometimes tried to dominate proceedings, and the reasons given for making decisions were not always valid. But there was certainly a lot of exploratory talk, as illustrated in the sequence. The children ask each other questions, they appeal for everyone's views, they try to justify their views rationally and by recourse to evidence. They try to reach agreement through the democratic process of a vote. When that fails, Ben proposes (with Emmeline's support) that they resolve the dilemma through the non-rational process of tossing a coin. But notice then what Oliver does – he objects, reminds the group of the ground rules agreed for the activity ("it's meant to be *thinking!*") and pulls in some additional relevant information for the group's consideration. Faced with this appeal, the group resume their rational debate.

I have given just one example, from one school, of how exploratory talk was encouraged amongst learners. My purpose is simply to illustrate a possibility made real, achieved through the sharing of knowledge between researchers, teachers and learners. But evidence for the importance of helping learners acquire, understand, use and appreciate the value of ground rules for conducting discussions which are rational, equitable and productive is emerging from sociocultural research elsewhere (see, for example, Baker-Sennett, Matusov, & Rogoff, 1992; Lyle, 1993).

## Summary and conclusions

Although talk amongst learners has tended to have a low status in formal education, recent research provides some good reasons for encouraging learners to talk and work together in educational activities. Talk is now recognized as more than a means for sharing thoughts: it is *a social mode of thinking*, a tool for the joint construction of knowledge by teachers and learners. (This concept and related matters are discussed and exemplified in more detail in Mercer, 1995.) However, research does not support the idea that talk and collaboration are inevitably useful, or that learners left to their own devices necessarily know how to make best use of their opportunities. A sociocultural perspective on classroom education supports the use of collaborative activity, but it also highlights the need for a rationale, in terms of both procedures and principles, for the activities learners are expected to do as part of their education. What is more, learners themselves need access to that rationale; and it has to be a rationale that they find convincing. Of course, learners, even those young ones entering infant school, are never blank slates on which their teachers must inscribe all educationally relevant skills. Most children over 9 or 10 may have all the language strategies they need to engage in exploratory talk (and so in educated discourse) without being expressly taught them. They may well already use them to good effect on occasion. Maybin (1994) suggests that children normally do more explaining and justifying in their informal conversations than when they are on task in class. But we also need to consider what is the function and *content* of such conversations. Justifying social or moral choices to friends, or even discussing the social norms of classroom life (Much & Schweder, 1978; Elbers, 1994), is not necessarily the same as using language as a social mode of thinking when making joint decisions in solving problems or choosing between alternative explanations for observed physical events. There are good reasons to believe that pupils and students are often unclear or unaware of what they are expected to be doing and achieving when they are on task in educational activities, and that teachers often provide little useful information about such things to children. And there are no good reasons for assuming that children already possess a good understanding and awareness of how best to go about "learning together" in the classroom.

There are communicative and intellectual dimensions to the organization of collaborative activities which are important if the activities are intended to contribute to children's educational progress. Simply sitting them down with a shared task may stimulate talk, but of what kind and quality? It may be that teachers – the organizers of collaborative activity – often do not have a clear notion of what kind of talk they are trying to encourage and for what reason. They may take the ground rules for granted or, perhaps under the influence of some progressive educational ideology, they may think that it is wrong to guide students' activity so precisely (Edwards & Mercer, 1987).

It would of course be naive to ignore the extent to which (as discussed in Mercer, 1995, Ch. 4) pupils resist, subvert and re-negotiate the ground rules and goals for classroom activity which are promoted by their teachers. But it is nevertheless the case that learners usually have to try to make sense of any activity as best they can, because they are given little help in understanding and appreciating the educational ground rules they are expected to follow. There is a weight of accumulated research evidence to support this view (Mercer & Edwards, 1981; Hull, 1985; Sheeran & Barnes, 1991; Phillips, 1992; Westgate & Corden, 1993; Elbers & Kelderman, 1994), and there are obvious implications in those findings for teachers' practice. But there is no evidence to suggest that explicit consideration of the ground rules of educational activities has become a normal part of classroom life in schools or other educational institutions anywhere in the world. I would suggest that this is not just a reflection of the failure of researchers to effectively disseminate their results to teachers, but an indication of the need for educational research to feed more directly into practical classroom applications. Given the growing evidence that learners do benefit from activities which give explicit consideration to educational ground rules (Brown & Palincsar, 1989; Prentice, 1991; Steel, 1991; Dawes et al., 1992), this is a pressing need. It may be that the kind of research which is more likely to produce results which will influence classroom processes is applied, interactive research of the kind described in this paper, based on a close working relationship between teachers and researchers.

## Acknowledgements

The SLANT (Spoken Language and New Technology) project was a joint venture of the University of East Anglia and the Open University, funded 1990–93 by the Economic and Social Research Council (ref. R000232731). This support, and the co-operation of schools in Buckinghamshire, Cambridgeshire, Northamptonshire and Norfolk, is gratefully acknowledged.

## References

Baker-Sennett, J., Matusov, E., & Rogoff, B. (1992). Sociocultural processes of creative planning in children's playcrafting. In P. Light & G. Butterworth (Eds.), *Context and cognition: Ways of learning and knowing* (pp. 93–114). London: Harvester-Wheatsheaf.

Barbieri, M., & Light, P. (1992). Interaction, gender and performance on a computer-based task. *Learning and Instruction, 2*, 199–213.

Barnes, D., & Todd, F. (1978). *Communication and learning in small groups*. London: Routledge & Kegan Paul.

Barnes, D., & Todd, F. (1995). *Communication and learning revisited.* New York, NY: Heinemann.

Bell, N., Grossen, M., & Perret-Clermont, A.-N. (1985). Sociocognitive conflict and intellectual growth. In M. W. Berkowitz (Ed.), *Peer conflict and psychological growth (New Directions in Child Development. no. 29)* (pp. 283–322). San Francisco, CA: Jossey-Bass.

Blaye, A., Light, P., Joiner, R., & Sheldon, S. (1991). Collaboration as facilitator of planning and problem solving on a computer-based task. *British Journal of Developmental Psychology, 9,* 471–483.

Brooks, G., Latham, J., & Rex, A. (1986). *Developing oral skills.* London: Heinemann.

Brown, A., & Palincsar, A. (1989). Guided, co-operative learning and individual knowledge acquisition. In L. Resnick (Ed.), *Knowing, learning and instruction* (pp. 393–451). New York, NY: Lawrence Erlbaum.

Bruner, J. (1985). Vygotsky: A historical and conceptual perspective. In J. Wertsch (Ed.), *Culture, communication and cognition: Vygotskian perspectives* (pp. 21–34). Cambridge: Cambridge University Press.

Croll, P. (1986). *Systematic classroom observation.* Lewes, Sussex: The Falmer Press.

Crook, C. (1991). Computers in the zone of proximal development: Implications for evaluation. *Computers in Education, 17*(1), 81–91.

Dawes, L. (1993, February). Special report: Talking points. *Junior Education.*

Dawes, L., Fisher, E., & Mercer, N. (1992). The quality of talk at the computer. *Language and Learning,* pp. 22–25.

Doise, W., & Mugny, G. (1984). *The social development of intellect.* Oxford: Pergamon Press.

Edwards, D., & Mercer, N. (1987). *Common knowledge: The development of understanding in the classroom.* London: Methuen/Routledge.

Edwards, A. D., & Westgate, D. (1994). *Investigating classroom talk* (2nd ed.). London: The Falmer Press.

Elbers, E. (1994). Sociogenesis and children's pretend play: A variation on Vygotskian themes. In W. de Graaf & R. Maier (Eds.), *Sociogenesis re-examined* (pp. 219–241). New York, NY: Springer.

Elbers, E., & Kelderman, A. (1994). Ground rules for testing: Expectations and misunderstandings in test situations. *European Journal of Psychology of Education, 9*(1), 111–120.

Elliot, J. (1991). *Action research for educational change.* Milton Keynes: Open University Press.

Fisher, E. (1993). Distinctive features of pupil-pupil talk and their relationship to learning. *Language and Education, 7*(4), 239–258.

Fletcher, B. (1985). Group and individual learning of junior school children on a microcomputer-based task. *Educational Review, 37,* 251–261.

Galton, M., & Williamson, J. (1992). *Group work in the primary classroom.* London: Routledge.

Habermas, J. (1979). *Communication and the evolution of society.* London: Heinemann.

Habermas, J. (1984). *The theory of communicative action* (Vol. 1). Cambridge: Polity Press.

Hasan, R. (1994). The texture of a text. In D. Graddol & O. Boyd-Barrett (Eds.), *Media texts: Authors and readers* (pp. 74–89). Clevedon: Multilingual Matters.

Hatano, G., & Inagaki, K. (1992). Desituating cognition through the construction of conceptual knowledge. In P. Light & G. Butterworth (Eds.), *Context and cognition: Ways of learning and knowing* (pp. 115–133). London: Harvester-Wheatsheaf.

Heath, S. B. (1982). *Ways with words.* Cambridge: Cambridge University Press.

Hewitt, R. (1989, November). *Oral assessment and the new oracy.* Paper presented at the CUE Symposium on Oracy and Assessment, Birkbeck College, London.

Howe, C. (Ed.). (1993). Special issue: Peer interaction and knowledge acquisition. *Social Development, 1*(3).

Hoyles, C., Healy, L., & Pozzi, S. (1992). Interdependence and autonomy: Aspects of groupwork with computers. *Learning and Instruction, 1,* 239–257.

Hoyles, C., Sutherland, R., & Healy, I. (1990). Children talking in computer environments: New insights on the role of discussion in mathematics learning. In K. Durkin & B. Shine (Eds.), *Language and mathematics education.* Milton Keynes: Open University Press.

Hull, R. (1985). *The language gap.* London: Methuen.

Jones, A., & Mercer, N. (1993). Theories of learning and information technology. In P. Scrimshaw (Ed.), *Language, classrooms and computers* (pp. 11–26). London: Routledge.

Lave, J. (1992). Word problems: A microcosm of theories of learning. In P. Light & G. Butterworth (Eds.), *Context and cognition: Ways of learning and knowing* (pp. 74–92). Hemel Hempstead: Harvester-Wheatsheaf.

Light, P. (1993). Collaborative learning with computers. In P. Scrimshaw (Ed.), *Language: Classrooms and computers* (pp. 40–56). London: Routledge.

Light, P., & Glachan, M. (1985). Facilitation of problem solving through peer interaction. *Educational Psychology, 5,* 217–225.

Light, P., & Littleton, K. (1994). Cognitive approaches to group work. In P. Kutnick & C. Rogers (Eds.), *Groups in schools.* London: Cassell.

Light, P., Littleton, K., Messer, D., & Joiner, R. (1994). Social and communicative processes in computer-based problem solving. *European Journal of Psychology of Education, 9,* 93–109.

Lyle, S. (1993). An investigation into ways in which children "talk themselves into meaning". *Language and Education, 7*(3), 181–197.

Maybin, J. (1994). Children's voices: Talk, knowledge and identity. In D. Graddol, J. Maybin, & B. Stierer (Eds.), *Researching language and literacy in social context* (pp. 131–150). Clevedon: Multilingual Matters.

Mercer, N. (1992). Culture, context and the construction of knowledge in the classroom. In P. Light & G. Butterworth (Eds.), *Context and cognition: Ways of learning and knowing* (pp. 28–46). London: Harvester-Wheatsheaf.

Mercer, N. (1994). The quality of talk in children's joint activity at the computer. *Journal of Computer Assisted Learning, 10*(1), 24–32.

Mercer, N. (1995). *The guided construction of knowledge: Talk amongst teachers and learners.* Clevedon: Multilingual Matters.

Mercer, N., & Edwards, D. (1981). Ground-rules for mutual understanding: A social psychological approach to classroom knowledge. In N. Mercer (Ed.), *Language in school and community* (pp. 30–46). London: Edward Arnold.

Mercer, N., Edwards, D., & Maybin, J. (1988). Putting context into oracy. In M. Maclure, T. Phillips, & A. Wilkinson (Eds.), *Oracy matters* (pp. 122–132). Milton Keynes: Open University Press.

Mercer, N., & Fisher, E. (1992). How do teachers help children to learn? An analysis of teachers' interventions in computer-based tasks. *Learning and Instruction, 2,* 339–355.

Messer, D., Joiner, R., Light, P., & Littleton, K. (1993). Influences on the effectiveness of peer interaction: Children's level of cognitive development and the relative ability of partners. *Social Development*, 2(3), 279–294.

Much, N. C., & Schweder, R. A. (1978). Speaking of rules: The analysis of culture in breach. In W. Damon (Ed.), *Moral development* (pp. 19–39). San Francisco, CA: Jossey-Bass.

Open University. (1991). *Talk and learning 5–16: An in-service pack on oracy for teachers*. Milton Keynes: The Open University.

Phillips, T. (1992). Why? The neglected question in planning small group activity. In K. Norman (Ed.), *Thinking voices: The work of the National Oracy Project* (pp. 148–155). London: Hodder & Stoughton.

Prentice, M. (1991). A community of enquiry. In *Talk and learning 5–16: An in-service pack on oracy for teachers* (pp. A28–A31). Milton Keynes: The Open University.

Rogoff, B. (1990). *Apprenticeship in thinking*. Oxford: Oxford University Press.

Sheeran, N., & Barnes, D. (1991). *School writing: Discovering the ground rules*. Milton Keynes: Open University Press.

Steel, D. (1991). Granny's garden. In *Talk and learning 5–16: An in-service pack on oracy for teachers* (pp. A226–A231). Milton Keynes: The Open University.

Wegerif, R. (1994). *Educational software and the quality of children's talk*. Centre for Language and Communications Occasional paper No. 40. Milton Keynes: The Open University.

Wells, G. (1992). The centrality of talk in education. In K. Norman (Ed.), *Thinking voices: The work of the National Oracy Project* (pp. 283–310). London: Hodder & Stoughton.

Wertsch, J. (Ed.). (1985). *Culture, communication and cognition: Vygotskian perspectives*. Cambridge: Cambridge University Press.

Westgate, D., & Corden, R. (1993). What we thought about things: Expectations, context and small group talk. *Language in Education*, 7(2), 115–122.

Wood, D. (1988). *How children think and learn*. Oxford: Basil Blackwell.

*This chapter is from my book* Words and Minds. *It is thus taken out of context ('context' is in fact one of the concepts I discuss in the chapter) but in this version I have tried to eliminate references to other parts of that book. I include it here for two reasons. First, unlike the other chapters, it includes examples of talk taken from social events outside the classroom, which show that the same concepts are relevant to understanding how spoken communication works in a range of settings. And secondly, the explanation it includes of how language is used for collective thinking came to underpin much of my subsequent research.*

# 4  Laying the foundations

*Mercer, N. (2000). Chapter 2 of* Words and Minds: How we Use Language to Think Together. *London: Routledge.*

To claim that we can observe and analyse people 'thinking together' might seem questionable. Surely, it might be objected, 'thinking' is a process that takes place inside individuals' heads, and all that can be observed and analysed is people using language to communicate information and ideas? My first response to this objection is to say that the notion of 'communication' does not capture the special quality of the joint intellectual activity I am concerned with here. 'Communication' encourages the view of a linear process whereby people exchange ideas, think about them individually and then again exchange the products of their separate intellectual efforts. This does not do justice to the dynamic interaction of minds which language makes possible. Of course people think individually, but one might similarly claim that 'dancing' is necessarily an individual process, because basically it is a matter of a person using their brain to co-ordinate their own body movements; yet we commonly talk of people 'dancing together', because we wish to recognize the nature of the joint, co-ordinated physical activity involved. I have introduced the term 'interthinking' in order to focus attention on the joint, co-ordinated intellectual activity which people regularly accomplish using language.

The fact that we can never really know what anyone else is thinking is a problem faced by all research on human cognition. Fortunately, the problem is a lesser one for me than for some kinds of psychological researchers, who are indeed trying to study thought processes inside individual people's heads. But it is also a problem that we all face in our everyday lives; and in both research and everyday life we deal with that problem in practical ways, by using whatever information we can to infer what other people think. Our lives may well depend on how well we can do this. In science and other kinds of investigative research, we deploy the same perceptive faculties and reasoning powers that we use in everyday life to the study of a particular topic or problem – but in a more rigorous and systematic way. We can look carefully at how people use language to try to solve problems, argue about different points of view, resolve differences and create shared knowledge and understanding. We can see whether their use of language reveals some common strategies or techniques for doing so. We can also see what outcomes their efforts achieve, and we can add to what we observe by asking people for their own insights into what they do. In this chapter, I will describe some of the ways in which people use language to strive to reach joint understanding, and in doing so I will also introduce some concepts that are useful for analysing the process of thinking collectively. The first of these concepts is 'context'.

## Context

The concept of 'context' is necessary for understanding how we use language to think together. This is rather unfortunate, because it is particularly difficult to produce a satisfactory definition of 'context' – and many people have tried.[1] No definition is widely accepted across the field of language studies, because anyone working in the field can always find good reasons for disagreeing with anyone else's definition. This state of affairs does not reflect an unusual state of chaos in the field, compared with other kinds of research, and it need not be an obstacle here. (Neuroscientists, psychologists and philosophers have similar problems with 'consciousness' and 'intelligence', as do physicists with 'time', but their research likewise continues.) I have my own conception of 'context', and Sequence 1 below will help me to begin to explain what this is. The sequence is an extract from a telephone conversation I recorded while doing some research on the language of work. How much sense can you make of it?

### Sequence 1: the GAT job

| | |
|---|---|
| CALLER: | Is Ellen there? It's Bill. |
| SECRETARY: | I'll put you through. |
| ELLEN: | Hello, Bill. |
| BILL: | Oh, hi. Just a quick, um, query. Umm. You, uh, with the GAT job. |
| ELLEN: | Yeh. |
| BILL: | Umm, you know we were talking about the, the range which it's possible, the salary range? |
| ELLEN: | Yeh. |
| BILL: | The two scales just join on, do they, end on? Or . . . |
| ELLEN: | Yeh. |
| BILL: | . . . you know the discretionary range. |
| ELLEN: | Yeh, well . . . |
| BILL: | (*interrupting*) Is that an overlap? |
| ELLEN: | Um. Strictly speaking it isn't. |

BILL:  Oh right.
ELLEN:  But we had someone appointed to the PTE . . .
BILL:  Yeh.
ELLEN:  . . . who was earning above the top of the lower scale, where
    . . .
BILL:  [Yeh.
ELLEN:  [. . . she came from.
BILL:  Yeh.
ELLEN:  And that was a short-term post and she was allowed to be
    appointed . . .
BILL:  [Aah.
ELLEN:  [. . . to a discretionary point, so that might be an option.
BILL:  Well, sounds to me a good one. Let's, yeh, let's go for that.

You may have guessed that this was a conversation between two people who work in the same business; they are in fact a manager (Bill) and an administrator (Ellen) in the same university. Their work often brings them into contact, and this is one reason why they can begin the conversation with few preliminaries or extended explanations. They both know the nature of each other's job, and in their conversation can build easily on the 'common knowledge' of their shared workplace and of past conversations they have had on related topics (hence the use of expressions like 'You know we were talking about . . .' and 'You know the discretionary range . . .'). They are continuing an earlier discussion of the point on a salary range at which an appointment could be made to a post in the university. The most obvious 'jargon' words are the acronyms (GAT and PTE), which, because they are not real English words at all, would be completely incomprehensible even to outsiders who were members of their language community. The phrase 'discretionary range' is made up of two English 'dictionary words', but the meaning of this phrase for the speakers in this conversation depends on some very specific, shared knowledge about the financial working practices of British universities. Because the speakers' past experience has prepared them well for this conversation, the 'jargon' used is certainly no problem. Indeed, using the specialized language of their professional community enables them to think together about the problem (how to find a suitable salary for a newly appointed person) and find an acceptable solution.

The specific information you probably lacked about the content and purpose of the conversation, and which you would need to make proper sense of it, was of course available to the speakers. They had no reason to make their meanings more explicit, because they were drawing on the common knowledge that they had accumulated from similar experiences and earlier conversations. That shared knowledge formed part of the *context* – the contextual foundation – that they created for their talk.

When dealing with spoken language, some researchers define 'context' in terms of the physical environment in which language is used, but that only provides some potential resources for our contextmaking. To return to Sequence 1: there are no good reasons for inferring that the furniture of Ellen and Bill's respective offices, or the telephone hardware they used to communicate, were important for the sense-making in their talk. Even in a face-to-face encounter, the context of a conversation between two people is not necessarily made up of the physical objects and events around the speakers. Present objects are potential contextual resources, but so are objects and events long gone, if speakers recall them and treat them as relevant. Today I stood near someone in the middle of a busy high street who was apparently conducting an intimate conversation on his mobile phone (I heard what he said quite clearly, as he used the usual bellowing style of mobile phone users in public places). Except for the speaker initially and briefly explaining where he was to his listener, the conversation I overheard seemed to rely not at all on the frantic urban life around the speaker for its contextual foundations, as it seemed to be concerned entirely with emotionally charged events that had taken place elsewhere. But then again, perhaps it did have some contextual function, in that the distant listener might be enabled to appreciate the speaker's sense of urgency in dealing with this matter by being aware of where he had felt driven to call from. The point is that what really counts as 'contextual' is a matter for participants in a conversation, and this is a problem for studying how we use language for making meaning together. For these kinds of reasons, I feel that we have to accept that 'context' is a mental phenomenon, and that it consists of *whatever information listeners (or readers) use to make sense of what is said (or written).*

We always make sense of language by taking account of the circumstances in which we find it, and by drawing on any past experience that seems relevant. If you pick up a scrap of paper from the floor, and see there are printed words in English on it, you will use the information you have about where you found it and your knowledge of the forms that printed English takes, as well as what the words 'say', to decide what they mean. So when I found a piece of card on our living room table, bearing the words '. . . full collection of these lovable . . .', it made perfect sense to me as part of the packaging for one of the many toy cats that inhabit my daughter's room. I used several different kinds of information to do this contextualizing – the location in which I found it was relevant, as was my memory of a new cat having been bought the previous day. As well as the actual content of printed language, the bright colours of the print and its surround helped me to relate it to the domain of children's toys. One of the most important skills of literacy is being able to decide what kind of text you are dealing with and using this information to contextualize it. It is because written texts can be fairly reliably contextualized in this way that Michael Halliday (the founder of systemic functional linguistics) suggested that types or genres of written text are associated with particular 'contexts of use', and that literate people are able to draw relevant information about 'context of use' from the distinctive form and content of a text in order to identify particular functional types or genres of written language (for example, assembly instructions, personal letters, news articles, and so on) and so make sense of them.[2] According to systemic linguists, a text (which may be someone's contribution to a conversation, or a piece of written language) has its 'context of use' defined when it is generated, and so carries the stamp of its intended function in its form. This approach has provided many interesting and useful insights into the relationship between the features and styles of language and its communicative function.

However, to understand the process of collective thinking, we need a different notion of 'context' from that used by Halliday and other systemic linguists. One reason is that they are concerned with features of texts, rather than the processes of people's thinking, and so their notion of context does not capture the essentially dynamic, temporal nature of the human mental process of *contextualizing*. By 'context of use', systemic linguists mean something that a text carries with it, wherever it goes, as an enduring, identifying characteristic. The producer of a written text or utterance is assumed to be able to determine this completely. The text on a toy's packaging therefore reflects its writer's ideas about its 'context of use'. However, if the focus of our interest is the development of shared understanding rather than features of texts, 'context' is better thought of as a configuration of available information that people use for making sense of language in particular situations. 'Context' is created anew in every interaction between a speaker and listener or writer and reader. From this perspective, we must take account of listeners and readers as well as speakers and writers, who create meanings together. For example, our interpretation of what we hear or read can be revised by gaining new, relevant information. We may make a different sense of the same text – say, a statement on the toy cat's packaging about the limited safety of the product for use by very young children – depending on what relevant information we had available at any time. Say we read it once, and then have a conversation with a lawyer friend who explains that toy manufacturers are always advised to include on their packaging a carefully worded 'disclaimer' about their responsibility for safety, regardless of realistic levels of risk. That conversation would enable us to *recontextualize* the statement and hence reassess our understanding of its meaning and function.

My conception of 'context' is also meant to explain the way in which people can co-operate in making sense. For communication to be successful, the creation of context must be a co-operative endeavour. Two people may well begin a conversation with enough prior shared knowledge to be able to achieve some initial joint understanding without making a great deal of information explicit. But as the conversation progresses, speakers must continue to provide relevant information, to the best of their judgements of need and relevance, if new shared knowledge is to be constructed. Speakers and writers have a responsibility for providing their listeners or readers with what they need to know, or at least with clues to help them access what they need to observe or remember. In this way, conversations run on contextual tracks made of common knowledge.

## Language and other systems for making context

Particularly useful insights into how language is used to get things done come from research on language use in work settings. This shows that language is not just an important tool for literate occupations like journalism or research, or in 'talk' occupations like broadcasting, counselling, teaching and the law, but also for a much broader range of activities. For example, research in Canada by the linguist Peter Medway has shown that even the construction industry relies heavily on language for getting things done. Building a house is not simply a matter of an architect drawing up plans and then handing them to the builder who converts them into three-dimensional reality. The whole process is one of explanation, interpretation and negotiation. Even the most carefully drawn plans have ambiguous interpretations, and the real world of work on a building site requires frequent redefinitions, reinterpretations and modifications of the plans 'on the hoof as the work progresses'. The talk transcribed in Sequence 2 below comes from an on-site recording made by Medway, of a conversation in which an architect (Joe) was negotiating with a heating consultant (Harry) over the location of a problematic piece of ducting. The ducting had turned out to be bulkier than anticipated in the design of the building, and Harry had previously suggested to Joe that this would require the ceiling of the building to be lower than planned. The conversation took place as Joe, Harry and Luc (the site supervisor) walked around the site. (*Because of noise on the site, some of the recorded speech was inaudible. Inaudible speech is marked by the symbol (. . .) and where the transcription is uncertain the words are in parentheses.*)

### Sequence 2: constructing the virtual building

JOE:      OK, next.
          (*He looks up towards the underside of the concrete slab. Harry walks a couple of steps, pointing upwards. Joe and Luc accompany him.*)
HARRY:  (. . .), right? (. . .) the ductwork coming down that way is supposed to (go through there).
JOE:      Well as you were saying yesterday on the phone, Harry that if (*9-second pause while Joe spreads out a roll of drawings and looks at them*) if we lower this part by three inches . . .
HARRY:  Yes.
JOE:      That will be fine, right?
HARRY:  This should be fine, (because) the ductwork can be penetrating through there OK (. . .)

JOE:     Because this is at twenty-six hundred and this is twenty-seven
         seventy-five. (*These are figures in mm. for the height of the ceiling
         taken from the drawings*)
HARRY:   That's right.[3]

This is an interesting example because of the way in which the talk is related
to the physical environment. As well as language, two other 'semiotic systems' (ways for making meaning) are involved. One is *gesture*, as when Harry
points to part of the construction, and the second is *drawing*, represented by
the set of architectural plans which Joe consults later. Language is often used
in conjunction with these other meaning-making tools, which can be used
to draw physical artefacts into the realm of the conversation. Although the
concrete slab to which Harry points had been there, above them, when they
began to speak, it was not necessarily part of the context for the conversation until he pointed to it. Many other bits of the partly constructed building
also surrounded them, but they were not in any obvious sense 'contextual'.
Similarly, once Joe had laid the drawings out in front of the three speakers,
it became possible for him to refer to parts of the drawing by simply saying
'if we lower this part by three inches' because he knew the drawings now
formed a contextual resource for the conversation. In doing this, he was
making good use of what linguists call *exophoric reference* – employing words
like 'that' and 'there' to refer to things which exist in the physical context of
the talk. Exophoric reference is a kind of linguistic 'pointing'.

    The discussion on the building site also drew on another kind of contex-
tual resource: that of past shared experience. We can see this in Joe's reference to the telephone conversation he had had with Harry the previous day
(in which Harry had suggested that the solution to their problem was to
lower the ceiling). But in fact, although the proposed solution is phrased in
terms of 'lowering' the ceiling, we should note that they are talking about
a ceiling that does not yet exist. They are not really talking about either the
edifice around them, or the graphical representation on the plans, but (as
Medway puts it) a *virtual* building that they are constructing together, ahead
of the real one, through their conversation.

    Another resource that Joe and Harry can use to build context is the com-
mon knowledge each has gained from their individual training and work
experience as a member of the construction industry. They are familiar with
its problems, working practices, technical drawings – and, like Bill and Ellen
in Sequence 1, they understand the technical terms and other ways of using
language that are employed to get the job done in their community of work.

## Contextual clues

From the point of view of a listener or reader, understanding will be limited by the quality and quantity of relevant knowledge we have for doing
the work of contextualization. But we are very good at hunting out such

relevant information. Given limited contextual resources, a listener or reader can often make quite good sense of language which contains elements with which they are quite unfamiliar. Look, for example, at the transcription below of someone talking in a radio interview. What sense can you make of it, and what clues do you use to do so?

> Mi salim eplikeson bilong mi na skul bod i considerim na bihain ekseptim mi na mi go long skul long fama.

To help you more, I can tell you that this is an example of an English pidgin language, the *Tok Pisin* ('talk pidgin') of Papua New Guinea. It is a transcription of part of a radio interview broadcast in 1972. The speaker is a student, who is telling the interviewer about his plans to study agriculture. Any reader who is familiar with English pidgins will no doubt have used that knowledge already to make some sense of what they read. According to the sociolinguist Suzanne Romaine who collected this example,[4] *Tok Pisin* developed in the time of the British Empire, when English began to be used as an official language in the region. First used as a means of communication between the indigenous population and their European colonizers, it eventually became the most important *lingua franca* for Papua New Guineans, who have around 750 indigenous languages between them. Like other English pidgins, its vocabulary is derived mainly from English, but its grammar reflects some features of the original local languages. The transcription shows the conventional, 'standardized' form of spelling used for *Tok Pisin* today, which represents in a fairly obvious way (for English speakers) how the words are pronounced (try speaking it out loud). Once you realize that some of the words are derived from English, and you have some idea of the theme being dealt with, you should be able to use this contextual information to make some sense of what is written there – without me telling you what any of the pidgin words actually mean. (See note 5 for some feedback on your attempt.)[5]

## Making context

In everyday life – unless we are finding our feet in a new language environment – we do not usually have to search hard for relevant contextual information to 'crack the code' of what we hear or read in the way that was necessary for making sense of the pidgin example above. We will be interacting with people who speak or write more or less the same variety of language and, because they have a similar life experience, much common knowledge can be taken implicitly for granted. But another rather different reason is that both speakers and listeners (or writers and readers) take an active role in building the contextual foundations for effective communication. If we are trying to communicate with someone, we strive to make the contextual foundations adequate. What is more, as our talk with someone continues, earlier conversation provides a shared contextual basis for the talk which follows. Like the operators of some strange, dual-controlled track-laying vehicle called 'language', conversational partners build the contextual foundations for their own communication as they go along.[6] They usually do this without much consciousness or awareness. Nevertheless, the process of joint contextualizing can be done well or badly, as the next two sequences illustrate. The first, Sequence 3, is from a session which my colleagues and I recorded, in which a girl and boy (both aged 15) are doing a problem-solving communication activity called 'Map'.[7] In this activity, which is done in pairs, partners are both given maps of the same area of British countryside. However, while the map held by one partner is recent and accurate, the other partner has an old map which does not show some recent, significant changes to the environment. For example, only the more recent map shows that a motorway now bisects the area and that a railway has been dismantled. Pairs sit back to back and have to imagine that the partner with the old map has telephoned the other in the course of a country walk to ask for help in reaching the village of Penfold beyond the obstacle of the motorway (which is unmarked on the older map).

## Sequence 3: Simon and Mandy and the map problem

SIMON: Hello Mandy?

MANDY: Hello?

SIMON: Yeh, right, I'm out in the country, um, at Chidding, in the phone box here, yeh?

MANDY: Yeh.

SIMON: OK? And I was on a walk up to Penfold, to have a wander round up there, and to my horror, there was a motorway there across the footpath. Now um, can you direct me from Chidding to Penfold so I can get there please?

MANDY: You go down Waldon Road.

SIMON: Oh, OK.

MANDY: Past the footpath, by Chidding Hall. And then . . .

SIMON: (*interrupting*) Hold on. Chidding Hall.

MANDY: Yeh. And then you go up [the footpath

SIMON: (*interrupting*)          [Hold on. Now where's Chidding Hall.

MANDY: Centre for Overseas Studies, by . . .

SIMON: Pardon? (*interrupting*)

MANDY: Centre for Overseas Studies. (*'Chidding Hall', but not 'Centre for Overseas Studies', is marked on Simon's map*)

SIMON: Oh right, got it.

MANDY: Then you go down a little bit more.

SIMON: Yeh (*hesitantly*).

MANDY: By a, to a footpath.

SIMON: A footpath. Ah, no I haven't got a footpath on here. Can you give me the co-ordinates, and I'll draw it in?

MANDY:   Um, C1.
SIMON:   C1. Is it near the railway line?
MANDY:   It's just across the road from the Booking Hall.
SIMON:   Where? (*sounding perplexed: the Booking Hall is marked on his older map as a railway station*)
MANDY:   Booking Hall.
SIMON:   Um, no I can't find Bicking Hall.

The sequence is fairly typical of Mandy and Simon's talk throughout the activity. They interacted in a friendly way, Simon asked a lot of questions and Mandy provided answers. But Mandy hardly ever asked Simon questions about what his map showed. She showed little evidence of being able to distance herself from her own perspective, based on the information provided by her map, and appreciate Simon's problem from his point of view. In response to his questions, she simply stated information that she had and repeated it when he enquired further. Whether this was for reasons of nervousness, lack of interest or a weakness in her communication skills I do not know; but Mandy's failure to take an active, collaborative role in building a contextual foundation of common knowledge meant that this pair did not do well on this problem. The next sequence shows two of their classmates also attempting to solve the same problem.

### Sequence 4: Sue and Tracy and the map problem

TRACY:   Does your, does your grid map go ABC along the bottom?
SUE:     ABC, yes.
TRACY:   And 1,2,3 along the side ?
SUE:     That's right.
TRACY:   And north points upwards?
SUE:     (*pause*) Yes.
TRACY:   Well that's all right then.
SUE:     OK. Have you got the canal?
TRACY:   Canal, um.
SUE:     Towpath?
TRACY:   I've got the track of the old railway, which is right up the [top.
SUE:                                                                    [Yeh
         well that's what I've got, because you've got the new one.
TRACY:   Oh 'derelict canal' is that it?
SUE:     Um (*sounding uncertain*).
TRACY:   Well it might just be 'canal' on your one, if it's an old one.

Tracy and Sue went about the activity in a very different way from Simon and Mandy. Sequence 4 comes from quite early on in their attempt and shows how they both set about finding out what information they had in common, and how their maps differed. By establishing that both maps used the same grid reference system, they were able to use this to build, quickly and very effectively, a shared contextual foundation for solving the problem together.

## Conversational ground rules

I now want to introduce another concept for understanding how we lay the foundations for joint intellectual activity: 'conversational ground rules'. The original use of the term 'ground rules' was in sport, to refer to the fact that a particular playing field or ground might have local conventions, perhaps created to take account of its special physical features, which visiting players would need to be made aware of and accept. It is now commonly used to mean special or local conventions of behaviour in any area of life. By 'conversational ground rules' I mean *the conventions which language users employ to carry on particular kinds of conversations.*[8] Conversational ground rules are part of the context of any conversation. They consist of the knowledge, which may not be made explicit by speakers, about how to 'do' certain kinds of talking. Generally speaking, for spoken language to be used for effective communication, participants need to have this kind of shared understanding and agreement about what to do to make it happen.

Look at Sequence 5 below. The first speaker is an occupational counsellor and the second is one of her clients, an unemployed man. The interview is taking place in an office in a city in England, and was recorded by my colleague Jo Longman during our research on occupational counselling.[9] The participants are engaged in the joint task of filling in a 'Personal Training Plan Form', on behalf of the client, which must include a basic *curriculum vitae* for the client and end with some specific recommendations for courses of occupational training. This form will be used by the counsellor to apply for job vacancies and training courses on behalf of the client. What kinds of ground rules do you think are being followed here?

### Sequence 5: doing things with fish

| | |
|---|---|
| COUNSELLOR: | You've not done any filleting, but you have worked with fish? |
| CLIENT: | Yeah. |
| COUNSELLOR: | So I need to know all the things that you've done with fish. |
| CLIENT: | Packing, that's one. Sorting out. |
| COUNSELLOR: | Sorting out, what do you mean by sorting out? |
| CLIENT: | Like grading with machinery doing it by (*inaudible*). |
| COUNSELLOR: | What do you do that by, size, how big they are, or weight? |
| CLIENT: | Weight. Barrowboy. |
| COUNSELLOR: | That means going down to the market and collecting the fish and taking it back. Right? |
| CLIENT: | Yeah. Skin the fish. |
| COUNSELLOR: | OK you were doing shop work in the video shop. So what does that involve? |

CLIENT:          Getting up in the morning!
COUNSELLOR:   Yeah that's the hardest part for me too.

As analysts of the conversation, we can infer from what is said that both participants have access to some relevant shared knowledge. Some of this knowledge is quite specific: the counsellor says 'OK you were doing shop work in the video shop', and the client responds in a way which suggests that this allusion, with its apparently abrupt change of conversational topic, makes perfect sense to him. (Because I have access to the complete interview, I know that the client had provided this information earlier in summarizing his past employment.) But at a more general level, from the smooth flow of talk and the lack of any obvious signs of confusion on the part of each participant, it is obvious that something in their past experience has prepared both participants for the experience of the special kind of conversation they are engaged in, which is a conversation in which one person asks the other about their life in order to produce a written account. That is, both the counsellor and her client seem to have some shared understanding of how an occupational counselling interview should be carried out. (This is not inevitably the case, of course: some other clients we recorded in the same setting seemed surprised and aggrieved at the intrusive questioning of the counsellor.)

We can also see that this particular episode reveals how the speakers organize the 'thinking together' that is necessary to come up with a completed Personal Training Plan Form at the end of the interview. Almost all the sequence is made up of questions and answers – Q–A, Q–A, Q–A, and so on. The counsellor does nearly all the talking, and she is the only one who asks questions. That is, the two conversationalists act out their roles by using language differently, but do so in such complementary ways that a clear pattern emerges – their discourse takes on a distinctive structure. This structure is conventional for the kind of language activity commonly called an 'interview'; the talk can be thought of as the product of both speakers using their knowledge of the ground rules for doing interviews. The structure is, to some extent at least, the result of practical requirements. To be able to get information that is sufficiently clear and comprehensible, the counsellor has to ask for basic information ('. . . you have worked with fish?') and clarify the responses made ('. . . what do you mean by sorting out?') so that they can be recorded. On his part, the client has to describe particular working practices in words – something that he may never have had to do before. We can make some inferences about what they both now know that they did not know at the beginning. By the end of the interview, the counsellor has gained considerable new information about the occupational life history of her client, and so this is now (subject to all the vagaries of human memory and interpretation) shared, common knowledge. In accord with the ground rules of such interviews, the counsellor tells the client little about her own employment history. In Sequence 5, only one piece of information about the counsellor is offered to the client (in the last line).

The conversation in Sequence 5 runs quite smoothly because both participants know and accept the ground rules that the counsellor will ask questions about the client's work history, and that the client will provide clear enough answers to enable the counsellor to fill in a Personal Training Plan Form. For the client to start asking detailed questions about the counsellor's employment history, or for the counsellor to begin dictating what should be written on the form to the client, would constitute a breaking of the ground rules currently being applied. But imagine a situation in which the client and counsellor discover that they both used to work for the same firm, and their conversation switches into a discussion of the people who worked there and their personal characteristics. If that happened, we might expect to see changes in the structure of talk (for example, a more even spread of questioning between the speakers) as well as in the content. We could then infer from the talk that the use of the ground rules which apply to 'interviews' had been temporarily suspended by both speakers, and a different set of ground rules, which apply when people are engaged in 'informal conversation', was being used instead.

## Cumulative talk

We can see an extract from an informal conversation in Sequence 6 below. Its structure is very different from that of Sequence 5, and I would like you to consider *how* it is different and *why* this might be so. I will provide you with some contextual information, in advance. The sequence is an extract from an informal conversation between two female, middle-class friends (K and C) in England (recorded by the sociolinguist Jennifer Coates). K is explaining that she is worried that her neighbour might be able to see into her house, because she saw him undressing in his living room.

### Sequence 6: screening trees

K: and I thought my God
C: yeh
K: if I can see him
C: he can see you
K: and I don't always just get undressed in my living room
C: (*laugh*)
K: you know I mean OK I'm sure he's not
C: peeping
K: peeping or anything
C: but he
K: but it just
C: you accidentally saw him
K: that's right
C: oh I don't blame you I think it needs screening trees round it.[10]

In this piece of talk, there are no questions and answers, and there is no argument. Instead, the speakers work together to produce a continuous stretch of mutually intelligible language ('if I can see him / he can see you / and I don't always just get undressed in my living room'). Contextual references to what they have already said, and to what they can both see as they speak, can be left implicit. So C says 'I don't blame you I think it needs screening trees round it' without needing to say what K might be 'blamed' for or what 'it' is. Coates suggests that the co-operative structure and implicit referencing of this kind of talk reflect one of its social functions, which is to establish and strengthen the solidarity and intimacy of the speakers. In my own research, I have usually called this kind of conversation *cumulative talk*, because speakers build on each other's contributions, add information of their own and in a mutually supportive, uncritical way construct shared knowledge and understanding. This kind of talk can be very usefully applied for getting joint work completed, as the next sequence shows. This is from a session which my colleagues and I recorded in a primary school classroom, where two 10-year-old girls, Katie and Anne, two friends, were working at the computer on the production of their own class newspaper. At the point at which the sequence begins, they have been working together on this task for a while and have already talked through various options for design and content. They have been engaged in the task for about an hour and a quarter and are trying to compose some text for their front page.

### Sequence 7: fantabuloso

KATIE:   Okay, so right then. What shall we write?

ANNE:   We can have something like those autograph columns and things like that and items, messages.

KATIE:   Inside these covers (*long pause*) Our fun-filled . . .

ANNE:   That's it!

KATIE:   Something . . .

ANNE:   Something like that!

KATIE:   Yeah.

ANNE:   Inside this fabulous fun-filled covers are – how can we have a fun-filled cover? Let me try.

KATIE:   Inside these (*long pause*). Hah huh (*laughs*).

ANNE:   You sound happy on this. Fantabuloso (*laughs*).

KATIE:   Inside these inside these fant, inside these fun-filled, no inside these covers these fantastic these brilliant . . .

ANNE:   Brilliant.

KATIE:   Is it brilliant?

ANNE:   No.

KATIE:   No. Fantast fantabuloso shall we put that?

ANNE:   Yeah (. . .) fantabluloso.

KATIE:   Fan-tab-u-lo-so.

ANNE:   Loso. Fantabuloso.
KATIE:  Fantabuloso oso.
ANNE:   Fantabuloso ho![11]

In this sequence, we see Katie and Anne asking each other questions. They also make suggestions and offer some reasons for the decisions they take. They are clearly using language to think together about this task, but like the speakers in Sequence 6, they are doing so in a mutually supportive, cumulative way. One particularly interesting feature of their talk, however, is that we can see them talking the text of their newspaper into existence. Some of what they say is simply a comment to their partner ('You sound happy . . .', 'That's it!', 'Yeah'), but other things they say are proposals for the text itself ('Inside these . . . ', 'Brilliant'). Anne first says 'Fantabuloso', and does so in a way that leaves it uncertain whether this is a comment or a proposal for the text. We can then see that this joke-word becomes shared property of the speakers. It is a part of the contextual foundation of their conversation, and so is a resource to which Katie can return shortly as they continue their search for a catchy opening phrase. Both then take up the word, establish joint agreement about its spelling and use it together in a brief, playful celebration of their success in finding a catchy word for their headline.

'Cumulative talk' is based on ground rules which encourage joint, additive contributions to the talk and relatively uncritical acceptance of what partners say. Katie and Anne, like K and C in Sequence 6, are not only thinking through a problem together, they are affirming and developing a friendship. In cumulative talk we can see one way in which the social and intellectual uses of language are combined. There are other kinds of talk, based on different ground rules, which are also commonly used in joint work-based activity. People do not usually make explicit the conversational ground rules that they are using; such rules are normally assumed to be understood, as they are part of the more general contextual foundations for using language that can be drawn from the broader cultural base of every language user's experience in their community.

## Creating a context for working together

Sequence 8 shows two other people navigating a way through a problem towards a solution. Read it and see what sense you can make of their conversation. (*Each speaker's words have been put in a column under their respective names.*)

### Sequence 8: negotiating some business

| Speaker A | Speaker B |
|---|---|
| We'd like to get some state business. | I will have to work out something, Joe, where you could visit with the trustees. |
| Do you control Mr Gordon? | He'll go along with a lot of the things I recommend. |

How do you and I develop a relationship?

I have a public relations firm . . . and I do business other than what I'm doing here.

I can give you $2,000 now, with a 50–50 split of the commission. I deal only with you. There's $4,000 a month possible on this.

Keep talking.

We'll deal on a case by case basis. Can you handle X Insurance Company politics?

Here's $2,000. Let's shake hands on it. Do we have a deal?

We have a deal.

There's 50 people I can send you. I have contacts in Boston.[12]

You probably guessed that this is a piece of business talk. The clues you used probably included the use of words like 'business' and 'trustees', the references to money changing hands and the classic business closing statement 'Let's shake hands on it'. However, although none of the words would in themselves be unfamiliar to you, you would be unlikely to know who the speakers, or the people they refer to ('the trustees', 'Mr Gordon'), are, and what events have led up to this particular conversation in which 'the deal' is struck. You therefore may not have guessed that it shows two people involved in the clandestine business of negotiating a bribe. It comes from the research of a sociolinguist, Roger Shuy, and is a conversation between an undercover agent for the American law enforcement agency the FBI, Joe Hauser (Speaker A, who secretly recorded the talk), and a trade union official who was a target of the FBI's enquiries in an operation known as Brilab (an acronym for 'Bribery of Labor Unions').

Shuy has studied many such secretly recorded, clandestine conversations, and has offered the following analysis of the structure of an archetypal 'bribe' transaction:

### Bribe event structure in actual bribe event

| Phases | Speaker A | Speaker B |
|---|---|---|
| Problem | We'd like to get some state business | I will have to work out something, Joe, where you could visit with the trustees. |
| | Do you control Mr Gordon? | He'll go along with a lot of the things I recommend. |
| | How do you and I develop a relationship? | I have a public relations firm . . . and I do business other than what I'm doing here. |

| | | | |
|---|---|---|---|
| *Proposal* | I can give you $2,000 now, with a 50–50 split of the commission. | Keep talking. | |
| | I deal only with you. | We'll deal on a case by case basis. | |
| | There's $4,000 a month possible on this. | Can you handle X Insurance Company politics? | |
| *Completion* | Here's $2,000. Let's shake hands on it. | | |
| | Do we have a deal? | We have a deal. | |
| *Extension* | | There's 50 people I can send you. I have contacts in Boston.[13] | |

Shuy claims that this 'phase' model can usefully be applied to all the tape-recorded data that he has seen presented by the FBI in bribery cases. Entry into each of the phases depends on the successful completion of the previous one. After some initial greetings (which might be considered to constitute a preliminary phase in themselves), a *problem* is presented by the first party. This usually amounts to a request for help. During this phase, the first party usually also checks on the other's authority and capacity to deliver. The next phase is the *proposal*, in which rewards are discussed and promises made. If things are going well, this phase may be used to build some kind of intimacy, with common acquaintances being mentioned, anecdotes told and so on. The final part of the negotiation is marked by entry into the *completion* phase, classically symbolized by the handshake and expressions like 'It's a deal'. There may then follow an *extension* phase, with future possibilities being introduced.

Shuy's method of analysis is intended as a practical one, and its use has influenced the course of some court cases and retrospectively cast doubt on the validity of the verdicts of others. As Shuy explains, for example, in a number of US bribery cases involving politicians and other public servants, it has been claimed by the state prosecution that the fact that a public servant has even engaged in a conversation with a would-be briber is sufficient to show that they are corrupt. Shuy suggests that juries are often easily persuaded by this line of argument, because people generally assume that two people talking together in reasonable tones, without explicit disagreement, must have shared values and purposes. Those accused of corruption are then convicted on the basis of what he calls 'conversational contamination'. However, he shows that a more careful analysis of events may reveal that the attempted bribery did not follow the model pattern, that the accused person did not collude in the bribe attempt, and the crucial stage of completion (in which 'the deal' is made) may never have materialized. An example is the following extract from a recorded conversation, between a US politician (Williams), accused of corruption, and an FBI agent (Farhart), masquerading as an Arab sheik seeking residence in the USA. In earlier conversation,

Williams has agreed to advise the sheik on how he might best present his case to immigration, but with no suggestion of impropriety:

FARHART: I will, for your help, uh, assistance, I would like to give you . . . some money for, for permanent residence.

WILLIAMS: No. No. No. No, when I work in that kind of activity, it is purely a public, not uh, No, within my position, when I deal with law and legislation, it's not within . . . (*telephone rings, interrupting*). My only interest is to see this come together.[14]

On this occasion a proposal for a bribe may have been made, but, using the transcript, Shuy showed that the normal bribe structure of events had not been completed; and in what was said the offer was clearly rejected. However, Shuy's analysis did not save Senator Williams, who was convicted and imprisoned on this and similar tape evidence (none of which, Shuy suggests, was any more convincing about the senator's guilt than the above example). Shuy comments that many American trial judges are unwilling to admit a linguist as expert witness in court because they claim that any normal person can understand a conversation when they first hear it, and that to analyse talk in depth is to impose false levels of meaning on 'common-sense' understandings. They also resist the idea that repeated listenings to a tape may reveal to observers new, but no less 'genuine', meanings than were apparent on the first listening. The casualties of this obstinate naivety are the victims of injustice.

## Intercultural conversations

Helen Marriott has carried out research on what she calls 'intercultural business negotiations', transactions which involve people from significantly different cultural backgrounds. Some of her data come from a video-recorded conversation, in English but held in Japan, between a Japanese food importer and an Australian cheese manufacturer. The speakers were both amenable to being recorded. Sequence 9 is an extract from their conversation. (*J = Japanese speaker, A = Australian, [indicates simultaneous speech, and (.) a pause of noticeable length.*)

### Sequence 9: selling to Japan

J: And eh what your object to eh visit to me, is that eh introduce for eh this

A: We'd like to sell to Japan

J: sell to Japan

A: yeh

J: uh huh

A: or make it in Japan.

J: mm ah here yes

A: Either way, whichever is the best.
J: mm
A: Maybe make it here for um six months and eh if it's acceptable
J: ah six, six months
A: well we could send some samples from [Australia
J:                                                      [in Melbourne uh huh
A: and just test the market (.) if it's good we could then make it in Japan
J: uh huh (.) uh huh
A: with a joint venture.[15]

Marriott found that there were significant differences between the two men's behaviour in the interaction. The Japanese man often sought clarifications, and periodically offered summaries of information discussed. That is, he used strategies to check that there was *shared understanding* of matters being negotiated – something which the Australian rarely did. After the recording Marriott interviewed them to gain their views of how the transactions had gone. Both men felt that the other had not talked in the ways they would expect, given their business role. So, for example, the Japanese man commented: '. . . in Japan maybe the salesman speak more more, more explanation about his company's and the condition of the trading.'[16] The Australian, on the other hand, felt that the brevity and non-committal nature of the Japanese man's reactions to his comments (as in the extract above) left him feeling 'that I don't really know what he's going to do. It finished a little bit unconcluded.'[17] Overall, then, it seems that the two men did not have a secure, shared set of ground rules for building a context for their work activity. The unfortunate consequence was that the two men failed to communicate effectively, and the Australian left feeling particularly dissatisfied with the outcome of the encounter. Although the Japanese speaker was very ready to admit to limitations in his use of English, Marriott suggests that this was not a major cause of misunderstanding. Instead she suggests that the different expectations held and interpretations made about the conversation by the two men reflected other, less obvious differences in their cultural backgrounds and experiences. To some extent, this may be a matter of Japanese and Australian people having different habitual conversational styles – ways of expressing intent, interest and so on, by words and gestures, vary considerably across societies. But Marriott emphasizes that explaining misunderstandings in terms of cultural experiences does not simply mean making generalized comparisons between Japanese and Australian ways of conversing. In the international business world of today other cultural factors besides national origin might be just as important for shaping speakers' ways of talking business and their interpretation of events. The Japanese man worked in a large, international organization: he had much more experience of intercultural business negotiations than the Australian, he had dealt a lot with foreign business people in Japan, and he had made several work trips abroad. The Australian, on the other hand, worked for his own small firm, had travelled little, and his previous work had not involved him in these kinds of negotiations. In other words, the Japanese businessman was probably more familiar with the conversational ground rules for carrying on such a business negotiation, and so for predicting its structure and outcomes.

Even when people may agree that they are all engaged in the same kind of talk activity, such as 'dinner conversation', they may not necessarily have the same understanding of how it should be carried out. In her research on informal conversations, the sociolinguist Deborah Tannen has shown how even people of fairly similar social backgrounds may follow different ground rules, and how this can lead to some misunderstandings. For example, she analysed the conversation of a group of friends who had come together in the USA for a Thanksgiving dinner party.[18] The group consisted of two Californians (both men), three New Yorkers (two men and Tannen herself) and an English woman. Much conversation apparently took place during the meal, but when Tannen asked the guests afterwards if they had enjoyed it, she got very different responses. The New Yorkers had found it lively and satisfying, but the others evaluated it much less favourably. They had felt intimidated and pushed into the conversational sidelines by their New Yorker friends. One of the Californians commented: 'I'm amazed at how you guys talk over each other, saying the same thing at the same time. When I have a conversation there are pauses.' The other said he felt threatened by the New Yorkers' continual barrage of direct questions like 'How do you know that?' and 'How did you feel?' It appeared that what Tannen called the 'New York Jewish highinvolvement' style of informal conversation was both unfamiliar and (on first encounter) unacceptable to her guests from California and England. That is, while the New Yorkers' ground rules might include those in the following list (and be justified in the ways in which I have justified them below), their guests would not expect to follow such rules (and would probably not be convinced by those justifications):

- Talk to relative strangers about personal matters (it shows that you are willing to trust them).
- Interrupt speakers if you have something urgent to contribute (it shows that you are enthused by what they have said).
- Ask people direct questions about their lives, interests, problems and so on (it shows that you are interested in them).
- Tell anecdotes about things that have happened to you (it shows that you lead an interesting life and will encourage other people to tell stories of their own).

## Frames of reference

We often only realize that ground rules exist when someone breaks them. I remember first becoming aware of this from reading about the work of the sociologist Harold Garfinkel.[19] Garfinkel encouraged students to carry out what he called 'breaching experiments', of which an example was to go home to their parents' houses and, without saying anything in explanation, behave as if they were boarders rather than members of the family. This difficult activity offers insights into the ways in which the students felt it necessary to modify their behaviour to be lodger-like (such as by asking for permission to use the telephone, rather than simply taking its availability for granted). It is also interesting to note how relatives reacted: Garfinkel's students were asked 'Are you sick?', 'What are you being so superior about?', 'Are you out of your mind or are you just stupid?' In this way, it is possible to see beneath what Garfinkel calls 'the obstinate reality of everyday life', the taken-for-granted assumptions that underpin almost all conversations and which we use every day as foundations for the joint creation of new knowledge.

My appreciation of the importance of implicit ground rules was also helped by the cross-cultural research of the psychologist Michael Cole and his colleagues, who in the 1960s studied literacy and reasoning amongst members of a Liberian people called the Kpelle. Reasoned debate and argument were apparently common and important parts of Kpelle culture, but most of the people had not attended school. Sequence 10 shows what happened when Cole's team (one of whom was acting as the 'experimenter') asked a member of the Kpelle (the 'subject') to solve a reasoning problem, involving the fictitious characters of Flumo and Yakpalo.

### Sequence 10: Flumo and Yakpalo

EXPERIMENTER:   Flumo and Yakpalo always drink cane juice (rum) together. Flumo is drinking cane juice. Is Yakpalo drinking cane juice?

SUBJECT:   Flumo and Yakpalo drink cane juice together, but the time Flumo was drinking the first one Yakpalo was not there on that day.

EXPERIMENTER:   But I told you that Flumo and Yakpalo always drink cane juice together. One day Flumo was drinking cane juice. Was Yakpalo drinking cane juice that day?

SUBJECT:   The day Flumo was drinking cane juice Yakpalo was not there on that day.

EXPERIMENTER:   What is the reason?

SUBJECT:   The reason is that Yakpalo went to his farm that day and Flumo remained in town on that day . . .[20]

We can see that the experimenter and subject apparently reached an *impasse*, because while one of them treated the conversation as a way of presenting a formal test of logic (in which the people mentioned, and their actions, are simply vehicles for presenting the problem), the other treated it as a fictional scenario with more open possibilities. As Cole and his colleagues point out, neither was behaving irrationally; it is simply that they were not contextualizing the talk about the story of Flumo and Yakpalo in the same way. This reflects their different 'schooled' and 'unschooled' backgrounds. In other words, the experimenter and the subject did not establish a *shared frame of reference*: their talk lacked shared contextual foundations, and they were not employing the same ground rules. This meant that they were not really engaged in the same kind of collective thinking activity. This reflected their different past cultural experiences of using language to represent and discuss intellectual problems.

We will all have discovered that, on some occasions, even people who are quite co-operatively and amicably involved in a conversation may misunderstand each other. An example from my own experience that puzzled me for a while was an occasion when I was watching television with an older relative, Auntie Mick. The programme we were watching was a game show (a type of programme I hate) in which the participants had to carry out daring kinds of activities, such as bungee jumping. As we watched, one particularly dislikable contestant (from my perspective) gestured wildly to the crowd and dived off in a reckless way in his bungee jump. Auntie Mick suddenly said: 'It's amazing that jerk doesn't break his neck!', to which my immediate response was 'Yes!', meaning that he certainly was a jerk and it was surprising that he survived such foolishness. It was only later that, on reflection, and taking account of her apparently uncritical enjoyment of the rest of the show, I realized that Auntie Mick was probably simply referring to the 'jerk' of the bungee rope, not to the character of the contestant. When I eventually asked her, she confirmed that this was what she had meant. Running over her sentence in my mind, I concluded that there was no obvious way, in terms of pronunciation or intonation, that these two possible meanings would necessarily sound different. Moreover, we were both familiar with the English language and the kind of television show we were watching. The misunderstanding which occurred clearly had something to do with shared contextual foundations, but was not of an obvious kind. I eventually concluded that one way of describing the basis of this trivial but intriguing misunderstanding was that – as in Cole's talk with the Kpelle – Auntie Mick and I were using different frames of reference. That is, although we could assume joint understanding in general terms of what we were watching and discussing, we were each tacitly making very different, value-laden interpretations of the events being shown. Amazingly, but misleadingly, Auntie Mick's sentence expressed both our quite different interpretations.

Most of the time when we use language we depend heavily on the assumption that the person with whom we are interacting has a similar understanding of the words we use, what we are trying to achieve by talking and the ways in which we should use language to make it happen. That is, in casual conversations and many other spoken language events (such as counselling sessions, interviews, sales encounters and lessons in school), we commonly assume that the people with whom we are dealing do not only share our understanding of the kind of interaction in which we are involved (what I have called the 'ground rules' for the talk), but also share other assumptions about values, purposes and ways of categorizing information which are important for building a shared frame of reference.

We may *not* make many assumptions about such shared understanding if we decide that we are dealing with someone who is a novice to the kind of encounter taking place – for example, if a counsellor or therapist knows that a new client is unfamiliar with what happens in counselling sessions and so will be unfamiliar with the kind of dialogue involved, or a teacher knows that they are dealing with a student from abroad who may be unfamiliar with the conventions of classrooms. But research has shown that counsellors, teachers, medical staff, police officers and others who are in control of conversations often act as if the people with whom they are dealing *are* familiar with the relevant ground rules, and do not help 'novices' by making the ground rules explicit (or explaining why they are following them). That is, the controlling interviewers too often fail to take an active-enough role in building shared contextual foundations for talk. This may put less experienced, less powerful participants in the conversation at a great disadvantage, limiting the scope and potential benefits for them of the talk. Moreover, interviewers may treat any failure to follow the ground rules on the part of the interviewees as stupidity or unco-operative behaviour. This is bound to have some unfortunate consequences for how well interviews are used as a means for enabling a 'professional' and a 'client' to share information and think together through a problem, and is undoubtedly one of the reasons why processes of guidance, justice and medical consultation go awry.[21]

One example of this kind of problem concerns the way in which people feel it is appropriate to respond to direct requests for information. The linguist Diana Eades describes how, in Australian Aboriginal communities, it is normal for speakers to say 'yes' in conversations even when they do not necessarily agree with what the speaker says, because their culture's ground rules use this simply as a way of helping the interaction along. However, police officers, lawyers and other interrogators from white Australian backgrounds sometimes interpret such remarks as signs of agreement, with some disastrous consequences.[22]

In Aboriginal cultures (and in many others, for example amongst some indigenous American people), it is also apparently not considered polite to engage in very direct requests for information. Yet such requests are a familiar feature of teacher-led talk in the classrooms of 'mainstream' Australian society. As researchers like Ian Malcolm[23] have observed, this means that there is often a 'ground rules mismatch' between white Australian teachers and the young Aboriginal children in their classes, with the teachers finding the children strangely reluctant to engage in the kinds of question-and-answer sessions which the teachers take for granted as a normal feature of classroom communication. These different perceptions by teachers and students about how talk should be used in the classroom can have serious educational consequences. A teacher needs continually to gauge the existing levels of understanding of students, check that students have been able to follow what they have heard or have read, and assess the progress they are making as they carry out activities. One of the main ways in which they do this is by talking with students. Students make better progress when they engage with their teacher in thinking through problems and issues, so that difficulties and misunderstandings come to the surface, and processes and procedures are talked through. In this way, education becomes a guided process of thinking with language, rather than merely a one-way transmission of information. But this process is unlikely to happen if teachers and students have not developed a joint understanding of the appropriate ground rules for talking together.

## Summary

Most of the time, when we speak with other people, we do so on the assumption that they are making sense. We also assume that they will make matters as clear as they think is necessary for us to understand them. We look into what they say for clues to the kinds of contextual resources we should draw on, we may ask for relevant additional information, and we may offer some ourselves. If such assumptions are false, then this will often emerge in the course of any continued conversation, and we can treat this as a 'special case' and revise our behaviour to take account of it.

In trying to make sense of what someone says, we never rely only on our knowledge of the basic meanings of words, or our familiarity with the grammatical constructions they use. As listeners, we always access some additional, contextual information, using any explicit guidance or hints provided by a speaker and drawing on any remembered past experience which seems relevant. As a conversation progresses, the content of what is said provides a contextual foundation for the talk which follows.

'Context', in the sense in which I am using the term, is not something that exists independently of people. In order to combine their intellectual efforts, people have to strive to create foundations of common, contextualizing knowledge. People do this by drawing on whatever information resources they think are relevant. These contextual resources are likely to be found in such things as:

- the physical surroundings;
- the past shared experience and relationship of the speakers;
- the speakers' shared tasks or goals;
- the speakers' experience of similar kinds of conversation.

Language also can be used to create its own context, as I will show in more detail in the next chapter. While the contexts that conversationalists build can never be fully accessible to an observer, we can infer some of what is being treated as 'contextual' by noticing the references speakers make (for example, to their environment and events past and present) and how the information they put into a conversation is treated as an accumulating basis of common knowledge as their conversation unfolds over time.

I called one kind of contextual resource that enables people to communicate effectively 'conversational ground rules'. If these rules are broken or if speakers are not following the same ones, misunderstandings can occur. Nevertheless, such occasions are interesting because they bring the normally implicit ground rules to the surface. Conversations also depend on speakers adopting, or creating, a common 'frame of reference' for considering available information and defining what they are trying to achieve together. Misunderstandings in conversations often result from weaknesses in the contextual foundations for collective thinking.

## Notes

1 David Crystal's *Dictionary of Linguistics and Phonetics* (Oxford, Blackwell, 1985, p. 71) explains that 'context' is sometimes used by linguists to refer to nothing more than the parts of a spoken utterance or written text which are near to a word on which they are focusing. But the term 'context of situation' is also used by linguists to refer to 'the whole set of external features *considered relevant* to the linguistic analysis of an utterance' (Crystal, 1985, p. 72). The way psychologists use the notion of 'context' also varies considerably. For example, it is interesting to compare the range of uses and definitions within two books with very similar titles: P. Light and G. Butterworth (eds) *Context and Cognition,* Hemel Hempstead, Harvester-Wheatsheaf, 1992; and A. C. Qhelhas and F. Pereira, *Cognition and Context,* special issue of *Análise Psicológica,* Lisbon, ISPA, 1998.

2 Halliday and Hasan (1989). Within the Hallidayan tradition of systemic functional linguistics, 'context' is tied to situations in which language texts are generated. For a short, clear explanation of this approach, see Martin (1993).

3 Adapted from Medway (1996, p. 109).

4 Cited in Romaine (1990, p. 197).

5 Most *Tok Pisin* words are derived from English words. For example, 'eplikeson' is really a variant of 'application', 'skul' of 'school', 'ekseptim' is derived from 'accept him' and 'long' from 'belong'. Using this knowledge, you may guess that 'skul long fama' can be roughly translated as 'school belong(ing to) farmers' – that is, an agricultural training institution. Suzanne Romaine offers the following complete translation into standard English of what the student says: 'I sent my application to the school board and then they considered and accepted me and I'm going to agricultural school.'

6 The educational researchers Edwards and Furlong were perhaps the first to express clearly this important idea of the reciprocal relationship between language and context: 'It is not a matter of the context determining what is said, because the process is reciprocal. [Speakers] create through talk the very context on which they rely to support that talk' (Edwards and Furlong, 1978, p. 57). In recent years, conversation analysts seem to be the researchers most aware of this. See, for example, Drew and Heritage (1992).

7 'Map' is one of several activities devised in the early 1980s by the National Foundation for Educational Research for the purpose of assessing the oral communication skills of British children. The sequences transcribed here were recorded by The Open University and can be heard on the audiocassette for *Talk*

*and Learning 5–16: An Inservice Pack on Oracy for Teachers,* Milton Keynes, The Open University, 1991.

8  For other examples of the use of ground rules in analysing language use, see Edwards and Mercer (1987), Sheeran and Barnes (1991) and Mercer (1995).

9  This research is reported in Mercer and Longman (1992, pp. 103–25) and Longman (1996, pp. 116–21).

10  Coates (1994, p. 181).

11  This sequence was recorded during the *Spoken Language and New Technology (SLANT)* project, which was a joint venture of the University of East Anglia and The Open University, funded by the Economic and Social Research Council. It involved schools in Buckinghamshire, Cambridgeshire, Northamptonshire and Norfolk, and is reported in Wegerif and Scrimshaw (1997).

12  Shuy (1993, p. 24).

13  Shuy (1993, p. 24).

14  Shuy (1993, p. 32).

15  Marriott (1995, pp. 260–1).

16  Marriott (1995, p. 263).

17  Marriott (1965, p. 262).

18  Tannen (1984). For a general discussion of conversational styles, see also Maybin (1996).

19  Garfinkel (1963).

20  This research is reported in Cole, Gay, Glick, and Sharpe (1971). This sequence is given as cited by Ulric Neisser in L.B.Resnick (ed.) *The Nature of Intelligence,* New York, Lawrence Erlbaum, 1976, pp. 135–6.

21  The talk of job-counselling interviews, and the problems of understanding that arise in them, are described in Mercer and Longman, 'Accounts'. Problems which arise in interrogations of suspects by police are discussed in Gudjonsson (1992). Research on medical consultations and other kinds of client-professional talk is described in Drew and Heritage (1992), *Talk at Work.*

22  Eades.

23  Malcolm (1982, pp. 115–34). For more on these kinds of cross-cultural language issues in education, see Mercer and Swann (1996).

# References

Coates, J. 'No gap, lots of overlap', in D. Graddol, J. Maybin, and B. Stierer (eds) *Researching Language and Literacy in Social Context,* Clevedon, Multilingual Matters, 1994, p. 181.

Cole, M., Gay, J., Glick, J., and Sharpe, D. *The Cultural Context of Learning and Thinking,* New York, Basic Books, 1971.

Drew, P., and Heritage, J. (eds) *Talk at Work: Interaction in Institutional Settings,* Cambridge, Cambridge University Press, 1992.

Eades, D. 'Communicative strategies in Aboriginal English', in J. Maybin and N. Mercer (eds) *Using English: From Conversation to Canon,* London, Routledge with the Open University, 1996.

Edwards, A. D., and Furlong, V. F. *The Language of Teaching,* London, Heinemann, 1978, p. 57.

Edwards, D. and Mercer, N. *Common Knowledge,* London, Methuen/ Routledge, 1987.

Garfinkel, H. 'A conception of, and experiments with, "trust" as a condition of stable concerted actions', in O. J. Harvey (ed.) *Motivation and Social Interaction,* New York, Ronald Press, 1963.

Gudjonsson, G. *The Psychology of Interrogations, Confessions and Testimony*, Chichester, John Wiley and Sons, 1992.

Halliday, M. A. K., and Hasan, R. *Language, Context, and Text: Aspects of Language in a Social-Semiotic Perspective*, London, Oxford University Press, 1989.

Longman, J. 'Professionals and clients: form filling and the control of talk', in J. Maybin and N. Mercer (eds) *Using English: From Conversation to Canon,* London, Routledge with the Open University, 1996, pp. 116–21.

Malcolm, I. 'Speech events in the Aboriginal classroom', *International Journal of the Sociology of Language,* 1982, vol. 36, pp. 115–34.

Marriott, H. 'Deviations in an intercultural business negotiation', in A. Firth (ed.) *The Discourse of Negotiation: Studies of Language in the Workplace,* London, Pergamon, 1995, pp. 260–1.

Martin, J. 'Genre and literacy—modeling context in educational linguistics', *Annual Review of Applied Linguistics,* 1993, vol. 13, pp. 141–72.

Maybin, J. 'Everyday talk', in J. Maybin and N. Mercer (eds) *Using English: From Conversation to Canon,* London, Routledge with the Open University, 1996.

Medway, P. 'Constructing the virtual building: language on a building site', in J. Maybin and N. Mercer (eds) *Using English: From Conversation to Canon,* London, Routledge with the Open University, 1996, p. 109.

Mercer, N. *The Guided Construction of Knowledge: Talk Amongst Teachers and Learners*, Clevedon, Multilingual Matters, 1995.

Mercer, N. and Longman, J. 'Accounts and the development of shared understanding in Employment Training Interviews', *Text,* 1992, vol. 12, no. 1, pp. 103–25.

Mercer, N., and Swann, J. (eds) *Learning English: Development and Diversity*, London, Routledge with The Open University, 1996.

Romaine, S. 'Pidgin English advertising', in C. Ricks and L. Michaels (eds) *The State of the Language*, London, Faber and Faber, 1990, p. 197.

Sheeran, Y. and Barnes, D. *School Writing: Discovering the Ground Rules,* Milton Keynes, Open University Press, 1991.

Shuy, R. *Language Crimes: The Use and Abuse of Language Evidence in the Courtroom*, London, Blackwell, 1993, p. 24.

Tannen, B. *Conversational Style: Analysing Talk Amongst Friends*, Norwood, NJ, Ablex, 1984.

Wegerif, R. and Scrimshaw, P. (eds) Computers *and Talk in the Primary Classroom,* Clevedon, Multilingual Matters, 1997.

*In the late 1990s the Open University began training teachers of English as a second or other language. As a result, I became involved with research in language classrooms, and first engaged with applied linguistics and studies of bilingual development. Through working with researchers and teachers in those fields, I realised that they were often dealing with aspects of classroom education that were not specific to the language classroom, and that a sociocultural perspective on teaching and learning was as relevant there as with any other curriculum subject. This chapter was written for a new postgraduate, international, distance education course for teachers created jointly with Macquarie University, in which I was fortunate enough to work closely with Chris Candlin, a leading figure in applied linguistics.*

# 5  Language for teaching a language

*Mercer, N. (2001). Language for teaching a language. In C.N. Candlin &* *N. Mercer (eds),* English Language Teaching in its Social Context. *London: Routledge, pp. 243–257.*

## Introduction

This chapter is about the use of language as a medium for teaching and learning, with special relevance to the teaching of English. However, many of the issues I will deal with, especially those in the early parts of the chapter, are not specific to the use of any particular language in the classroom, or the teaching of any particular curriculum subject. Of course, languages of instruction and curricula vary from country to country, from region to region and even from school to school. Teachers differ in their style and approach, and their classes are made up of individuals of various personal characteristics and cultural backgrounds, who differ in the ways they respond to teachers and particular styles of teaching. But, as I will explain, observational research suggests that some ways that language is used in interactions between teachers and students are common features of classroom life throughout the world. I will illustrate some of these features of classroom language with real-life examples, and discuss their possible educational functions. In the latter part of the chapter, I will use the theoretical perspective of socio-cultural psychology to relate the earlier analysis of classroom language to a consideration of the nature and quality of classroom education. In these ways, I hope to demonstrate the practical educational value of a careful analysis of the interactive process of teaching-and-learning.

## Language and teaching

Wherever they are and whatever they are teaching, teachers in schools and other educational institutions are likely to face some similar practical tasks. They have to organise activities to occupy classes of disparate individuals, learners who may vary considerably in their aims, abilities and motivations. They have to control unruly behaviour. They are expected to teach a specific curriculum, a body of knowledge and skills which their students would not normally encounter in their out-of-school lives. And they have to monitor and assess the educational progress the students make. All these aspects of teachers' responsibilities are reflected in their use of language as the principal tool of their responsibilities. As examples of this, I would like you now to consider two transcribed sequences of classroom talk, Sequences 1 and 2. For each in turn, consider:

1   Can you identify any recurring patterns of interaction in the talk between teacher and pupils?
2   What would you say were the main functions of the teacher's questions in each of the sequences? Do the sequences differ at all in this respect?

I have made my own comments after both the sequences.

(Note: in the transcriptions words spoken particularly emphatically are underlined. Words which were unclear during transcription are in curled brackets { }. The onset of simultaneous speech is marked with a square bracket [.)

### Sequence 1: toy animals

This sequence was recorded in an English lesson in a Russian primary school. The teacher has just set up a collection of soft toy animals in front of the class.

T:   Have you got any toy animals at home? Be quick. Raise your hand (*she raises her own hand*) and show me. Have you got any toy animals? S-{Name of child}
S:   (*Standing up*) I have got a cat, a
T:   No, sit down, in your place.
S:   Yes, I have.
T:   I have got many?
S:   Toys at home.
T:   Toy <u>animals</u> at home.

### Sequence 2: personal qualities

This next sequence comes from a TESOL class for young adults in a college in London. A little earlier, the teacher had asked each of the students to list their own personal qualities, both positive and negative.

T:   Who would like to tell the class about their personal qualities? Dalia?
D:   I am polite, friendly, organised, trustworthy, responsible but sometimes I am impatient and unpunctual. Sometimes (*laughs*).
T:   Good, isn't it? (*Addressing the class*) Thank you, Dalia. That was good. Now can you tell me the positive qualities you have just said.
D:   Yeah?

T:  That is, friendly, um, organised.
D:  {Right}
T:  How is it helping you . . .
D:  Yeah?
T:  . . . with your friends [in the class?
D:                           [It help me to get along with people and to under-
    stand them and help them.
T:  That's good. And what about the, the not very positive ones [like punctual
D:                                                               [Sometimes
T:  What happens then?
D:  Sometimes I lose my friend basically of that because I lose my temper
    very quickly.
T:  And what happens with me? I don't smile at you that much do I ?

## Comments on Sequences 1 and 2

Sequence 1 illustrates some patterns which typify most classroom talk. First, the teacher took longer turns at speaking than any students. Second, she asked all the questions. Observational research has shown that in classroom conversations teachers usually ask the great majority of questions, usually – as in this case – to elicit some kind of participatory response from the students. She then *evaluates* the replies they give. She is also using questions to direct the topic or content of the talk towards issues that she wishes to focus attention on. Looking more carefully at Sequence 1, we can see that there is a structural pattern to the talk: a *teacher's question* is followed by a *student response*, followed in turn by some *teacher feedback or evaluation*. This structural element of classroom talk was first described by the linguists Sinclair and Coulthard (1975; see also Mehan, 1979; Van Lier, Chapter 5 of this book) and is usually known as an Initiation-Response-Feedback (IRF) exchange. For example:

T:  . . . Have you got any toy animals? S-{Name of child}   I
S:  (*Standing up*) I have got a cat, a                      R
T:  No, sit down, in your place.                             F

IRF exchanges can be thought of as the archetypal form of interaction between a teacher and a pupil – a basic unit of classroom talk as a continuous stretch of language or 'text'. They do not typify the pattern of talk in all classroom activities; other kinds of talk involving different patterns of exchanges (e.g. in which students ask questions of teachers, or of other students) may happen too. And outside the most formal and traditional of classrooms, they may not often be found in their classic, simple form. But IRFs have been observed as a common feature in classrooms the world over, and in other languages besides English.

In Sequence 1, the IRF exchanges are being used to perform a common function in classrooms, one that is almost certainly familiar to you from your own schooldays: a teacher is eliciting from learners their knowledge of the relevant curriculum subject (in this case, English). Research shows that this particular kind of use of question-and-answer by a teacher – asking questions to which the teacher knows exactly what answers she seeks – is the most common function of IRFs in classrooms. Here students are essentially trying to provide the information that the teacher expects them to know. As the classroom researchers Edwards and Westgate say:

> Most classroom talk which has been recorded displays a clear boundary between knowledge and ignorance. . . . To be asked a question by someone who wants to know is to be given the initiative in deciding the amount of information to be offered and the manner of telling. But to be asked by someone who already knows, and wants to know if you know, is to have your answer accepted, rejected or otherwise evaluated according to the questioner's beliefs about what is relevant and true.
>
> (1994, p. 48)

Teachers need to check students' understanding of procedural, factual matters, and that is commonly the function of IRF exchanges. Sequence 1 illustrates also how 'feedback' from a teacher may also be used to control students' behaviour. These are quite legitimate functions of teacher-talk, and all teachers might expect to use language in this way quite frequently. But the danger of relying heavily and continuously on traditional, formal question-and-answer reviews for guiding learning is that students then get little opportunity for using language in more creative ways – such as experimenting with new types of language constructions.

As in much classroom talk, in Sequence 2 we can also see IRF exchanges occurring, though here as slightly more complex, linked structures, in which the student interjects during the teacher's elicitations, perhaps seeking clarification, which the teacher provides. And if we consider the content and function of the question-and-answer exchanges in the two sequences, we can see that something rather different is going on in each of them. In Sequence 1, the teacher is asking her primary school pupils to produce English sentences which conform to the models she has in mind. The children respond by trying to provide these 'right answers'. The teacher in Sequence 2 is not doing that. Instead, she is asking questions to encourage the students to elaborate, in English, on what they have written. In this way, the teacher is not so much trying to elicit particular forms or structures of English, but rather encouraging the student to use English in a practical, communicative manner. I am not suggesting that either teacher is using their questioning techniques to better or worse effect, but simply illustrating the fact that IRF exchanges can be made to serve a variety of pragmatic, educational functions.

## Techniques for teaching

Having identified the archetypal structure of teacher–student talk, I will next describe some specific ways of interacting with students which are commonly used by teachers. I call these 'techniques', because I believe that they represent teachers attempting to shape language into a set of suitable tools for pursuing their professional goals. I will illustrate each technique and consider how they can contribute to the process of teaching-and-learning. The techniques are summarised in Table 5.1.

### Eliciting knowledge from learners

We have seen that when a teacher initiates an IRF sequence, this usually has the function of eliciting information from a student. If this is simply a straightforward request, we can describe the teacher's verbal act as a *direct elicitation*. But teachers also often engage in what can be called *cued elicitation*, which is a way of drawing out from learners the information they are seeking – the 'right' answers to their questions – by providing visual clues and verbal hints as to what answer is required. Here is an example recorded in an English lesson in a Zimbabwean primary school. The teacher has set up a number of objects on her desk, and also has a set of cards on which various consonants ('b', 'f', 'j' etc.) are written. The children have to come to the front of the class and match the consonants to the name of an object.

### Sequence 3: say the sound

TEACHER: (*to child*):   Say the sound.
CHILD:   b-b-b
TEACHER:   b-b-b is for?

(*Child does not answer. Teacher waves her hand over the nearest objects, one of which is a book*)

CHILD:   b-b-b is for book.
TEACHER:   Well done!

*Table 5.1* Some techniques that teachers use

---

**. . . to elicit knowledge from learners**
Direct elicitations
Cued elicitations

**. . . to respond to what learners say**
Confirmations
Rejections
Repetitions
Reformulations
Elaborations

**. . . to describe significant aspects of shared experience**
Amplifications
Explanations
'We' statements
Recaps

---

The use of cued elicitation as a teaching technique is widespread. It can be traced to the Socratic dialogues constructed by Plato (Edwards, 1988). By using this technique, the teacher avoids simply giving the child the right answer. Sequence 3 also illustrates how non-verbal communication – the use of gestures and other signs – can be an important component of classroom talk.

### Responding to what learners say

As illustrated by the sequences above, one of the ways that teachers sustain dialogues with their students is to use what students say as the basis for what they say next. In this way, the learners' own remarks are incorporated into the teaching-learning process. The most obvious way of doing this is through *confirmation* (as, for example, a teacher's 'Yes, that's right' to a pupil's answer). *Repetitions* of things learners say are another way, one which allows the teacher to draw to the attention of a whole class an answer or other remark which is judged by the teacher to have educational significance.

Teachers often paraphrase or *reformulate* a pupil's remark, usually so as to offer the class a revised, tidied-up version of what was said which fits in better with the point that the teacher wishes to make or the form of response being sought. For example, in this extract from Sequence 1:

S:   Yes, I have.
T:   I have got many?
S:   Toys at home.
T:   Toy <u>animals</u> at home.

There are also *elaborations*, when a teacher picks up on a cryptic statement made by a pupil and expands and/or explains its significance to the rest of the class. Wrong answers or unsuitable contributions may be explicitly *rejected* by a teacher. But we should also note a popular technique that teachers have for dealing with wrong answers – simply ignoring them.

### Describing shared experience

Classroom activities often rely on students reading instructions, whether in print or on a computer screen. It is important that they understand properly what is expected of them, if the activity is to succeed. Teachers therefore often *amplify* instructions with the intention of making them clearer and less ambiguous. Other texts may also contain information which students need to make sense of before they continue any further. In classrooms it is common to hear teachers *explaining* these texts to students as either a preliminary to activities or if some confusion about them seems to arise. For example, in this extract from a Spanish lesson for adult students:

*Sequence 4: ser and estar*

TEACHER:  It says (*reading from text*) 'This is one of the main difficulties for English-speaking learners' meaning the two verbs *ser* and *estar* which both, uh, translate as 'to be' in English. (*Reading again*) '*Ser* means to exist while *estar* means to be situated'. That sounds horribly complicated, I think to start by thinking of *ser* as being about permanent things and *estar* as temporary ways of being. *Vamos a ver* . . . (*He continues in Spanish*)

An important task for a teacher is to help learners see how the various activities they do, over time, contribute to the development of their understanding. Education cannot be merely the experience of a series of consecutive events, it must be a developmental process in which earlier experiences provide the foundations for making sense of later ones. For those involved in teaching and learning, continuous shared experience is one of the most precious resources available. There are many ways that teachers try to create continuities in the experience of learners – by sequencing activities in certain ways, by dealing with topics in order of difficulty and so on. Teachers can help learners perceive *continuity* in what they are doing. Through language there is the possibility of repeatedly revisiting and reinterpreting that experience, and of using it as the basis for future talk, activity and learning.

'*We*' *statements* (as in a teacher saying to a class 'last week we learned how to measure angles') are often used when teachers are trying to represent past experience as relevant to present activity. They show how teachers help learners see that they have significant past experience in common and so have gained shared knowledge and collective understanding which can be drawn upon to progress further. Teachers also often *recap* shared classroom experience from earlier in a lesson, and from previous lessons, usually emphasising the points or events they consider of most educational significance.

I have described and illustrated each of the techniques as separate items, each with an obvious function; but this is a simplification, for the sake of clarity of exposition, of the relationship between language form, function and context. An analyst of classroom discourse has to recognise that (a) any particular utterance can perform more than one function (so that, as in the first part of Sequence 3, a *repetition* can also be an *elicitation*); (b) any particular technique can serve more than one pedagogic purpose, and be used effectively or otherwise; and (c) the functional meaning of any interaction for participants may be shaped by contextual factors not available to the analyst (such as information gained from their shared past experience of interaction; see Breen, 2001, for further discussion of such matters). However, despite these caveats, I have found the identification of these techniques a useful, practical aid to analysis.

## Interaction in bilingual and multilingual settings

In the next part of the chapter I will consider some aspects of teacher–student interaction in classrooms where English is being used as a classroom language, but is not the first language of the children. I hope to show through these examples some of the qualities these bilingual settings have in common with monolingual classrooms, while also pointing out some of the special interactional features they may generate. There are two main sorts of situation which can be included here. The first occurs in countries where English is not the usual everyday language, and the mother tongue of most of the children is not English. The second is where pupils whose mother tongue is not English enter schools in a predominantly English-speaking country. I will provide examples from both of these types of situation.

In any situation where English is used as a classroom language but is not the main language of children's home or community, teachers may have the multiple task of teaching (a) the English language, (b) the educational ground rules for using it in the classroom and (c) any specific subject content. Jo Arthur (1992) carried out observational research on teaching and learning in primary school classrooms in Botswana. English was used as the medium of education, but it was not the main language of the pupils' local community. She observed that when teachers were teaching mathematics, they commonly used question-and-answer sessions as opportunities for schooling children in the use of appropriate 'classroom English' as well as maths. For example, one primary teacher commonly insisted that pupils reply to questions 'in full sentences', as shown below:

### Sequence 5: how many parts?

| | |
|---|---|
| TEACHER: | How many parts are left here (first pupil's name)? |
| FIRST PUPIL: | Seven parts. |
| TEACHER: | Answer fully. How many parts are there? |
| PUPIL: | There are . . . there are seven parts. |
| TEACHER: | How many parts are left? Sit down my boy. You have tried. Yes (second pupil's name)? |
| SECOND PUPIL: | We are left with seven parts. |
| TEACHER: | We are left with seven parts. Say that (second pupil's name). |
| SECOND PUPIL: | We are left with seven parts. |
| TEACHER: | Good boy. We are left with seven parts. |

(Arthur, 1992, pp. 6–7)

Sequence 5 is made up of a linked series of IRF exchanges. For example:

How many parts are left here? [Initiation]
Seven parts [Response]
Answer fully [Feedback/Evaluation]

The Botswanan students therefore needed to understand that their teacher was using these exchanges not only to evaluate their mathematical understanding, but also to test their fluency in spoken English and their ability to conform to a 'ground rule' that she enforced in her classroom – 'answer in full sentences'. Arthur comments that for pupils in this kind of situation, the demands of classroom communication are complicated because their teacher is attempting to get them to focus on both the medium (English) and the message (maths). Arthur reports that such dual focus is common in Botswanan classrooms, as the following sequence from another lesson shows:

### Sequence 6: the continent of Africa

T:   In which continent is your country? In which continent is your country? Give an answer
P1:  In Africa is my country
T:   He says in Africa is my country. Who could frame her sentence? In Africa is my country
P2:  Africa is my continent
T:   My question was in which continent is your country?
P3:  Its continent is in Africa
T:   It is in the continent of Africa. everybody
PS:  It is in the continent of Africa

(Arthur, 1992, p. 13)

### Bilingual code-switching in the classroom

In circumstances where one language is being used as a classroom language, but where the pupils' first language is a different one, a teacher may sometimes 'code-switch' to the first language if they judge it necessary. (We saw this kind of switch taking place between Spanish and English in Sequence 4 above.) Sometimes the first language may be used only for asides, for control purposes or to make personal comments. However, when code-switching amounts to translation by the teacher of the curriculum content being taught, its use as an explanatory teaching strategy is somewhat controversial. On the one hand, there are those who argue that it is a sensible, common-sense response by a teacher to the specific kind of teaching and learning situation. Thus in studying its use in English-medium classrooms in Hong Kong, Angel Lin (2001) explains a particular teacher's use of code-switching as follows:

> by always starting in L1, Teacher D always starts from where the student is – from what the student can fully understand and is familiar with.
>
> (p. 282)

Researchers of bilingual code-switching (as reviewed by Martyn-Jones, 1995) have often concluded that it is of dubious value as a teaching strategy, if one of the aims of the teaching is to improve students' competence in English. Thus Jacobson comments:

> the translation into the child's vernacular of everything that is being taught may prevent him/her from ever developing the kind of English language proficiency that must be one of the objectives of a sound bilingual programme.
>
> (Jacobson, 1990, p. 6)

It seems, however, that teachers often use code-switching in more complex ways than simply translating content directly into another language. On observing classrooms in Hong Kong, Johnson and Lee (1987) observed that the switching strategy most commonly employed by teachers had a three-part structure as follows:

1   'Key statement' of topic in English
2   Amplification, clarification or explanation in Cantonese
3   Restatement in English

They comment that 'direct translation was comparatively rare; the general effect was of a spiralling and apparently haphazard recycling of content, which on closer examination proved to be more organised than it appeared.' (1987, p. 106). The implication here is that such teachers are pursuing the familiar task of guiding children's understanding of curriculum content through language, but using special bilingual techniques to do so.

An interesting study of code-switching in bilingual classrooms in Malta was carried out by Antoinette Camilleri (1994). She showed that code-switching was used as a teaching technique by teachers in a variety of ways. Look for example at these two extracts from the talk of a teacher in a secondary school lesson about the production and use of wool, and based on a textbook written in English. The teacher begins by reading part of the text. (*A translation of talk in Maltese is given in the right hand column.*)

### Sequence 7: wool

### Extract 1

England Australia New Zealand and
Argentina are the best producers of wool
*dawk l-aktar li għandhom* farms *li j*           they have the largest number
*rabbu n-nagħaggħas-suf* O.K. England           of farms and the largest
*tgħiduli minn licma post* England               number of sheep for wool
*għandhom* Scotland *magħrufin tant*             O.K. England where in England
*għall-*wool *u ġersijiet tagħhom* O.K.           we really mean Scotland they
                                                  are very well-known for their
                                                  woollen products

## Extract 2

wool *issa* it does not crease but it has to be washed with care *issa din importanti ma għidtilkomx illi jekk ikolli nara xagħra jew sufa waħda* under the microscope *ghandha qisha ħafna* scales *tal. ħuta issa jekk ma naħ slux sewwa dawk l-is*cales *jitgħaqqdu go xulxin u indaħħ gersi daqshekk gol-* washing machine *u noħorgu daqshekk għax jixxrinkjali u jitgħaqqad kollu*

now this is important didn't I tell you that if I had a look at a single hair or fibre it has many scales which if not washed properly get entangled and I put a jersey this size into the washing machine and it comes out this size because it shrinks and gets entangled

(Adapted from Camilleri, 1994)

Camilleri notes that the first extract shows the teacher using the switch from English to Maltese to expand or *amplify* the point being made, rather than simply repeat it in translation. In the second extract, she *explains* the English statement in Maltese, again avoiding direct translation. Camilleri comments that the lesson therefore is a particular kind of literacy event, in which these are 'two parallel discourses – the written one in English, the spoken one in Maltese' (p. 12).

Studies of code-switching in classrooms have revealed a variety of patterns of bilingual use (Martyn-Jones, 1995). For example, Zentella (1981) observed and recorded events in two bilingual classes in New York schools, one a first grade class (in which the children were about six years old) and the other a sixth grade (in which the average age would be about 12). The pupils and teachers were all native Spanish speakers, of Puerto Rican origin, but the official medium for classroom education was English. One of the focuses of her analysis of teacher–pupil interactions was IRF sequences. Both Spanish and English were actually used by teachers and pupils in the classes, and Zentella was able to show that there were three recurring patterns of language-switching in IRF sequences, which seem to represent the use of certain 'ground rules' governing language choice. These are summarised below:

| Rules governing language choice | Teacher initiation | Student reply | Teacher feedback |
|---|---|---|---|
| 1 Teacher and student: | English | Spanish | English |
| 'follow the leader' | Spanish | Spanish | Spanish |
| 2 Teacher: 'follow the child' | English | Spanish | Spanish |
| | Spanish | English | English |
| 3 Teacher: 'include the child's | English | Spanish | both languages |
| choice not yours' | Spanish | English | both languages |

(Adapted from Zentella, 1981)

From this example, we can see that distinctive patterns of language use emerge in bilingual classrooms, but these can be interpreted as adaptations of the common IRF structure and language strategies used by teachers in monolingual settings. What is more, the distinctive patterns of switching which emerge in teacher-talk can be explained in terms of the special communicative resources that arise in a modern language classroom and the ways that teachers decide to respond to these special circumstances. The extent to which code-switching between English and another language occurs in a particular setting will therefore be influenced by factors such as (a) the degree of fluency in English that members of a particular class have achieved; (b) the bilingual competence of teachers; (c) the specific teaching goals of teachers; and – crucially – (d) the attitudes of both children and teachers to the practice of code-switching and to the languages involved.

## What learners have to understand about classroom language

When students enter an English-medium or EFL classroom having grown up speaking another language, it may be difficult for both teachers and children to distinguish between two 'learning tasks' – acquiring a basic fluency in English and learning the social conventions of using English as a classroom language. Some patterns of classroom language – such as IRF sequences – are likely to be familiar to any student who has had experience of school, even if they had encountered them in another language. As I noted earlier, however (in the comparison of Sequences 1 and 2), IRFs can be used for different purposes, some of which may not be familiar to students from their previous educational experience (say, if they have arrived as immigrants in an English-speaking country having been educated elsewhere in another language). Depending on their experiences within their own language communities, students might also be unfamiliar with some other conventions or 'ground rules' for using English that are associated with particular social settings inside and outside school.

For these reasons, it can be difficult for a teacher to tell whether a new pupil who is not fluent in English, and who appears to be having difficulties with using the language in the classroom, is struggling with general aspects of using English or having difficulties with grasping the 'local' ground rules for classroom language use. This kind of difficulty may arise in relation to the learning of written as well as spoken English, and is well illustrated by the research of Alex Moore (1995), who studied the progress of children of non-English-speaking immigrant families entering secondary schools in Britain.

Because of his close and continuous involvement in classroom events as a kind of 'action researcher' (Elliot, 1991), Moore was able to observe, describe and analyse teaching and learning over several weeks or months in one class. One of his special 'case studies' was of the progress of a Sylheti boy of 15 who had been in Britain one year since coming from Bangladesh (where he had been educated in Bengali). Moore focused on Mashud's class-room education in writing English. Mashud had quite a few problems with 'surface features' of English such as handwriting, spelling and grammatical structures, but was an enthusiastic writer. However, Moore and Mashud's teacher (Mrs Montgomery) both noticed that:

> his work had a particular idiosyncrasy in that whenever he was set creative writing – or even discursive writing – assignments, he produced heavily for-mulaic fairy-story-style moral tales which were apparently – according to information volunteered by other Sylheti pupils in the class – translations of stories he had learnt in his native tongue.
>
> (Moore, 1995, p. 362)

Despite being a willing pupil, Mashud seemed unable to transcend this tra-ditional style of genre and write in the genres that his teachers knew would be required of him in the British education system and in wider society. Further consideration led Moore and Mrs Montgomery to some hypotheses about why this was so:

> It has to be said that neither Mrs Montgomery or I knew enough about Bangladeshi or Sylheti story-telling traditions to be able to expound with any degree of confidence on the cause of Mashud's particular way of going about things. The key to our future pedagogy, however [. . .] lay in Mrs Montgomery's very wise recognition that *'there could be* the most enormous difference between what Mashud has been brought up to value in narratives and what we're telling him he should be valuing'.
>
> (Moore, 1995, p. 366)

This insight into Mashud's difficulties with genres of writing was supported by a more careful analysis of Mashud's texts, which had a linear, additive, chronological structure associated with oral, rather than literate cultural traditions (Ong, 1982). The outcome was the teacher designing activities for Mashud which would support or 'scaffold' (Bruner, 1986; Maybin, Mercer and Stierer, 1992) his development as a writer of English:

> If we responded appropriately, Mashud would, we hoped, learn some-thing of what was valued in expressive writing in his new school, and how that was different from – though no better than – what he may have learned to value at school in Bangladesh.
>
> (Moore, 1995, p. 368)

This approach proved successful, as during the remaining period of Moore's research Mashud showed clear progress in coming to understand and cope with the demands of writing in the genres of English required in the Brit-ish school system. Describing research with children in a Spanish-English bilingual program in Californian schools, Moll and Dworin (1996) also highlight the important role of a teacher in helping learners make the best educational use of their bi-cultural language experience in developing their literacy skills in the second language.

## A socio-cultural perspective on classroom interaction

I now wish to relate the above discussion of language as the medium of teaching-and-learning to a consideration of the quality of education. To do this, I will draw on a particular approach to human learning and development which is known as *socio-cultural psychology*. This approach has emerged during the final decades of the twentieth century from a belated appreciation of the pioneering research on the relationship between language and cognitive development carried out by the Russian psychologist Lev Vygotsky (for example, Vygotsky, 1962). Vygotsky worked in Moscow in the 1920s and 30s, in an institution for children who had special educational needs, but his ideas on the process of teaching and learning have much broader educational relevance than the specific institutional settings in which he put them into practice. Vygotsky gave language a special, important role in human cognitive development, describing human individuals and their societies as being linked by language into a historical, continuing, dynamic, interactive, spiral of change. Led by the example of Jerome Bruner (1985, 1986), a considerable body of research has now emerged which uses a 'neo-Vygotskian', socio-cultural perspective in the analysis of educational processes. Some of the most significant and distinctive implications of adopting a socio-cultural perspective on classroom education are, I believe, as follows:

1    *Language is our most important pedagogic tool.* Although they do not necessarily make this explicit, I suggest that the most influential socio-cultural theorists of cognitive development (as represented by such as Bruner, 1986; Wertsch, 1991; Rogoff, 1990) ascribe three important functions to language: (a) as *a cognitive tool* whose acquisition enables children to gain, process, organise and evaluate knowledge; (b) as *a cultural tool*, by which knowledge is shared, stored and made available to successive generations; (c) as *a pedagogic tool* by which intellectual guidance is provided to children by other people. These roles are inextricably intertwined. To this specification of the roles of language we might add the comment: learning how to use language effectively as a cultural tool is an important educational goal for native speakers as well as second language learners. So language is both the tool for carrying out teaching-and-learning and also that which is meant to be learnt and taught.

2    *Education is a dialogical, cultural process.* The development of students' knowledge and understanding is shaped by their relationships with

teachers and other students, and by the culture in which those relationships are located (Newman, Griffin and Cole, 1989; Gee, 1996). The educational success students achieve is only partly under their own control, and only partly under the control of their teachers. This is where the socio-cultural concept of 'scaffolding', which I mentioned briefly earlier, is useful. The essence of this concept, as developed by Bruner (1986), Wood (1988) and others, is that an effective teacher provides the kind of intellectual support which enables learners to make intellectual achievements they would never accomplish alone; and one way they do so is by using dialogue to guide and support the development of understanding.

3 *Language carries the history of classroom activity into its future.* The socio-cultural perspective suggests that if we want to understand the process of learning, we must study not only what a learner does but also the activities of parents, teachers, peers who create – indeed, constitute – the dynamic context of their learning experience (Edwards and Mercer, 1987; Hicks, 1996). Rogoff (1990) talks of children being involved in a process of 'guided participation' in the intellectual life of their communities, which implies the necessary involvement of others. For similar reasons, I have described the process of teaching-and-learning as 'the guided construction of knowledge' (Mercer, 1995). This is a process which is carried on over time, so that, as the language researcher Janet Maybin (1994) has put it, the talk on any occasion between a teacher and their regular class of students can be considered part of the 'long conversation' of their relationship. Language is a tool for building the future out of the past: the meaningfulness of current and future joint activities of teachers and learners depends on the foundations of their common knowledge (Mercer, 2000).

4 *Classroom interaction follows implicit 'ground rules'.* The socio-cultural perspective emphasises that everyday human activity depends heavily on participants being able to draw on a considerable body of shared knowledge and understanding, based on their past shared experience or similar histories of experience. The conventions or 'ground rules' which ensure that speakers and listeners, writers and readers are operating within the same genres of language are rarely made explicit, but so long as participants can safely assume shared knowledge, the language of everyday interaction follows its conventional patterns. If the contextual foundations of shared knowledge are lacking – such as when students' home backgrounds have not prepared them well for making sense of the language and culture of the classroom – misunderstandings may easily arise and persist unresolved (Heath, 1983; LoCastro, 1997). Making the 'ground rules' of classroom activity explicit can help overcome misunderstandings and misinterpretations, and there is growing evidence that students' progress is significantly enhanced if teachers do so (Christie, 1990; Mercer, Wegerif and Dawes, 1999).

## Conclusion

Recordings and transcriptions of classroom talk, analysed from a socio-cultural perspective, offer us glimpses of the social, cultural, communicative process of education being pursued and, with varying degrees of success, accomplished. They may capture illustrations of the best practice, in which teachers enable students to achieve levels of understanding which might never, or at least not nearly so quickly, have been achieved without a 'scaffolding' guidance; they as often reveal misunderstandings being generated, and opportunities for guided development being squandered. As teachers, as well as researchers, we can learn much from what they reveal. It is of course unrealistic to expect any busy teacher to monitor and evaluate every interaction in their classroom; but recent research (in areas of the curriculum other than language teaching) has shown that through a better understanding of the use of language as a pedagogic tool, teachers can help students improve their curriculum-related learning and their use of language as a tool for constructing knowledge (Brown and Palincsar, 1989; Wegerif, Rojas-Drummond and Mercer, 1999; Mercer, Wegerif and Dawes, 1999). A socio-cultural perspective has only quite recently been brought to bear on teaching and learning in the modern language classroom (see Van Lier (2001), Gibbons (2001) and Breen (2001)), but I am convinced that its application will have significant practical implications for this field of educational endeavour.

## References

Arthur, J. (1992) 'English in Botswana classrooms: Functions and constraints', *Centre for Language in Social Life Working Papers No.46*. University of Lancaster, UK.

Breen, M. (2001) 'Navigating the discourse: On what is learned in the language classroom', in C.N. Candlin & N. Mercer (eds), *English Language Teaching in its Social Context*. London: Routledge.

Brown, A. and Palincsar, A.S. (1989) 'Guided, cooperative learning and individual knowledge acquisition', in L. Resnick (ed.) *Knowing, Learning and Instruction*. New York: Lawrence Erlbaum.

Bruner, J.S. (1985) 'Vygotsky: A historical and conceptual perspective', in J.V. Wertsch (ed.) *Culture, Communication and Cognition: Vygotskian Perspectives*. Cambridge: Cambridge University Press.

Bruner, J.S. (1986) *Actual Minds, Possible Worlds*. London: Harvard University Press.

Camilleri, A. (1994) *Talking Bilingually, Writing Monolingually*. Paper presented at the Sociolinguistics Symposium, Lancaster University, March 1994.

Christie, F. (1990) *Literacy for a Changing World*. Melbourne: Australian Council for Educational Research.

Edwards, A.D. and Westgate, D. (1994) *Investigating Classroom Talk* (Second Edition). London: The Falmer Press.

Edwards, D. (1988) 'The Meno', in M. Billig, S. Condor, D. Edwards, M. Gane, D. Middleton and A. Radley (eds.) *Ideological Dilemmas: A Social Psychology of Everyday Thinking*. London: Sage.

Edwards, D. and Mercer, N. (1987) *Common Knowledge: The Development of Understanding in the Classroom*. London: Methuen/Routledge.

Elliot, J. (1991) *Action Research for Educational Change*. Milton Keynes: Open University Press.

Gee, J.P. (1996) 'Vygotsky and current debates in education: Some dilemmas as afterthoughts to *Discourse, Learning and Schooling*', in D. Hicks (ed.) *Discourse, Learning and Schooling*. Cambridge: Cambridge University Press.

Gibbons, P. (2001) 'Learning a new register in a second language', in C.N. Candlin & N. Mercer (eds.), *English Language Teaching in its Social Context*. London: Routledge.

Heath, S.B. (1983) *Ways With Words: Language, Life and Work in Communities and Classrooms*. Cambridge: Cambridge University Press.

Hicks, D. (1996) 'Contextual enquiries: A discourse-oriented study of classroom learning', in D. Hicks (ed.) *Discourse, Learning and Schooling*. Cambridge: Cambridge University Press.

Jacobson, R. (1990) 'Allocating two languages as a key feature of a bilingual methodology', in R. Jacobson and C. Faltis (eds.) *Language Distribution Issues in Bilingual Schooling*. Clevedon: Multilingual Matters.

Johnson, R.K. and Lee, P.L.M. (1987) 'Modes of instruction: Teaching strategies and students responses', in R. Lord and H. Cheng (eds.) *Language Education in Hong Kong*. Hong Kong: The Chinese University Press.

Lin, A. (2001) 'Doing-English-lessons in the reproduction or transformation of social worlds?' In C.N. Candlin & N. Mercer (eds.), *English Language Teaching in its Social Context*. London: Routledge.

LoCastro, V. (1997) 'Politeness and pragmatic competence in foreign language education', *Language Teaching Research*, Vol. 1, No. 3, pp. 239–268.

Martyn-Jones, M. (1995) 'Code-switching in the classroom', in L. Milroy and P. Muysken (eds.) *One Speaker, Two Languages: Cross Disciplinary Perspectives on Code-switching*. Cambridge: Cambridge University Press.

Maybin, J. (1994) 'Children's voices: Talk, knowledge and identity', in D. Graddol, J. Maybin and B. Stierer (eds.) *Researching Language and Literacy in Social Context*. Clevedon: Multilingual Matters.

Maybin, J., Mercer, N. and Stierer, B. (1992) '"Scaffolding" learning in the classroom', in K. Norman (ed.) *Thinking Voices*. London: Hodder and Stoughton.

Mehan, H. (1979) *Learning Lessons: Social Organization in the Classroom*. Cambridge, MA: Harvard University Press.

Mercer, N. (1995) *The Guided Construction of Knowledge: Talk Amongst Teachers and Learners*. Clevedon: Multilingual Matters.

Mercer, N. (2000) *Words and Minds: How We Use Language to Think Together*. London: Routledge.

Mercer, N., Wegerif, R. and Dawes, L. (1999) 'Children's talk and the development of reasoning in the classroom', *British Educational Research Journal*, Vol. 25, No. 1, pp. 95–113.

Moll, L. and Dworin, J. (1996) 'Biliteracy development in classrooms: Social dynamics and cultural possibilities', in D. Hicks (ed.) *Discourse, Learning and Schooling*. Cambridge: Cambridge University Press.

Moore, A. (1995) *The Academic, Linguistic and Social Development of Bilingual Pupils in Secondary Education: Issues of Diagnosis, Pedagogy and Culture*. Unpublished Ph.D. thesis, The Open University.

Newman, D., Griffin, P. and Cole, M. (1989) *The Construction Zone*. Cambridge: Cambridge University Press.

Ong, W. (1982) *Orality and Literacy*. London: Methuen.

Rogoff, B. (1990) *Apprenticeship in Thinking.* Oxford: Oxford University Press.

Sinclair, J. and Coulthard, M. (1975) *Towards an Analysis of Discourse: The English Used by Teachers and Pupils.* London: Oxford University Press.

Van Lier, L. (2001) 'Constraints and resources in classroom talk: issues of equality and symmetry' in C.N. Candlin & N. Mercer (eds), *English Language Teaching in its Social Context.* London: Routledge.

Vygotsky, L.S. (1962) *Thought and Language.* Cambridge, MA: MIT Press. (Originally published in Russian in 1934.)

Wegerif, R., Rojas-Drummond, S. and Mercer, N. (1999) 'Language for the social construction of knowledge: Comparing classroom talk in Mexican pre-schools', *Language and Education*, Vol. 13, No. 2, pp. 133–150.

Wertsch, J. (1991) *Voices of the Mind: A Socio-Cultural Approach to Mediated Action.* Cambridge, MA: Harvard University Press.

Wood, D. (1988) *How Children Think and Learn.* Oxford: Basil Blackwell.

Zentella, A.C. (1981) '*Ta bien*, you could answer me in *cualquier idioma*: Puerto Rican codeswitching in bilingual classrooms', in R. Duran (ed.) *Latino Language and Communicative Behavior.* Norwood, NJ: Ablex Publishing Corporation, pp. 109–132.

*In this publication from the turn of the century I explain why I felt a new concept was needed within sociocultural theory (which I also refer to as CHAT, Cultural Historical Activity Theory) that was more social, and more dialogic, than Vygotsky's 'Zone of Proximal Development'. My proposal was the concept of the 'Intermental Development Zone', which I hoped would help create a theoretical link between conversational interaction and individual learning. The 'Talk Lessons' programme I refer to later in the chapter is what has become better known as 'Thinking Together' (https:// thinkingtogether.educ.cam.ac.uk).*

# 6   Developing dialogues

*Mercer, N. (2002). Developing dialogues. In G. Wells & G. Claxton (eds), Learning for Life in the 21st Century: Sociocultural Perspectives on the Future of Education. Oxford: Blackwell, pp. 141–153.*

This chapter is about how children learn to use language as a tool for thinking, collectively and alone, and how other people use language to help them do so. I want to argue two main points: firstly, that the prime aim of education ought to be to help children learn how to use language effectively as a tool for thinking collectively; and secondly, that classroom-based involvement in culturally based ways of thinking collectively can make a significant contribution to the development of individual children's intellectual ability. To do so, I first draw on research about parent-child interaction to discuss the relationship between children's engagement in dialogue and the development of their understanding. I then shift the focus to schools. Drawing on classroom-based research, I describe classroom-based education as a dialogic process, in which both talk between teachers and learners and talk amongst learners have important roles to play. In these ways I intend to illustrate the practical educational value of research based on a sociocultural or CHAT perspective. But as well as serving some useful practical ends, I also hope to show how this kind of research can provide answers to some intriguing theoretical questions about the relationship between thought, language and social activity.

   The founding father of sociocultural research, Lev Vygotsky (1978), proposed that there is a close relationship between the use of language as a cultural tool (in social interaction) and the use of language as a psychological tool (for organizing our own, individual thinking). He also suggested that our involvement in joint activities can generate new understandings which we then 'internalize' as individual knowledge and capabilities. Although developmental psychologists have treated his claims about the connections between 'intermental' and 'intramental' activity with great interest, surprisingly little evidence has been offered to support or refute them. Towards the end of this chapter I will describe some classroom-based research which has provided such evidence.

## Development from a sociocultural perspective

The central idea underpinning the sociocultural perspective on human intellectual development is that individual development is integrated with the
longer-term historical development of our species; and that language plays
a vital role in achieving this integration. Psychological and anthropological studies of adult-child relations, observed in many cultures, support the
view that growing up is an 'apprenticeship in thinking', an induction into
ways with words and ways of thinking which is achieved through dialogue.
(For example, Heath, 1983; Rogoff, 1990, 1995; Wells, 1992.) This research
has highlighted the importance of the role that parents and other people
play in helping children learn, in the course of everyday joint activity. However, little of that research has been concerned with the activity of adults
as self-conscious teachers or instructors, or the ways children seek guidance or information to improve their understanding. Adults do not only
allow children to participate in family activities, they also deliberately provide them with information and explanations and instruct them in ways to
behave. And children, for their part, may take active roles in soliciting help
or obtaining information and transforming what they are given into their
own new understanding. They can also contest what they are told, by adults
or other children, and gain understanding from engaging in argument.

I can begin to illustrate these points through the following sequence of
dialogue. It comes from a conversation with my daughter Anna, which happened when she was 2 years old. At that time, I was regularly recording our
talk in joint activities. On this occasion, the topic of our conversation had
continued from a little earlier the same evening when, for the first time, she
had seen bats flying round the house. I had pointed to the eaves, where I had
said the bats slept.

*Sequence 1: bats in the roof*

ME:       What did you think of the bats?
ANNA:   What?
ME:       Did you like the bats?
ANNA:   Yeh.
ME:       Think of those bats now, they're out flying around now. Aren't they?
ANNA:   They not going – are they lying on the roof?
ME:       What about them?
ANNA:   Lie on the roof.
ME:       Oh yeh.
ANNA:   They not, but not inside.
ME:       Yeh, I think they do go inside the roof.
ANNA:   But not in.
ME:       You don't think so?
ANNA:   Not in!

ME:     Not in the roof? I think they go inside the roof. That's where they go to sleep in the day.

ANNA:     (*sounding confused*) But they, they not going inside it.

ME:     Why? (*laughing*) Why do you think that?

ANNA:     (*also laughing*) But they are not going inside it.

ME:     They can get inside it. There are little kind of holes round the edge of the roof, at the top of the walls, and they creep in there.

ANNA:     They go there to bye-byes now?

ME:     Yeh- no, they go to bye-byes in the day. They're just coming out now.

ANNA:     Are they not going to bye-byes now?

ME:     No, they go to bye-byes in the day, in the morning, and they fly around all night. They get up at night and go out.

It seems that our earlier conversation, while watching the bats, had left Anna with some intellectual dissatisfaction with what she had heard me explain about the lifestyle of the bats. This motivated her to ask whether the bats' habit was to sleep lying on the roof, thus questioning my own earlier statement that they slept inside it. As can be seen from the transcript, when I would not confirm her existing belief, she reiterated it four times, continuing to do so until I offered a more elaborated explanation of how the bats might enter the roof. She seemed to accept this explanation as reasonable, because in her next statement she asked if the bats were now going 'there' to sleep. As we continued on this topic, it became apparent to me that she did not understand that the bats were nocturnal, and so I tried also to explain this feature of their lifestyle.

One thing that interests me about Sequence 1 is that both explanations which I provided were about matters raised by her, not by me. The information children gain through language may sometimes be, or at least appear to be, incompatible with experience gained in other ways, or with their existing understandings which have been formed through past experience. Language provides both a means for generating a motivating kind of cognitive conflict and also a means for resolving it. Using language, children can actively test their understanding against that of others, and may use argument to elicit relevant information and explanations from adults and other children about what they perceive – and what they want to know.

## Adult guidance

Observations by researchers of the casual adult-child interactions of everyday life have revealed that adults often rely on particular techniques or guidance strategies for generating a common frame of reference during an episode of teaching-and-learning. For example, Wertsch (1985) observed parents of young children using two rather similar techniques. The first, which he calls 'establishing a referential perspective', is when an adult responds to a child's apparent lack of comprehension by referring to other shared knowledge.

Imagine, for instance, that while on a country walk a parent says to a child 'Look, there's a tractor'. If this reference fails (that is, the child doesn't seem to realize which object is being referred to), the adult may then say something like 'Can you see, that big green thing with enormous wheels in the field?' In doing this, the adult is drawing on resources of common knowledge to build a shared contextual frame of reference, based on the reasonable assumption that the child's understanding of basic features like colour and appearance will help them identify the strange object in question. Coupled with this technique, adults use a kind of reverse process which Wertsch calls 'abbreviation'. This is when, over the course of time, an adult begins to assume that new common knowledge has been successfully established and so, when talking to the child, makes progressively more abbreviated or cryptic references to what is being discussed. For example, the next time the same parent and child are out in the countryside, the parent may first point out 'another big green tractor', but then later just refer to 'the tractor'. In these ways, by creating common knowledge and then gradually assuming its existence, the adult first provides a 'scaffolding' to support the child's developing understanding and then dismantles it as the child becomes able to sustain their new understanding independently. It is important to note that from such experiences the child can gain not only a better understanding of the experience being discussed with the adult, but also of how language can be used effectively as a tool for describing and consolidating shared experience.

Research in schools has revealed that teachers also depend on the use of particular linguistic strategies for guiding, monitoring and assessing the activities they organize for their pupils (in ways described in Edwards and Mercer, 1987; Mercer, 1995). All teachers ask their pupils a lot of questions. Most teachers also regularly offer their classes recaps – summaries of what they consider to be the salient features of a past event – which can help students to relate current activity to past experience. Teachers also often elaborate and reformulate the contributions made to classroom dialogue by pupils (for example, in response to a teacher's questions) as a way of clarifying what has been said for the benefit of others, and also of making connections between the content of children's utterances and the technical terminology of the curriculum (Lemke, 1990; Wells, 1999). These strategies seem to be in common use throughout the world, even though teaching styles and ways of organizing classrooms vary within and across cultures (see Edwards and Westgate, 1994, and Mercer, 1995, for a review of relevant research).

Of course, as with the tools of any trade, teachers can use these common discursive strategies relatively well or badly. To make such an evaluation, we need to consider what their intended educational purpose might be. For a teacher to teach and a learner to learn, both partners need to use talk and joint activity to create a shared framework of understanding from the resources of their common knowledge and common interests or goals. Talk is the principal tool for creating this framework, and by questioning, recapping, reformulating, elaborating and so on teachers are usually seeking to draw pupils into a shared understanding of the activities in which they are engaged. I find it useful to think of this shared understanding as an 'intermental development zone' (IDZ) in which educational activity takes place. The IDZ is a dynamic frame of reference which is reconstituted constantly as the dialogue continues, so enabling the teacher and learner to think together through the activity in which they are involved. If the quality of the IDZ is successfully maintained, misunderstandings will be minimized and motivations will be maximized. If this is successful, the teacher will be able to help the learner transcend their established capabilities and to consolidate their experience in the zone as improved capability and understanding. If the dialogue fails to keep minds mutually attuned, however, the IDZ collapses and the scaffolded learning grinds to a halt.

The IDZ is a mutual achievement, dependent on the interactive participation and commitment of both teacher and learner; but a teacher must take special responsibility for its creation and maintenance. It is a continuing, contextualizing framework for joint activity, whose effectiveness is likely to depend on how well a teacher can create and maintain connections between the curriculum-based goals of activity and a learner's existing knowledge, capabilities and motivations. (I discuss the relationship between the idea of the IDZ and the well-established sociocultural concepts of 'scaffolding' and the Zone of Proximal Development in Mercer, 2000, Chapter 6.) In the next section I will describe some ways in which teachers can most successfully develop an IDZ with their pupils and help them make the most of their educational experience.

## Some characteristics of effective teaching

For several years now, I have been involved in research on how teachers use language as the principal tool of their trade. Based in primary schools in England and in Mexico, one of the aims of this research has been to improve the quality of classroom education. The Mexican strand of this research, led by Sylvia Rojas-Drummond at the Autonomous University of Mexico (UNAM), has compared teachers in state schools whose pupils had been found to develop particularly well in reading comprehension and mathematical problem-solving, with teachers in similar schools whose pupils have not made such significant achievements. Using video recordings of classroom interactions, the Mexican researchers and I tried to discover if the better teachers differed from those who were less successful in the ways they interacted with their pupils. Essentially, we were trying to see if the better teachers were providing a more effective 'scaffolding' for their pupils' learning. We were also interested in what kinds of learning teachers appeared to be encouraging.

Our analysis covered several features of classroom interaction, including teachers' uses of questions. We looked at the content of tasks, activities and discussions, at the extent to which teachers encouraged pupils to talk together and at the kinds of explanations and instructions teachers provided to pupils for the tasks they set them. The results of this time-consuming and complex analysis (described in more detail elsewhere: Rojas-Drummond, Mercer & Dabrowski, 2001; Rojas-Drummond & Mercer, 2004) can be summarized as follows. We found that the more effective teachers could be distinguished by the following characteristics:

(1) They used question-and-answer sequences not just to test knowledge, but also to guide the development of understanding. These teachers often used questions to discover the initial levels of pupils' understanding and adjust their teaching accordingly, and used 'why' questions to get pupils to reason and reflect about what they were doing.
(2) They taught not just 'subject content', but also procedures for solving problems and making sense of experience. This included teachers demonstrating the use of problem-solving strategies for children, explaining to children the meaning and purpose of classroom activities, and using their interactions with children as opportunities for encouraging children to make explicit their own thought processes.
(3) They treated learning as a social, communicative process. As I mentioned, earlier research has shown that most teachers make regular use of a set of conventional dialogic techniques – question-and-answer sessions, recaps, reformulations and so on. The more effective teachers used these effectively to do such things as encouraging pupils to give reasons for their views, organizing interchanges of ideas and mutual support amongst pupils and generally encouraging pupils to take a more active, vocal role in classroom events.

The findings of our research are in accord with those of other researchers (see for example Brown and Palincsar, 1989). This has encouraged my colleagues and me – and the teachers with whom we have been working closely in both the UK and Mexico – to believe that it is useful for teachers to become aware of the techniques they use in dialogue and what they are trying to achieve through using them. Teachers have found this approach useful for examining their own practice. Even very good teachers, who probably do these things without being aware that they do so, seem nevertheless to appreciate gaining this meta-awareness.

As I suggested earlier, effective teaching does not simply depend on the use of particular language techniques, it depends on how they are used to create and maintain IDZs. The better Mexican teachers and those who were less effective were all using elicitations, recaps, reformulations and other conventional features of the everyday language of classroom life. The crucial difference between the two sets of teachers was how and when they used them, and what they used them to teach. They differed significantly in the extent they used dialogue to help children see the relevance of past experience and common knowledge, and in the opportunities they provided for children to explain their own understanding or misunderstanding. When setting up activities or reviewing them with children, the most effective teachers used language to support and guide the children's activity. They also encouraged more active and extended participation in dialogue on the part of the children.

The extent to which the children themselves contribute to the establishment and maintenance of an IDZ is of course crucial. That is, the 'ground rules' of classroom interaction must offer them legitimate opportunities to express their uncertainties and reveal their confusions, and to request information and explanations from others who are more knowledgeable. We concluded that the quality of children's educational experience is significantly affected by the extent to which their dialogue with the teacher gives what they are doing in class a continuity of meaning (so that activity is contextualized by the history of past experience) and a comprehensible and worthwhile purpose.

These findings encouraged us to conclude that a good primary school teacher is not simply the instructor or facilitator of the learning of a large and disparate set of individuals, but rather the creator of a particular quality of intermental environment – a 'community of enquiry' (Lipman, 1970; Wells, 1999) in which students can take active and reflective roles in the development of their own understanding. In such classrooms, the students are apprentices in collective thinking, under the expert guidance of their teacher. I will return to these matters shortly, after some consideration of talk among children when a teacher or other 'expert' adult is not involved.

## Talk among learners

A sociocultural perspective helps us appreciate the reciprocal relationship between individual thinking and the collective intellectual activities of groups. We use language to transform individual thought into collective thought and action, and also to make personal interpretations of shared experience. Not only the intellectual development of early childhood but the whole of human life depends on the maintenance of a dynamic relationship between the 'intramental' and the 'intermental'. So far, I have focused on how the pursuit of intermentality figures in the relationships between adults as 'experts' and children as 'novices'. But as well as learning from the guidance and example of adults, children (and novices of all ages) also learn the skills of thinking collectively by acting and talking with each other. Any account of intellectual development which was based only on the study of dialogues between older and younger generations of a community would therefore be inadequate. Members of a younger generation use language among themselves to generate their own, shared understandings and to pursue their own interests. Each generation is active in creating the new knowledge they want, and, in doing so, the communal resources of the language toolkit may be transformed. Yet even the rebellious creativity of a new generation is, in part, the product of a dialogue between generations.

Language offers children a means for simulating events together in play, in ways which may enable the participants to make better sense of the actual experiences on which the play is based. Elbers (1994) provides some excellent examples of children engaged in this kind of play activity. Like many children, when they were aged 6 and 7, his two daughters enjoyed setting up play 'schools' together with toy animals. They would act out scenarios in which, with one of them as the teacher, the assembled creatures would act out the routines of a school day. But Elbers noticed that one typical feature of their play school was that incidents that disrupted classroom life took place with surprising frequency. Here is one such example (translated by Elbers from the Dutch). Margareet is the elder girl, being nearly 8 years old, and here takes the role of the teacher. Elisabeth, her younger (6-year-old) sister, acts out the role of a rather naughty pupil.

### Sequence 2: play school

| | |
|---|---|
| MARGAREET: | Children, sit down. |
| ELISABETH: | I have to go to the toilet, Miss. |
| MARGAREET: | Now, children, be quiet. |
| ELISABETH: | I have to go to the toilet. |
| MARGAREET: | I want to tell you something. |
| ELISABETH: | (*loud*) I have to go to the toilet! |
| MARGAREET: | (*chuckles*) Wait a second. |
| ELISABETH: | (*with emphasis*) Miss, I have to go to the toilet!! |
| MARGAREET: | OK, you can go. |
| ELISABETH: | (*cheekily*) Where is it? (*laughs*) |
| MARGAREET: | Over there, under that box, the one with the animals on, where the dangerous animals . . . (*chuckles*) under there. |
| ELISABETH: | Really? |
| MARGAREET: | Yes. |

(Elbers, op. cit. p. 230)

In this sequence we can see a child appropriating an adult's way with words. 'Now, children, be quiet' is exactly the kind of teacher-talk that Margareet will have heard every day in 'real' school. But Elbers suggests we can also interpret this sequence as an example of children reflecting together on the rules which govern their behaviour in school, and how the robustness of these rules can be tested. They can play with ideas of power and control without risking the community sanctions which such behaviour would incur in 'real life'. Teachers normally have to be obeyed, and children are not meant to leave the class during lessons – but given the legitimate excuse of having to go to the toilet, how can a child not get her way? Sometimes, in setting up this kind of activity, the girls (out of role) would discuss how best to ensure that such disruptive incidents occurred. For example:

*Sequence 3: setting up the play school*

MARGAREET:    You should choose four children who always talk the most; those children must sit at the front near the teacher. It'll be fun if they talk.

ELISABETH:    (*to one of the toy pupils*) You, you sit here and talk, right?

MARGAREET:    The desks are behind each other, then they can only. then I have to turn round all the time, if the children talk.

(Elbers, op. cit. p. 231)

These kinds of examples illustrate something important about how language use in play activities may contribute to children's development. Language can be used by them to simulate social life, to create virtual contexts in which they can practise using the genres of their culture to think together about their shared experience in the communities in which they are cultural apprentices. That is, language enables children to think together about social experience; and social experience enables them to acquire and practise ways of using language to think collectively. For children, playing with discourses is an important way of assimilating the language resources of the community in which they are growing up. This kind of 'adult' talk is particularly common in the classroom 'home' corner in the early years of school.

## Learning to engage in collective reasoning

In everyday life outside school, the 'ground rules' of everyday communication are usually taken for granted, and there is little meta-discussion or joint reflection on how things are normally done. This indicates a clear and useful role for schools, which are special institutional settings created for guiding intellectual development and understanding. Education should help children gain a greater awareness and appreciation of the discourse repertoire of wider society and how it is used to create knowledge and to get things done. Some valuable, practical ways of using language may not be used much in the informal activities of everyday childhood life, and so children can hardly be expected to learn them there. School life should give them access to ways of using language which their out-of-school experience may not have revealed. It should help them extend their repertoire of language genres and so enable them to use language more effectively as a means for learning, pursuing interests, developing shared understanding and – crucially – reasoning and solving problems together. There is little evidence, however, that this role is recognized within most education systems, or carried out by most teachers. The use of language as a toolkit for collective reasoning is not a common topic in classroom talk, nor does it figure explicitly in any school curriculum I have seen. In all levels of education, from primary school to university, students usually seem to be expected to work out the 'ground rules' of effective discussion for themselves.

Classroom research has also shown very clearly that in most of the dialogue between teachers and pupils, it is rare for pupils to ask the teacher questions, and even less common for pupils to challenge explanations or interpretations of events that are offered by teachers. That is, the kind of interrogative exchange that took place between Anna and myself in Sequence 1 would be unlikely to occur in a classroom. Reasons for this, in terms of power relations and conventional norms of social behaviour, are not hard to find; but the fact is that teacher-pupil dialogues do not offer much opportunity for pupils to practise their use of language as a tool for reasoning more generally. A more suitable setting for productive argumentative dialogue, one might expect, would be collaborative activity amongst pupils without a teacher present. However, observational research in classrooms suggests that when pupils are allowed to work together in groups most of their talk is either disputational or blandly and unreflectively co-operative, only involving some of the children and providing no more than a brief and superficial consideration of the relevant topics (Barnes and Todd, 1995; Bennett and Cass, 1989; Wegerif and Scrimshaw, 1997).

Over the last 10 or so years, Lyn Dawes, Rupert Wegerif, Karen Littleton and I have been working closely with primary teachers in the UK to develop a practical programme of 'Talk Lessons' for children aged 8–11. The Talk Lessons are designed with a careful balance of teacher-led and group-based activities. Drawing from the research on teacher-pupil communication which I described earlier, we have designed teacher-led whole-class activities to raise children's awareness of how they talk together and how language can be used in joint activity for reasoning and problem-solving. These teacher-led activities are coupled with group-based tasks, in which children have the opportunity to practise ways of talking and collaborating, and these in turn feed into other whole-class sessions, in which teachers and children reflect together on what has been learned. The group tasks include topics directly relevant to the National Curriculum for English, science and citizenship (cf. Dawes, 1997, 1998, for a teacher's account of these lessons and activities in a curriculum context). We have also created computer-based activities using specially designed software (as described in Wegerif, Mercer and Dawes, 1998; the Talk Lessons and associated software are available as Dawes, Mercer and Wegerif, 2000).

In order to evaluate the Talk Lessons programme, we made comparisons between children in 'target' classes (those using the Talk Lessons) and 'control' classes (of similar children in schools not involved in the programme). One specific kind of comparison we made was to video-record groups of both target and control children doing the same computer-based activities. This comparison reveals striking differences between the two sets of children. Children who took part in the programme are seen to discuss issues in more depth and for longer, participate more equally and fully, and provide more reasons to support their views. (The findings of this research are reported in detail in Mercer, Wegerif and Dawes, 1999; our methods of analysis are described in Wegerif and Mercer, 1997.) Our analysis of recordings of the group activities shows that the improved ability of the 'target' children to think together critically and constructively can be related directly to the structure and content of their talk.

Our 'target' and 'control' classes were also both given a psychological test, the Raven's Progressive Matrices, which has been commonly used as a general measure of non-verbal reasoning (Raven, Court and Raven, 1995). As an additional way of assessing any effects of the Talk Lessons on children's problem-solving skills, we gave both sets of children this test before the target children did the Talk Lessons, and then again after the series of lessons had been completed. A group of children in each target class was also video-recorded, before and after the programme, as they tackled the test. In this way we were able to observe, analyse and assess these children's joint problem-solving activity. When we compared groups in 'target' classes who had failed on specific problems in the pre-lessons test with their successes in the post-lessons test, we could see from the transcripts of their discussions how the quality of their collective reasoning had enabled them to do so. Here, for illustration, are two sequences from the talk of children in the same group. They are doing one of the Raven's puzzles (D9). Sequence 6 was recorded before they did the series of Talk Lessons, while Sequence 7 was recorded after they had done so.

### *Sequence 6: Graham, Suzie and Tess doing Raven's test item D9 (before the Talk Lessons)*

| | |
|---|---|
| TESS: | It's that |
| GRAHAM: | It's that, 2 |
| TESS: | 2 is there |
| GRAHAM: | It's 2 |
| TESS: | 2 is there Graham |
| GRAHAM: | It's 2 |
| TESS: | 2 is there |
| GRAHAM: | What number do you want then? |
| TESS: | It's that because there ain't two of them |
| GRAHAM: | It's number 2, look one, two |
| TESS: | I can count, are we all in agree on it? |
| | (*Suzie rings number 2 – an incorrect choice – on the answer sheet*) |
| SUZIE: | No |
| GRAHAM: | Oh, after she's circled it! |

### *Sequence 7: Graham, Suzie and Tess doing Raven's test item D9 (after the Talk Lessons)*

| | |
|---|---|
| SUZIE: | D9 now, that's a bit complicated it's got to be |
| GRAHAM: | A line like that, a line like that and it ain't got a line with that |

TESS:       It's got to be that one
GRAHAM:   It's going to be that don't you think? Because look all the rest
          have got a line like that and like that, I think it's going to be that
          because . . .
TESS:       I think it's number 6
SUZIE:      No I think it's number 1
GRAHAM:   Wait no, we've got number 6, wait stop, do you agree that it's
          number 1? Because look that one there is blank, that one there
          has got them, that one there has to be number 1, because that is
          the one like that. Yes. Do you agree?
          (*Tess nods in agreement*)
SUZIE:      D9 number 1 (*She writes '1', which is the correct answer*)

In Sequence 6, we can see that Tess does offer a reason – a good reason –
for her view, but Graham ignores it and she seems to give up in the face of
his stubbornness. Suzie has taken the role of writer and she says little. At
the end, having ringed the answer Graham wanted, she disagrees with it. It
is not the right answer; but they all move on to the next problem anyway.
Sequence 7 illustrates some ways that the talk of the same children changed
after the programme of Talk Lessons and how this helped them to solve the
problem. Graham responds to opposition from Tess by giving an elaborated
explanation of why he thinks 'number 1' is the correct choice. This clear
articulation of reasons leads the group to agree on the right answer. Such
explanations involve a series of linked clauses and so lead to longer utterances. All three children are now more equally involved in the discussion.
They make more effective rhetorical use of language for expressing their
opinions and persuading others of their value. Compared with their earlier
attempt, language is being used more effectively by the group as a tool for
thinking together about the task they are engaged in.
    The quality of the discussion of the children who were most successful in
solving the Raven's problems can be related to the concept of 'exploratory
talk', a way of using language for reasoning which was first identified by
the pioneering British educational researcher Douglas Barnes (e.g. Barnes
and Todd, 1995). My own conception of this way of communicating is as
follows:

> Exploratory talk is that in which partners engage critically but construc-
> tively with each other's ideas. Relevant information is offered for joint
> consideration. Proposals may be challenged and counter-challenged but,
> if so, reasons are given and alternatives are offered. Agreement is sought
> as a basis for joint progress. Knowledge is made publicly accountable
> and reasoning is visible in the talk.

There are good reasons for wanting children to use this kind of talk in
group activities, because it is a very functional kind of language genre, with

speakers following ground rules which help them share knowledge, evaluate evidence and consider options in a reasonable and equitable way. That is, exploratory talk represents a way in which partners involved in problem-solving activity can use language to think collectively – to 'interthink' effectively, with their activity encapsulated in an intermental zone of their own construction. Other experimental and observational studies have demonstrated the value of talk of this kind in problem-solving (Teasley, 1997; Lyle, 1993; see also Littleton and Light, 1999). As a result of some recent convergence between sociocultural research and systemic functional linguistics, the relationship between the language genres of a community, the organization of social activity and the pursuit of education has become clear (Gibbons, 2001; Russell, 1997; Wells, 1999). Exploratory talk is embodied in some important social practices, such as those used in science, law and business, and it is reasonable to expect that education should help every child to become aware of its value and become able to use it effectively.

## From the intermental to the intramental

The comparisons between the talk of the children in target and control classes, and between the 'before' and 'after' talk of children in the target classes, confirmed that the Talk Lessons were changing the ways language was used as a tool for collective reasoning. In a nutshell, the lessons led to the children using more 'exploratory talk', and the increased use of this kind of talk was associated with improved joint problem-solving. But, as I mentioned at the very beginning of this chapter, the results of this research also provide some evidence about Vygotsky's hypothesis about the link between social activity (the 'intermental') and individual development (the 'intramental'). This aspect of the research depended again on the use of the Raven's test. Two versions of this test are available and so, as well as giving one version of the test to groups of children in both target and control classes before and after the Talk Lessons programme had been implemented (with the target classes), we also set each child in the target and control classes the other version of the test as an individual problem-solving activity. We found that target children became significantly better at doing the problems individually, when compared with the control children. That is, the children who had experienced the Talk Lessons appeared to have improved their reasoning capabilities by taking part in the group experience of explicit, rational, collaborative problem-solving. This is despite the fact that these children had no more experience or training in doing the Raven's puzzles, together or alone, than the children in the control classes.

Of course, we cannot be sure exactly what the target children learned from their experience that made the difference. It may be that some gained from having new, successful problem-solving strategies explained to them by their partners, while others may have benefited from having to justify and make explicit their own reasons. But a more radical and intriguing possibility is that children may have improved their reasoning skills by 'internalizing' the ground rules of exploratory talk, so that they became able to carry on a kind of silent rational dialogue with themselves. That is, the Talk Lessons may have helped them become more able to generate the kind of rational thinking which depends on the explicit, dispassionate consideration of evidence and competing options. That interpretation is consistent with Vygotsky's claims about the link between the social and the individual; collective thinking has a shaping influence on individual cognition.

## Conclusions

One of the strengths of bringing a sociocultural perspective to bear on education, I believe, is that it encourages us to recognize that the quality of education cannot be explained in terms of 'learning' or 'teaching' as separate processes, but rather in terms of the interactive process of 'teaching-and-learning'. (The English language offers no elegant way of referring to this process. Interestingly, Vygotsky had at his disposal the Russian word *obuchenie*, which means both teaching and learning.) While the focus of attention of educational research may at any particular time be on the teacher or on the learner, we need to consider the active contributions of both these partners to *obuchenie* in any account of events and their outcomes. I have introduced the notion of an 'intermental development zone' to highlight the way that the success of education can be very dependent on partners creating and maintaining shared knowledge resources and a common frame of reference for their joint activity. For an applied researcher or teacher who is concerned with assessing and improving the quality of education, a sociocultural perspective helps avoid any tendency to attribute problems or solutions to the separate actions of teachers or learners, or to account for events without reference to the historical, cultural and institutional frameworks in which they take place.

In relation to classroom education, a sociocultural perspective may also help us transcend the persistent, unfortunate and unhelpful debate about the relative benefits of teacher-led, whole-class sessions and activities where learners work together without the teacher in small groups. Group activities offer learners good opportunities to practise and evaluate ways of using language to think collectively, away from the teacher's authoritative presence. But they need first to be guided in how to talk and work together if these activities are to be of most benefit for their learning; and they may later need the intellectual leadership of a teacher to help them consolidate what they have learned from their joint efforts and relate it to the curriculum and other cultural reference frames. Thus, in the Talk Lessons programme, teachers organize and lead activities, provide children with information and guidance and help them recognize and reflect on what they have learned. They talk explicitly with children about the goals of classroom activities. Each teacher models 'exploratory' ways of talking for the children in whole-class sessions – for example, asking 'Why?' at appropriate times, giving examples of reasons for opinions and checking that a range of views is heard. The success of the Talk Lessons programme depends very much, I believe, on its careful balance between teacher-led, whole-class sessions and 'talk groups' in which children work and talk together, without constant teacher supervision, on problem-solving activities. The organized continuity of this experience helps children to consolidate learning and gain educational benefit from their experience – and hopefully helps them understand better how language can be used, in many kinds of social situation, for thinking together and getting things done.

The sociocultural or CHAT perspective on intellectual development asserts that we are essentially social, communicative creatures who gain much of what we know from others and whose thoughts and actions are shaped by our interactions. It also highlights the ways that, through involvement in the taken-for-granted normality of social life, each new generation is influenced by the habits of its predecessors. The role of language as a cultural toolkit for joint intellectual activity is emphasized by this perspective – and so is the relationship between the social and psychological uses of language. All these ideas can be traced back to the original work of Vygotsky. But we need now to go further, following Vygotsky's pioneering example by developing a more radical conception of the relationship between language and thinking. My own suggestion is that we focus our attention directly upon language as a means for thinking collectively – a process which we might, by analogy with 'interaction', call 'interthinking' (Mercer, 2000). This would involve the study of many other kinds of social interaction, not only those which are in any obvious sense 'educational'. Such studies could help us to bring the intellectual, developmental, pragmatic, social and cultural functions of language within one theoretical framework. We could then, with increasing confidence, apply this framework in educational and other applied fields of research.

## References

Barnes, D. and Todd, F. (1995) *Communication and Learning Revisited*. Portsmouth, NH: Boynton-Cook.

Bennett, N. and Cass, A. (1989) The effects of group composition on group interactive processes and pupil understanding. *British Educational Research Journal*, Vol. 15, pp. 119–132.

Brown, A. and Palincsar, A. S. (1989) Guided, co-operative learning and individual knowledge acquisition. In L. Resnick (Ed.), *Knowing, Learning and Instruction*. New York: Lawrence Erlbaum.

Dawes, L. (1997) Teaching talking. In R. Wegerif and P. Scrimshaw (Eds.), *Computers and Talk in the Primary Classroom*. Clevedon: Multilingual Matters.

Dawes, L. (1998) Developing exploratory talk. In L. Grugeon, L. Hubbard, C. Smith and L. Dawes (Eds.), *Teaching Speaking and Listening in the Primary School*. London: David Fulton Press.

Dawes, L., Mercer, N. and Wegerif, R. (2000) *Thinking Together: Activities for Teachers and Children at Key Stage 2*. Birmingham: Questions Publishing Co.

Edwards, A.D. and Westgate, D.P.G. (1994) *Investigating Classroom Talk* (Second, revised edition). London: Falmer Press.

Edwards, D. and Mercer, N. (1987) *Common Knowledge: The Development of Joint Understanding in the Classroom*. London: Methuen/Routledge.

Elbers, E. (1994) Sociogenesis and children's pretend play: A variation on Vygotskian themes. In W. de Graaf and R. Maier (Eds.), *Sociogenesis Re-examined*. New York: Springer.

Gibbons, P. (2001) Learning a new register in a second language. In C. Candlin and N. Mercer (Eds.), *English Teaching in Social Context*. London and Milton Keynes: Routledge with the Open University.

Heath, S. B. (1983) *Ways With Words: Language, Life and Work in Communities and Classrooms*. Cambridge: Cambridge University Press.

Lemke, J. (1990) *Talking Science: Language, Learning And Values*. Norwood, NJ: Ablex.

Lipman, M. (1970) *Philosophy for Children*. Montclair, NJ: Institute for the Advancement of Philosophy for Children.

Littleton, K. and Light, P. (Eds.). (1999) *Learning With Computers: Analysing Productive Interaction*. London: Routledge.

Lyle, S. (1993) An investigation in which children talk themselves into meaning. *Language and Education*, Vol. 7, No. 3, pp. 181–196.

Mercer, N. (1995) *The Guided Construction of Knowledge: Talk Amongst Teachers and Learners*. Clevedon: Multilingual Matters.

Mercer, N. (2000) *Words and Minds: How We Use Language to Think Together*. London: Routledge.

Mercer, N., Wegerif, R. and Dawes, L. (1999) Children's talk and the development of reasoning in the classroom. *British Educational Research Journal*, Vol. 25, No. 1, pp. 95–111.

Raven, J., Court, J. and Raven, J. C. (1995) *Manual for Raven's Progressive Matrices and Vocabulary Scales*. Oxford: Oxford Psychologists Press.

Rogoff, B. (1990) *Apprenticeship in Thinking: Cognitive Development in Social Context*. New York: Oxford University Press.

Rogoff, B. (1995) Observing sociocultural activity on three planes: Participatory appropriation, guided participation and apprenticeship. In J.W. Wertsch, P. del Rio and A. Alvarez (Eds.), *Sociocultural Studies of Mind*. Cambridge: Cambridge University Press.

Rojas-Drummond, S., Mercer, N. and Dabrowski, E. (2001) Collaboration, scaffolding and the promotion of problem solving strategies in Mexican pre-school students. *European Journal of Psychology of Education*, Vol. XV, No. 3, pp. 179–196.

Rojas-Drummond, S. and Mercer, N. (2004) Scaffolding the development of effective collaboration and learning. *International Journal of Educational Research*, Vol. 39, 99–111.

Russell, D. (1997) Rethinking genre in school and society: An activity theory analysis. *Written Communication*, Vol. 14, No. 4, pp. 504–554.

Teasley, S. (1997) Talking about reasoning: How important is the peer group in peer collaboration? In L. Resnick, R. Slj, C. Pontecorvo and B. Burge (Eds.), *Discourses, Tools and Reasoning: Essays on Situated Cognition*. Berlin: Springer Verlag.

Vygotsky, L. S. (1978) *Mind in Society: The Development of Higher Psychological Processes.* Cambridge, MA: Harvard University Press.

Wegerif, R. and Mercer, N. (1997) Using computer-based text analysis to integrate quantitative and qualitative methods in the investigation of collaborative learning. *Language and Education,* Vol. 11, No. 4, pp. 271–286.

Wegerif, R., Mercer, N. and Dawes, L. (1998) Software design to support discussion in the primary classroom. *Journal of Computer Assisted Learning,* Vol. 14, pp. 199–211.

Wegerif, R. and Scrimshaw, P. (Eds.). (1997) *Computers and Talk in the Primary Classroom.* Clevedon: Multilingual Matters.

Wells, G. (1992) *The Meaning Makers: Children Learning Language and Using Language to Learn.* London: Hodder and Stoughton.

Wells, G. (1999) *Dialogic Inquiry: Towards a Sociocultural Practice and Theory of Education.* Cambridge: Cambridge University Press.

Wertsch, J. V. (ed.) (1985) *Culture, Communication and Cognition: Vygotskian Perspectives.* Cambridge: Cambridge University Press.

*When we wrote this chapter, my co-authors and I pointed out that most schools in the UK provided little or no training for their students in how to use spoken language effectively; and we argued that they really should, for the several reasons we set out in the chapter. As I write now, early in 2019, the situation at last seems to be improving. Efforts to give oracy more parity with literacy and numeracy in the mainstream curriculum are gaining momentum in the UK (and in several other countries); an Oracy Network has been set up in the UK, which is gaining political support. And the kind of collaborative problem solving we were organizing for the children involved in the research described in this chapter is now being assessed (albeit through a computer-based simulation) by the PISA international tests of educational attainment.*

# 7 Reasoning as a scientist

## Ways of helping children to use language to learn science

*Mercer, N., Dawes, R., Wegerif, R., & Sams, C. (2004). Reasoning as a scientist: ways of helping children to use language to learn science.* British Educational Research Journal *(Carfax Publishing), 30, 3, 367–385.*

## Abstract

Sociocultural researchers have claimed that students' learning of science is a discursive process, with scientific concepts and ways of reasoning being learned through engagement in practical enquiry and social interaction as well as individualized activity. It is also often claimed that interacting with partners while carrying out scientific investigations is beneficial to students' learning and the development of their understanding. The research we describe investigated the validity of these claims and explored their educational implications. An experimental teaching programme was designed to enable children in British primary schools to talk and reason together and to apply these skills in their study of science. The results obtained indicate that (a) children can be enabled to use talk more effectively as a tool for reasoning and (b) talk-based activities can have a useful function in scaffolding the development of reasoning and scientific understanding. The implications of the findings for educational policy and practice are discussed.

## Introduction

Educational researchers who adopt a sociocultural perspective have commonly depicted science education as a discursive process, whereby novices (students) are inducted into a way of representing and understanding phenomena (using language and other representational means) by those more expert in the field. Thus, Lemke (1990) proposed that science education should enable students to become 'fluent speakers of science', while Leach and Scott suggest that students should be helped by their science teacher to 'make sense of the talk which surrounds them, and in doing so, relate it to their existing ideas and ways of thinking' (Leach and Scott, 1995, p. 44). Contemporary sociocultural theorists (e.g. Wertsch, 1991; Wells, 1999; Daniels, 2001) follow Vygotsky (e.g. 1978) in emphasizing the importance of language use and social interaction within communities for the development of educated ways of making sense of the world, such as those associated with science. As Vygotsky put it, intermental (social) activity will promote intramental (individual) intellectual development. This claim, having an obvious plausibility, has been widely accepted. However, other than our own findings presented previously (Mercer et al., 1999), any empirical evidence offered for its validity has been, at best, indirect. Our earlier research showed that the induction of children into an explicit, collaborative style of reasoning, which we call *Exploratory Talk*, led to gains in children's individual scores on the Raven's Progressive Matrices test of non-verbal reasoning. These gains, first demonstrated for children in Year 5 in British primary schools, were subsequently replicated in other year groups and in primary schools in Mexico (Rojas-Drummond et al., 2001). However, our earlier studies did not investigate whether this induction was beneficial to children's learning in science. To the best of our knowledge, no direct relation has been demonstrated between encouraging students to engage in certain ways of using spoken language and their improved understanding or attainment in science. One group of studies has shown that discussion can contribute to the development of conceptual understanding in science (Howe et al., 2000), but that research did not encourage the pragmatic use of particular forms of dialogue. Nevertheless, Howe *et al.*'s work is interesting and very relevant here. Their findings provide support for the value of discussion and investigation by children without the authoritative presence of a teacher, while also showing that expert involvement can have a crucial and beneficial influence for guiding children's activity in productive directions. On the basis of their experimental comparisons of different types of hypothesis testing task (with children aged 9–11), they specify some conditions for a kind of activity which effectively promotes the development of both conceptual and procedural knowledge. These are hypothesis testing activities with a four-part structure, in which (a) pupils first debate their conceptual understanding and reach a consensus about the hypothesis to be investigated (with the pursuit of consensus a key requirement), (b) next subject their consensual positions to expert guidance (by a teacher) about how to pursue a practical controlled investigation of their hypothesis, (c) perform the investigation and (d) discuss the outcomes together to draw conclusions. These conclusions have strong and direct relevance to the design of our own study, which, like those of Howe *et al.*, involved the use of computer-based group activities.

### The aims and focus of the research

The research we describe in this article was designed to test sociocultural claims about the significance of discursive induction for the study of science. The research also had the practical aim of improving children's ability to use language as a tool for reasoning and to improve their attainment in science and mathematics. (For reasons of space and clarity, this article will only deal with science.) The study was based in primary schools in south-east England and involved the implementation and evaluation of an experimental teaching programme for children in Year 5 (ages 9–10). One link between the learning of science and the use of language is the development of a specialized vocabulary for representing concepts and describing processes. In addition, spoken language provides a familiar medium through which a child can describe their conceptions of phenomena in order that teachers assess a level of understanding (Ollerenshaw and Ritchie, 1998). However, supporting the learning of vocabulary and descriptive skills was not the main focus of our research. Instead, our experimental programme aimed to develop children's use of language as a tool for reasoning together and to enable them to use the discussion skills they developed in carrying out science activities. This focus reflects the historical origins of the project in a series of earlier projects concerned with talk and reasoning in the classroom.

## Contexts for teaching and learning science

There are two main contexts in which spoken language can be related to the learning of science in schools. The first is teacher-led interaction with pupils. A sociocultural account of cognitive development emphasizes the guiding role of more knowledgeable members of communities in the development of children's knowledge and understanding, and in their induction into the discourses associated with particular knowledge domains. The concept of 'scaffolding', as originally used by Wood et al. (1976), is relevant here, as are the concepts of 'guided participation' (Rogoff, 1990), 'the guided construction of knowledge' (Mercer, 1995) and 'dialogic teaching' (Alexander, 2003). For educational researchers, sociocultural theory highlights the role of teachers in helping children develop new ways of describing and conceptualizing experience.

The second context is that of peer group interaction. Working in pairs or groups, children are involved in interactions which are more 'symmetrical' than those of teacher–pupil discourse and so have different kinds of opportunities for developing reasoned arguments, describing observed events, etc. In science education, such collaboration can be focused on practical investigations, which also have great potential value for helping children to relate their developing understanding of abstract ideas to the physical world. Computer-based science activities can offer similar opportunities in virtual environments. The research of Howe et al. (2000), described earlier, has shown that under certain conditions computer-based activities for groups of children are effective in promoting the development of scientific understanding; but discussions amongst groups of young science students may not always be productive and useful. Observational research in British primary schools has shown that the talk which takes place when children are asked to work together is often uncooperative, off-task, inequitable and ultimately unproductive (Galton and Williamson, 1992; Wegerif and Scrimshaw, 1997).

A possible explanation for the doubtful quality of much collaborative talk is that children do not bring to this task a clear conception of what they are expected to do, or what would constitute a good, effective discussion. This is not surprising, as many children may rarely encounter examples of such discussion in their lives out of school – and teachers rarely make their own expectations or criteria for effective discussion explicit to children (Mercer, 1995). Children are rarely offered guidance or training in how to communicate effectively in groups. Even when the aim of talk is made explicit – 'Talk together to decide'; 'Discuss this in your groups' – there may be no real understanding of *how to* talk together or for what purpose. Children cannot be expected to bring to a task a well-developed capacity for reasoned dialogue. This is especially true for the kinds of discursive skills which are important for learning and practising science: describing observations clearly, reasoning about causes and effects, posing precise questions, formulating hypotheses, critically examining competing explanations, summarizing results, and so on. On this basis, we began this research with the hypothesis that children studying science would benefit from teacher guidance of two main kinds. Firstly, and most obviously, they need to be helped to gain relevant knowledge of natural phenomena, investigative procedures, scientific concepts and terms – the content of science. Teachers commonly expect to provide this kind of guidance. Secondly, they need to be helped to learn how to use language to enquire, reason and consider information together, to share and negotiate their ideas and to make joint decisions. This kind of guidance is not usually offered. We therefore designed a teaching programme which would enable teachers to integrate these two kinds of guidance.

## Method

The research involved the design, implementation and evaluation of a programme of lessons. We will describe the intervention programme, the design of the study, how data was gathered and the methods used to analyse it.

### The intervention programme

As mentioned earlier, our research has shown that language skills associated with improved reasoning can be effectively taught and learned. That earlier research involved the creation and evaluation of talk-based classroom activities. An intervention programme was designed for the present study which built directly upon that earlier research. A key feature of this 'Thinking Together' programme was the systematic integration of teacher-led interaction and group-based interaction. The main aims of the programme were:

(i)   to raise children's awareness of the use of spoken language as a means for thinking together;

(ii) to enable children to develop their abilities to use language as a tool for thinking, both collectively and alone;

(iii) to enable children to apply the tool of language effectively to their study of the science and mathematics curriculum.

More specifically, the programme was intended to ensure that children became able to carry out the kind of discussion we call *Exploratory Talk*. This is talk in which:

- all relevant information is shared;
- all members of the group are invited to contribute to the discussion;
- opinions and ideas are respected and considered;
- everyone is asked to make their reasons clear;
- challenges and alternatives are made explicit and are negotiated;
- the group seeks to reach agreement before taking a decision or acting.

Barnes and Todd (1977, p. 126) in their classic study of group work describe this sort of talk, which is not commonly heard, but which has great educational value:

> It is a collective relationship that we observed in our small group discussions. Members were free to shift the topic, to try out new formulations and to explore alternatives, since none of the questions asked concealed positional claims to impose a frame on the discussion – to guide its direction or to judge the relevance of answers. The members of our groups cast their bread upon the waters. They were each other's resources and most of their utterances were contributions to thinking.

Each teacher was provided with 12 detailed lesson plans. These lessons involved a teacher-led introduction, a group discussion activity and a final 'sharing' plenary session. The aims of the lessons were to do with the teaching and learning of explicit talk skills such as critical questioning, sharing information or negotiating a decision. These related closely to the Speaking and Listening component of the National Curriculum for English. The first five lessons were aimed at raising children's awareness of how talk could be used for working together and establishing in each class a set of 'ground rules' for discussion which would generate talk of an 'exploratory' kind. The further seven lessons encouraged children to apply their developing discussion skills to the study of the science and mathematics curriculum for Year 5. Each lesson applied a specific talk skill and targeted a specific concept in science.

Some lessons involved computer-based activities. One of the software items chosen was Granada's *Science Explorer II*. This provides sets of problems and simulated experimental environments and was already in use in all the project schools. The topics of 'light' and 'sound' (which are included in the National Curriculum scheme of work for Year 5) were the focus for these activities. For example, in one *Science Explorer* activity children are given the problem of soundproofing a room against the singing of an operatic neighbour using such materials as wood, metal and cork. In relation to the study of light, the activity requires them to make a light-proof screen from a set of materials including tissue paper, writing paper and card. The task is to select a type of (virtual) material and predict the number of sheets which will block out light. The group then test their prediction in the simulated environment. The content and level of these problems are suited well to the Year 5 Science curriculum in English schools, as prescribed for the classes involved in our study.

Although we gathered data from activities based on several types of software, in this article our illustrative examples of talk come from the use of *Science Explorer*. In the context of the intervention, children were prompted to discuss their predictions and findings while engaged in the activity.

A necessary condition for the implementation of the intervention programme was that teachers would effectively model and guide the development of children's language skills. Accordingly, each participating teacher received training in the Thinking Together approach, based on videotaped examples and activities derived from earlier related projects. Once the intervention was under way, this training was reinforced through regular visits to schools by one of the research team, which on some occasions included demonstrating activities and teaching techniques. Researchers tried to ensure that all the lessons in the programme were carried out in each school. This was achieved for the initial five lessons, but for a variety of practical reasons some teachers were unable to fit all the later lessons into their class's activities.

## Design of the study

The effects of this programme on talk, reasoning and learning were studied through observation and formal assessment of children in experimental classes, with pre- and post-intervention comparisons being made with children in matched control classes in other local schools with similar catchments. Seven classes of children in Year 5 (aged 9–10) in primary schools in Milton Keynes participated actively by following the Thinking Together intervention programme. These classes were designated 'target classes'. There were 196 children in the target classes at the beginning of the study, but with children arriving and departing from classes during the intervention period, 109 of the original children completed the programme. (Milton Keynes has a high rate of population movement, within the city as well as in and out of it.) A matched set of control classes in other, similar local schools was identified. These classes consisted of 210 children at the beginning of the study, with 121 of those still being in the control classes by the time the last data collection was made. Control classes did not participate in the Thinking

Together programme, but followed the same prescribed English and science National Curriculum and also used the *Science Explorer* software, but not necessarily as a basis for regular group activities.

The teachers of the target classes were given training relating to the first part of the project on an initial training day, and the first five lessons were completed by the end of the first term (which also saw the completion of the pre-intervention observations and assessment). Teachers of control classes did not receive training but were aware that the results of the research would be made available to them on its completion. We have no reason to believe there was any relevant exchange of ideas between target and control schools during the period of study. The complete set of lessons (including those concerned with mathematics, which are not discussed here) was implemented in the target schools over the autumn and spring school terms, with the total duration of the intervention (i.e. from the pre-testing to the post-testing) being 23 weeks.

### Data collection

The data gathered consisted of:

(i) pre- and post-intervention video recordings of a 'focal group' in each target and control class carrying out computer-based activities;
(ii) video recordings of other groups of children in target schools engaged in joint activities during Thinking Together lessons;
(iii) video recordings of teacher-led whole class sessions during Thinking Together lessons;
(iv) audio-recordings of interviews with teachers and children;
(v) children's scores on the Raven's Progressive Matrices test of non-verbal reasoning;
(vi) children's scores on tests of knowledge and understanding in science (based on a set of assessment tasks for Year 5, known as 'optional SATs', which are made available to schools in England and Wales by the Qualifications and Curriculum Authority).

Pre- and post-intervention data was gathered for all of these in target schools, with pre- and post-intervention data for (i), (iv) and (v) also gathered in the control schools.

Interviews and video-recorded interactions were transcribed. The data we gathered was intended to inform us about:

(a) the teacher's role in scaffolding children's use of language and their learning of science;
(b) the nature and content of children's discussions;
(c) the outcomes of our intervention on the quality of children's discussion;
(d) the outcomes of our intervention on children's understanding of science.

To study the teachers' activities in guiding children's use of talk and learning, we video-recorded all the target class teachers carrying out at least two of the prescribed lessons. (For reasons of space, we cannot discuss the analysis of the teacher's role in this article: see Rojas-Drummond and Mercer, 2004, for more on that topic.) In order to study the effects of the Thinking Together programme on curriculum-related learning, we compared target and control children's understanding of National Curriculum science topics that they had studied during the period when the intervention took place. We describe this assessment in more detail below.

## Methods of analysis

### Qualitative analysis of children's talk in groups

Using the video-recorded data, qualitative and quantitative methods of discourse analysis were used to investigate changes in the quality of children's talk and collective reasoning. The methodology for making this kind of comparison, described fully in Wegerif and Mercer (1997), combines a detailed qualitative analysis of language used by each group of children in specific episodes of joint activity with a quantitative computer-based analysis of the whole corpus of recorded group talk. These methods were used to make two kinds of comparisons:

(a) between the talk of children in control classes and target classes doing curriculum-based activities at a stage when the 'ground rules' for talk had been established in target classes; and
(b) between the pre-intervention and post-intervention talk of children in target classes while involved in similar activities.

We hoped in this way to feel confident that any differences observed in the quality of children's talk (in ways that related to our hypotheses) were attributable to the intervention.

The recorded data of children talking as they carried out activities in the Thinking Together programme was subject to joint qualitative analysis by the research team. The main aim of the analysis was to gauge the extent to which the discussions of children in the target classes came to resemble Exploratory Talk. However, the analysis had more subtle aspects than this may seem to suggest. We were not interested in simply identifying stretches of talk as 'exploratory' and coding them accordingly. Indeed, our view is that the nature of language – in which any one grammatical form can be used to fulfil a range of pragmatic functions – renders any coding scheme of dubious value if used separately from a more contextually sensitive, ethnographic type of analysis. Our aim is to consider the extent to which children are using language appropriately and effectively as a tool for thinking together. In making that analysis, the definition of Exploratory Talk serves as an 'ideal type' – a typification of reasoning embodied in talk. The features of Exploratory Talk, as described earlier, are therefore used as a point of reference for the consideration of the quality of the talk of each group.

One focus of the qualitative analysis was on changes in children's use of talk while engaged in science investigations. This involved the examination of the pre- and post-intervention talk of children in target classes as they engaged in computer-based science investigations using *Science Explorer II* and related to the Year 5 curriculum. The aim of this analysis was to determine if children's joint engagement with the task changed in the predicted ways following the intervention: that is, if they used more talk of an 'exploratory' kind and applied it productively to a scientific task.

This detailed qualitative discourse analysis of talk by the researchers was used in combination with other methods to determine whether children in target classes began to use more Exploratory Talk and apply it appropriately through participating in the project. One additional method was a 'blind assessment'. The purpose of this was to avoid biased judgements arising from the research team's expectations about the outcomes of the intervention. To enable this, one group of children in each target and control class was observed and recorded using the same piece of software in the same activity at the beginning and again at the end of the programme. It was originally intended that the activity to be used for this 'blind' pre/post comparison would also be based on a *Science Explorer* activity. However, on reflection it was agreed that the use of one of the activities devised for the project programme would not constitute a fair test, as the target children could be influenced positively by their greater familiarity with discussions based on the *Science Explorer* environment. A decision was therefore taken to base comparisons of children's talk on recordings of focal groups carrying out a 'moral dilemma' activity based on software called *Kate's Choice* (designed by a member of the research team and tested in earlier, related research) since this would be novel to all the children involved.

A set of 12 tapes and transcripts of the pre- and post-intervention discussions of six focal groups in target classes as they carried out one computer-based activity was modified to eliminate all clues as to location and time of recording. Two Open University researchers not involved in the project, but who were familiar with the analytic method and with classroom interaction, studied this data. They were asked to jointly (a) identify episodes of talk which had the characteristics of Exploratory Talk; (b) note the extent of these within the recorded event; and (c) use their findings to decide which discussions were 'pre-intervention' and which were 'post-intervention'.

## Quantitative analysis of differences in talk

A quantitative analysis of pre/post differences in the talk of target groups was made using the same *Kate's Choice* data. As in our previous research, one aspect of this analysis focused on the relative extent to which children used 'indicator words' which qualitative analysis in earlier research had shown were associated with reasoning. The indicator words selected were 'because', 'if', 'I think', 'would' and 'could'. Previous research had also shown that the more children explain and justify their views, the longer their utterances will tend to be. We therefore compared the relative mean length of pre-/ post-intervention utterances in the focal groups when involved in the same type of activity.

## Evaluating knowledge and understanding of the science curriculum

Improvements in subject-related knowledge and understanding were assessed in the following ways. Firstly, as mentioned earlier, we used problems taken from the 'optional SATS' tests for Key Stage 2 provided by the QCA. These covered areas of the curriculum studied by children in both target and control classes. Secondly, a 'concept map' activity was devised to assess individual understanding of scientific terms and their relationships (as used in some earlier research on science education (Russell and Watt, 1990) and computer use in schools (Harrison et al., 2002)). This activity was based on the topics of 'food' and 'healthy eating', which were studied by both target and control classes. Children were provided with a list of key words and were asked to make a concept map by linking words and annotating these links. Children's responses were scored for the number of links and labels in their concept map which related appropriately to the relevant curriculum knowledge. For example, a link between the word *healthy* and the word *fruit* would score one point, and an appropriate annotation on that link such as '*vitamins*' or '*fibre*' would score another point. The same activity was given to target and control classes at the beginning and at the end of the school year. Additional evidence came from teachers' assessments of children's progress made over the same period.

## Changes in the quality of collective and individual reasoning

As mentioned earlier, our previous research had indicated that teaching children to use Exploratory Talk helped them to solve the non-verbal reasoning problems of the Raven's Progressive Matrices test more effectively (Mercer et al., 1999; Wegerif et al., 1999). We compared pre- and post-intervention performances of target and control classes working on the problems of the Raven's test in groups and as individuals. We have used this finding to argue in support of a Vygotskian, sociocultural account of the relationship between language use and intellectual development. That is, we believe that by engaging in guided, spoken reasoning with their peers, children can assimilate a way of thinking which helps them to reason better when working alone. The Raven's test is an appropriate measure for supporting this claim, as its scores correlate highly with other tests of reasoning and with measures of academic achievement (Raven et al., 1995). However, in the earlier research, small sample size meant that although findings for individuals were statistically significant, findings for group scores did not achieve statistical significance (though they were in the predicted direction). This represented a weakness in the evidence we offered for the link between intermental activity and intramental development. In the current project we therefore attempted the test of this sociocultural hypothesis again, with a larger sample of children. Again, the Raven's test was used to compare the pre- and post-intervention for both individual and group performances of target and control classes.

## Results

Our main hypothesis was that if teachers focused on the direct teaching of ways of using talk effectively for joint reasoning and on the development of children's awareness of the importance and value of this use of talk during science activities, this would raise children's achievement in the study of science. We also predicted effects of the intervention on the quality of children's talk and interaction and on their non-verbal reasoning. Analysis of the data supported these predictions, as explained below.

### *Changes in the quality of talk and collaborative activity*

#### *Qualitative analysis of talk*

We have selected brief but representative sections of the many hours of talk we recorded to illustrate the patterns we discerned in our analysis. The two examples below illustrate the kinds of differences between the talk of target and control groups that we observed. In the first example, a group in a control school are working on a *Science Explorer* investigation into the effectiveness of materials for providing soundproofing.

#### *Transcript 1: control school group: Keep it Quiet*

| | |
|---|---|
| HANNAH: | (*reads from screen*) Keep it Quiet. Which material is the best insulation? Click 'measure' to take a sound reading. Does the pitch make a difference? |
| DARRYL: | No we don't want clothes. See what one it is then. (*points to screen*) |
| HANNAH: | No it's cloth. |
| DARRYL: | Oh it's cloth. |
| HANNAH: | Go down. This is better when Stephanie's in our group. |
| DARRYL: | Metal? |
| HANNAH: | Right try it. |
| DEBORAH: | Try what? That? |
| HANNAH: | Try 'glass'. |
| DARRYL: | Yeah. |

DEBORAH:   No one.
HANNAH:    Now.
DARRYL:    (*interrupts*) Measure.
HANNAH:    Now measure. Hold. (*turns volume control dial below screen*)
DARRYL:    Results, notes.
HANNAH:    Results. We need to go on a different one now. Results.
DARRYL:    Yeah, you need to go there so you can write everything down.
HANNAH:    I'm not writing.

For comparison, the next transcript is of a group of children who have been involved for two terms in the Thinking Together programme. They are engaged in a *Science Explorer* activity about the effectiveness of materials for blocking out light.

### Transcript 2: target school group: blocking out light

ROSS:    OK. (*reads from screen*) Talk together about a plan to test all the different types of paper.
ALANA:   Dijek, how much did you think it would be for tissue paper?
DIJEK:   At least ten because tissue paper is thin. Tissue paper can wear out and you can see through, other people in the way, and light can shine in it.
ALANA:   OK. Thanks.
ALANA:   (*to Ross*) Why do you think it?
ROSS:    Because I tested it before!
ALANA:   No, Ross, what did you think? How much did you think? Tissue paper. How much tissue paper did you think it would be to block out the light?
ROSS:    At first I thought it would be five, but second –
ALANA:   Why did you think that?
ROSS:    Because when it was in the overhead projector you could see a little bit of it, but not all of it, so I thought it would be like, five to block out the light.
ALANA:   That's a good reason. I thought, I thought it would be between five and seven because, I thought it would be between five and seven because normally when you're at home if you lay it on top, with one sheet you can see through but if you lay on about five or six pieces on top you can't see through. So that's why I was thinking about five or six.

The talk of the group in Transcript 1 indicates that the children are not working cooperatively except at the most superficial level. They do not share knowledge, build on each other's suggestions, provide reasons for their proposals or seek joint agreement. The contributions are monosyllabic and minimal. It does not seem that the participants are at all engaged with one another's thinking. This kind of talk is not uncommon in primary classrooms and illustrates a need for the guided development of children's skills in communicating and thinking together. In Transcript 2 the children's discussion has many of the features of Exploratory Talk. They ask each other for information and opinions, seek reasons and provide them, share their thoughts and evaluate proposals that are made. Challenges are constructive, and all members of the group are involved in working towards a joint decision. The children's use of the structures they have recently been taught may seem a little formulaic (for example, Alana's repeated 'Why do you think that?'), but they are using the strategies appropriately and purposefully. Opinions are treated with respect. Each speaker has the opportunity to develop their ideas as they speak. Indeed, it appears that the talk precipitates thinking. The two researchers who carried out the 'blind assessment' exercise identified the transcribed discussions correctly as 'pre-' and 'post-intervention' for five out of the six classes.

### Quantitative analysis of talk

Table 7.1 shows the relative incidence of indicator words in target children's talk while doing *Kate's Choice*, before and after their involvement in the Thinking Together lessons.

It can be seen that there is a greatly increased incidence of the words indicative of Exploratory Talk in the children's discussions after the intervention. The children's greater use of such words reflects their increased attempts to share each other's thoughts before deciding on a course of action and moving on through the programme. In earlier research, we had found that the more children explain and justify their views, the longer their utterances tend to be. The association between increased utterance length and more explanation and justification was confirmed in the present study by the qualitative analysis of a sample of transcripts. We therefore also counted the number of utterances in all the talk data which exceeded 100 characters when transcribed (excluding text read from the computer screen). The results of this analysis, provided in Table 7.2, are indicative of the more elaborated contributions to the discussions made by children post-intervention.

*Table 7.1* Relative incidence of indicator words: *Kate's Choice*

| Indicator word | Pre-intervention talk in focal groups in target classes | Post-intervention talk in focal groups in target classes |
| --- | --- | --- |
| because | 13 | 50 |
| I think | 35 | 120 |
| would | 18 | 39 |
| could | 1 | 6 |
| Totals | 65 | 215 |

*Table 7.2* Relative incidence of long utterances during *Kate's Choice*

|  | Pre-intervention talk; target classes | Post-intervention talk; target classes |
| --- | --- | --- |
| Utterances 100 + characters | 1 | 46 |

*Table 7.3* Results for the SATs science questions

|  | Numbers | Pre-intervention: mean scores | Post-intervention: mean scores |
| --- | --- | --- | --- |
| Target classes | 119 | 3.97 | 5.70 |
| SD |  | 2.323 | 2.442 |
| Control classes | 129 | 4.22 | 5.04 |
| SD |  | 1.997 | 2.206 |
| Effect size | 0.29 |  |  |

$F(1, 245) = 10.305$; two-tailed $p = .002$.

## Evaluating knowledge and understanding of the science curriculum

The results of the assessment based on science SATs questions are shown in Table 7.3. The numbers of children are less than the total number who participated, because to ensure validity of statistical analysis it was necessary to exclude those children for whom no pre/post match was possible due to departures during the project and absences at the times of testing. It was also unfortunate that because of staffing problems in one school at the time of the post-intervention assessment, one class had to be excluded. Nevertheless, the results indicate that the scores of target classes increased significantly more than those of the control classes. This supports the view that the intervention had a positive effect on the target children's study of the relevant parts of the science curriculum.

The concept mapping exercise was used as a test of the extent to which children in the target classes became, over the period of the intervention, relatively more able to perceive relationships between different scientific concepts – or at least the terms representing them. The results of the exercise are summarized in Table 7.4, which indicates the impact of the intervention in the predicted direction. Because the intervention did not involve any special teaching about the relationships between concepts or terms, the target children's superior post-intervention performance in producing concept maps seems most appropriately attributed to the improved quality of their collective reasoning about the relevant subject matter.

Overall, the results show that the children in the target classes gained significantly better scores in science than those in control classes, thus providing evidence for the effectiveness of the intervention in improving children's study of the science curriculum.

*Table 7.4* Results of the Science Concept Mapping Exercise

| | Numbers | Pre-intervention: mean scores | Post-intervention: mean scores |
|---|---|---|---|
| Target classes | 115 | 1.52 | 6.02 |
| SD | | 1.455 | 3.364 |
| Control classes | 129 | 1.08 | 3.97 |
| SD | | 1.473 | 2.756 |
| Effect size | 0.74 | | |

$F(1, 241) = 17.471$; two-tailed $p = 0.000$.

*Table 7.5* Group performances of children in target and control classes on the Raven's test

| | Pre-intervention: mean scores | Post-intervention: mean scores |
|---|---|---|
| Target classes | 20.08 | 23.62 |
| SD | 4.052 | 2.413 |
| Control classes | 19.90 | 22.36 |
| SD | 3.423 | 2.290 |
| Effect size | 0.55 | |

$F (1,76) = 6.281$; two-tailed $p = 0.014$.

## Changes in the quality of collective and individual reasoning

The mean scores of children carrying out the Raven's test are shown in Table 7.5. Pre- and post-intervention comparisons of groups of children in the target and control classes working on the Raven's test were made using an analysis of covariance with pre-intervention results as covariate, post-intervention results as dependent variable and condition as fixed. It can be seen that the target pupils performed significantly better than the control pupils after the intervention, taking into account the pre-intervention performance levels of both groups.

In the school environment, some changes in the pre/post membership of groups were inevitable. Such changes could be assumed to reduce the covariance between the pre- and post-test scores, which would mostly decrease the accuracy of the corrected post-score measures (in the analysis of covariance) by introducing 'noise'. This would normally make it harder to detect a significant difference due to the treatment condition. It is possible the group composition changes may not have been random and could have introduced bias into the analysis of covariance, but this cannot be detected or corrected. Taking these two considerations into account, the results for the groups are indicative of the intended effect of the intervention.

Pre/post comparisons of individual children in the target and control classes doing the Raven's test were also made using an analysis of covariance with pre-intervention results as covariate, post-test results as dependent variable and condition as fixed. The mean scores are shown in Table 7.6. Although the differences are not large, the target children performed significantly better than the control children after the intervention, taking into account pre-intervention performance levels.

As mentioned earlier, our previous studies had shown statistically significant increases in individual scores on this test, but not in corresponding group scores. These new results provide statistical evidence of changes in both group and individual reasoning. They thus provide support for the general sociocultural hypothesis that the intermental activity of using language as a tool for reasoning collectively can influence the development of individual thinking and learning. They also support the more specific hypothesis that a programme of activities for encouraging the use of Exploratory Talk had specific, predicted positive effects on the quality of children's reasoning. Moreover, these effects are demonstrated by a test which was not similar in content or format to any activities in the Thinking Together programme, meaning that the target children were no more familiar with the test than the control children. This therefore also supports the view that the discursive and reasoning skills gained by the target children were not highly task-specific or context-bound, but represented a transferable competence. By involvement in a class undertaking the teaching and learning of talk skills, the children had gained the kinds of generalizable communication and thinking skills which are commonly advocated as a desirable outcome of educational experience.

In order to evaluate longer-term effects, sample 'spot check' video recordings of activities with children from two target schools have been made, almost one year after the end of the intervention. These showed that individuals and groups were still able to recall the ground rules and use Exploratory Talk appropriately when carrying out problem-solving activities. One of our intentions has been to follow Adey and Shayer's (1993) example by post-testing for the impact of the intervention in future years, by tracing target classes on measures of academic attainment. However, as mentioned earlier, there are high rates of mobility of participating children and teachers in Milton Keynes, and this makes it difficult to track any one cohort of

*Table 7.6* Individual performances of children in target and control classes on the Raven's test

|                 | Pre-intervention: mean scores | Post-intervention: mean scores |
|-----------------|-------------------------------|--------------------------------|
| Target classes  | 16.26                         | 18.90                          |
| SD              | 3.981                         | 3.542                          |
| Control classes | 15.60                         | 17.88                          |
| SD              | 4.357                         | 3.702                          |
| Effect size     | 0.27                          |                                |

$F_{(1,224)} = 6.065$; two-tailed $p = 0.015$.

children. There is also the problem of the lack of continuation of the Thinking Together approach as participating teachers leave a school or as children move to other schools, with the likely result that the discourse habits which the approach has encouraged in children will not be reinforced. Nevertheless, our continued involvement with Milton Keynes schools should make it possible to assess continuing effects on practice and achievement.

## Discussion and conclusions

The research reported here has demonstrated that an experimental teaching programme enabled children in primary schools to work together more effectively, improve their language and reasoning skills and reach higher levels of attainment in their study of science. We have replicated and strengthened our earlier findings, which supported the sociocultural claim that language-based, social interaction (intermental activity) is a developmental influence on individual thinking (intramental activity). But the results provide support of other kinds for the sociocultural perspective on education, and hence for the validity of sociocultural theory as the basis for an applied psychology of education. By showing that children's increased use of certain ways of using language leads to better learning and conceptual understanding in science, we have provided empirical support for the conception of science education as induction into a community of discourse or practice (Lemke, 1990; Leach and Scott, 1995).

The intervention programme was carefully designed to include both teacher-led activities and activities in which children worked together in groups; and as the teachers in target schools were trained to provide guidance of a particular kind, and the group discussion in target schools was expressly based on 'ground rules' which were not made available to control classes, our study does not enable the effects of these two factors to be distinguished. But our theoretical position supports the view that separating these two types of interaction is incompatible with the provision of an effective educational experience; it would not be possible to design an intervention compatible with our sociocultural hypotheses without combining these two elements. Moreover, the complementary effects of both types of interaction for primary science education have been well demonstrated by other very relevant research (particularly that of Howe et al., 2000, as discussed in the earlier part of this article). Our findings therefore add to the evidence that the development of scientific understanding is best assisted by a careful combination of peer group interaction and expert guidance, and provide an example of how that combination can be successfully achieved.

These findings have relevance for current debates about the role of educational research for providing a base of evidence for informing educational practice. They demonstrate that the pursuit of applied, practical educational research need not entail the loss of a theoretical dimension in favour of mere evaluative description. Theoretically informed ideas about teaching and learning can be transformed into empirical investigations, which can then provide new insights into 'what works' – and thus provide an evidential base for practice of the most robust kind. Practice is best informed if it has both theoretical and empirical support.

Evidence of the positive effects of our intervention on children's talk and attainment has been provided by several complementary strands of our analysis. However, there are also other observed effects, more subtle and harder to measure precisely, on ways teachers work with their classes, on groups undertaking joint activities and on individual children. The teachers in the project schools have created talk-focused classrooms in which the children, as Barnes and Todd (1977) put it, are 'each other's resource'. But this does not mean teachers abdicated responsibility for guiding the construction of knowledge; their role in enabling children to gain a better understanding of interpersonal communication and curriculum content was crucial. Rather, it created conditions in which the educational purposes of teacher-led and group-based activities become clearer to all involved. Teachers report that their relationship with their class benefits, as the class gains an ethos based on shared purposes for activity and, especially, for collaboration. The class atmosphere becomes more open, interested and engaging.

Providing children with 'rules' for talk may seem constraining. But if children agree on ground rules and then implement them, this can represent a kind of freedom. The usual social conditions for talk – for example, the dominance of participants who talk most and most forcefully – are suspended. The social status of individuals can be neutralized by the ground rules, creating an intellectual environment which is more equitable – though of course it is also one in which everyone's ideas are open to critical examination. More confident children gain the opportunity to hear a wider range of views. Quieter children find that their contribution is sincerely requested and valued. One of the simplest but most profound benefits for children is the idea that challenging each other is not just accepted but encouraged. In many situations, challenges can be threatening. In the target groups, however, a challenge leads to an exchange of reasoning and a better understanding of another's position. The insight that this is possible may be generalized to other situations. Teachers have reported that participating children find it easier to resolve conflict in situations outside the classroom. Our findings indicate that if teachers provide children with an explicit, practical introduction to the use of language for collective reasoning, then children learn better ways of thinking collectively and better ways of thinking alone. The implications for educational practice are clear.

In order that the results of the project can inform educational practice, a set of lesson plans called *Thinking Together in Maths and Science* has been created and will be published as a companion volume to our earlier publication (Dawes et al., 2000). This will incorporate guidelines for the effective use of existing educational software as a basis for group activity. Draft multimedia material for the professional development of teachers on the implementation of the Thinking Together approach has also been produced. It sets out the structure of the Thinking Together programme and the teaching strategies involved in implementing it, using video sequences of classroom interaction from the project data to illustrate ways of modelling and scaffolding children's questioning and reasoning. This has been used to conduct professional development sessions for schools and workshops at conferences, and it also provides the basis for an Open University online in-service course for teachers. Related projects, building on the methods and results described here, have begun in Milton Keynes schools for Key Stages 1 (ages 6–7) and 3 (ages 12–13).

In the UK, findings from our earlier research have already informed the official guidance and training materials provided for teachers in relation to English and the national strategies in literacy and the foundation subjects (e.g. Department for Education and Skills, 2002; QCA, 2003) and have been presented to a House of Commons Select Committee on Education and Skills. However, across the curriculum subjects there is considerable variation in terms of official policy, teacher guidance and classroom practice in the extent to which it is recognized that the quality of teaching and learning is dependent on the quality of classroom dialogues. It is our hope that the findings reported here will encourage greater recognition of this in the teaching of science.

## Acknowledgements

The researchers gratefully acknowledge the support of the Nuffield Foundation (Project EDU/00169/G) and the participation of teachers and children in Milton Keynes schools. We also register our appreciation of the expert advice and assistance of Dr Martin Le Voi of The Open University in carrying out and verifying the statistical analysis.

## References

Adey, P. and Shayer, M. (1993) An exploration of long-term far-transfer effects following an extended intervention programme in the high school science curriculum, *Cognition and Instruction*, 11(1), 1–29.

Alexander, R. (2003) Talk in teaching and learning: International perspectives, in *New Perspectives on Spoken English in the Classroom: Discussion Papers* (London, Qualifications and Curriculum Authority).

Barnes, D. and Todd, F. (1977) *Communication and Learning in Small Groups* (London, Routledge & Kegan Paul).

Daniels, H. (2001) *Vygotsky and Pedagogy* (London, RoutledgeFalmer).

Dawes, L., Mercer, N. and Wegerif, R. (2000) *Thinking Together: A Programme of Activities for Developing Thinking Skills at Key Stage 2* (Birmingham, Questions Publishing).

Department for Education and Skills (DfES). (2002) *Training Materials for the Foundation Subjects: Key Stage 3 National Strategy* (London, DfES).

Galton, M. and Williamson, J. (1992) *Group Work in the Primary Classroom* (London, Routledge).

Harrison, C., Comber, F., Fisher, T., Haw, K., Lewin, C., Lunzer, E., McFarlane, A., Mavers, D., Scrimshaw, P., Somekh, B. and Watling, R. (2002) *The Impact of Information and Communication Technologies on Pupil Learning and Attainment* (The ImpaCT II Study). ICT in Schools Research and Evaluation Series No.7 (Coventry, British Educational Communications and Technology Agency /Department for Education and Skills). Available online at: www.becta.org.uk/research/reports/docs/ImpaCT2 strand1_report.pdf

Howe, C., Tolmie, A., Duchak-Tanner, V. and Rattray, C. (2000) Hypothesis testing in science: Group consensus and the acquisition of conceptual and procedural knowledge, *Learning and Instruction*, 10(4), 361–391.

Leach, J. and Scott, P. (1995) The demands of learning science concepts: Issues of theory and practice, *School Science Review*, 76, 47–51.

Lemke, J. (1990) *Talking Science: Language, Learning and Values* (Norwood, NJ, Ablex).

Mercer, N. (1995) *The Guided Construction of Knowledge: Talk Amongst Teachers and Learners* (Clevedon, Multilingual Matters).

Mercer, N., Wegerif, R. and Dawes, L. (1999) Children's talk and the development of reasoning in the classroom, *British Educational Research Journal*, 25(1), 95–111.

Ollerenshaw, C. and Ritchie, R. (1998) *Primary Science: Making It Work* (London, David Fulton).

Qualifications and Curriculum Authority (QCA). (2003) *New Perspectives on Spoken English in the Classroom: Discussion Papers* (London, QCA).

Raven, J., Court, J. and Raven, J. C. (1995) *Manual for Raven's Progressive Matrices and Vocabulary Scales* (Oxford, Oxford Psychologists Press).

Rogoff, B. (1990) *Apprenticeship in Thinking* (New York, Oxford University Press).

Rojas-Drummond, S. and Mercer, N. (2004) Scaffolding the development of effective collaboration and learning, *International Journal of Educational Research*, 39(1–2), 99–110 (Special Issue on Group Work, edited by P. Blatchford and P. Kutnick).

Rojas-Drummond, S., Mercer, N. and Dabrowski, E. (2001) Collaboration, scaffolding and the promotion of problem solving strategies in Mexican pre-schoolers, *European Journal of Psychology of Education*, XVI(2), 179–196.

Russell, T. and Watt, D. (1990) SPACE (The Science Process and Concept Exploration Project), Research *Report: Growth* (Liverpool, Liverpool University Press).

Vygotsky, L. S. (1978) *Mind in Society: The Development of Higher Psychological Processes* (Cambridge, MA, Harvard University Press).

Wegerif, N., Mercer, N. and Dawes, L. (1999) From social interaction to individual reasoning: An empirical investigation of a possible socio-cultural model of cognitive development, *Learning and Instruction*, 9, 493–516.

Wegerif, R. and Mercer, N. (1997) Using computer-based text analysis to integrate quantitative and qualitative methods in the investigation of collaborative learning, *Language and Education*, 11(4), 271–287.

Wegerif, R. and Scrimshaw, P. (Eds) (1997) *Computers and Talk in the Primary Classroom* (Clevedon, Multilingual Matters).

Wells, G. (1999) *Dialogic Inquiry: Towards a Sociocultural Practice and Theory of Education* (Cambridge, Cambridge University Press).

Wertsch, J. (1991) *Voices of the Mind: A Socio-cultural Approach to Mediated Action* (Cambridge, MA, Harvard University Press).

Wood, D., Bruner, J. and Ross, G. (1976) The role of tutoring in problem-solving. *Journal of Child Psychology and Child Psychiatry*, 17, 89–100.

*This chapter represents my first detailed explanation of the mixed method approach to analysing classroom talk which Rupert Wegerif and I developed and used in our joint research. This methodology was unique at that time, I believe, because it combined qualitative discourse analysis methods (as used by sociolinguists), computer-based methods for analysing texts (as developed in corpus linguistics) and controlled comparisons and statistical analyses of effects (as commonly carried out by psychologists). We had to think of a name for it and so, to reflect the theoretical foundations of our research, we chose 'sociocultural discourse analysis'.*

# 8   Sociocultural discourse analysis

## Analysing classroom talk as a
## social mode of thinking

*Mercer, N. (2005). Sociocultural discourse analysis: analysing classroom talk as a social mode of thinking.* Journal of Applied Linguistics *(Equinox Publishing), 1, 2, 137–168.*

## Abstract

This paper describes a methodology for the analysis of classroom talk, called sociocultural discourse analysis, which focuses on the use of language as a social mode of thinking – a tool for teaching-and-learning, constructing knowledge, creating joint understanding and tackling problems collaboratively. It has been used in a series of school-based research projects in the UK and elsewhere, and its use is illustrated with data from those projects. The methodology is expressly based on sociocultural theory and, in particular, on the Vygotskian conception of language as both a cultural and a psychological tool. Its application involves a combination of qualitative and quantitative methods and enables the study of both educational processes and learning outcomes.

## 1 Introduction

In this article I will describe and discuss a methodology for analysing talk which colleagues and I have developed in recent years. As I will explain, I am using the term 'methodology' to refer to an integrated set of methods and procedures. It has been designed to serve a particular research interest, which basically is to understand how spoken language is used as a tool for thinking collectively. We have mainly used it to study how people pursue joint educational activities. I call this methodology 'sociocultural discourse analysis' to distinguish it from other approaches and because it is based on a sociocultural perspective on the nature and functions of language, thinking and social interaction. From this perspective, language is regarded as a cultural and psychological tool for getting things done. The methodology has been used to analyse teacher-student and student-student interactions, and I will draw on data from both for illustrative examples. Several colleagues have been influential in the development and use of the methodology, and I will refer to our joint publications wherever appropriate.

A wide range of methods for analysing talk are now available (as discussed, for example, in Edwards and Westgate, 1994 Mercer, Littleton and Wegerif, 2004). Such methods cannot be judged as intrinsically better or worse for analysing talk, at least in abstract terms: any method can only be judged by how well it serves the investigative interests of a researcher, how adequately it embodies the researcher's theoretical conception or model of language in use and their beliefs about what constitutes valid empirical evidence. A methodology represents the interface between theory and particular research questions, and the use of particular methods and procedures in an investigation represents a methodology in action. It determines not only how data is analysed, but what kind of data is gathered. I will begin by explaining in more detail the theoretical foundations of the type of discourse analysis my colleagues and I employ.

## 1.1 A sociocultural perspective

Research into the processes of teaching, learning and cognitive development has been transformed in the last 20 years by the emergence of a theoretical perspective which is usually called 'sociocultural', but is also sometimes described as 'socio-historical' and (more recently) 'cultural-historical'. (See for example Wertsch, 1985; Daniels, 2001; Wells and Claxton, 2002.) Its origins are mainly in the work of the Russian psychologist Vygotsky (e.g. 1978). Sociocultural research is not a unified field, but those within it treat communication, thinking and learning as related processes which are shaped by culture. The nature of human activity is that knowledge is shared and people jointly construct understandings of shared experience. Communicative events are shaped by cultural and historical factors, and thinking, learning and development cannot be understood without taking account of the intrinsically social and communicative nature of human life. From a sociocultural perspective, then, humans are seen as creatures who have a unique capacity for communication and whose lives are normally led within groups, communities and societies based on shared 'ways with words', ways of thinking, social practices and tools for getting things done. Education is seen as a dialogic process, with students and teachers working within settings which reflect the values and social practices of schools as cultural institutions. A sociocultural perspective highlights the possibility that educational success and failure may be explained by the quality of educational dialogue, rather than simply in terms of the capability of individual students or the skill of their teachers. It encourages the investigation of the relationship between language and thinking and also of the relationship between what Vygotsky (1978) called the 'intermental' and the 'intramental' – the social and the psychological – in the processes of learning, development and intellectual endeavour.

## 1.2 Language as a tool for collective thinking

Many human activities involve not just the sharing of information and the coordination of social interaction, but also a joint, dynamic engagement with ideas amongst partners. When working together, we do not only interact, we 'interthink' (Mercer, 2000). Some sociocultural researchers have investigated how, in particular encounters or through a series of related encounters, two or more people use language to combine their intellectual resources in the pursuit of a common task. Good examples would include Middleton and Edwards's (1990) study of collective remembering, Elbers's (1994) research on children's play and that of O'Connor and Michaels (1996) on the orchestration of classroom group discussions. Discourse analysts of other theoretical persuasions, such as conversation analysts, have also studied the processes of joint intellectual activity. However, few researchers have tried to relate the content, quality and temporal nature of dialogue during joint activities to outcomes such as the success or failure of problem-solving, or to specific learning gains for participants (a notable exception being the work of Kumpulainen and Wray, 2002). Yet the relationship of dialogue processes to outcomes is of crucial interest, with possible practical implications not only in educational settings. Studying the joint construction of knowledge can also tell us more about the nature of spoken language, because such joint knowledge-building is an essential requirement of conversational interaction. Conversations are founded on the establishment of a base of common knowledge and necessarily involve the creation of more shared understanding. Conversational partners use language to travel together from the past into the future, mutually transforming the current state of their understanding of the topic(s) of their conversation. To do so, they need to build a contextual foundation for the progress of their talk; talk is also the prime means for building that contextual foundation. Gee and Green (1998) refer to this aspect of language use as 'reflexivity'. If one is interested in how talk is used to enable joint intellectual activity, one must be concerned with the ways that shared knowledge is both invoked and created in dialogue. This concern was central in the development of the methodology I describe here, especially in the earliest stages when Edwards and I were working on the research reported in *Common Knowledge* (Edwards and Mercer, 1987).

## 1.3 The dynamic and contextualised nature of talk as collective thinking

Talk which mediates joint intellectual activity poses a considerable methodological challenge for a discourse analyst because of its reflexivity. Any specific interaction in which two people are engaged in solving a problem together has a *historical aspect* and a *dynamic aspect*. Historically, the interaction is located within a particular institutional and cultural context. Speakers' relationships also have histories. Things that are said may invoke knowledge from the joint past experience of those interacting (e.g. their recall of previous activities they have pursued together), or from the rather different kind of 'common knowledge' which is available to people who have had similar, though separate, past experiences. This knowledge may be more or less culturally specific. For example, two people conversing who had at different times studied linguistics at Lancaster University could safely assume much shared understanding of both the subject and the locations in which it was studied, even if this had been gained quite separately. The *dynamic* aspect of collective thinking refers to the fact that the basis of common knowledge upon which shared understanding depends is constantly being developed. The contextual base is in a constant state of flux, as immediate shared experiences and corresponding conversational content provide the resources for building future conversational context. A key problem for researchers concerned with understanding how talk is used for the joint construction of knowledge (or, indeed, with understanding how conversational communication functions at all) is gaining an understanding of how speakers construct the contextual foundations of their talk. We can only do this in a partial, limited fashion, by sampling their discourse over time and by drawing in our analysis on any common resources of knowledge we share with the speakers. But however difficult it may be to find a solution, the problem cannot be avoided.

## 2  Sociocultural discourse analysis

As I mentioned earlier, I use the term 'sociocultural discourse analysis' to refer not just to one particular method, such as the qualitative, interpretative procedure which my colleagues and I employ in our analysis of specific events, but to the methodology as whole (which involves several methods, both qualitative and quantitative, as I shall explain). It seemed necessary to name it in this way because the term 'discourse analysis' is used to refer to several different approaches to analysing language (both spoken and written) and to quite different methods. Within linguistics, its use usually indicates an interest in the organisation and functions of continuous text. It can signify research on monologic texts as well as on dialogue. Within sociology, psychology, anthropology and educational research, it usually refers to the analysis of episodes of talk in social context. In sociology 'discourse' can also be used to refer to the general social climate of ideas associated with a topic rather than specific conversations, and so some discourse analysis may amount to a branch of cultural studies.

The sociocultural discourse analysis I describe here has been influenced by the work of language researchers in several disciplines, but has its own special characteristics. It differs from 'linguistic' discourse analysis in being less focused on language itself and more on its functions for the pursuit of joint intellectual activity. As in linguistic ethnography and conversation analysis, reports of the analysis are usually illustrated by selected extracts of transcribed talk, to which the analyst provides a commentary. And like some linguistic analyses – but unlike much ethnographic research – it incorporates a concern with the lexical content and the cohesive structure of talk, especially across the contributions of individual speakers, because word choices and cohesive patterning can represent ways that knowledge is being jointly constructed. It differs from conversation analysis (as exemplified for example by the work in Drew and Heritage, 1992: see also Schegloff, 1997) because cognition and the social and cultural context of talk are considered legitimate concerns. Indeed, as I mentioned earlier, dialogue is treated as a form of intellectual activity – as a social mode of thinking. Unlike discursive psychology – at least the version with which I am most familiar – the sociocultural analysis I describe here is concerned not only with the processes of joint cognitive engagement, but also with their developmental and learning outcomes (cf. for example Edwards and Potter, 1992: 19). Other educational researchers have also devised useful approaches to the analysis of talk based on a sociocultural perspective and have used them in the pursuit of their own research questions. Examples can be found in Lyle (1993, 1996), Hicks (1996), Gee and Green (1998), Wells (1999), Alexander (2000) and Kumpulainen and Wray (2002). While their methods share some features with those I describe here, I do not of course claim to represent their methodologies or underlying rationale.

### 2.1 The complementary use of qualitative and quantitative methods

Within the social sciences, a common distinction which is made between research studies and, indeed, between researchers is whether they use qualitative or quantitative methods. The choice between these types of methods often seems to be ideological as much as methodological, with quantitative researchers claiming to uphold the more 'scientific', 'rigorous' approach and qualitative researchers claiming the more 'human', interpretative stance. My own view is that the ideological associations of methods are often an obstacle to sensible research design, limiting the range of options available. Different kinds of methods enable different kinds of research questions to be addressed and different kinds of evidence to be obtained. Each has strengths and weaknesses. Focusing on the analysis of talk, the relative strengths and weaknesses of the various qualitative and quantitative methods for analysing talk can be summarised as follows.

### 2.1.1 Quantitative analysis

This type of method most obviously includes the coding scheme approach known as 'systematic observation' in which utterances are allocated to pre-defined categories, but also would include any other methods which involve measuring the relative frequencies of occurrence of particular words or patterns of language use. These methods provide an efficient way of handling a lot of data; for example a researcher can 'survey' a lot of classroom language relatively quickly. Numerical comparisons can be made, which may then be subjected to a statistical analysis. However, the actual talk data may be lost early in the analytic process. In systematic observation studies, all you work with are your coded categories, and the ways these have been pre-determined can limit the analyst's sensitivity to what actually happens. Categories are usually treated as mutually exclusive, even though utterances commonly have more than one possible functional meaning. Moreover, a static coding of types of utterance cannot handle the dynamic nature of talk and so cannot deal with the ways that meaning is constructed amongst speakers, over time, through interaction.

### 2.1.2  *Qualitative analysis*

Here I would include ethnography, sociolinguistic studies and conversation analysis. These methods rely on the close, detailed consideration of carefully transcribed episodes of talk. Categories used are often generated through the analysis: they are outcomes, not prior assumptions brought in to sort the data. The examples of talk provided to any audience for the research are real: they are not asked to take on trust the validity of an abstracted categorisation scheme. A positive feature of this kind of approach for analysing talk as collective thinking is that the actual talk remains the data throughout the analysis, and so the processes of the joint construction of knowledge can be examined in detail. The development of joint understanding, or the persistence of apparent misunderstandings or different points of view, can be pursued through the continuous data of recorded/transcribed talk. However, qualitative methods are difficult to use with large sets of data, because the analysis is so time-consuming. (It is commonly estimated that transcribing and analysing 1 hour of talk using such methods will take between 5 and 12 hours of research time.) As a result, datasets are often small, and so it is difficult to use such analyses to make convincing generalisations. Researchers are open to charges of selecting particular examples to make a case.

Having assessed their various strengths and weaknesses, my colleague Wegerif and I decided to explore the complementary use of qualitative and quantitative methods of analysing talk (as first discussed in Wegerif and Mercer, 1997). One of our motivations was to combine the detailed analysis of talk in specific events with a comparative analysis of dialogue across a representative sample of cases. For this latter kind of analysis, we needed to deal fairly easily and quickly with quite a large language corpus (such as one consisting of over 20 hours of transcribed conversation). To do so, we combined interpretative methods with the use of computer-based text analysis. Concordance software enables any text file to be scanned easily for all instances of particular target words. Commonly used examples are *Monoconc*, *Wordsmith* and *Conc 1.71*. Recent versions of qualitative data analysis packages such as *NVivo* also offer some similar facilities. A concordancer allows a researcher to move almost instantly between occurrences of particular words and the whole transcription. This enables particular words of special interest to be 'hunted' in the data, and their relative incidence and form of use in particular contexts to be compared. Not only can the repetition and frequency of occurrence of items be measured, but the analysis can also indicate which words tend to occur together (collocations) and so help reveal the way words gather meanings by the company that they keep. The results of such searches can be easily presented in tabular form. Collocations and repetitions can reveal some of the more subtle, local meanings that words have gathered in use, meanings which are not captured by literal definitions.

An important and valuable aspect of this analysis is that the basic data remains throughout the whole process. By integrating this method with other methods, the analysis can be both qualitative (focusing on the relationship between particular interactions which occur at different times in the data) and quantitative (assessing the relative incidence of 'key words' or collocations of words in the data as a whole, or comparing their incidence in data subsets). Initial exploratory work on particular interactions can be used to generate hypotheses which can then be tested systematically on a large text or series of related texts. For example, a researcher may want to see if a technical term introduced by a teacher is taken up by students later in their group-based activity. And by locating all instances and collocations of a term in the transcription file, the way it is used by teachers and students in relation to their joint activity can then be considered (see for example Monaghan, 1999; Wegerif and Mercer, 1997; Mercer, 2000: Chapter 3). I will illustrate this feature later in the paper.

## 3 Linking processes to outcomes

Most analyses of talk in educational settings have been exclusively concerned with the processes of education, not with educational outcomes or effects. This again seems often to reflect researchers' commitment to certain types of research paradigms, with little overlap between those who use quantitative, experimental type methods to assess effects/outcomes and those who use qualitative methods to focus on processes. My colleagues and I have tried to transcend this methodological divide, because we have as much interest in educational outcomes (of classroom dialogue) as in educational processes. For example, we have investigated the relationship between the ways that teachers talk with students and the learning that students can subsequently demonstrate (as described for example in Rojas-Drummond, Mercer and Dabrowski, 2001; see also Mercer, 2000: Chapter 6). We have also related variations in styles of talk amongst groups of children to their different rates of success in problem-solving and to the educational attainment of the individuals involved (e.g. Mercer, Dawes, Wegerif and Sams, 2004). In this way, we have not only taken advantage of the affordances of different methods and paradigms, but have also provided a variety of empirical support for the conclusions of our research which has been accepted as valid by a wider range of audiences. I will return to these matters also later in the paper.

## 4  Analysing collective thinking in the classroom

As mentioned earlier, our methodology has been used to analyse both teachers' talk with students and students' talk amongst themselves in paired or group activities. The analyses of teacher-student dialogue came first, and they generated an account of the different discursive techniques teachers typically and frequently used as the 'tools of their trade' (Mercer, 1995). All teachers ask their students a lot of questions, creating the Initiation-Response-Follow up/Feedback (IRF) exchanges first described so graphically by Sinclair and Coulthard (1975). They also regularly offer their classes *recaps* – summaries of what they consider to be the salient features of a past event – which can help students to relate current activity to past experience. These may be *literal* or *reconstructive*, the latter being where the teacher 'rewrites history', presenting a version of events which perhaps fits in better with his/her teaching plans. Teachers also often *elaborate* and *reformulate* the contributions made to classroom dialogue by students (for example in response to a teacher's questions) as a way of clarifying what has been said for the benefit of others and also to make connections between the content of children's utterances and the technical terminology of the curriculum. They often mark experiences as significant in the experience of the class by using 'we' (as in 'When we did the experiment last week'). A list of techniques I have identified is presented in Table 8.1.

These techniques seem to be in common use throughout the world, even though teaching styles and ways of organising classrooms vary within and across cultures (see Edwards and Westgate, 1994; Mercer, 1995; Alexander, 2000). Of course, as with the tools of any trade, teachers can use these common discursive techniques relatively well or badly. To evaluate the use of techniques, we need to consider what their intended educational purpose

*Table 8.1*  Some techniques that teachers use (from Mercer, 1995: 34)

---

*to elicit knowledge from learners*
  Direct elicitations
  Cued elicitations
*to respond to what learners say*
  Confirmations
  Repetitions
  Elaborations
  Reformulations
*to describe significant aspects of shared experiences*
  'We' statements
  Literal recaps
  Reconstructive recaps

---

might be. For a teacher to teach and a learner to learn, both partners need to use talk and joint activity to create a shared framework of understanding from the resources of their common knowledge and common interests or goals. Talk is the principal tool for creating this framework, and by questioning, recapping, reformulating, elaborating and so on teachers are usually seeking to draw pupils into a shared understanding of the activities in which they are engaged. As mentioned above, the purpose of identifying these techniques has been to pursue an interest in the ways teachers guide the joint construction of knowledge. Other kinds of research interests (in, say, classroom control and discipline) would of course generate different typologies.

Our early observational studies of children's talk in groups (Fisher, 1992; Dawes, Fisher and Mercer, 1992; Mercer, 1994, 1995) also created a typology, by which my colleagues and I described children's talk as being more or less like three archetypical forms: Disputational, Cumulative and Exploratory:

- *Disputational talk*, which is characterised by disagreement and individualised decision making. There are few attempts to pool resources, offer constructive criticism or make suggestions. Disputational talk also has some characteristic discourse features – short exchanges consisting of assertions and challenges or counter assertions ('Yes, it is.' 'No it's not!').
- *Cumulative talk*, in which speakers build positively but uncritically on what the others have said. Partners use talk to construct a 'common knowledge' by accumulation. Cumulative discourse is characterised by repetitions, confirmations and elaborations.
- *Exploratory talk*, in which partners engage critically but constructively with each other's ideas. Statements and suggestions are offered for joint consideration. These may be challenged and counter-challenged, but challenges are justified and alternative hypotheses are offered. Partners all actively participate, and opinions are sought and considered before decisions are jointly made. Compared with the other two types, in Exploratory talk knowledge is made more publicly accountable and reasoning is more visible in the talk.

As with the description of teachers' talk strategies, the three types of talk were not devised to be used as the basis for a coding scheme (of the kind used in systematic observation research). We have had no wish to reduce the data of conversation to a categorical tally, because such a move into abstracted data could not maintain the crucial involvement with the contextualised, dynamic nature of talk which is at the heart of our sociocultural discourse analysis. Rather, the typology offers a useful frame of reference for making sense of the variety of talk in relation to our research questions. While recognising its relative crudeness, we have found that the typology is a very useful heuristic device. In an initial consideration of the data, it particularly helps an analyst perceive the extent to which participants in a joint activity are at any stage (a) behaving cooperatively or competitively and (b) engaging in the critical reflection or in the mutual acceptance of ideas. It is also very useful for explaining the principles and outcomes of discourse analysis to 'users' of research, such as teachers. Our original intention was to refine the typology into a more subtle and extensive scheme for differentiating talk in terms of its variety and adequacy for carrying out different types of joint intellectual activity, but my own view now is that this would not be a particularly worthwhile development. It is hard to see what value a much more complex differentiation would offer, and the elegant simplicity of a three-part list would be lost.

The reader might like to test the application of the typology by considering each of the following short examples of discussions, Transcripts 1–3 below (to which I will also provide my own commentary).

## 4.1 A note on transcription

For all kinds of discourse analysis, it is important that the transcription of speech is a faithful representation of what is actually said, to the extent that speakers' utterances are not misrepresented and as much information relevant to the analysis is included as is practically possible. But as with methods of analysis, no one particular convention for transcribing speech is intrinsically better than another. Transcription choices should be determined by the research questions being addressed and the claims which will be made on the basis of the analysis. For example, in our research we have not usually recorded details of the length of pauses made by speakers (as is often done, for example, in the transcripts of conversation analysts). We decided that information about the lengths of pauses was not relevant to the questions we were addressing. The format we have usually adopted in recent times is that shown in the examples below, in which standard punctuation is used to represent the grammatical organisation of the speech as interpreted by the researcher. As shown in the later examples (Transcripts 4–7) any comments about other features of the talk and non-verbal aspects of the encounter judged as relevant to the analysis are recorded in a third column. Non-word utterances such as 'mm'/'ooh' are included when they are judged to have a communicative function (e.g. to show surprise or agreement, or to extend a speaker's turn in the face of possible interruptions). Words spoken emphatically are in italics. Simultaneous speech is shown by the use of brackets ( [ ) preceding each utterance. Where the accurate transcription of a word is in doubt, it is followed by a question mark in parentheses (?). Utterances which cannot be understood are marked [unintelligible].

In all three of the transcripts below, the participants are primary school children working at the computer. They are all engaged in the joint task of making up a conversation between two cartoon characters portrayed on a computer screen and also have to decide what the characters are thinking as they speak. They then type the words into the relevant 'speech' and 'thought' bubbles. (Whenever it seemed to the researchers that the children were speaking the voices of the characters, the words have been placed in inverted commas.)

## Transcript 1: Jo and Carol

CAROL:  Just write in the next letter. 'Did you have a nice English lesson'

JO:  You've got to get it on there. Yes that's you. Let's just have a look at that. 'Hi, Alan did you have a nice English lesson. Yes thank you, Yeah. Yes thank you it was fine.'

CAROL:  You've got to let me get some in sometimes.

JO:  You're typing.

CAROL:  Well you can do some, go on.

JO:  'Yes thank you'

CAROL:  [unintelligible]

JO:  You're typing. 'Yes thank you' 'I did, yeah, yes, thank you I did.'

CAROL:  You can spell that.

JO:  Why don't *you* do it?

CAROL:  No, because *you* should.

## Transcript 2: Sally and Emma

SALLY:  Yeah. What if she says erm erm 'All right, yeah.' No, just put 'Yeah all right.' No, no.

EMMA:  No. 'Well I suppose I could.'

SALLY:  'spare 15 p.' Yeah?

EMMA:  Yeah.

SALLY:  'I suppose.'

EMMA:  'I suppose I could spare 50p.'

SALLY:  '50?'

EMMA:  Yeah. 'Spare 50 pence.'

SALLY:  '50 pence.'

EMMA:  '50 pence.' And Angela says 'That isn't enough I want to buy some-thing else.'

SALLY:  Yeah, no no. 'I want a drink as well you know I want some coke as well.'

EMMA:  'That isn't enough for bubble gum and some coke.'

SALLY:  Yeah, yeah.

## Transcript 3: Tina, George and Sophie

GEORGE:  We've got to decide.

TINA:  We've got to decide together.

GEORGE:  Shall we right, right, just go round like [take

TINA:                                                                       [No, go round. You say what you think, and she says.

GEORGE:     I think she should be saying 'Did you steal my money from me?'
TINA:       Your go.
SOPHIE:     I think we should put 'I thought that my money's gone missing and I thought it was you.'
GEORGE:     'I think it was you.'
SOPHIE:     Which one?
TINA:       Now what was it I was going to say, Um, um.
GEORGE:     No because she's *thinking*, so we need to do a thought. So we could write her saying
SOPHIE:     'My money's gone [missing so'
TINA:                       [I was going to say if we're doing the one where she's saying, this is *saying* not thinking.
SOPHIE:     'My money's gone do you know where it is?'
TINA:       No, [on the saying one she could say
GEORGE:         [You should be saying
TINA:       Like she could be thinking to say to Robert, she could be saying 'Do you know where's my money?' 'Do you know anything about my money going missing?'
GEORGE:     Yeh, what, yeh that's good. When she's thinking I think she should be thinking 'Oh my money's gone missing and its definitely Robert.'
TINA:       Yeh.
SOPHIE:     No 'cos she's *saying* it to him isn't she?
TINA:       [No she's *thinking* at the moment.
GEORGE:     [No she's *thinking*.
TINA:       *That's* the speech bubble.

## 4.2 Commentary: Transcripts 1, 2 and 3

The talk in Transcript 1 has characteristics of Disputational talk. Both participants take an active part, but there is little evidence of joint, cooperative engagement with the task. Much of the interactional talk consists of commands and assertions. The episode ends with a direct question and answer, but even this exchange has an unproductive, disputational quality.

Transcript 2 has features of Cumulative talk. There is no dispute, and both participants contribute ideas which are accepted. We can see repetitions, confirmation and elaborations. The interaction is cooperative, but there is no critical consideration of ideas.

Transcript 3 has characteristics of Exploratory talk. It begins with Tina and George making explicit reference to their task as requiring joint decision making, and they attempt to organise the interaction so that everyone's ideas are heard. They then pursue a discussion of what is appropriate content for the character's 'thought' and 'speech' bubbles in which differing opinions are offered and visibly supported by some reasoning (for example 'No, because she's *thinking*, so we need to do a thought.' '. . . if we're doing the one where she's saying, this is *saying* not thinking.'). However, their reasoning is focused only on this procedural issue: they do not discuss explicitly or critically the proposed content of the character's thoughts and words. Later parts of the discussion also have a disputational quality, as the participants simply seem to assert and counter-assert that a character is either thinking or speaking. Were the space available to include longer examples, I could show that their later discussion also has some Cumulative features.

## 5 The methodology in action

I will describe the methodology in action by providing an account of the procedures for gathering data within a typical project and then use transcripts to illustrate how the data gathered is analysed. In recent projects, we have had the following main interests:

(i) the nature and functions of teacher-student dialogue as a means for guiding children's joint activity and learning;
(ii) the quality of children's talk during group-based activities as a medium for joint problem-solving and learning;
(iii) the relationship between teacher-student and student-student dialogues, focusing on such issues as if/how teacher-student dialogue can be seen to inform students' subsequent group activity and whether their group talk shows that students have been inducted into specific forms of discourse;
(iv) the relationship between the quality of students' engagement in classroom dialogue and learning outcomes;
(v) designing ways for teachers to improve the quality of classroom dialogue as an educational process.

These interests have meant that we have usually recorded both teacher-student and student-student dialogue in the same classrooms. In the most recent projects we have compared classrooms in which teachers were asked to use a specially designed programme of discourse strategies and activities with classrooms in which no interventions were made. Typically, we gather data in classrooms over a period of not less than 10 weeks. The talk data consists of video-recordings and associated field notes. One or two 'target' groups of (usually) three children in each of the project classes are recorded, with each group being recorded several times over the observational period. Recordings are also made of the whole-class, teacher-led sessions which precede and follow each group activity. The nature and timing of these recordings are designed not only to enable us to look at the way children talk and interact in groups (and how this may change over time), but also so that we gain information about the temporal development of shared understanding in the class as a whole. These recordings are transcribed, initially, by a professional transcriber, whose electronic file is then corrected by a member of the research team in light of a careful reviewing of each recording. Some comments about non-verbal aspects and other potentially relevant information about the events (e.g. as supplied by a teacher) are added at this stage.

The next step is a detailed analysis of the talk of the groups of children. Typically, this begins with members of the team watching recordings together, each with a transcript (which may be revised again in this process). We might first watch a series of recordings of groups made before the intervention begins (the implementation of an experimental teaching programme) and then move on to post-intervention recordings. We also look at the recordings and transcripts of teacher-led sessions from the same classes. This viewing is of course directed by our research questions. After such communal viewing sessions, individual members of the team carry out their own analyses of particular lessons or series of lessons.

In much recent research, the initial guiding framework for our analysis of children's group talk has been the typology of Disputational, Cumulative and Exploratory talk referred to earlier. One of our main interests has been in the extent to which the children engage in talk which has 'Exploratory' features and the extent to which the nature of their interaction enables them to engage productively in the task. A second interest has been in how the quality of their interaction changes over time under the influence of a teacher as a 'discourse guide' (Mercer, 1995: Chapter 5). This has involved analysing a related series of whole-class sessions, group talk by children and occasions when a teacher has intervened in a group's activities.

It is not possible in an article such as this to include a great deal of transcript data. This means some aspects of the analysis, especially those concerned with the temporal development of collective activity through and across recorded sessions, cannot be fully explained. Nevertheless, some exemplification and explanation is possible. Transcripts 4–7 below are taken from the data of a recent project based in British primary schools. Most of this data has already been through the collective team viewing stage, and some papers including the analyses which emerged from those sessions and subsequent related analyses have been published. However, the particular extracts of data included here have not been included together in any earlier publication, and the commentaries I will provide on them represent my own analysis, generated for this paper. Transcript 4 is part of a whole-class session that was recorded a few weeks into the observational period of a project based in primary (Year 5) classrooms in England. In it, the teacher is setting up a group activity in which the children will work together on a computer-based science investigation. This lesson was the sixth in a series in which the teacher had been expressly encouraging the children to become more aware of how they talked and worked together. In a previous lesson (which we had also recorded) she had established with the children a set of 'ground rules' for how they should talk and work together in their groups. These included:

1   Members of groups should seek agreement before making decisions.
2   Group members should ask each other for their ideas and opinions ('What do you think?').
3   Group members should give reasons for their views and be asked for them if appropriate ('Why do you think that?').

The teacher told us that she had two main goals for the session: to ensure that the children knew what to do in the computer-based activity and to ensure that the ground rules were in the forefront of their minds as they worked together. In this extract, she is focusing on the ground rules.

### Transcript 4: teacher-led session 1. Rehearsing the ground rules

| | |
|---|---|
| TEACHER: | Before you go on to the next step on the computer what do you need to make sure that the whole group has done? Oh! More hands up than that. Emma? | |
| EMMA: | Agreed. |
| TEACHER: | Agreed. The whole group needs to agree. | *Teacher writes 'everybody agrees' on board.* |
| | OK one of my speech bubbles. I wonder what kind of things we might hear each other saying during today's lesson? | |
| | | *Teacher draws a speech bubble. Points to a child.* |
| BOY: | What do you think? | |
| TEACHER: | What do you think? | *Teacher writes 'What do you think?' in speech bubble.* |
| | Anything else you might hear people saying as we have today's lesson? Kaye. | |
| KAYE: | What is your idea? | *Teacher draws a speech bubble and writes 'What is your idea?' in it.* |
| TEACHER: | Brilliant! What's your idea? Ooh, Sydney. | |
| SYDNEY: | Why do you think that? | |
| TEACHER: | Excellent. Well done. | *Teacher draws a speech bubble and writes 'Why do you think that?' in it.* |

|   |   |   |
|---|---|---|
| | Any other things we might hear people say? Ruby. | |
| RUBY: | I'm not too sure on that idea. What do you think? | *Teacher draws a new speech bubble.* |
| TEACHER: | Brilliant. Well done. What do we need to remember in our groups? Kiera? | |
| KIERA: | That everybody gets a turn to talk | |
| TEACHER: | Everybody gets a turn to talk. | *Teacher points to a child.* |
| GIRL: | Everybody needs to share their opinions | |
| TEACHER: | Yeah – and are we all the same? | |
| CLASS: | No | |
| TEACHER: | Will there be someone in your group that perhaps wants to talk all the time? | |
| CLASS: | Yes | |
| TEACHER: | Will there be someone in your group who doesn't want to talk at all? | |
| CLASS: | Yes! | |
| TEACHER: | How are you going to get that person who doesn't want to talk at all to say something? Shane? What do you think? How are you going to get that person who sits there and doesn't say anything to say something in your group? Help him out Tyber. | |
| TYBER: | Ask them. | |
| TEACHER: | Ask them – brilliant. What about that person who talks ALL the time? | |
| | | *Emphasises with actions* |
| BOY: | Tell him to shut up. | |
| TEACHER: | Ooh! Are you? I hope not because that's not positive language is it? What could you do to help them out? Kiera. | |
| KIERA: | Ask them and then ask somebody else and then ask the other person. | *Teacher silences an interruption with a gesture.* |
| TEACHER: | Brilliant. Making sure that you ask everybody in the group. Excellent. Kaye? | |

## 5.1 Commentary: Transcript 4

The characteristic IRF structure of classroom talk is apparent here (as is the common feature that the teacher does most of the talking). There are of course many features of this interaction that are worthy of comment, but I will focus on the temporal quality of the dialogue and in particular the teacher's orientations to past shared experience and to future activity. The teacher begins by orientating the children to the immediate future, to the computer-based activity they will begin shortly. In that same first remark (a *direct elicitation*) she also orientates them to the past – to the 'ground rules' which she had discussed with them in the previous lesson. The children respond by offering their ideas, which we can see are also drawn from the shared experience of the previous lesson. The teacher provides evaluative comments in the form of *confirmations* (e.g. 'Excellent. Well done.'), repetitions ('What do you think' and 'Everybody gets a turn to talk'). She *reformulates* one child's remark:

KIERA:   Ask them and then ask somebody else and then ask the other person.
TEACHER:   Brilliant. Making sure that you ask everybody in the group. Excellent.

She also consolidates this common knowledge publicly in a different mode, by writing it in speech bubbles on the board. In sociocultural terms, the board is being used as a cultural tool for this purpose, and its use highlights the multimodal quality of much educational dialogue. (See Bourne and Jewitt, 2003, for a discussion of this kind of multimodality.) So we can see that this is an exercise in collective remembering and the consolidation of learning, driven by the pedagogic goals of the teacher. It is also worth noting that the teacher also provides some models of the kind of talk she is encouraging: towards the end of the episode she asks Shane 'What do you think?' We can see how the teacher and children are drawing on recent past experience to establish ways that the children will talk and think together in the forthcoming computer-based task. With regard to the future, note the teacher's reference to 'positive language' in the final stage of the extract, which I will refer to later.

The next transcript comes from a recording of a group of three children later on in the same lesson as Transcript 4, as they work together on a computer-based investigation into the relative effectiveness of different materials for providing sound insulation. The software allows them to carry out simulated tests, and they have already investigated the soundproofing properties of some materials – cork, wood and paper – earlier in the activity. A novel feature of the extract as a piece of classroom discourse is that the computer is also a speaker. In the role of a 'talking bug' whose words both appear in text on the screen and are spoken out loud, it sets out the problem for the children.

### Transcript 5: group work 1. Blocking out sound

COMPUTER:   Now can you help me with a problem?
I live in a hole in the ground and every morning the birds wake me up with their high-pitched singing.

| | |
|---|---|
| SYLVIA: | He should build it [with |
| COMPUTER: |                   [I want to block out the sound with things I have found lying on the ground – stones, leaves, thick tree bark, sticks. How do I design a fair test to find out which is best? Talk together. When you have agreed, then click on 'continue'. |
| BEAU: | Well [inaudible] will block out this |
| SYLVIA: | What it's like cork? |
| KIERA: | But it's not. We've got to find out differences(?). |
| SYLVIA: | Wood. Lots of sticks are [inaudible] wood |
| BEAU: | Sssh |
| COMPUTER: | Every morning the birds wake me up with their high-pitched singing. Click continue when you have finished. Click this button to print what you have written. |

*Teacher tells class they have 2 minutes to complete this stage of the activity. The 'return' key is pressed, which causes the computer to restate the problem. Reads screen.*

| | |
|---|---|
| BEAU: | Click on this |
| SYLVIA: | I want |
| COMPUTER: | I want to block out the sound with things I have found lying on the ground – stones, leaves, thick tree bark, sticks. How do I design a fair test to decide which one is best? Talk together. When you have agreed, then click on 'continue'. |
| BEAU: | Um every morning, block out the, block the hole up and use one type of material. |
| SYLVIA: | Use thick tree bark and stones and sticks. |
| KIERA: | No, look. We have to find out a way – we have to find out a way – to make ['sure'?]. Well, we'd have to use |
| BEAU: | We'd have to make a fair test, right? |
| KIERA: | Well a fair test was, we'd have to use, what did you say a fair test was? |

*Turns to Beau.*

| BEAU: | All the materials and one day go away and choose [one | |
| SYLVIA: |                 [These are all the materials you've got | *Points to screen.* |
| KIERA: | Yeah but let Beau carry on with what he was saying. What were you saying? | |
| BEAU: | Use one material every day when you wake up or when she wakes up and see which one blocks out the sound most. | |
| KIERA: | Or have you got your own opinion? Do you agree? | *Turns to Sylvia.* |
| SYLVIA: | Yes | *Long hesitation before speech.* |
| KIERA: | I agree as well. I think that's all of us agree. | *Children nod.* |

### 5.2 Commentary: Transcript 5

In this extract all three children engage with the task. Kiera, in particular, shows a concern with establishing a joint understanding of exactly what they are expected to do ('We've got to find out different . . .'; 'No, look. We have to find out a way . . .'; 'Well a fair test was, we'd have to use.'). She also is the group member who shows most explicit concern with the group's adherence to the 'ground rules' which were established in the earlier whole-class session ('Yeah but let Beau carry on with what he was saying. What were you saying?'; 'Or have you got your own opinion? Do you agree?'). In this way, her remarks embody the recent educational experience of the group – and as such will serve to evoke the memory of that experience for the other members. Her contributions are most responsible for any resemblance the group's discussion in this episode has to Exploratory talk. ('Partners all actively participate and opinions are sought and considered before decisions are jointly made.') Other aspects of recently created common knowledge are also apparent in the group's talk – for example, the references by Sylvia to wood and cork early in the extract can be understood as attempts to relate this new simulation task to the knowledge gained from those which they have recently completed. In these various ways, we can see how the children's joint intellectual activity depends crucially on the historical foundations of earlier talk in the whole-class session and group activity. The talk is used to make joint sense of the current task and to maintain the quality of interaction defined by the class's ground rules.

This kind of data and analysis of course offers opportunities for pursuing other topics besides the use of talk itself. For example, we have used this kind of data to examine the teaching and learning of science (Mercer, Dawes, Wegerif and Sams, 2004). In a more extended analysis (i.e. using more of the available data) one might look more critically at the extent to which the teacher has used dialogue to help the children establish an adequate understanding of the scientific principles and procedures which they are expected to draw on in the computer-based tasks.

*Transcript 6: teacher-led session 2*

Transcript 6 is from the next recorded lesson of the same class (about a week later). There were, of course, other lessons between the recordings, in which the researchers were not present. In this whole-class session, at the beginning of the lesson, the teacher is setting up another group activity, this time involving the task of putting numbers into sets.

| | | |
|---|---|---|
| TEACHER: | Can you remember what we had to sort in our science lesson? | |
| CHILD: | Food. | |
| TEACHER: | Food. Brilliant! We had to sort it into different categories didn't we? This time we're going to be sorting numbers. So that's our objective – 'Sorting Numbers'. | *Writes objective on board.* |
| | I'm going to work with Donal and Alan today and in my group I've decided I'm going to sort the numbers by multiples of three, and I don't care what they think. What's the matter Michaela? | *Teacher takes on role of child with grumpy expression.* |
| MICHAELA: | You should, um, decide as a group. | |
| TEACHER: | Oh super. There's one of our ground rules already 'Decide as a group'. | *Writes this on board.* |
| | OK. How am I going to do that? Because I want to sort my numbers by multiples of three. How am I going to make sure that we decide that as a group? | |
| KIERA (?): | Ask them what they think. Also, when you ask what they think, don't turn your back on them because that's not positive body language. | *Teacher writes.* |
| TEACHER: | You mentioned positive body language. What other type of language do we need to make sure is positive? Not just our body language – come on Sydney – join in please. What other sort of language do we need to make sure is positive? | |
| CHILD: | The way we talk. | |
| TEACHER: | The way we talk! Am I going to say 'I'm going to sort these in multiples of three!'? | |
| CHILD: | No. | |

| | | |
|---|---|---|
| TEACHER: | Michael, what would you say if you were in my situation? | |
| MICHAEL: | Um, 'I want to sort them by multiples of three. What do you think about?' | |
| TEACHER: | That would be a good thing to say. | |
| MICHAEL: | Miss, it would be a lot easier if everyone sorted them by multiples of one, then you wouldn't sort them by anything. | |
| TEACHER: | That's very true. You are a very good mathematician, Michael. | |
| CHILD: | Um, you could say, 'Please can we sort out [inaudible]' | |
| TEACHER: | Super, well done. My pen's going to run out, isn't it? | *Writes on board.* |
| | Can anybody think of one more ground rule that we think is important? Nirmal? | |
| NIRMAL: | Ask for their opinion. | |
| TEACHER: | Ask for an opinion. Ask what they think. I can put 'Opinion' – that's a much better word than ask what they think. Well done. One more ground rule that's important. Go on then Sydney? | *Writes 'Opinion' on board.* |
| SYDNEY: | Be prepared to change your idea. | |
| TEACHER: | Well done. Why is that so important? Why should we need to be prepared to change our idea? | |
| CHILD: | Somebody else might think different to you. | |
| TEACHER: | Somebody else might? | |
| CHILD: | Somebody else might have a different opinion | |
| TEACHER: | Is your opinion necessarily going to be the best? | |
| CHILDREN | No. | |
| TEACHER: | No? So we need to change. Be prepared. Fantastic. OK, as I'm wandering around the classroom and looking and watching and listening to what you are doing, I wonder what sort of things I might hear you saying? Go on. Tell your partner one thing you might say. Bernice, can you tell Sydney? And . . . stop! Ready? Looking this way. Donal's group. Share one of the things I might hear you say. | *Writes 'Be prepared to change' on board. Children talk to each other.* |
| DONAL: | What do you think? | |
| TEACHER: | 'What do you think?' Brilliant – Emma? | *Writes this on board.* |

| | | |
|---|---|---|
| EMMA: | Why do you think that? | |
| TEACHER: | 'Why do you think that?' That's another good one, not just what but why do you think that? Brilliant. Anything else I might hear you saying as I wander round? Joe? | *Writes on board.* |
| JOE: | Yes and No. | |
| TEACHER: | Yes and No. OK. People agreeing and disagreeing. Would you expand on just saying 'yes' or would you expand on just saying 'no'? Pardon? | *Inaudible remark from child.* |
| GIRL: | You'd say why. | |
| TEACHER: | 'Yes' and then 'why'. Ooh, all my pens are running out. 'yes' and then 'why' and 'no' and then 'why'. | *Writes 'why' on board.* |
| GIRL: | I'm prepared to change my idea because you're so cool. | |
| TEACHER: | I'm prepared to change my idea because you're so cool! Can you think of a better explanation than just because you're so cool? Because it's better – because it sounds more plausible – it sounds more interesting – Michael? | |
| MICHAEL: | If you were by my group you'd probably hear 'Ah, but' and 'if' a lot because if one has one idea and another has another idea, we say 'ah, but, this, this, this, this' or 'ah, but this' – | |
| TEACHER: | But, you're then still explaining 'why'. Well done. | |
| KIERA: | You could have 'What's your opinion?' because you're asking [inaudible]. | |
| TEACHER: | Excellent. 'What's your opinion?'. Goodness me, I'm going to run out of board space. Uh, uh. Ssh, ssh. Nirmal? | *Writes on board.* |
| NIRMAL: | 'Do you like that idea?' | |
| TEACHER: | 'Do you like that idea?' | *Writes on board.* |
| CHILD: | 'Why do you like that idea?' | |
| TEACHER: | Brilliant. One more then. Sylvia? Pardon? | *Inaudible response.* |
| SYLVIA: | 'Do we all agree?' | |
| TEACHER: | That's the crucial one isn't it 'Do we all agree?' That's what you were going to say was it? 'Do we all agree?' | *Writes 'Do we all agree?' on board.* |

## 5.3 Commentary: Transcript 6

The teacher begins this session with a common type of *elicitation* – an appeal to the children's memory of past activity. This is one way in which teachers try to help children see the continuity of educational experience and to encourage them to recall knowledge of past events which is relevant to current or future activity. She here tries to establish the similarity between two potentially disparate activities, by invoking the generic category of action of 'sorting'. As in the session represented in Transcript 4, she again here makes a switch of topic from the formal curriculum content (maths) to that of how the children will work and talk together in groups. Her role play of the uncooperative partner is an unusual form of *cued elicitation* for invoking children's collective memory of the 'ground rules', which should by now be a well-established part of the common knowledge and local culture of this class. (A search through the data for this teacher would enable us to see if this kind of role play was a common technique in her repertoire: if it was, this would help explain the readiness with which Michaela responds to the cue.) The teacher responds to Michaela's remark with a confirmation and an explicit reference to 'our ground rules', so marking them as the common property of the class. She then uses a series of IRF exchanges to draw out once again – in this public forum – the main rules from members of the class. Her own utterances often include *repetitions* ('Do you like that idea?') and *reformulations/elaborations* of children's remarks ('Ask for an opinion. Ask what they think.').

Early in the extract, a child responds with a reference to 'positive body language', which the teacher picks up and elaborates in her next turn. We saw that this notion of 'positive language' was used by the teacher in Transcript 4. We can interpret the child's use of this term as an example of the appropriation by a student of a new expression from the teacher, albeit in a teacher-led encounter. The data has granted us a glimpse of the historical process of the teaching and learning of a type of technical term. However, a computer-based search for the word 'positive' in all the data for this class showed that this was the only recorded instance of a child using the term: the teacher used it five times, always collocated with 'language', in two of five recorded lessons. There was not therefore much evidence of the children taking up this expression and making active use of it in discussing their own interactions. Other terms and phrases used by the children, though less distinctive, also may share a similar history: 'Decide as a group'; 'ask for their opinion'; 'what do you think?'; 'why do you think that?', while quite common English phrases, will almost certainly have acquired a special resonance for members of the class through the discussion of the 'ground rules' early in this series of lessons. In all the recorded data for this class, the teacher uses the phrase 'what do you think' five times, while the children use it 18 times, of which 15 occurrences are found during group work. The rate of usage of this phrase increases in group activity as time progresses.

One part of this extract that particularly interests me is towards the end when the teacher is asking members of the class if they might say more than simply 'Yes' or 'No' to someone else's idea – the section that begins with the teacher saying 'Would you expand on just saying "Yes". . .?' An unidentified girl comments that she might explain that someone's idea has changed her mind because the speaker is 'so cool'. The teacher picks up on this, seeming dissatisfied with a reason which is not based on rational evaluation – though she does not really make this very clear, perhaps so as to avoid seeming too critical of the girl's comments. Michael then offers a brief account of some words he thinks would be frequently heard in his group, explaining that (if I may reformulate his remarks) these reflect the fact that different opinions are debated. We can see from this that Michael has gained an insight into the ways that the use of certain words reflects a certain kind of talk and a certain kind of mutual engagement with ideas. The teacher does not appear to recognise the potential significance of this contribution for the class's study of talk. Although she says 'Well done' she continues to pursue her point about the need to explain 'why'. This is perhaps unfortunate, but perfectly understandable: the process of discourse analysis offers insights which a speaker can hardly be expected to gain in the heat of conversational exchange. Nevertheless, this is the kind of issue which the analysis could be used to raise with a group of teachers in a professional development session based on the research. More positively, though, in such a session I would also be likely to draw attention to the ways this teacher successfully engages the class in explicit consideration of how they talk and to her efforts (in this extract and in other recorded sessions) to consolidate children's developing knowledge and understanding about how talk can be used to think collectively.

The final example, Transcript 7, is taken from later in the same lesson as Transcript 6. In it, three children in the class are embarking on the number sorting activity.

### Transcript 7: group work 2

| ALAN: | 'Sort. Type in category.' Shall we do multiples of one? No, they'd all be mult, of – | *Reads and points to screen. Looks at Neelam.* |
|---|---|---|
| NIRMAL: | Five? | |
| ALAN: | No, three. No, yeah, no? Multiples of three, alright. Is M,U,L, mul-multi | *Looks at the others to check.* *They nod agreement. Begins to type.* |
| NIRMAL: | Mul, it's TY | |
| ALAN: | Multi-pl, multiples of four, yeah? | *Typing.* |
| NIRMAL: | Four or three? | *Leans round to ask Neelam.* |

| ALAN: | Four or three. What do you think? | *Asks Neelam.* |
|---|---|---|
| NEELAM: | Four | |
| ALAN: | Four. Yeah. Yeah? | *Types.* |
| NIRMAL: | Shall I start? Is eighteen a multiple of four? | |
| NEELAM: | Four, eight, twelve | |
| ALAN: | Ss | |
| NIRMAL: | Yes it is. Four times four | |
| ALAN AND NEELAM: | No, no, no, no, no | |
| NIRMAL: | Sixteen | |
| ALAN: | No, no, no, no. | |
| NEELAM: | No, it's sixteen. | *Nirmal puts it in the 'no' box.* |
| NIRMAL: | Is fifteen? | |
| ALAN: | No | |
| NEELAM: | No | *Nirmal puts it in the 'no' box.* |
| NIRMAL: | Is nine? | |
| ALAN: | No. | |
| NEELAM: | No. | |
| NIRMAL: | Why do you think that? | |
| ALAN: | Um | |
| ALAN AND NEELAM: | Because | |
| ALAN: | Because it goes four, eight then twelve so it misses nine out. | |
| NEELAM: | 'Cos if you do four times five it isn't – | |
| NIRMAL: | And, and only, and only the even numbers end in zero, two, four, six, eight. | |
| ALAN: | Yeah. And four is even. | *Nirmal drops it in the box.* |

## 5.4 Commentary: Transcript 7

This transcript includes many indications of the temporal relationship of this episode of talk with those we have already considered – for example, the use of the phrases associated with the ground rules ('What do you think?' 'Why do you think that?'). But what does it reveal about how this group of children are thinking together? They are definitely on task and working in a very collaborative manner. They ask many questions of each other, using them to check responses to ideas, to elicit opinions and to resolve differences of opinion. This manner of conversing can be seen to contribute to their success in the task. A good illustration concerns the discussion about what is a multiple of four. It is clear that Nirmal has not begun this activity with a good grasp of the four times-table. But through the discussion with Alan and Neelam he not only establishes correct answers, he elicits reasons for their claims:

> Why do you think that?
> Because it goes four, eight then twelve so it misses nine out.

He then concludes the episode with what looks like a realisation of how these facts accord with his own knowledge about even numbers:

> And, and only, the even numbers end in zero, two, four, six, eight.

The discussion in this group has many of the features of Exploratory talk. Although we cannot be confident in making claims about learning from this evidence alone, we can see that this illustrates how, in a supportive group environment, children who are the more able in a subject may enable the progress of less able partners.

## 6 Quantitative aspects of analysis

Some quantitative aspects of the methodology cannot be illustrated through transcript extracts, as they involve the data corpus as a whole. In some studies we have assessed the effects of an intervention (known as the *Thinking Together* programme) in which teachers expressly encouraged the use of 'ground rules' for encouraging Exploratory talk amongst the members of their classes. More specifically, we wanted to see if this intervention produced observable changes in the nature of the children's talk. We used a computer-based concordance analysis to count the relative incidence of key words and phrases which the qualitative analysis had shown are associated with the use of Exploratory talk and so identified variations over time within groups and between groups who had or had not been involved in the *Thinking Together* programme. Examples of such key words are 'if', 'because', 'I think' and 'agree' (which we have seen used in Transcripts 3 and 7 of groups presented above). We searched for these in the combined transcript data of recordings for six groups of three children. Three of these groups were in target classes (those who had been involved in *Thinking Together*) and three were in matched control classes in other schools (who had pursued a normal curriculum). We had recorded all the groups *before* and *after* the intervention period, as they tackled a standardised set of problems (*Raven's Progressive Matrices*). The results of this analysis are shown in Tables 8.2a and 8.2b below. An analysis of variance revealed that the difference between the target and control conditions was statistically significant ($F = 5.547$: one-tailed $p = 0.039$). In accord with the outcomes of the qualitative analysis, this supported the view that the intervention had changed the children's talk behaviour.

Another quantitative feature of the methodology was also referred to earlier in the paper, namely the assessment of learning outcomes for *individual*

*Table 8.2a* Total incidence of key linguistic features in the talk of Target and Control groups while engaged in the Raven's test, before and after the implementation of the *Thinking Together* programme

| Key feature | Target groups | | Control groups | |
|---|---|---|---|---|
| | *Pre* | *Post* | *Pre* | *Post* |
| because | 62 | 175 | 92 | 66 |
| agree | 7 | 89 | 13 | 21 |
| I think | 51 | 146 | 31 | 52 |
| Totals | 110 | 411 | 136 | 139 |

*Table 8.2b* Incidence of key linguistic features in the talk of each Target and Control group while engaged in the Raven's test, before and after the implementation of the Thinking Together programme (Adapted from Mercer, Wegerif & and Dawes, 1999)

| | *Target 1* | | *Target 2* | | *Target 3* | | *Control 1* | | *Control 2* | | *Control 3* | |
|---|---|---|---|---|---|---|---|---|---|---|---|---|
| | *Pre* | *Post* | *Pre* | *Post* | *Pre* | *Post* | *Pre* | *Post* | *Pre* | *Post* | *Pre* | *Post* |
| because | 25 | 100 | 12 | 45 | 25 | 30 | 34 | 25 | 28 | 17 | 30 | 24 |
| agree | 7 | 87 | 0 | 0 | 0 | 2 | 12 | 20 | 1 | 0 | 0 | 0 |
| I think | 7 | 87 | 0 | 12 | 44 | 47 | 27 | 44 | 3 | 5 | 1 | 3 |
| Totals | 39 | 174 | 12 | 57 | 69 | 79 | 73 | 89 | 32 | 22 | 31 | 2? |

children who had, or who had not, been participants in the *Thinking Together* programme. As with the measures of relative incidence of key terms, this depended on the use of a quasi-experimental research design whereby children in target classes in which the intervention had taken place were compared in their performance with children in matched control classes on the same talk activities and outcome measures. Although there is not space to discuss this aspect of the methodology in any detail, the kinds of results obtained are illustrated in Table 8.3.

## 7 Discussion and conclusions

In this paper, I have tried to explain how a particular methodology was created for the analysis of talk as a social mode of thinking. Its nature reflects both

(i) a particular perspective on the nature and functions of language and its relationship to individual and collective intellectual activity and
(ii) a particular set of research questions about how language is used to enable joint intellectual activity and carry out the process of teaching-and-learning in school.

*Table 8.3* Children's performances on a test of their study of the science curriculum (Adapted from Mercer, Dawes, Wegerif & and Sams, 2004)

|  | Numbers | Pre-intervention: mean scores | Post-intervention: mean scores |
| --- | --- | --- | --- |
| Target classes | 119 | 3.97 | 5.70 |
| SD |  | 2.323 | 2.424 |
| Control classes | 129 | 4.22 | 5.04 |
| SD |  | 1.997 | 2.206 |
| Effect size | 0.29 |  |  |

$F(1, 245) = 10.305$; two-tailed $p = 0.002$

I have illustrated the procedures of this sociocultural discourse analysis, using data extracts from research in which it was employed to show how it can reveal ways that language is used for thinking collectively in educational settings. I have focused mainly on the temporal aspects of the discursive processes whereby teaching-and-learning is carried out and intellectual problems are tackled, in order to show how the methodology can be used to track the development of common knowledge amongst the teacher and students of a class, to examine the ways that a teacher seeks to guide students through a series of related educational activities and to induct them into new ways of using language as a tool for thinking together. I have also shown how the analysis can be used to assess the quality of the interactions of students, to study how the quality of interactions may change over time and – an important feature – to make quantitative assessments of those changes and of the outcomes (in terms of learning and problem-solving) of engagement in different types of dialogue. Finally, I have described its use to assess the impact of a planned intervention in which the results of earlier observational research were used to design and implement a teaching programme for improving the quality of classroom dialogue as an educational tool.

I have used educational examples, but this methodology has relevance to the study of collective thinking activities in other settings. Through a sociocultural discourse analysis we are able to examine and assess the linguistic process whereby people strive for intersubjectivity. We can see how they use language to introduce new information, orientate to each other's perspectives and understandings and pursue joint plans of action. Various methods for studying talk also deal with these concerns. But the methodology I have described here also enables those processes of communication to be related to thinking processes and to learning outcomes. In this way, we can examine what is achieved through involvement in discussions, in classrooms and elsewhere – and perhaps offer constructive advice about how discussions can be made more effective. Constraints of space have inevitably limited what I could show of the methodological procedures, but I hope that what I have provided is sufficient to enable other researchers to understand this methodology, to examine it critically and perhaps build upon it in the pursuit of their own research questions.

# References

Alexander, R. (2000) *Culture and Pedagogy: International comparisons in primary education*. Oxford: Blackwell.

Bourne, J. and Jewitt, C. (2003) Orchestrating debate: A multimodal analysis of classroom interaction. *Reading, Language and Literacy* 23(2): 64–72.

Daniels, H. (2001) *Vygotsky and pedagogy*. London: Routledge/Falmer.

Dawes, L., Fisher, E. and Mercer, N. (1992) The quality of talk at the computer. *Language and Learning* 10: 22–25.

Drew, P. and Heritage, P. (eds.). (1992) *Talk at work: Interaction in institutional settings*. Cambridge: Cambridge University Press.

Edwards, A. D. and Westgate, D. P. (1994) *Investigating Classroom Talk* (2nd edn). London: The Falmer Press.

Edwards, D. and Mercer, N. (1987) *Common knowledge: The development of joint understanding in the classroom*. London: Methuen.

Edwards, D. and Potter, J. (1992) *Discursive Psychology*. London: Sage.

Elbers, E. (1994) Sociogenesis and children's pretend play: A variation on Vygotskian themes. In W. de Graaf and R. Maier (eds.) *Sociogenesis Re-examined*. New York: Springer.

Fisher, E. (1992) Characteristics of children's talk at the computer and its relationship to the computer software. *Language and Education* 7(2): 187–215.

Gee, J. P. and Green, J. (1998) Discourse analysis, learning and social practice: A methodological study. *Review of Research in Education* 23: 119–169.

Hicks, D. (1996) Contextual enquiries: A discourse-oriented study of classroom learning. In D. Hicks (ed.) *Discourse, Learning and Schooling*. Cambridge: Cambridge University Press.

Kumpulainen, K. and Wray, D. (eds.). (2002) *Classroom Interaction and Social Learning: From Theory to Practice*. London: Routledge-Falmer.

Lyle, S. (1993) An investigation into ways in which children 'talk themselves into meaning'. *Language and Education* 7(3): 181–197.

Lyle, S. (1996) An analysis of collaborative group work in the primary school and the factors relevant to its success. *Language and Education* 10(1): 13–32.

Mercer, N. (1994) The quality of talk in children's joint activity at the computer. *Journal of Computer Assisted Learning* 10: 24–32.

Mercer, N. (1995) *The Guided Construction of Knowledge*. Clevedon: Multilingual Matters.

Mercer, N. (2000) *Words and Minds: How We Use Language to Think Together*. London: Routledge.

Mercer, N., Dawes, R., Wegerif, R. and Sams, C. (2004) Reasoning as a scientist: Ways of helping children to use language to learn science. *British Educational Research Journal* 30(3): 367–385.

Mercer, N., Littleton, K. and Wegerif, R. (2004) Methods for studying the processes of interaction and collaborative activity in computer-based educational activities. *Technology, Pedagogy and Education* 13(2): 193–209.

Mercer, N., Wegerif, R. and Dawes, L.(1999) Children's talk and the development of reasoning in the classroom. *British Educational Research Journal* 25(1): 95–111.

Middleton, D. and Edwards, D. (1990) Conversational remembering: A social psychological approach. In D. Middleton and D. Edwards (eds.) *Collective Remembering*. London: Sage.

Monaghan, F. (1999) Judging a word by the company its keeps: The use of concordancing software to explore aspects of the mathematics register. *Language and Education* 13(1): 59–70.

O'Connor, C. and Michaels, S. (1996) Shifting participant frameworks: Orchestrating thinking practices in group discussion. In D. Hicks (ed.) *Discourse, Learning and Schooling*. Cambridge: Cambridge University Press.

Rojas-Drummond, S., Mercer, N. and Dabrowski, E. (2001) Collaboration, scaffolding and the promotion of problem-solving strategies in Mexican pre-schoolers. *European Journal of Psychology of Education* XVI(2): 179–196.

Schegloff, E. (1997) Whose text? Whose context? *Discourse and Society* 8(2): 165–187.

Sinclair, J. and Coulthard, M. (1975) *Towards an Analysis of Discourse: The English Used by Teachers and Pupils*. London: Oxford University Press.

Vygotsky, L.S. (1978) *Mind in Society: The Development of Higher Psychological Processes*. Cambridge, MA: Harvard University Press.

Wegerif, R. and Mercer, N. (1997) Using computer-based text analysis to integrate quantitative and qualitative methods in the investigation of collaborative learning. *Language and Education* 11(4): 271–286.

Wells, G. (1999) *Dialogic Enquiry: Towards a Sociocultural Practice and Theory of Education*. Cambridge: Cambridge University Press.

Wells, G. and Claxton, G. (eds.). (2002) *Learning for Life in the 21st Century*. Oxford: Blackwell.

Wertsch, J. V. (ed.). (1985) *Culture, Communication and Cognition: Vygotskian Perspectives*. Cambridge: Cambridge University Press.

*It is a truism to say "learning takes time," but – as I learned as an undergraduate – much of the early psychological research on learning consisted of giving people things to remember and then immediately assessing their success. Yet we all know that learning a skill, or gaining a deep understanding of a subject, is normally a cumulative, iterative, and often interactive process. An insightful comment by one of my academic heroes, Douglas Barnes (quoted in the article), made me decide to explore this aspect of classroom learning in more depth, using data my colleagues and I had gathered in recent projects.*

# 9 The seeds of time

## Why classroom dialogue needs a temporal analysis

*Mercer, N. (2008). The seeds of time: why classroom dialogue needs a temporal analysis.* Journal of the Learning Sciences *(Routledge),* 17, 1, 33–59.[1]

## Abstract

The process of teaching and learning in school has a natural long-term trajectory and cannot be understood only as a series of discrete educational events. Classroom talk plays an important role in mediating this long-term process, and in this article I argue that more attention should be given to the temporal dimension of classroom dialogue, both empirically and theoretically, if we are to appreciate how children gain an education from their classroom experience. I explore this topic using data from recent applied, interventional research in United Kingdom primary schools and examine how classroom talk is used to represent past shared experience, carry ideas forward from one occasion to another, approach future activities, and achieve learning outcomes. The article ends with a discussion of the theoretical, methodological, and educational implications of making this kind of temporal analysis.

> If you can look into the seeds of time
> And say which grain will grow and which will not
> Speak, then, to me . . .
> (*Macbeth*, Act 1, Scene 3)

In this article, I examine how the passage of time is embodied in classroom talk and how this embodiment contributes to the process of teaching and learning. I begin by elaborating this topic, arguing for its significance, discussing relevant prior research, and considering some methodological and theoretical issues involved in studying it. I then present the first of several transcripts from a related series of events and use an analysis of the transcribed talk to begin to explore these issues and discuss what is involved in making a temporal analysis. Following the consideration of more examples of talk involving both teacher–student and student–student dialogue, I draw conclusions about the importance of the temporal dimension for analyzing the discursive process of teaching and learning and discuss the theoretical and methodological developments that will be required if this topic is to be pursued.

Most of my research has been carried out in primary/elementary schools. In such schools, a teacher and the members of a class normally stay together for the whole of a school year. Their classroom life is organized into lessons that may be as short as half an hour or as long as two hours; but any one lesson usually represents part of a series dealing with a topic or a set of related topics, taking place at quite regular intervals. Moreover, although the efforts of the learners (and the teacher) in each lesson may be focused on specific learning outcomes, there is a cumulative quality to the educational process. Particular tasks will be set in the context of an overarching curriculum, some topics will take more than one session to pursue, and the achievement of some kinds of skills and understanding may be prerequisites for more advanced work. The treatment of topics and development of skills may be planned by teachers as a staged process.

As Douglas Barnes (1992) observed, "Most learning does not happen suddenly: we do not one moment fail to understand something and the next moment grasp it entirely" (p. 123). It is widely accepted that becoming educated is not simply a matter of accumulating information; it involves the gradual induction of students into new perspectives on the world and the development of new problem-solving skills and new ways of using language for representing knowledge and making sense of experience. In British schools, at least, some of the most important assessment is designed to test students' cumulative, integrated understanding of a subject and not just their recall of specific items from discrete lessons. From a student's perspective, school work should ideally have a cohesive, cumulative quality in which specific activities and their goals can be seen to form part of a greater whole, as part of a purposeful educational journey.

The continuity of personnel and the linking of the content of lessons can be expected to provide some coherence to children's experience of classroom education. However, for all students some discontinuity and incoherence will be inevitable, caused by such factors as absences of students from crucial lessons in a sequence; the use of inappropriate pedagogic strategies; students' difficulties in keeping up with the pace of activities; and the effects of lack of concentration, boredom, and distractions of many kinds. Bereiter (1997) highlighted the problems that may be caused by teachers and students pursuing goals that are based on different implicit time frames. Alexander (2000), Crook (1999), and several other educational researchers have argued that coherent knowledge and purposeful understanding will not naturally emerge for students from their continuous immersion in classroom life: They have to be pursued actively as pedagogic goals, through the use of appropriate teaching strategies. Language is our prime tool for making collective sense of experience, and the extent to which students will perceive cohesion and coherence in their classroom work may be heavily dependent on how dialogue mediates that activity. Talk with a teacher, and with other students, is perhaps the most important means for ensuring that a student's engagement in a series of activities contributes to his or her developing understanding of science, mathematics, or any other subject as a whole. In order to understand how classroom education succeeds and fails as a process for developing students' knowledge and understanding, we therefore need to understand the temporal relationship between the organization of teaching and learning as a series of lessons and activities and how it is enacted through talk. To put it another way: As learning is a process that happens over time, and learning is mediated through dialogue, we need to study dialogue over time to understand how learning happens and why certain learning outcomes result. We may then see more clearly how the precious resource of the time that a teacher and a class spend together can be used to good effect in the pursuit of children's education, or how it may be squandered.

The significance of the temporal dimension of discourse for the development of knowledge and understanding has been recognized by several researchers (e.g., Alexander, 2000, chapter 15; Cobb, 1999; Crook, 1999; Erickson, 1996; Issroff, 1999; Lemke, 2001; Nystrand, Wu, Gamorgan, Zeiser, & Long, 2003; Roth, 2001, 2005, 2006; Wells, 1999, chapter 3), but relatively few studies have expressly examined the relationship between time, talk, and learning in classroom life. One possible reason, as Littleton (1999) suggested, is that studying the dialogues of teaching and learning over an extended period of time poses serious methodological and theoretical challenges. As is apparent from one of the few studies of this topic (by Rasmussen, 2005, who analyzed the talk over some months in a Norwegian primary classroom), just gathering the relevant data requires the researcher's substantial commitment of his or her own time for continual recording and observation – and then some theoretical and methodological innovation is needed for the subsequent analysis.

Methodologically, there is little guidance available for studying the temporal development of talk, and not just within educational research. On consulting several excellent and well-regarded methodological texts representing various approaches including sociolinguistics, discursive psychology, conversation analysis, and systemic functional linguistics (Christie, 2002; Edwards & Westgate, 1994; Gee, 1999; Potter & Wetherell, 1994; ten Have, 1999), I found no substantial treatment of this topic. However, I found some useful advice in publications by Gee and Green (1998) and Scott, Mortimer, and Aguiar (2006). Gee and Green described one of the functions of talk as "connection building," whereby intertextual links are made by speakers in their joint meaning making. Following other researchers such as Bloome and Egan-Robertson (1993), they identified this as an important characteristic of classroom discourse and suggested that useful insights can be gained into how classroom talk functions by addressing such questions as the following:

> What sorts of connections (intertextual ties) are proposed, recognized, acknowledged, and interactionally made to previous or future interactions

(activity) and to texts, to other people, ideas, things, institutions and discourses outside the current interaction?

Which processes, practices and discourses do [speakers] draw on from previous events/situations to guide the actions in the current situation (e.g., text construction)?

(Gee & Green, 1998, p. 141)

Scott et al. (2006), reporting a study of talk in school science lessons, offered the following advice:

To understand the purpose of a specific teaching activity in a sequence of lessons it is necessary to determine how this particular activity fits with the whole sequence. . . . [Our] analysis of the discourse of science lessons involves an iterative process of moving backwards and forwards through time, trying to make sense of the episodes as linked chains of interactions.

(p. 610)

Also within an analysis of learning in science lessons, Roth (2006) offered the valuable insight that it is only by pursuing the trajectory of students' learning over time that an analyst can begin to recognize the potential significance of the apparent repetition of certain actions (such as procedures in a practical scientific investigation) as part of the learning process. The same act repeated cannot be assumed to be "the same" act in repetition, because it builds historically on the earlier event. This insight applies as much, of course, to the consideration of verbal acts – and so problematizes the use of categories such as "types of questions" and other atemporal coding schemes for studying the educational functions of discourse. The question "What causes rusting?" would have very different meanings and functions if asked by a science teacher in an introductory whole-class discussion before any work on oxidation had been done by the class, at the end of a series of group-based experiments, or in a revision session just before a public examination.

At a different level of analysis, Christie (1999) showed how teachers use talk to manage the timing and sequencing of events in the classroom. My own earlier research described discursive strategies commonly used by teachers to refer to past events and so consolidate relevant experience being shared with their students. For example, they use *recaps*, or summaries of what they consider to be the most salient features of a past event for the current activity (Edwards & Mercer, 1987; Mercer, 1995). Recaps can be *literal* or *reconstructive*, the latter being where the teacher "rewrites history," presenting a modified version of events that fits his or her current pedagogic concerns. Teachers also frequently use *elicitations* to activate students' recall about past events (e.g., "Who can tell me what they found out about the moon in the last lesson?"). It is common, too, for them to mark past shared experiences as significant and relevant by using *we statements* (as in "Remember when we looked at the map of Italy?"). In those ways teachers invoke common knowledge and highlight the continuities of educational experience, trying to draw students into a shared, cumulative, and progressive understanding of the activities in which they are engaged. In his influential research on culture and pedagogy, Alexander (2000, 2004) suggested that one indicator that teacher–student talk deserves to be called *dialogic* is that the teacher uses talk to provide a cumulative, continuing, contextual frame to enable students' involvement with the new knowledge they are encountering.

## A theoretical basis for the temporal analysis of educational dialogue

Not only methodological development, but also some theoretical development is required if we are to use a temporal analysis of classroom dialogue to understand the process of teaching and learning. As Roth (2006) pointed out, despite the significance of time and temporality as constituent aspects of human experience, learning theories generally do not take them into account. He commented:

> Learning theorists take an . . . atemporal perspective of learning, by mapping prior knowledge and subsequent knowledge in an atemporal space, much like mathematicians conduct mathematics in a space that has no time.
>
> (p. 234)

Within most psychological and educational research there is little recognition of how language really functions to allow the dialogic, temporal process of meaning making that is at the heart of education. It is only in linguistic research that we find a clearer conceptualization of how meaning is carried through time by language users, using such concepts as *intertextual referencing* (Agha & Wortham, 2005; Bloome & Egan-Robertson, 1993; Gee & Green, 1998; Shuart-Faris & Bloome, 2005) and *textual cohesion* (e.g., Christie, 2002; Gibbons, 2002; Martin & Rose, 2003). There is also relevant work under the heading of *indexicality* (Hanks, 2001; Silverstein & Urban, 1996). However, such research has not been concerned with understanding cognitive development or learning processes, or measuring educational outcomes, so although it offers useful concepts, they are not embedded in an appropriate theoretical framework. There is a gap in contemporary educational theory where there should be a conceptual framework for explaining "becoming educated" as a temporal, discursive, dialogic process.

An appropriate base for developing a theory of school-based learning as a temporal, dialogic process might be provided by the sociocultural perspective built upon the foundations of the work of Vygotsky (e.g., Daniels, 2001; Vygotsky, 1978; Wells & Claxton, 2002; Wertsch, 1984, 1985). Not only does this perspective recognize language as a key psychological and cultural tool, but also, as Lemke (2001) explained, "Sociocultural approaches to learning and development are not just about social interaction. . . . They are more significantly about the role of longer time-scale constancies and how they constrain, afford and intrude into moment-by-moment activity" (p. 19). Within sociocultural theory, the Vygotskian concept of the zone of proximal development figures prominently as a means for describing the way a child's intellectual capacity changes over time to reach new levels with the dialogic support or *scaffolding* of an adult or more capable peer (Vygotsky, 1978; Wertsch, 1984). But the zone of proximal development is essentially a static concept, representing an individual mental state at any point rather than a dynamic, dialogic process (as Wells, 1999, p. 102, also concluded). We need ways of describing how intersubjectivity (in the sociocultural sense of this term as used by Wertsch, 1984) is pursued, maintained, or lost in the course of classroom talk. In earlier work I introduced a new concept, the *intermental development zone* (IDZ), to focus on the way that a teacher and learner (or group of learners) can stay attuned to one another's changing states of knowledge and understanding over the course of an educational activity (Mercer, 2000, chapter 6). My aim was to conceptualize cognitive development and learning interactively – to understand teaching and learning as an intermental process. For a teacher to teach and a learner to learn, talk and joint activity must be used to create a shared communicative space, the IDZ, constructed from the resources of their common knowledge and shared purposes. In this intermental zone, which is reconstituted constantly as the dialogue continues, the teacher and learner(s) negotiate their way through the activity in which they are involved. My own metaphorical image of the IDZ is as a kind of bubble in which teacher and learner move through time. The IDZ thus represents the dynamic, reflexive maintenance of a purposeful, shared consciousness by a teacher and learner, focused on the task at hand and dedicated to the objective of learning. It is constructed in talk by explicit references to shared experience (present, past, and future) and common tasks and goals, but it can also be sustained by tacit invocations of common knowledge that may only be intelligible to the participants. Its existence is dependent on the contextualizing efforts of those involved. If their dialogue fails to keep participating minds mutually attuned and focused on the task, the IDZ bubble collapses, and the scaffolding of learning stops. Like the notions of the zone of proximal development and scaffolding (as introduced by Wood, Bruner, & Ross, 1976), the notion of the IDZ focuses attention on how a learner's understanding progresses under guidance through an activity, but it attends more to the dynamics of joint educational activity action and to the way that talk can be used to maintain intersubjectivity and pursue common purposes. For example, if during a problem-solving task in which a learner is having some difficulties a teacher appeals to the learner's memory of carrying out a previous task as being relevant to the task at hand, and if the learner then takes up this reference and draws some accurate comparisons between the old and new tasks in a way that indicates that the reference has been understood, we could infer that an IDZ was in existence. I illustrate the use of this concept through examples later.

In her recent research on children's talk during project work, Rasmussen (2005) used the concept of *participation trajectory* (adapted from the work of Dreier, 1999, 2003) to highlight the pattern of children's involvement in a particular, extended classroom activity from its inception to its conclusion some weeks later. The concept helps a researcher perceive a series of observed events as a journey for those involved, and so heightens sensitivity to continuities and discontinuities in children's educational experience. Dreier's (2003) own recommendation is that we should "move from studying how a person deals with one particular situation to how a person conducts his or her life in a trajectory of participation in and across social contexts (such) as one's home, school, workplace and so forth" (p. 21). The concept has also been used to good effect by Payler (2005) in her study of young children's transition from preschool to primary school, revealing how discontinuities in their educational experience, exacerbated by the different pedagogic approaches used by teachers in the two institutions, had significant effects on the quality of their participation and learning. However, although this concept very usefully encourages and enables a temporal focus on the social nature of learning, it is focused on individual patterns of involvement in social processes. The kind of trajectory with which I am concerned here is not of individual social actors moving across settings (such as home and school), but of speakers moving together through a series of related interactions within the same institution (school). It is not a participation trajectory, but a *dialogic trajectory*.

## Into the classroom

To provide a concrete basis for the rest of my discussion of temporality, I use several extracts of transcribed talk.[2] These all come from a series of lessons recorded in one primary classroom in southeast England over a period of 4 months as part of a recent project on talk and collaborative activity in science and math education in which several schools were involved (as reported in more detail in Dawes, 2004; Mercer & Sams, 2006; Mercer, Dawes, Wegerif, & Sams, 2004). The first is Extract 1, below. Please read it now, without further introduction, and consider what sense you can make of the observed event from the transcript alone.

### Extract 1: introductory whole-class session, March 18

TEACHER:  Before you go on to the next step
on the computer what do you need
to make sure that the whole group
has done? Oh! More hands up than
that. Emma?

EMMA:  Agreed.

| | |
|---|---|
| TEACHER: | Agreed. The whole group needs to agree. | *Teacher writes "everybody agrees" on board.* |
| | OK one of my speech bubbles. I wonder what kind of things we might hear each other saying during today's lesson? | *Teacher draws a speech bubble. Points to a child.* |
| AXEL: | What do you think? | |
| TEACHER: | What do you think? Anything else you might hear people saying as we have today's lesson? Kaye? | *Teacher writes "What do you think?" in speech bubble.* |
| KAYE: | What is your idea? | *Teacher draws a speech bubble and writes in it "What is your idea?"* |
| TEACHER: | Brilliant! What's your idea? Oh, Sydney? | |
| SYDNEY: | Why do you think that? | |
| TEACHER: | Excellent. Well done. Any other things we might hear people say? Rebecca? | *Teacher draws a speech bubble and writes "Why do you think that?"* |
| REBECCA: | I'm not too sure on that idea. What do you think? | |
| TEACHER: | Brilliant. Well done. What do we need to remember in our groups? Kiera? | *Teacher draws a new speech bubble.* |
| KIERA: | That everybody gets a turn to talk | |
| TEACHER: | Everybody gets a turn to talk. | *Teacher points to Anna.* |
| ANNA: | Everybody needs to share their opinions | |
| TEACHER: | Yeah – and are we all the same? | |
| CHILDREN: | No | |
| TEACHER: | Will there be someone in your group that perhaps wants to talk all the time? | |
| CHILDREN: | Yes. | |
| TEACHER: | Will there be someone in your group who doesn't want to talk at all? | |
| CLASS: | Yes! | |
| TEACHER: | How are you going to get that person who doesn't want to talk at all to say something? Shane? What do you think? How are you going to get that person who sits there and doesn't say anything to say something in your group? Help him out Tyber. | |

| | | |
|---|---|---|
| TYBER: | Ask them. | |
| TEACHER: | Ask them – brilliant. What about that person who talks *all* the time? | *Emphasizes "all."* |
| ALAN: | Tell him to shut up. | |
| TEACHER: | Ooh! Are you? I hope not because that's not positive language is it? What could you do to help them out? Kiera? | |
| KIERA: | Ask them and then ask somebody else and then ask the other person. | *Teacher silences an interruption with a gesture.* |
| TEACHER: | Brilliant. Making sure that you ask everybody in the group. Excellent. Kaye? | |

I expect that readers could make a good deal of sense of what was going on in the observed lesson from the transcript. For those who study classroom interaction, it would have many familiar linguistic features. A researcher's interpretation of a piece of conversational data will itself have a historical quality, as new data will be compared with past experience of similar language events. But to gain more than a superficial understanding of this extract as a representation of an educational event, some additional background information is needed. In a journal article such as this, I normally offer some information to readers in advance of the extract, as follows (with the precise content dependent on the focus of the article).

### Extract 1: background information

Extract 1 comes from the data of an interventional research project, set in English primary schools, and focuses on the development of children's use of spoken language as a tool for reasoning in science and mathematics. The participants were a teacher and her usual class of 10- to 11-year-olds, and the extract is part of the recording that was made of an introductory whole-class session to a math lesson. The children were sitting in groups of three or four at their tables, looking toward the teacher, who was standing at the front of the class. In the series of lessons we were recording, the teacher was expressly concerned not only with children's learning of the curriculum (and in particular science and math), but also with the development of the children's abilities to talk, reason, and work well together in groups. As part of the project intervention, she had worked with members of the research team in the previous weeks to set up a programme of activities called *Thinking Together* (Dawes, Mercer, & Wegerif, 2003) for raising the children's awareness of how they talked and worked in groups. This was the sixth in a series of lessons in which the use of talk for reasoning had been given special attention. In the previous one (which we also recorded), she had discussed with children how they could most effectively work together to solve problems, drawing on the concept of *Exploratory Talk* that had been developed through earlier phases of this research from the work of Barnes and Todd (1977). Exploratory Talk is

> discussion in which partners engage critically but constructively with each other's ideas. Relevant information is offered for joint consideration. Proposals may be challenged and counter-challenged, but if so reasons are given and alternatives are offered. Agreement is sought as a basis for joint progress. Knowledge is made publicly accountable and reasoning is visible in the talk.
>
> (Mercer, 2000, p. 98)

In that previous lesson, the teacher had drawn from her discussion with her class the following three points, writing them up on the board as she did so:

1 Members of groups should seek agreement before making decisions.
2 Group members should ask each other for their ideas and opinions ("What do you think?").
3 Group members should give reasons for their views, and be asked for them if appropriate ("Why do you think that?").

She then put up on the wall of the classroom a set of *ground rules for talk*, which represented the essence of Exploratory Talk and which had been elaborated in the earlier teacher-led whole-class discussion of talking in groups. The notion of ground rules for talk, like that of Exploratory Talk, is an element of the Thinking Together programme based on earlier research (e.g., Edwards & Mercer, 1987; Mercer, 1995) and had been introduced to the teacher by the researchers. These rules were as follows:

**Our ground rules for talk**

We share our ideas and listen to one another.
We talk one at a time.
We respect each others' opinions.
We give reasons to explain our ideas.
If we disagree we try to ask "why?"
We always try to agree at the end.

There were thus two types of objectives devised by the teacher for this lesson, concerned with the study of mathematics and with encouraging the use of Exploratory Talk. Immediately after this introductory plenary, the children began to work on math problems together in small groups using a computer programme called *Function Machine*. Their math objective was to work out how to solve the problem of what function had been applied to each number they put in to the "machine" by considering the number that it produced as an output. The specific talk objective was to use the ground rules in doing this task, related to the broader objective (pursued over a series of lessons) of developing skills for effective collaboration. Just before the start of Extract 1, the teacher had written both objectives on the board and explained them.

As the background information above explains, members of the research team had been involved in the planning that generated the educational content for this extract. This meant that the researchers were involved in its history and so, rather unusually, we could draw on past experience shared with the teacher when making sense of what was said and done. We were thus able to infer that in her talk the teacher is drawing directly upon prior experience shared with her class. She uses questions to draw out from the children not only relevant comments on how they should interact, but also a collective recall of previous lessons – and most specifically, to establish a shared understanding of the ground rules for talk. We can see her characteristic teacher's use of *we* in this respect: "What do we need to remember in our groups?" She elicits *models of speech acts* that would represent an appropriate use of the ground rules to which they have agreed: the phrases "What do you think?" and "Why do you think that?" She then encodes these models in the more permanent language mode of writing (her "speech bubbles"), which could then travel through time as a shared resource for the class as they pursue their activity.

Several of the teacher's questions signify temporality, for example the following:

- "Before you go on to the next step on the computer what do you need to make sure that the whole group has done?"
- "I wonder what kind of things we might hear each other saying during today's lesson?"
- "Will there be someone in your group that perhaps wants to talk all the time?"

These utterances seem designed to highlight for students the ways that knowledge gained in past activity can be used to anticipate future needs. This one extract therefore shows a teacher using talk to attempt to build the future of her students' educational experience on the foundations of their shared history. Before we leave Extract 1, please note one of the teacher's last remarks ("I hope not because that's not positive language is it?") because I discuss it later.

## The temporal context of classroom talk

Talk that mediates joint intellectual activity poses a considerable methodological challenge for a discourse analyst, because any interaction has two aspects, both of which have a temporal quality: a *historical aspect* and a *dynamic aspect*. Historically, the interaction will be located within a particular institutional and cultural context. Speakers' relationships also have histories. Things that are said may invoke knowledge from the joint past experience of those interacting (e.g., their recall of previous activities they have pursued together) or from the rather different kind of common knowledge that is available to people who have had similar, though separate, past experiences. (For example, two people conversing who had studied linguistics at the same university could safely assume much shared understanding of both the subject and the locations in which it was studied, even if they had not been contemporaries.)

The dynamic aspect refers to the fact that conversations are not planned, they emerge. Speakers' contributions are contingent on what their partners say, and speakers will not even know in advance exactly what they are going to say and for how long they will speak (Roth, 2006, p. 251). The basis of common knowledge upon which shared understanding depends is constantly being developed as participants in a continuing conversation interact. The nature of the shared knowledge being invoked in any dialogue is therefore potentially quite complex. It is in a state of flux, as immediate shared experiences and corresponding conversational content provide the resources for building the temporal foundations of future talk. A profound problem for researchers concerned with the joint construction of knowledge (and, indeed, with understanding how conversational communication works at all) is inferring what knowledge resources speakers are using. Speakers may make explicit references to shared past experience or other types of common knowledge, but they often invoke such historical, temporal resources only implicitly. As Littleton (1999) commented, "Observable interactions are likely to have unobservable determinants in the histories of individuals, groups and institutions" (p. 182). Lemke (2001) likewise observed, "Time is not Galilean in such systems; the longer term, the nonproximate event, may be more relevant to the next move than the immediately preceding event" (p. 23). However, we can only deal with this phenomenon in a partial, limited fashion by sampling discourse over time and by drawing in our analysis on any resources of knowledge we share with the speakers.

We also need to take into account that educational dialogue in classrooms is a cultural artifact, and its special nature is embodied in its distinctive, functional qualities as a speech genre (or set of genres) that has been so well described by generations of classroom researchers. As I mentioned earlier, some characteristic features of that genre, such as teachers' recaps, are designed to invoke knowledge from the joint past experience of those interacting (i.e., their recall of previous activities they have pursued together).

To make educational sense of a particular classroom interaction, then, it would help to know not only what happened within the interaction, but also what happened before it, what the participants were expecting to happen, and what they learned from it. That is, it would be useful to have information about the following:

1  *The shared history of the participants.* It helps to know whether a teacher and a class have worked together before, if there have been previous lessons on this topic, and if the students have encountered this particular kind of task before (and so could be expected by the teacher to have some relevant past experience). This can, and should, strongly influence an analyst's interpretation of the meaning and significance of utterances for the participants – for example regarding the function of questions in which the teacher appears to be seeking information from the learner (i.e., are these stimulated recall questions, or attempts to gauge the understanding of a learner with whom the teacher is unfamiliar?). Access to recordings of prior lessons could thus be a crucial resource. However, it is not a comprehensive history of an event or the shared experience of the participants that analysts need, but rather those aspects of shared knowledge that the participants treat as relevant to their current task and so invoke in their dialogue. For instance, in Extract 1, the teacher's question "What do you need to make sure that the whole group has done?" would have a very different meaning for members of a class who have spent a previous lesson discussing what a group should do to work effectively than for those of a class that was just beginning to do so on this occasion. The very same teacher elicitation could, depending on the local history of the exchange, invoke very different kinds of responses from a student. This issue also relates to the next point.

2  *The temporal development of the dialogue.* We not only need background information about shared experience prior to the observed event, we also want information about the progress of the talk itself. A conversation is like a sophisticated type of dual-control (or multi-control) track-laying vehicle: Its participating "drivers" use the history of their encounter to build the foundations for its future path as it proceeds. Conversations run on contextual tracks made of common knowledge (as discussed in more detail in Mercer, 2000, chapters 2 and 3).

In their seminal study of classroom talk, Barnes and Todd (1977) explained how when a group of children are working together

> meanings for what is going on in the conversation are constructed not from any one utterance on its own, but from cycles of utterances, perhaps over quite lengthy sections of the interaction. Now these cycles are not readily isolable: they adhere to the interaction between utterances, and the speaker-hearer's intentions for, and interpretation of, these utterances. When we analyze talk, what we are trying to do is to feel our way into the meanings the participants made for the interaction as it happened. But the meanings which the participants made were not stable. They were fluid and changing, built up out of the existing knowledge and expectations which they brought to the

situation, along with their own implicit summary of what went on in the conversation, and their reaction to that summary. Meanings change in the course of on-going events in the conversation, which lead to a reinterpretation of what has gone on so far.

(p. 17)

This dynamic aspect of conversational interaction is what Gee (1999) called its *reflexivity*. It is the historically cumulative, reflexive nature of conversation that requires "explicitness" to be treated as a relative concept, because speakers need only be as explicit as is necessary for effective communication (Grice, 1975). If people conversing share a relatively advanced understanding of a technical subject, much basic knowledge about it can be left implicit, even if the relevant knowledge has been gained quite separately by the participants. They also build joint semantic resources for implicit reference as they continue to interact. Of course, speakers do not necessarily follow Gricean maxims. Inappropriate judgements about explicitness are a common source of misunderstandings, in classrooms as in other settings. A temporal perspective may help us understand this problematic aspect of the joint construction of knowledge.

3   *The trajectory of the event.* As well as the history of the event, it would also help to have some information about how participants perceive its projected future. For example, do the participants know that they have up to an hour or so to spend together on the problem, or is this event jointly perceived as a brief encounter? Is there evidence of a shared perception of the trajectory among participants? Is there any evidence that the educational activity is regarded as part of a longer educational journey, or is it seen as a "one-off" event?

4   *The educational outcomes of the event.* The goal of some research into language and social interaction may be no more than an understanding of the nature of the process observed. But for educational researchers like myself, there is also usually an interest in the educational value of any teaching-and-learning interaction. To put it bluntly, I often want to know if there is evidence that any students have been educated as a result of the dialogue I observe. I might also want to explain why participation in the same educational, discursive events has apparently led to different educational outcomes among students. One way of exploring this is to track back from observable outcomes through the history of those events.

Of course, as researchers we will never have all of the information we might want for making a temporal analysis, but that does not justify ignoring the information that we can obtain. We can make efforts to gain some of it by observing and recording series of events over time, rather than single events; by talking to the participants; and by gathering other kinds of documentary data such as timetables, teachers' lesson plans, students' work, and so on. And to use this information effectively, we also need a clear conceptualization of educational dialogue as a temporal process.

## Back to the classroom

We now return to the primary classroom that figured in Extract 1. Extract 2 (below) took place 10 days later, on the next occasion when that class was recorded. Again, it is taken from whole-class session at the start of a lesson, before the children began a group-based activity.

*Extract 2: introductory whole-class session, March 29*

| | | |
|---|---|---|
| TEACHER: | Can you remember what we had to sort in our science lesson? | |
| ANNA: | Food. | |
| TEACHER: | Food. Brilliant! We had to sort it into different categories didn't we? This time we're going to be sorting numbers. So that's our objective – sorting numbers. | *Writes this objective on board.* |
| | I'm going to work with Donal and Alan today and in my group I've decided I'm going to sort the numbers by multiples of three, and I don't care what they think. What's the matter Maya? | *Teacher takes on role of child with grumpy expression.* |
| MAYA: | You should, um, decide as a group. | |
| TEACHER: | Oh super. There's one of our ground rules already, "Decide as a group." OK. How am I going to do that? Because I want to sort my numbers by multiples of three. How am I going to make sure that we decide that as a group? | *Writes "Decide as a group" on board.* |
| KIERA: | Ask them what they think. Also, when you ask what they think, don't turn your back on them because that's not positive body language. | *Teacher writes "Ask them what they think."* |
| TEACHER: | You mentioned positive body language. What other type of language do we need to make sure is positive? Not just our body language – come on Sydney – join in please. What other sort of language do we need to make sure is positive? | |
| CHILD: | The way we talk. | |
| TEACHER: | The way we talk! Am I going to say "I'm going to sort these in multiples of three!"? | |

| | |
|---|---|
| CHILD: | No. |
| TEACHER: | Maya, what would you say if you were in my situation? |
| MAYA: | Um, "I want to sort them by multiples of three. What do you think about it?" |
| TEACHER: | That would be a good thing to say. [*and then a little later*] |

| | | |
|---|---|---|
| TEACHER: | OK, as I'm wandering around the classroom and looking and watching and listening to what you are doing, I wonder what sort of things I might hear you saying. Go on. Tell your partner one thing you might say. Bernice, can you tell Sydney? And . . . stop! Ready? Looking this way. Donal's group. Share one of the things I might hear you say. | *Children talk to each other.* |
| DONAL: | What do you think? | |
| TEACHER: | What do you think? Brilliant – Emma? | *Emphasizes the word "you" and writes "What do you think?" on board.* |
| EMMA: | Why do you think that? | |
| TEACHER: | Why do you think that? That's another good one, not just what but why do you think that? Brilliant. | *Writes "Why do you think that?" on board.* |

There is a familiar quality about the opening sequence of Extract 2. As in Extract 1, the teacher is beginning a whole-class session by checking the students' recall of how they are expected to work in a group. She begins this session with an appeal to the children's memory of past activity by making an intertextual link to earlier dialogue: "Can you remember what we had to sort in our science lesson?" This appeal is responded to accordingly by one of the students. We can see here an exemplification of both the historical aspect and the dynamic aspect of classroom talk, as participants draw on their shared past experience to build the contextual foundations for their continuing interaction. As I mentioned earlier, an elicitation of this kind is one of several dialogic tools teachers commonly use to try to help children see the continuity of educational experience and to encourage them to recall knowledge of past events that is relevant to current or future activity.

The teacher provides positive feedback on Anna's response ("Food") and then recaps the previous activity: "We had to sort it into different categories didn't we?" In contrast, her next remark is future oriented: "This time we are going to be sorting numbers. So that's our objective – sorting numbers." By invoking the generic category of sorting, she marks as similar two class-room activities (one past and one in the immediate future) that might have seemed quite disparate to the students. Drawing on such shared experiential resources a teacher can use dialogue to set up and maintain an IDZ (as discussed earlier) to support learning, enabling participants to take a shared perspective on a task and pursue common (or at least compatible) goals. This may help students to perceive a series of activities as stages on a learning journey rather than as disconnected events.

Next, the teacher makes a very different kind of statement: "I'm going to work with Donal and Alan today and in my group I've decided I'm going to sort the numbers by multiples of three, and I don't care what they think." She is role-playing a child, and this seems an unusual kind of teacher-talk. But we see that Maya responds in a way that the teacher treats as appropriate – the flow of the interaction is smoothly maintained. Maya's response, "You should, um, decide as a group," shows that she is familiar with the teacher's rhetorical strategy and understands its pedagogic function. Her response also shows that she realizes that this dramatic characterization is not a diversion from the current topic, but an illustration of a transgression of the ground rules – and so demands a critical comment. The fact that the teacher and student can go directly into this role playing, without any explicit introduction, illustrates particularly well the historically contextualized, reflexive nature of talk in classrooms. The collaborative success of this bit of dialogue suggests that an IDZ is being maintained: Both teacher and student are operating within a shared frame of reference that supports the pursuit of the problem set by the teacher.

Later in the extract the teacher asks, "How am I going to make sure that we decide that together as a group?" Kiera's response, "Ask them what they think," paraphrases what the teacher had written up in a speech bubble in the earlier lesson (and that is now included as a permanent notice with the ground rules for talk on the classroom wall). Kiera then goes on to mention the need for "positive body language." The teacher picks this up and highlights "(an)other type of language" that "we need to make sure is positive." As earlier observers of this class, we can infer that a routine has been established for opening these lessons – an inference we can check against our data. We also see here the use by a child of a term (*positive language*) used by the teacher at the very end of Extract 1. It is very unlikely that a child's use of such a special term has any source but the teacher, and our historical data support the interpretation of this as appropriation by the child.

We next go to another introductory plenary session, a month later. The teacher is asking the children for comments on how they will work together.

### Extract 3: introductory whole-class session, April 26

TEACHER:   What would happen if I didn't check everyone agrees with the idea? I wonder what would happen – Emma? [*her reply is inaudible*] Yes, you'd be dominating the group. You'd be making decisions that not everybody perhaps has had a chance to think through.

LUKE:      Positive body language.
TEACHER:   What was that one you just said? Positive body language. Brilliant. That's not something I'm going to hear is it? No – it's something I can see. How do I see positive body language Donal?
DONAL:     Looking at people and then you can see if they are nodding.
TEACHER:   If you are looking at somebody it's going to be much more polite and show more respect than if you've got your back to somebody when they are talking.

We see here again the use of the term *positive body language*, reappearing like an echo of lessons past. It is a special term, a piece of technical vocabulary for talking about talk as a topic of study, that provides lexical evidence of the historical continuity of the dialogue in this class as a microcommunity of discourse. In these ways, we see that the talk of each lesson can be considered as a part of one long conversation among the members of this class (Maybin, 2005). The repetition of the term *positive body language* is a *cohesive tie* (Halliday & Hasan, 1976), linking the talk of the series of lessons into one extended text. A search for the word *positive* in all of the talk data for this class showed that there were just two instances of a child using the term collocated with the word *language* – in Extracts 2 and 3, in whole-class sessions. The teacher used it five times, always collocated with *language*, in two of the five recorded lessons. There was no recorded evidence of children taking up this expression and making active use of it in their groups without the teacher, though as reflection on ways of talking was not ever specified as part of such activity this is not surprising. However, Donal's explanation of the term suggests that its meaning is commonly understood. We therefore have some temporal evidence of this class developing *through* educational dialogue a shared vocabulary for talking *about* educational dialogue.

## Talk among students

So far, I have only presented extracts from teacher-led, whole-class sessions. But of course educational dialogues also take place among children, and such dialogues were a prime focus of attention in the research that provided the data I am using. In British schools, as in many other countries, students are commonly put into groups to carry out activities of a problem-solving type. But what sense do they make of the injunction to "work together," and to what extent are their expectations shaped by the teacher's instructions, examples, and guidance? Research in British schools by myself and colleagues over more than a decade supports the view that a shared understanding about how to talk and work effectively in groups is rare among primary children (Mercer, 1995, 2000; Mercer & Littleton, 2007; Wegerif & Scrimshaw, 1997). Talk during group work that could be described as "exploratory" is not common: Talk more commonly resembles the competitive and uncooperative argumentation we have called *disputational talk* or the friendly but uncritical discussion we have called *cumulative talk*. Examples of explicit reasoning, and of co-reasoning, as exemplified by the use of requests for information, challenges, and attempts to seek agreement, are hard to find. It was on the basis of such observations that we designed the interventional Thinking Together programme, in which teachers were encouraged to raise children's awareness of how they used talk to get things done, to set up ground rules for talk, and to guide and model the use of Exploratory Talk.

The next three extracts all come from group activities in the same classroom and the same series of lessons, when students were working together in groups of three without the teacher. The first, Extract 4, is from a group activity that directly followed Extract 2, the plenary on March 29. Three children are working together on math problems in which they have been given a series of numbers with one of the series missing and have to work out the missing number. At the point the extract begins, they are starting a new problem. Alan is making the first guess at what the missing item might be. The bold parts of the text relate to my subsequent comments.

### Extract 4: group work, March 29

| ALAN: | Four. **What do you think?** |
|---|---|
| MUJ: | Yes, four |
| NEERAN: | Is fifteen a multiple of four? No four fours are sixteen. |
| ALAN: | Yes it is. No. No. |
| MUJ: | No |
| ALAN: | Is nine? |
| MUJ: | No |
| NEERAN: | **Why do you think that?** |
| ALAN: | Because it goes four, eight then twelve, so it misses nine out. |

In Extract 4, we see Alan and Neeran asking "What do you think?" and "Why do you think that?" These are literal reproductions of the model questions put up on the board by the teacher in a previous lesson (as explained earlier in the section "Extract 1: Background Information") and provided by other children (Donal and Emma) as responses to the teacher in Extract 2. Now it might be expected that such questions would be commonly heard in group activity in any primary classroom; they are, after all, no more than everyday phrases with everyday meanings. However, the observational research mentioned above suggests that such an expectation is not justified. The kind of dialogue we have called Exploratory Talk is rare, and so are questions such as "What do you think?", "Why do you think that?", and "Do you agree?" that are associated with it. Moreover, preintervention recordings made in the classroom that provided the data used here were consistent with those observations. It is therefore a reasonable inference that the children in Extract 4 are following the class's ground rules for talk that were established around a month ago. Alan and Neeran's questions illustrate what I have called the historical aspect of dialogue: They index the past experience of the class as a community of inquiry (Wells, 1999). This gives them a different meaning than if they were uttered in another class where no special preparation for thinking together in groups had taken place. Their function is not only to carry forward the discussion, but also to invoke agreed norms for behavior within this community. In that sense the ground rules have shaped what I have called the dynamic aspect of the talk, and they provide resources for the maintenance of an IDZ. The talk embodies prior learning by the children about the use of language as a cultural and cognitive tool, and it can also be seen to embody the teacher's objectives for this series of lessons, as described in the earlier section "Extract 1: Background Information," for developing effective collaboration in groups. The available temporally extended data thus provide information about the dialogic trajectory of activity in this class. An analysis of educational dialogue that took no account of the temporal dimension, with its historical and dynamic aspects, could provide only a relatively impoverished understanding of what was going on in Extract 4 and would have little useful to say about what learning was expected of the children and what had been learned.

The next two transcripts are from the activity of two different groups in the same class. Extract 5 was recorded almost a month after Extract 4; the final example, Extract 6, was recorded slightly more than a month after that. In both cases the children are involved in solving a math problem in which they have to select an appropriate number to enter into a computer-based calculation. I present them and comment on them together. Again, bold text relates to my comments, which follow.

### Extract 5: group work, April 26

| | |
|---|---|
| KYLIE: | Let's just try a smaller number. **Who agrees we try a smaller number? I agree** (*Tony and Maya raise their hands*) |
| REBECCA: | I don't |
| KYLIE: | So – what number? Maya, you choose a number |
| MAYA: | Six |
| KYLIE: | **Do we all agree on six?** Tony and Maya? Yes Rebecca? |
| REBECCA: | No, try that other one |
| KYLIE: | We are! **Do you agree on six?** |
| REBECCA: | No |
| KYLIE: | **Why?** |

### Extract 6: group work, June 7

| | |
|---|---|
| SOFIA: | Five, seven and five equals twelve. So put five. |
| BEAU: | **Do you agree?** |
| KIRSTY: | Yes, and then we need to sort this out. (*and then a little later*) |

SOFIA:   I know, **why don't we use the seven again?**
KIRSTY:  **What do we do now?**
SOFIA:   **What do you think** we should do?
KIRSTY:  I don't know, it's too hard. I have never done this before.
BEAU:    I haven't done this before.
SOFIA:   **What can we remember?** A blank square. All I can remember is numbers. Eight add one is nine.

In these two extracts we again see children using questions such as "What do you think?" and "Do you agree?," which can be traced directly back to the establishment of the ground rules in their class (by now several months earlier). We can also see them use other related but different expressions: "Who agrees we try a smaller number?," "What do we do now?," and "What can we remember?" These can be read as evidence that they have not followed the ground rules only in a mechanistic way, by simply parroting the model speech acts offered by the teacher, but rather they have learned how to apply the rules in an appropriate, creative way in their discussions. In Extract 6, Sofia's final remark, "What can we remember?," is interesting in itself, from a temporal perspective, because it is an appeal to the relevant shared knowledge of her group gained through earlier classroom activities, which might allow them to "re-cognize" (as Roth, 2006, put it) the apparently new problem they are facing.

A temporal analysis supports the claim that the nature and quality of the children's discussion in Extracts 5 and 6 has been shaped by past events, namely the whole-class and small-group sessions of the Thinking Together lessons in which their teacher established the ground rules for talk and guided the development of their skills in using language as a tool for reasoning. I present here only specific examples, but the programme of research from which these data come has shown that the relative incidence of children's use of talk of an "exploratory" kind increases significantly in the experimental classrooms where the Thinking Together programme has been implemented, becoming much more frequent than in matching control classes (as assessed by methods described in Mercer, 2004; Wegerif & Mercer, 1997). That research has also provided quantitative evidence of significant pre/postintervention improvements in problem solving and curriculum learning in science and math for children whose teachers implemented the programme (as reported for the project that included the class represented in the current article in Dawes, 2004; Mercer et al., 2004; Mercer & Sams, 2006). In contrast with the findings of some other similar interventional research (notably Hogan, 1999), we have therefore demonstrated that raising children's awareness of how they use language to reason collectively helps them to reason more effectively as individuals. Moreover, a close examination of the talk data has enabled us to track the temporal development of the dialogue within particular groups of children as they attempted to solve problems, so that we could see how their deliberations led to correct or incorrect solutions. This means that we have independent evidence that children's appropriation of the ground rules does not merely induce a superficial form of verbal behaviour, but helps them use language more effectively as a tool for thinking, collectively and alone.

By examining both the process and the outcomes of the extended dialogues of teachers and children, it is possible to draw more valid and useful conclusions about the significance of classroom interaction than if the analysis is focused only on processes (as is often the case in sociolinguistic research and conversation analysis) or only on outcomes (as is often the case in more psychological, experimental-style investigations). In this particular case, the qualitative, temporal analysis of talk had a crucial role, when used in complement with quantitative measures of outcomes, in explaining how teachers can effectively help develop children's skills in using language as a cultural and cognitive tool.

## Discussion

I have used data from an interventional classroom research project in this article, but not to argue for the effectiveness of a particular intervention. Rather, I have used those data to illustrate my argument that the relationship between time, talk, and learning is intrinsically important to classroom education and deserves further exploration. The coherence of educational experience is dependent on talk among participants, and so analyses of the ways that their continuing shared experience is represented and the ways that talk itself develops and coheres over an extended period are required if we are to understand the process of teaching and learning.

Concepts such as reflexivity, intertextuality, dialogic trajectory, and IDZ, as discussed earlier, can be used to highlight the interactional, dynamic, self-contextualizing nature of classroom education. In broader terms, a sociocultural perspective provides an appropriate theoretical base for developing a more temporally sensitive understanding of teaching and learning. But stronger conceptual links need to be built between the different levels of human activity identified by sociocultural theory – the cultural, the psychological, and the social – so that we do not treat the cultural context of educational activity as static and given, but explain how it is sustained and renewed through the creative activities of people in conversation and embodied in the products of joint intellectual endeavor (cf. Sawyer, 2001). Making progress will require taking account of what Lemke (2001) has called the "multiple timescales" of human social activity, development, and learning, so that we are "as willing to look at biography and history as at situations and moments, as methodologically and theoretically prepared to study institutions and communities as to study students and classrooms" (p. 25).

Methodologically, we need better ways of analyzing classroom talk as a continuing, social mode of thinking, ways that reveal how the joint construction of knowledge is achieved over time. Talk that mediates continuing joint intellectual activity poses a considerable methodological challenge for a discourse analyst because of its reflexivity. I have suggested that every conversational interaction has a historical aspect and a dynamic aspect. Historically, the interaction is located within a particular institutional and cultural context, and speakers' relationships also have local and more specific histories. Speakers may invoke any knowledge from the past experience of all those interacting, whether gained separately or jointly. The dynamic aspect refers to the fact that talk is inherently reflexive: its contextual base is in a constant state of flux, as immediate shared experiences and corresponding conversational content provide the resources for building future conversational context. A key problem for researchers concerned with explaining how talk is used for the joint construction of knowledge (or, indeed, with understanding how conversational communication functions at all) is understanding how speakers build contextual foundations for their talk. We can only do this in a partial, limited fashion, by sampling their discourse over time and by drawing in our analysis on any resources of common knowledge we share with the speakers. But however difficult it may be to find a solution, the problem cannot be avoided. We need to reveal how the joint construction of knowledge is achieved by participants over time, because the process of teaching and learning depends on the development of a foundation of common knowledge.

A temporal analysis can help us see how students' ideas change through the extended process of interaction with a teacher and other students, and how new concepts, ways of using language, and ways of solving problems are appropriated. Although my focus has been on talk, my argument for the significance of the temporal dimension in the study of educational events and processes has a wider relevance, with implications for the kind of information we need to gather. If, as researchers, we want to appreciate the educational value of an observed interaction between a teacher and a class of students, we should seek available information about what happened before that interaction and what happened subsequently. It would also be helpful to know what the participants expected from the event and to make some assessment of what the students learned from it. This is no more than common sense, but it is nevertheless not consistent with some research methodologies. Analytic methods that do not recognize or deal with the temporal development of talk, its reflexivity, and its cohesive nature over longer timescales than one episode or lesson will inevitably fail to capture the essence of the educational process. Methods for analyzing discourse in which the analyst simply attends to the relationship between contributions made by participants in one recorded conversation, without applying available information about previous related interactions and historically contextual knowledge shared by participants (as seems to be advocated by some conversation analysts; e.g., Schegloff, 1997), will not work. The use of coding schemes in which utterances with the same syntactic form and/ or explicit content are taken to have the same pragmatic or semantic value, regardless of their location in the temporal sequence of communication, is also inappropriate. And rather than trying, in the interests of objectivity, to distance ourselves as analysts from the perspectives of those inside in the long conversations of teaching and learning, we should rather try to gain access to the relevant interpretative knowledge used by those insiders. As Roth (2001) said, in advocating the dual role of teacher–researcher, knowing a school culture from the inside allows researchers to appropriate participants' competence systems and so enables a richer interpretation of observed language and events.

Teachers use talk to sow seeds from which, in time, may grow the understanding of their students. Dialogues with teachers, and with their fellows, enable students to consolidate and develop their understanding over time, so that they can build new understanding upon the foundations of past experience. Good teachers will almost certainly conceptualize a learning trajectory for their students, albeit implicitly, and will know how dialogue can be used to transform this conception into social action. Some other teachers, and many of those training to be teachers, may not fully realize that they are responsible for the temporal cohesion of the educational experience of their students and lack skill in acting out this responsibility. They might be helped by being offered practical insights into this aspect of classroom dialogue. As educational researchers, we need to understand more about the temporal processes and outcomes of educational dialogues, because only then will we be able to help teachers to see how the resource of the time they spend with their students can be used to best effect.

## Notes

1 The data examples used in this article are from the project Language, Thinking and ICT in the Primary Curriculum, which was financed by Grant EDU/00169/G from the Nuffield Foundation. The research was carried out by Lyn Dawes, Steve Higgins, Claire Sams, Rupert Wegerif, and myself. The participation in this research of teachers and children in Milton Keynes schools, and the support of Milton Keyne Borough Council and the Nuffield Foundation, are acknowledged with thanks. I am extremely grateful for the constructive comments on earlier drafts of this article provided by Lyn Dawes, Judith Kleine Staarman, Karen Littleton, and Ingvill Rasmussen; and many thanks to Caroline Coffin, Janet Maybin, Karen Littleton, and Ian Wilkinson for providing valuable bibliographic resources and references for exploring the topic of temporality. The reviewers for the *Journal of the Learning Sciences* also helped the development of this article by providing very clear and useful comments.
2 The transcripts used here were taken from video recordings of a series of lessons (each about 45 min long) that were videorecorded in one teacher's class in a primary school in southeast England. I used a very simple transcription format, in which speech is rendered as grammatical phrases and sentences, to represent the sense that I, as a researcher with access to the raw data, made of what was said. Information about nonverbal aspects of communication judged pertinent to the analysis is included in a third column (or in parentheses). My judgement was that the inclusion of additional information at my disposal, such as length of pauses or other prosodic and contextual details, would be distracting to readers and irrelevant to the issues I am addressing.

# References

Agha, A., & Wortham, A. (Eds.). (2005). Discourse across speech-events: Intertextuality and interdiscursivity in social life [Special issue]. *Journal of Linguistic Anthropology, 15*(1).

Alexander, R. (2000). *Culture and pedagogy: International comparisons in primary education*. Oxford, UK: Blackwell.

Alexander, R. (2004). *Towards dialogic teaching: Rethinking classroom talk*. Cambridge, UK: Dialogos.

Barnes, D. (1992). The role of talk in learning. In K. Norman (Ed.), *Thinking voices: The work of the National Oracy Project* (pp. 123–128). London: Hodder & Stoughton.

Barnes, D., & Todd, F. (1977). *Communication and learning in small groups*. London: Routledge & Kegan Paul.

Bereiter, C. (1997). Situated cognition and how to overcome it. In D. Kirschner & J. Whitson (Eds.), *Situated cognition: Social, semiotic and psychological perspectives* (pp. 281–300). Hillsdale, NJ: Erlbaum.

Bloome, D., & Egan-Robertson, A. (1993). The social construction of intertextuality and classroom reading and writing. *Reading Research Quarterly, 28*, 303–333.

Christie, F. (1999). The pedagogic device and the teaching of English. In F. Christie (Ed.), *Pedagogy and the shaping of consciousness* (pp. 156–184). London: Continuum Press.

Christie, F. (2002). *Classroom discourse analysis: A functional perspective*. London: Continuum Press.

Cobb, P. (1999). Individual and collective mathematical learning: The case of statistical data analysis. *Mathematical Thinking and Learning, 18*(1), 46–48.

Crook, C. (1999). Computers in the community of classrooms. In K. Littleton & P. Light (Eds.), *Learning with computers: Analysing productive interaction* (pp. 102–117). London: Routledge.

Daniels, H. (2001). *Vygotsky and pedagogy*. London: Routledge/Falmer.

Dawes, L. (2004). Talk and learning in classroom science. *International Journal of Science Education, 26*, 677–695.

Dawes, L., Mercer, N., & Wegerif, R. (2003). *Thinking together: A programme of activities for developing speaking, listening and thinking skills for children aged 8–11*. Birmingham, UK: Imaginative Minds.

Dreier, O. (1999). Personal trajectories of participation across contexts of social practice. *Outlines: Critical Social Studies, 1*, 5–32.

Dreier, O. (2003). Learning in personal trajectories of participation. In N. Stephenson, H. Radtke, R. Jorna, & H. Stam (Eds.), *Theoretical psychology: Critical contributions* (pp. 20–29). Concord, Canada: Captus University Publications.

Edwards, A. D., & Westgate, D. (1994). *Investigating classroom talk* (2nd ed.). London: Falmer Press.

Edwards, D., & Mercer, N. (1987). *Common knowledge: The development of understanding in the classroom*. London: Methuen/Routledge.

Erickson, F. (1996). Going for the zone: The social and cognitive ecology of teacher-student interaction in classroom conversations. In D. Hicks (Ed.), *Discourse, learning and schooling* (pp. 29–62). Cambridge, UK: Cambridge University Press.

Gee, J. P. (1999). *An introduction to discourse analysis: Theory and method*. London: Routledge.

Gee, J. P., & Green, J. (1998). Discourse analysis, learning and social practice: A methodological study. *Review of Research in Education, 23*, 119–169.

Gibbons, P. (2002). *Scaffolding language, scaffolding learning: Teaching second language learners in the mainstream classroom.* Portsmouth, NH: Heinemann.

Grice, H. (1975). Logic and conversation. In P. Cole & J. Morgan (Eds.), *Syntax and semantics: Volume 3. Speech acts* (pp. 61–82). New York, NY: Academic Press.

Halliday, M. A. K., & Hasan, R. (1976). *Cohesion in English.* London: Longman.

Hanks, W. F. (2001). Indexicality. In A. Duranti (Ed.), *Key terms in language and culture* (pp. 180–183). Oxford: Blackwell.

Hogan, K. (1999). Thinking aloud together: A test of an intervention to foster students' collaborative scientific reasoning. *Journal of Research in Science Teaching, 36,* 1085–1109.

Issroff, K. (1999). Time-based analysis of students studying the Periodic Table. In K. Littleton & P. Light (Eds.), *Learning with computers: Analysing productive interaction* (pp. 46–61). London: Routledge.

Lemke, J. (2001). The long and the short of it: Comments on multiple timescale studies of human activity. *Journal of the Learning Sciences, 10,* 17–26.

Littleton, K. (1999). Productivity through interaction: An overview. In K. Littleton & P. Light (Eds.), *Learning with computers: Analyzing productive interaction* (pp. 179–194). London: Routledge.

Martin, J., & Rose, D. (2003). *Working with discourse: Meaning beyond the clause.* London: Continuum Press.

Maybin, J. (2005). *Children's voices: Talk, knowledge and identity.* Basingstoke, UK: Palgrave Macmillan.

Mercer, N. (1995). *The guided construction of knowledge: Talk amongst teachers and learners.* Clevedon, UK: Multilingual Matters.

Mercer, N. (2000). *Words and minds: How we use language to think together.* London: Routledge.

Mercer, N. (2004). Sociocultural discourse analysis: Analysing classroom talk as a social mode of thinking. *Journal of Applied Linguistics, 1*(2), 137–168.

Mercer, N., Dawes, R., Wegerif, R., & Sams, C. (2004). Reasoning as a scientist: Ways of helping children to use language to learn science. *British Educational Research Journal, 30,* 367–385.

Mercer, N., & Littleton, K. (2007). *Dialogue and the development of children's thinking: A sociocultural approach.* London: Routledge.

Mercer, N., & Sams, C. (2006). Teaching children how to use language to solve maths problems. *Language and Education, 20,* 507–527.

Nystrand, M., Wu, L., Gamorgan, A., Zeiser, S., & Long, D. (2003). Questions in time: Investigating the structure and dynamics of unfolding classroom discourse. *Discourse Processes, 35,* 135–198.

Payler, J. (2005). *Exploring foundations: Sociocultural influences on the learning processes of four year old children in a pre-school and reception class.* Doctoral thesis, University of Southampton, Southampton, UK.

Potter, J., & Wetherell, M. (1994). *Discourse and social psychology.* London: Sage.

Rasmussen, I. (2005). *Project work and ICT: Studying learning as participation trajectories.* Doctoral thesis, University of Oslo, Oslo, Norway.

Roth, W.-M. (2001). Situating cognition. *Journal of the Learning Sciences, 10,* 27–61.

Roth, W.-M. (2005). *Talking science: Language and learning in science.* Lanham, MD: Rowman & Littlefield.

Roth, W.-M. (2006). *Learning science: A singular plural perspective.* Rotterdam, The Netherlands: Sense.

Sawyer, K. (2001). *Creating conversations: Improvisation in everyday discourse.* Cresskill, NJ: Hampton Press.

Schegloff, E. (1997). Whose text? Whose context? *Discourse and Society, 8*(2), 165–187.

Scott, P., Mortimer, E., & Aguiar, O. (2006). The tension between authoritative and dialogic discourse: A fundamental characteristic of meaning making interactions in high school science lessons. *Science Education, 90,* 605–631.

Shuart-Faris, N., & Bloome, D. (Eds.). (2005). *Intertextuality and research on classroom education.* Greenwich, CT: IAP.

Silverstein, M., & Urban, G. (Eds.). (1996). *Natural histories of discourse.* Chicago, IL: University of Chicago Press.

ten Have, P. (1999). *Doing conversation analysis: A practical guide.* London: Sage.

Vygotsky, L. S. (1978). *Mind in society: The development of higher psychological processes.* London: Harvard University Press.

Wegerif, R., & Mercer, N. (1997). Using computer-based text analysis to integrate quantitative and qualitative methods in the investigation of collaborative learning. *Language and Education, 11*(4), 271–286.

Wegerif, R., & Scrimshaw, P. (Eds.). (1997). *Computers and talk in the primary classroom.* Clevedon, UK: Multilingual Matters.

Wells, G. (1999). *Dialogic enquiry: Towards a sociocultural practice and theory of education.* Cambridge, UK: Cambridge University Press.

Wells, G., & Claxton, G. (Eds.). (2002). *Learning for life in the 21st century.* Oxford, UK: Blackwell.

Wertsch, J. (1984). The zone of proximal development: Some conceptual issues. In B. Rogoff & J. Wertsch (Eds.), *Children's learning in the zone of proximal development: New directions in child development* (pp. 7–18). New York, NY: Jossey-Bass.

Wertsch, J. V. (Ed.). (1985). *Culture, communication and cognition: Vygotskian perspectives.* Cambridge, UK: Cambridge University Press.

Wood, D., Bruner, J., & Ross, G. (1976). The role of tutoring in problem-solving. *Journal of Child Psychology and Child Psychiatry, 17,* 89–100.

*In 2009 I was invited to write a methodological review by the editor of the* British Journal of Educational Psychology, *Andrew Tolmie; and having found that postgraduate students at Cambridge and the Open University seemed to find useful a comparison of the ways that researchers from different disciplinary backgrounds analysed classroom talk, I decided to make that the basis for my article. I was also encouraged to write a dispassionate piece on this topic after having seen how proponents of different approaches – such as conversation analysis, linguistic ethnography, corpus linguistics and experimental psychology – could be surprisingly dismissive of the value of each other's approaches. My own belief is that fundamentalist attachments to particular methodologies or disciplines are never helpful. We should use whichever methods are best for answering our research questions.*

# 10 The analysis of classroom talk
## Methods and methodologies

*Mercer, N. (2009). The analysis of classroom talk: methods and methodologies*. British Journal of Educational Psychology *(Wiley)*, 80, 1–14.

## Abstract

This article describes methods for analysing classroom talk, comparing their strengths and weaknesses. Both quantitative and qualitative methods are described and assessed for their strengths and weaknesses, with a discussion of the mixed use of such methods. It is acknowledged that particular methods are often embedded in particular methodologies, which are based on specific theories of social action, research paradigms, and disciplines; and so a comparison is made of two contemporary methodologies, linguistic ethnographyand sociocultural research. The article concludes with some comments on the current state of development of this field of research and on ways that it might usefully progress.

In this paper, I will describe some methods for analysing the talk and interaction of teachers and students, discussing their various affordances and limitations. One obvious way that methods vary is whether they provide qualitative or quantitative results, and so I will use that distinction as a major organizing principle. In educational research generally, the selection of a method seems often to reflect researchers' attachment to different epistemological theories, disciplinary traditions, and research paradigms. So in the study of classroom talk, different paradigms of enquiry, or methodologies, can be distinguished; and these embody certain tenets or principles about the nature of educational talk and how it can best be studied. For example, two influential approaches to the study of classroom talk in the UK are *linguistic ethnography* and *sociocultural research*. They have arisen from different disciplinary traditions, and those traditions not only influence researchers' methodological choices, but also the framing of their research questions and their conceptions of how educational research should relate to practice. Before describing particular methods, then, I will briefly describe these two rather different approaches.

Linguistic ethnography has a heritage of social anthropology and descriptive linguistics. Studies are typically observational, non-interventional, and qualitative. The essence of this approach is well explained in a paper by some leading exponents (Rampton et al., 2004); Creese (2008) and Tusting and Maybin (2007) are also very informative. Illustrative examples of this kind of research are Lefstein (2008), Maybin (2006), and Rampton (2007). Researchers normally employ the ethnographic and sociolinguistic methods I describe later in this article, which involve the close and detailed examination of classroom talk in its social and cultural context. They are unlikely to use any form of experimental method, or to use statistical analysis. Indeed, they are likely to feel quantitative, pre/post analyses of changes in talk or of learning gains are antithetical to a proper exploration and understanding of classroom communication. They have addressed research questions such as the following:

- How does classroom discourse enable, or inhibit, the expression of identities?
- How are the languages/language varieties of different cultures recognized and used in schools?
- Is current educational policy sensitive to the linguistic and cultural reality of school life?

Linguistic ethnographers commonly emphasize that language and social life are mutually shaping; that talk is always referential, interpersonal, emotive, and evaluative; that socialization is a never-ending process, mediated through talk and interaction; that language genres are important features of educational culture; and that children use talk, in classrooms as much as anywhere else, to negotiate and explore their identities. They also often argue that social situations are unique, and so generalizations of the kind commonly made by quantitative researchers are of dubious validity.

Sociocultural researchers, on the other hand, are more likely to affiliate to research traditions in social and developmental psychology and pedagogical studies, with strong attachments to the work of Vygotsky (1978; see also Daniels, 2001; Wertsch, 1985). A rationale for using this theoretical frame for studying classroom talk is provided by Alexander (2000) and Mercer and Littleton (2007). Illustrative examples of research are Black (2007), Howe, McWilliam, and Cross (2005), Skidmore (2006), Smith, Hardman, Wall, and Mroz (2004), and the collection edited by Mercer and Hodgkinson (2008). Nuthall's distinctive work also has much in common, theoretically and methodologically, with this line of enquiry (Nuthall, 1999, 2007; see also Collins & O'Toole, 2006). Sociocultural studies may be observational, interventional, and/or quasi-experimental. Researchers quite often combine qualitative and quantitative methods (as described under 'Mixed methods' later in the article). They have addressed questions such as:

- How does dialogue promote learning and the development of under standing?
- What types of talk are associated with the best learning outcomes?
- Does collaborative activity help children to learn, or assist their conceptual development?

Sociocultural researchers commonly emphasize that language is a cultural and psychological tool which (in Vygotskian terms) links the *intermental* and *intramental* – so, for example, classroom dialogue could have an important influence on the development of children's reasoning. They also typically emphasize that knowledge and understanding are jointly created, that talk allows reciprocity and mutuality to be developed through the continuing negotiation of meaning, and that education depends upon the creation and maintenance of intersubjectivity or 'common knowledge'. An implication often drawn is that teachers need to guide and scaffold learning, balancing the control of dialogue between teachers and students (Myhill, Jones, & Hopper, 2005). I would suggest that it is because of the directly 'applied' orientation of many sociocultural researchers that they are positively inclined towards the use of pre/post interventional designs, seeking to measure differential effects of talk on problem solving, learning, and conceptual change.

Having focused on the differences between these two methodologies, it is worth noting that they also have some shared principles. Researchers in both groups are thus likely to agree that classroom education cannot be understood without due attention to the nature and functions of talk (and that means there must be a qualitative element to the analysis); that cultural and local norms shape the processes of teaching and learning; and that in the classroom, meanings are continually renegotiated through talk and interaction over variable periods of time. The implication is that one-off, 'snapshot' studies of classroom talk are unlikely to yield as valid results as those which involve continuous and repeated observations, such as over a series of lessons. Both groups of researchers are likely to be critical of forms of classroom research which do not appear to recognize the importance of these principles – for example, through the use of simplistic coding schemes which treat all similar-looking utterances as repeated instances of the same event (at least if used without the correctional influence of a proper qualitative analysis, as discussed in more detail in later sections). They would probably also agree that the careful observation of classroom life commonly reveals much of interest that will not normally have been apparent to the teachers involved.

To some extent, then, it is difficult to completely separate methods from methodologies. Some researchers, indeed, would probably argue that we should not. Nevertheless, in the rest of this article, I will attempt to describe methods which are in common use simply in terms of their procedures and functionalities.

## Quantitative methods

Quantitative methods are those which use coding schemes to reduce the data of transcribed talk to counts of a specified set of features. The most well-known is 'systematic observation', but increasingly common is the use of computer-based text analysis to measure relative frequencies of occurrence of particular words or patterns of language use.

### Systematic observation

A well-established type of research on classroom interaction is known as 'systematic observation'. It essentially involves allocating observed talk (and sometimes non-verbal activity such as gesture) to a set of previously specified categories. The aim is usually to provide quantitative results which can be subjected to statistical analysis. For example, the observer may record the relative number of 'talk turns' taken by teachers and students, or measure the extent to which they produce types of utterance as defined by the researcher's categories (such as particular types of questions used by teachers). The basic procedure for setting up systematic observation is that researchers use their research questions and initial observations of classroom life to construct a set of categories into which all relevant talk (and any other communicative activity) can be classified. Observers are then trained to identify talk corresponding to each category, so that they can sit in classrooms or work from video-recordings and assign what they see and hear to the categories. Researchers may develop their own categorizing system, or they may take one 'off the shelf'. An example is Underwood and Underwood (1999), who used Bales' (1950) interaction analysis schedule to analyse the dialogue between children as they negotiated their way through a computer task. Teasley's (1995) work offers an interesting example of the use of this type of method applied to the study of collaborative learning. In her study, the talk of children working in pairs on a problem-solving task was recorded and transcribed, and each utterance attributed to 1 of 14 mutually exclusive categories. These categories included such functions as 'prediction' and 'hypothesis'. Transcripts were coded independently by two coders, and the level of agreement measured to ensure reliability. A count of categories of talk in different groups was correlated with outcome measures on the problem-solving activity in order to draw conclusions about the kinds of utterances which promote effective collaborative learning.

Many experimental studies of collaborative interactions use statistical techniques to ascertain whether there is any evidence of an association between the relative occurrence of particular features of classroom talk and students' success on task or learning gain. For example, correlation techniques were used by Barbieri and Light (1992) and Howe and Tolmie (1999) to determine whether there was any evidence of an association between particular features of learners' talk while working together on computer-based tasks and their success on task and learning gain. Similarly, regression analyses have enabled researchers such as Underwood and Underwood (1999) to determine which, if any, facets of the paired or group interaction were successful predictors of on-task performance.

As well as allowing an examination of any associations between aspects of collaborative activity and measures of outcome, the use of coding schemes for analysing talk also affords other distinct advantages. A lot of data can be processed fairly quickly. This allows researchers to survey life in a large sample of classrooms without analysing it all in detail, and to move fairly quickly and easily from observations to analysis. Systematic observation has undoubtedly provided interesting and useful findings regarding the nature of interactions amongst children working in pairs or groups (e.g. Bennett & Cass, 1989).

However, it is also important to recognize that methods which use only coded talk data have some inherent limitations. The most serious are the problems of dealing with ambiguity of meanings, the temporal development of meanings, and the fact that utterances with the same surface form can have quite different functions. Coding schemes normally require observers to put together all observed utterances which share the same surface features. So, for example, if a teacher asks a class the 'closed' question 'What is the capital of Peru?', it might seem to be unproblematic in its meaning and function, and so easy to code. But if a teacher asked that question before beginning a unit of work on Latin America, it could be being used to assess what relevant initial knowledge students have brought to this topic. If, on the other hand, it was asked at the end of the unit, it would probably have the very different function of assessing what students had learned from recent lessons. And yet again, the same question could be asked simply to rouse a dozing pupil, without any particular expectation by the teacher that the response would demonstrate learning. Although coding schemes could, in principle, be refined to handle such contextual variations, they rarely have been. There are also difficulties in determining the appropriate size of the unit of analysis to be coded – especially as the phenomenon under study involves a continual, evolutionary process of negotiation and re-negotiation of meaning between participants. For example, is the most meaningful unit a question or question-and-answer? Crook (1994) highlights a further difficulty, pointing out that a collaboration could be rich in instances of supposedly 'productive' talk, in the sense that there is evidence of conflict, predicting, questioning, and so on, and yet not lead to any worthwhile outcome. A simple count of such coded language features would not capture the extent to which talk is mobilized towards a particular goal or the creation of shared knowledge. Used in isolation, it would effectively reduce collaborations to atemporal 'inventories of utterances' (Crook, 1994, p. 150).

Studying and understanding the temporal dimensions of collaborative activity amongst students represents a considerable theoretical and practical challenge, and of course no method is perfect. But categorical coding schemes are generally inappropriate tools to use without the complementary use of a qualitative analysis, if there is an interest in studying the processes by which teachers and students build shared understandings. In order to gain a fuller understanding of the processes of collaborative work, researchers need methods which recognize that collaborative experiences are typically more than just brief, time-limited, localized sessions of joint activity. When researchers observe a class or group of students working together, the interaction observed is located within a particular historical, institutional, and cultural context. Students and teachers have relationships with histories, which shape the fluid process of classroom interaction. As Crook (1999) also comments, any productivity of interaction observed within a particular session may arise from circumstances that have previously been established. This point is echoed by Light and Light (1999) and Scott (2007), who note that interactions in any one observed session are likely to have determinants in the histories of individuals, groups, and institutions.

### Computer-based text analysis

Research in linguistics, in recent decades, has been revolutionized by the development of computer facilities for analysing large databases of written or spoken (transcribed) language. Software packages known as 'concordancers' enable any text file to be scanned easily for all instances of particular target words. (Commonly used examples are Monoconc, Wordsmith, and Conc 1.71. Recent versions of qualitative data analysis packages such as NVivo offer some similar facilities.) Not only can their frequency of occurrence be measured, but the analysis can also indicate which words tend to occur together, and so help reveal the way words gather meanings by 'the company that they keep'. The results of such searches can be presented as tabular concordances. One practical application of this method (outside educational research) has been in compiling dictionaries. Lexicographers now can base their definitions on an analysis of how words are actually used in a large databank (or 'corpus') of naturally occurring written and/or spoken language. Concordances can reveal some of the more subtle meanings that words have gathered in use, meanings which are not captured by literal definitions. These methods have more recently been taken up by classroom researchers.

Once recorded talk has been transcribed into a word file, a concordancer allows a researcher to move almost instantly between occurrences of particular words and the whole transcription. This enables particular words of special interest to be 'hunted' in the data, and their relative incidence and form of use in particular contexts to be compared. The basic data for this kind of analysis, throughout, remains the whole transcription. By integrating this method with other methods, the analysis can be both qualitative (targeting particular interactions or extended episodes) and quantitative (comparing the relative incidence of 'key words', or of types of interaction as might a systematic observer). Initial exploratory work on particular short texts (or text extracts) can be used to generate hypotheses, which can then be tested systematically on a large text or series of related texts. For example, a researcher may want to see if a technical term introduced by a teacher is taken up by students later in a lesson, or in their group-based activity. By locating all instances of the term in the transcription file, the ways it is used by teachers and students can then be considered (see, for example, Mercer, 2000; Monaghan, 1999; Wegerif & Mercer, 1997).

In summary, then, the strengths and weaknesses of quantitative methods are as follows:

## Strengths

- An efficient way of handling a lot of data; a researcher can survey a lot of classroom language relatively quickly and analyse a representative sample of events;
- enable numerical comparisons to be made across and within data samples, which can then be subjected to a statistical analysis.

## Weaknesses

- Actual talk, as data, may be lost early in the analysis. A researcher works only with predefined categories, and so new insights which might be gained from repeated considerations of the original data will be missed;
- the use of pre-determined categories or other target items can limit analysts' sensitivity to what actually happens; and
- coding which depends on the decontextualized identification of language features cannot handle the ways that the meaning of any utterance will depend on its history within the observed dialogue and perhaps in previous encounters between participants.

## Qualitative methods

These are methods which aim to reveal the nature, patterns, and quality of spoken interactions. They include ethnographic and sociolinguistic methods, and the method known as 'conversation analysis'. In practice, the first two often appear to be combined. The third tends to be kept distinct.

### Ethnographic analysis

Ethnographic methods are an adaptation of methods developed by social anthropologists and sociologists in non-educational fields (see e.g. Hammersley, 1982; Woods, 1983, for accounts of this). Ethnographic analysis aims for a rich, detailed description of observed events, through the researchers' continuous and close involvement in the social environment they are studying. A classic example is Heath's (1983) study of children's language and literacy in and out of school in the southern USA. Compared with the use of a quantitative method like systematic observation, this inevitably limits the sheer amount of classroom interaction which can be analysed; and in any case, the aim is for depth of analysis rather than a more superficial analysis of a large data set. It is therefore typical for studies which use ethnographic methods to study life in just a few classrooms. For example, Maybin (2006) used radio microphones to capture all the talk of a set of primary schoolchildren during their schooldays, both in lessons and in break periods, over several months. This data enabled her to show how children took up and developed certain ideas, themes, and ways of accounting for experience together as they interacted, and to discern the influence of past experience and of adults and parents in this meaning-making. Some researchers using ethnographic methods have only taken field notes of what was said and done, but nowadays it is common practice to tape-record talk, to transcribe those recordings, and to report the analysis by including short illustrative extracts from transcriptions. Today, ethnographic methods are increasingly merged with the sociolinguistic methods described below.

## Sociolinguistic discourse analysis

Some methods for researching talk in educational contexts have their roots in linguistics or, more precisely, sociolinguistics. Sociolinguistics is concerned, broadly, with the relationship between the forms and structures of language and its uses in society. (See Swann, Mesthrie, Deumert, & Leap, 2000, for a general introduction to this field.) Sociolinguistic research is normally qualitative, and often resembles ethnographic research; but it can also incorporate the methods of descriptive linguistics – such as the identification of distinctive sound patterns (phonology), grammatical constructions, or vocabulary items. Moreover, quantitative methods may also sometimes be employed. For example, sociolinguists have compared the extent to which girls and boys dominate classroom interactions (French & French, 1988; Swann, 2007), and recorded the incidence of switches from one language to another in the course of educational events (Edwards & Sienkewicz, 1990). The style of sociolinguistic discourse analysis which has become most popular in the USA is well represented by the work of Gee and Green (1998), and by the collection of articles edited by Hicks (1996).

It is worth noting that the term 'discourse analysis' has no precise meaning; it is used to refer to several different approaches to analysing language (both spoken and written) and hence to some quite different methods. Within linguistics, it sometimes indicates an interest in the way language is organized in units longer than sentences. Educational research following this approach has focused on the structural organization of classroom talk. The classic investigation of Sinclair and Coulthard (1975) showed that in teacher-led lessons the language has characteristics which mark it out as a distinct, situated language variety, and one which assigns particular roles to speakers (see also Stubbs, 1983; Willes, 1983). They devised a method for categorizing all talk in a lesson into a hierarchical system of 'acts', 'moves', and 'exchanges' and 'transactions'. The basic unit of teacher–pupil communication in this system is the 'IRF exchange', in which a teacher Initiates an interaction (typically by asking a question), the student Responds (usually by providing an answer), and the teacher then provides some Follow-up or feedback (for example, by confirming that the answer was correct). The IRF exchange was also identified at about the same time by Mehan (1979), who called it an 'IRE' (with 'E' standing for 'evaluation'). This 'triadic unit' has since been used by many classroom researchers, although few employ the whole of Sinclair and Coulthard's rather complex hierarchical system. A somewhat different method for analysing talk is based on *systemic functional grammar* (SFG), the creation of the linguist Halliday (1993). As the name implies, an SFG-based approach to analysing classroom language allows a researcher to consider how the special educational functions of classroom language relate to its grammatical structure and its textual organization (for example, Gibbons, 1998; Iedema, 1996).

## Conversation analysis

Conversation analysis (commonly abbreviated to CA) really deserves to be described as a methodology, rather than just a method. Its roots are in a radical sociology called ethnomethodology, which emerged during the 1960s through a dissatisfaction with the focus of the then dominant sociology on the structural organization of society on a grand scale (Garfinkel, 1967; Sacks, Schegloff, & Jefferson, 1974). Ethnomethodology aimed instead to explain how the social world operates through people's actions, by focusing on how social interaction is achieved, minute by minute, through everyday talk and non-verbal communication, and how people 'account for' their social experiences. CA is a demanding methodology, because it uses a very detailed and laborious style of analysis and sets very strict criteria for the kinds of interpretations which an analyst can make from the data of recorded talk; and it also involves the use of a very specific and detailed method of transcription (as explained in Drew & Heritage, 1992). Widely used in the analysis of talk in work-related settings (see, for example, Drew & Heritage, 1992), CA has still to be applied to any great extent in classroom research (but see Baker, 1997; Markee, 2000; Stokoe, 2000).

In summary, then, the strengths and weaknesses of qualitative methods are as follows:

## Strengths

- Any transcribed talk remains throughout the analysis (rather than being reduced to categories at an early stage) and so the researcher does not have to make initial judgments about meanings which cannot be revised;

- any categories emerging are generated by the analysis, not by codings based on prior assumptions;
- in research reports, examples of talk and interaction can be used to show concrete illustrations of your analysis: researchers do not ask readers to take on trust the validity of abstracted categorizations;
- the development of joint understanding, or the persistence of apparent misunderstandings or different points of view, can be pursued through the continuous data of recorded/transcribed talk; and
- because the analytic scheme is not established *a priori*, the analysis can be expanded to include consideration of any new aspects of communication that emerge in the data.

## Weaknesses

- It is difficult to use these methods to handle large sets of data, because they are so time consuming. It is commonly estimated that transcribing and analysing 1h of talk using such methods will take between 5 and 12 h of research time;
- it can be difficult to use such analyses to make convincing generalizations, because only specific illustrative examples can be offered; and
- researchers are open to charges of selecting particular examples to support their arguments.

# Mixed methods

The combined use of quantitative and qualitative methods has become more common in educational research, as in related fields like social psychology and sociolinguistics. In part, this seems to reflect a developing realization amongst researchers that each type of approach has its virtues, and that the integrity of the research enterprise need not involve making an ideological commitment to one or the other. But so far as I am aware, there is only one 'mixed methods' approach which has been given a specific name: sociocultural discourse analysis.

## *Sociocultural discourse analysis*

'Sociocultural' discourse analysis differs from 'linguistic' discourse analysis in being less concerned with the organizational structure of spoken language, and more with its content, function, and the ways shared understanding is developed, in social context, over time (as described in more detail in Mercer, 2005, 2008). As with ethnography and CA, reports of such research are usually illustrated by selected extracts of transcribed talk, to which the analyst provides a commentary. The basic data thus remains throughout the whole process, as with most qualitative methods. But this qualitative analysis is then integrated with quantitative analysis. This might involve using a concordancer to assess the relative incidence of 'key words' or collocations of words in the data (as described under 'sociolinguistic discourse analysis' above). Qualitative analyses of particular interactions can also be used to generate hypotheses which can then be tested systematically, and quantitatively, on a large text or series of related texts. For example, a researcher may want to see if a technical term introduced by a teacher is taken up by students later in their group-based activity. And by locating all instances and collocations of a term in the transcription file, the way it is used by teachers and students in relation to their joint activity can then be considered (see, for example, Mercer, 2000: Chapter 3; Wegerif & Mercer, 1997). A sociocultural method has been used to analyse and evaluate the talk of children working together in pairs or groups (Lyle, 1993, 1996; Mercer & Littleton, 2007), sometimes on computer-based activities (Kumpulainen & Mutanen, 1999; Wegerif & Scrimshaw, 1997).

## Conclusions

The analysis of classroom talk brings with it many challenges for researchers, and no method (or methodology) devised so far is without its limitations. But new entrants to this field of research can take advantage of the considerable amount of work, over some decades, that researchers of several disciplines have put into the development of methods for analysing interaction. There is no virtue in re-inventing wheels, or in ignoring the methodological problems with which others have grappled (and which they have at least partly overcome).

With their various strengths and weaknesses, it may seem logical to use two or more methods of analysing talk in a complementary way. In doing so, however, it is important to recall a point made earlier in this paper – that different methods may embody different conceptions of the nature of talk and what counts as a valid analysis. As Snyder (1995) argues on the basis of her studies of children's computer literacy, the successful combination of different methods depends on research being underpinned by a 'sensitive, flexible theoretical framework' for understanding the complexity of real-life events. Given such a framework, I believe there are ways of combining at least some methods which will satisfy most reasonable concerns about validity and methodological consistency. While underlying conceptions of what constitutes a valid course of enquiry are bound to be influential, and rightly so, my own view is that some choices of method – such as whether to use qualitative or quantitative methods, or to use an experimental design or naturalistic observations – should not be too easily determined by ideological commitments. I find arguments that only qualitative research can deal with the human reality of school life, or that only quantitative research amounts to real science, equally unconvincing. Instead, researchers should accept that various methods – and methodologies – have their distinctive strengths and weaknesses, and that by asking 'What do I need to do to answer my research questions?' an open-minded researcher may avoid simplistic choices. From this stance, the most effective forms of enquiry may involve the complementary use of more than one type of method, so that weaknesses are counterbalanced and evidence of more than one kind is generated. An increasing number of researchers seem to share this point of view.

It is worth noting that more researchers also seem to be involving teachers as co-researchers in the analysis of classroom talk and interaction, usually with the aim of helping teachers gain new insights into their everyday experiences and practice (see, for example, Armstrong & Curran, 2006; Hennessy & Deaney, 2009). More classroom researchers also use specially designed software, such as AtlasTi, NVivo, and ObserverXT, to organize and annotate their digitally recorded data. (Though as one sometimes has to remind students, any such software is just an organizational tool; it does not come with an in-built methodology and does not do the analysis for you!) But beyond these contemporary developments, how might this field of study most usefully develop, in methodological terms? Some might say that researchers should not just focus on talk itself, but instead make 'multimodal' analyses which treat talk as one of several communicative modes (along with gaze, gesture, written texts, pictures, video, and so on) as only in that way can the richness of classroom interaction be properly appreciated (see, for example, Jewitt, Kress, Ogborn, & Tsartsarelis, 2004). I have engaged in some multimodal analysis myself, when studying how teachers use interactive whiteboards, and have some sympathy with that argument (Gillen, Kleine Staarman, Littleton, Mercer, & Twiner, 2007). But language remains for me the prime cultural tool of the classroom. Spoken language enables, in unique ways, the development of relationships amongst teachers and learners and the development of children's reasoning and understanding; so I would not subscribe to an analytic approach which diluted its significance to that of just one of several modes.

I believe the toughest methodological challenge we face is to properly recognize that talk functions in a temporal context (as explained in more detail in Mercer, 2008). Classroom education is normally a continuing, cumulative experience for the participants, an experience which even researchers involved in longitudinal observational studies can only sample, only partly share. Participants draw on their shared history all the time when they communicate. Moreover, as a leading pioneer of research into classroom talk reminded us recently, 'Most learning does not happen suddenly' (Barnes, 2008, p. 4). If we want to understand how it happens through talk in classrooms, we need to operate on a suitable timescale – and of course use appropriate methods for collecting and analysing data. Approaches which rely only on brief encounters with classroom life, or on the atemporal coding of utterance types and content references, can never do justice to what teachers and learners achieve, or fail to achieve, every working day.

Regarding what we might most usefully use available methods to do, a pressing need is to provide more strong empirical evidence of how involvement in talk affects educational outcomes. There is evidence – some of which has been available for a while – that teachers' use of certain interactional strategies with students has beneficial effects on their curriculum learning and skills in comprehending texts (Brown & Palincsar, 1989; Chinn, Anderson, & Waggoner, 2001; Kyriacou & Issitt, 2008; Rojas-Drummond, Mercer, & Dabrowski, 2001; Wolf, Crosson, & Resnick, 2006). It has also been shown that certain features of discussion amongst students are associated with the development of their individual reasoning and understanding of curriculum topics (Howe et al., 2005; Mercer & Littleton, 2007). We also know that the ways teachers use talk in the classroom have a significant effect on how their students evaluate talk and use it as a tool for their own learning (Fisher & Larkin, 2008; Webb, Nemer, & Ing, 2006). But if this line of educational research is to have a major impact on educational policy and the training of teachers, we need more large scale studies which use a combination of qualitative analysis and quantitative assessments to consolidate and extend that evidence base and to show more clearly how talk can enable classroom education to be successful.

## Acknowledgements

Thanks to Karen Littleton, Rupert Wegerif, Judith Kleine Staarman, and Lyn Dawes for their involvement in earlier work which has informed this article. Thanks also to the organizers and participants in the ESRC-funded seminar *Linguistic Ethnography and Sociocultural Psychology in Conversation* at the Open University, 16 February 2008, which provided the basis for my comparison of those two approaches.

## References

Alexander, R. (2000). *Culture and pedagogy: International comparisons in primary education*. Oxford: Blackwell.

Armstrong, V., & Curran, S. (2006). Developing a collaborative mode of research using digital video. *Computers and Education, 46*, 336–347.

Baker, C. (1997). Ethnomethodological studies of talk in educational settings. In B. Davies & D. Corson (Eds.), *Encyclopedia of language and education, vol. 3: Oral discourse and education* (pp. 43–52). The Hague: Kluwer.

Bales, R. (1950). *Interaction process analysis*. Chicago, IL: The University of Chicago Press.

Barbieri, M., & Light, P. (1992). Interaction, gender and performance on a computer-based task. *Learning and Instruction, 2*, 199–213.

Barnes, D. (2008). Exploratory talk for learning. In N. Mercer & S. Hodgkinson (Eds.), *Exploring talk in school* (pp. 1–15). London: Sage.

Bennett, N., & Cass, A. (1989). The effects of group composition on group interactive processes and pupil understanding. *British Educational Research Journal, 15*, 19–32.

Black, L. (2007). Interactive whole class teaching and pupil learning. *Language and Education, 21*, 271–283.

Brown, A., & Palincsar, A. S. (1989). Guided, co-operative learning and individual knowledge acquisition. In L. Resnick (Ed.), *Knowing, learning and instruction* (pp. 393–451). New York, NY: Erlbaum.

Chinn, C., Anderson, R., & Waggoner, M. (2001). Patterns of discourse in two kinds of literature discussion. *Reading Research Quarterly, 36*, 378–411.

Collins, S., & O'Toole, V. (2006). The use of Nuthall's unique methodology to better understand the realities of children's classroom experience. *Teaching and Teacher Education, 22*, 592–611.

Creese, A. (2008). Linguistic ethnography. In K. A. King & N. H. Hornberger (Eds.), *Encyclopedia of language and education, vol. 10: Research methods in language and education* (2nd ed., pp. 229–241). New York: Springer Science + Business Media LLC.

Crook, C. (1994). *Computers and the collaborative experience of learning*. London: Routledge.

Crook, C. (1999). Computers in the community of classrooms. In K. Littleton & P. Light (Eds.), *Learning with computers: Analysing productive interaction* (pp. 102–117). London: Routledge.

Daniels, H. (2001). *Vygotsky and pedagogy*. London: Routledge/Falmer.

Drew, P., & Heritage, J. (Eds.), (1992). *Talk at work*. Cambridge: Cambridge University Press.

Edwards, V., & Sienkewicz, T. (1990). *Oral cultures past and present: Rappin' and Homer*. Oxford: Basil Blackwell.

Fisher, R., & Larkin, S. (2008). Pedagogy or ideological struggle? An examination of pupils' and teachers' expectations for talk in the classroom. *Language and Education, 22*, 1–16.

French, J., & French, P. (1988). Sociolinguistics and gender divisions. In N. Mercer (Ed.), *Language and literacy from an educational perspective, vol. 1: Language studies* (pp. 66–81). Milton Keynes: Open University Press.

Garfinkel, H. (1967). *Studies in ethnomethodology*. Englewood Cliff, NJ: Prentice Hall.

Gee, J. P., & Green, J. (1998). Discourse analysis, learning and social practice: A methodological study. *Review of Research in Education, 23*, 119–169.

Gibbons, P. (1998). Classroom talk and the learning of new registers in a second language. *Language and Education, 12*, 99–118.

Gillen, J., Kleine Staarman, J., Littleton, K., Mercer, N., & Twiner, A. (2007). A 'learning revolution'? Investigating pedagogic practice around interactive whiteboards in British primary schools. *Learning, Media and Technology, 32*, 243–256.

Halliday, M. A. K. (1993). Towards a language-based theory of learning. *Linguistics and Education, 5*, 93–116.

Hammersley, M. (1982). The sociology of the classroom. In A. Hartnett (Ed.), *The social sciences in educational studies* (pp. 33–45). London: Heinemann.

Heath, S. B. (1983). *Ways with words: Language, life and work in communities and classrooms*. Cambridge: Cambridge University Press.

Hennessy, S., & Deaney, R. (2009). The impact of collaborative video analysis by practitioners and researchers upon pedagogical thinking and practice: A follow-up study. *Teachers and Teaching: Theory and Practice, 15*, 617–638.

Hicks, D. (1996). *Discourse, learning and schooling*. Cambridge: Cambridge University Press.

Howe, C. J., McWilliam, D., & Cross, G. (2005). Chance favours only the prepared mind: Incubation and the delayed effects of peer collaboration. *British Journal of Psychology*, 96, 67–93.

Howe, C. J., & Tolmie, A. (1999). Productive interaction in the context of computer supported collaborative learning in science. In K. Littleton & P. Light (Eds.), *Learning with computers: Analysing productive interaction* (pp. 24–45). London: Routledge.

Iedema, R. (1996). Save the talk for after the listening: The realisation of regulative discourse in teacher talk. *Language and Education*, 10, 118–135.

Jewitt, C., Kress, G., Ogborn, J., & Tsartsarelis, C. (2004). Exploring learning through visual, actional and linguistic communication: The multimodal environment of science classroom. *Educational Review*, 1, 6–16.

Kumpulainen, K., & Mutanen, M. (1999). The situated dynamics of peer group interaction: An introduction to an analytic framework. *Learning and Instruction*, 9, 449–473.

Kyriacou, C., & Issitt, J. (2008). *What characterizes effective teacher–pupil dialogue to promote conceptual understanding in mathematics lessons in England in Key Stages 2 and 3?*, EPPI-Centre Report no. 1604R. Social Science Research Unit: Institute of Education, University of London.

Lefstein, A. (2008). Changing classroom practice through the English national literacy strategy: A micro-international perspective. *American Educational Research Journal*, 45, 701–737.

Light, P., & Light, V. (1999). Reaching for the sky: Computer supported tutorial interaction in a conventional university setting. In K. Littleton & P. Light (Eds.), *Learning with computers: Analysing productive interaction* (pp. 162–178). London: Routledge.

Lyle, S. (1993). An investigation into ways in which children 'talk themselves into meaning'. *Language and Education*, 7, 181–197.

Lyle, S. (1996). An analysis of collaborative group work in the primary school and the factors relevant to its success. *Language and Education*, 10, 13–32.

Markee, N. (2000). *Conversation analysis*. New York, NY: Erlbaum.

Maybin, J. (2006). *Children's voices: Talk, knowledge and identity*. Basingstoke: Palgrave Macmillan.

Mehan, H. (1979). *Learning lessons: Social organization in the classroom*. Cambridge, MA: Harvard University Press.

Mercer, N. (2000). *Words and minds: How we use language to think together*. London: Routledge.

Mercer, N. (2005). Sociocultural discourse analysis: Analysing classroom talk as a social mode of thinking. *Journal of Applied Linguistics*, 1, 137–168.

Mercer, N. (2008). The seeds of time: Why classroom dialogue needs a temporal analysis. *Journal of the Learning Sciences*, 17, 33–59.

Mercer, N., & Hodgkinson, S. (Eds.), (2008). *Exploring classroom talk*. London: Sage.

Mercer, N., & Littleton, K. (2007). *Dialogue and the development of children's thinking*. London: Routledge.

Monaghan, F. (1999). Judging a word by the company its keeps: The use of concordancing software to explore aspects of the mathematics register. *Language and Education*, 13, 59–70.

Myhill, D. A., Jones, S., & Hopper, R. (2005). *Talking, listening, learning: Effective talk in the primary classroom*. Maidenhead: Open University Press.

Nuthall, G. (1999). Learning how to learn: The evolution of students' minds through the social processes and culture of the classroom. *International Journal of Educational Research, 31*(3), 139–256.

Nuthall, G. (2007). *The hidden lives of learners*. Wellington: NZCER Press.

Rampton, B. (2007). Neo-Hymesian linguistic ethnography in the United Kingdom. *Journal of Sociolinguistics, 11*, 584–607.

Rampton, B., Tusting, K., Maybin, J., Barwell, R., Creese, A., & Lytra, V. (2004). *UK linguistic ethnography: A discussion paper*. Retrieved from www.ling-ethnog.org. uk/ documents/discussion_paper_jan_05.pdf

Rojas-Drummond, S., Mercer, N., & Dabrowski, E. (2001). Collaboration, scaffolding and the promotion of problem solving strategies in Mexican pre-schoolers. *European Journal of Psychology of Education, 16*, 179–196.

Sacks, H., Schegloff, E. A., & Jefferson, G. (1974). A simplest systematics for the organisation of turn-taking for conversation. *Language, 50*, 696–735.

Scott, P. (2007). Questions about teachers' goals, learners' roles and the co-construction of knowledge. Forum: A sociocultural perspective on mediated activity in third grade science. *Cultural Studies of Science Education, 1*, 497–515.

Sinclair, J., & Coulthard, M. (1975). *Towards an analysis of discourse: The English used by teachers and pupils*. London: Oxford University Press.

Skidmore, D. (2006). Pedagogy and dialogue. *Cambridge Journal of Education, 36*, 503–514.

Smith, F., Hardman, F., Wall, K., & Mroz, M. (2004). Interactive whole class teaching in the national literacy and numeracy strategies. *British Educational Research Journal, 30*, 395–411.

Snyder, I. (1995). Multiple perspectives in literacy research: Integrating the quantitative and qualitative. *Language and Education, 9*, 22–31.

Stokoe, E. (2000). Constructing topicality in university students' small-group discussion; a conversation analytic approach. *Language and Education, 14*, 184–203.

Stubbs, M. (1983). *Discourse analysis: The sociolinguistic analysis of natural language*. Oxford: Basil Blackwell.

Swann, J. (2007). Designing 'educationally effective' discussion. *Language and Education, 21*, 342–359.

Swann, J., Mesthrie, R., Deumert, A., & Leap, W. (2000). *Introducing sociolinguistics*. Edinburgh: Edinburgh University Press.

Teasley, S. (1995). The role of talk in children's peer collaborations. *Developmental Psychology, 31*, 207–220.

Tusting, K., & Maybin, J. (2007). Ethnography and interdisciplinarity: Opening the discussion. *Journal of Sociolinguistics, 11*, 575–583.

Underwood, J., & Underwood, G. (1999). Task effects in co-operative and collaborative learning with computers. In K. Littleton & P. Light (Eds.), *Learning with computers: Analysing productive interaction* (pp. 10–23). London: Routledge.

Vygotsky, L. S. (1978). *Mind in society: The development of higher psychological processes*. Cambridge, MA: Harvard University Press.

Webb, N., Nemer, K., & Ing, M. (2006). Small-group reflections: Parallels between teacher discourse and student behavior in peer-directed groups. *Journal of the Learning Sciences, 15*, 63–119.

Wegerif, R., & Mercer, N. (1997). Using computer-based text analysis to integrate quantitative and qualitative methods in the investigation of collaborative learning. *Language and Education, 11*, 271–286.

Wegerif, R., & Scrimshaw, P. (Eds.), (1997). *Computers and talk in the primary classroom.* Clevedon: Multilingual Matters.

Wertsch, J. V. (1985). *Vygotsky and the social formation of mind.* Cambridge, MA: Harvard University Press.

Willes, M. (1983). *Children into pupils: A study of language in early schooling.* London: Routledge and Kegan Paul.

Wolf, M., Crosson, A., & Resnick, L. (2006). *Accountable talk in reading comprehension instruction.* CSE Technical Report no. 670. Learning and Research Development Center, University of Pittsburgh.

Woods, P. (1983). *The sociology of the school.* London: Routledge and Kegan Paul.

*Several of my research projects have looked at the use of talk in the teaching and learning of science, but the project that generated this chapter is the only one in which I (along with my co-authors Lyn and Judith) had the marvellous opportunity to work with the science educator Phil Scott (and his colleague Jaume Amettler) of the University of Leeds. Working with this team helped me understand properly the value and truth of Phil's conviction that the best science teaching combines authoritative presentation and instruction with truly interactive teacher-student dialogue.*

*Keywords: observation study; primary education; science education; talk in classrooms*

# 11 Dialogic teaching in the primary science classroom

*Mercer, N., Dawes, L. & Kleine Staarman, J. (2009). Dialogic teaching in the primary science classroom.* Language and Education *(Taylor and Francis),* 23, 4, 1–17.

## Abstract

This paper describes research on dialogue between teachers and pupils during primary school science lessons, using talk from two classrooms to provide our examples. We consider whether teachers use dialogue to make education a cumulative, continuing process for guiding the development of children's understanding. Case studies of two teachers, using observational data taken from a larger data set, are used to illustrate their use of talk as a pedagogic tool. We also consider the differing extent to which the two teachers highlight for pupils the educational value of talk, and the extent to which they attempt to guide pupils' own effective use of talk for learning. Implications are drawn for evaluating the ways teachers use dialogue, and for professional development. An example is provided of an activity which has been found to help teachers implement dialogic teaching, and which illustrates how such an approach involves organising the structural variety of talk.

## Introduction

This paper has emerged from a recent project entitled 'Dialogic teaching in science classrooms', with colleagues Jaume Ametller and Phil Scott. The research involved detailed analyses of teacher–student interaction in science classrooms at primary and secondary levels. In this paper, we will use selected data from the classrooms of two primary school teachers who used talk in rather different ways. This selective use of data allows us to work within the space limitations of an article such as this to exemplify and discuss our findings from the project as a whole. We will begin by examining how, and the extent to which, the two teachers used dialogue to

- explore pupils' current understandings of topics;

- make explicit a learning trajectory for pupils, by relating past activities to those in the present and future;
- build links between the content of earlier discussions and current concerns;
- model, and make explicit to pupils, ways of using talk for sharing ideas, reasoning and developing shared understanding.

Having compared the practices of the teachers, we will draw some general conclusions and discuss the educational implications of our findings. We will then provide an example of the kind of pedagogic activities we have been developing, on the basis of those findings, to enable teachers to use talk effectively in the teaching of science.

Our investigations were partly inspired by the concept of 'dialogic teaching' as described by Alexander (2008a), in which a pedagogic approach, underpinned by specific principles, can be enacted through a range of possible talk strategies (Alexander provides a list of 47 indicators). Alexander argues that this approach, with its emphasis on the active, influential and sustained participation of pupils in classroom talk, will achieve the best educational results (Alexander 2000). A key indicator of dialogic teaching is that classroom talk should have a cumulative quality. This means that the communication between teacher and pupils should contribute to the cohesive, temporal organisation of pupils' educational experience and hence to the progressive development of their understanding.

Dialogic teaching also involves raising pupils' awareness of the potential educational power of talk so that they develop a meta-awareness of the use of talk for learning. This converges with our own previous work on science education, on whether developing children's awareness and skill in using talk as a tool for problem-solving helps their learning and the development of their scientific understanding (Mercer, Dawes, Wegerif, and Sams 2004). The implication is that an effective teacher of science will not only be concerned with helping children understand the content of the science curriculum but will also help them understand better the dialogic processes involved in studying and practising science. Thus Lemke's (1990) proposition that science education should make pupils fluent speakers of science could be elaborated to become 'science education should make pupils self-aware, fluent and reflective speakers of science'.

Another strong influence on our research has been Mortimer and Scott's (2003) work on teacher–student talk in secondary science classrooms. They use the concept of *communicative approach* to characterise how teachers use language to develop students' ideas in science. Mortimer and Scott use two dimensions to define the ways teachers and students communicate: *interactive–non-interactive* and *dialogic–authoritative*. During interactive communication both teacher and students contribute, while in non-interactive communication only the teacher speaks. Thus in interactive episodes the teacher typically engages students in a series of questions and answers, whilst in non-interactive teaching the teacher presents ideas in a 'lecturing' style. The dialogic–authoritative dimension is concerned with the extent to which both the teacher's and students' points of view are represented. The most 'authoritative' talk would be represented by the teacher's presentation of the authoritative canon of scientific knowledge. Talk is considered to be more dialogic the more it represents the students' points of view and the discussion includes their and the teacher's ideas. So a sequence in which several students explained their ideas about a phenomenon and discussed with the teacher and the rest of the class how those ideas related to scientific knowledge would be judged interactively/dialogically. There is no implication in Mortimer and Scott's scheme that any single type of communicative approach is intrinsically superior; the implication is rather that the quality of teaching will depend on a teacher's strategic use of interactive and dialogic approaches at different stages of a lesson or series of lessons.

An underlying assumption of our research, also taken from Mortimer and Scott, has been that the study of science inevitably involves the juxtaposition of everyday and scientific ideas. The meaningful learning of science must entail movement from the existing everyday ideas of children towards a more scientific point of view. Other research has provided evidence that talk about scientific phenomena can be an important motor for conceptual change (as discussed in Driver, Newton, and Osborne 2000; Kelly, Brown, and Crawford 2000; Lemke 1990; Ogborn, Kress, Martins, and McGillicuddy 1996). The continuing, dynamic process of classroom communication thus provides a means for helping children to develop, over time, a scientific perspective which they can apply to explain a range of phenomena.

There is much support from research for teachers giving attention to how they use talk to guide pupils' understanding, and for actively involving pupils in that process. However, research also shows that this seems to have had relatively little impact on the quality of classroom talk, which is still commonly dominated by closed questions, short pupil responses and little direct attention being given to the use of talk for teaching-and-learning (see, for example Galton 2007; Smith, Hardman, Wall, and Mroz 2004). On the basis of interviews with British primary teachers, Fisher and Larkin (2008) suggest that this reflects teachers' views of what counts as 'good' classroom talk, in which pupils' use of talk to explore ideas and help learning is less commonly mentioned than is their adherence to norms of politeness and 'good grammar'. We were therefore interested to see if teachers who expressed an interest in 'dialogic teaching', and who volunteered to take part in a project on it, would show a high level of awareness and skill in using talk as an educational tool.

## Methods

Our research was carried out in five primary schools and three secondary schools in two regions of England, with the participation of six primary (year 5/6/7) and six secondary teachers (year 7). Video and audio recordings of three consecutive science lessons (total duration, three to six hours) were made in all classrooms. All the teachers expressed an interest in dialogic teaching and volunteered to participate in the project knowing that this was its focus. All were considered by their local authority and schools to be 'good practitioners'. The lesson topics were selected through discussion with each teacher, which were based on the normal (national) curriculum. Lessons were planned by the teachers, and in accordance with our original plans, we made no interventions as to how lessons were taught or pupils' learning was assessed. However, we did share with teachers some information about 'dialogic teaching' drawn from the work of Alexander (2000) and from Mortimer and Scott (2003). We made it clear that our interest was to see how teachers used talk to teach science. In this paper, we will draw on data from recordings of two teachers, for reasons we explain below. These teachers, due to the involvement of their schools, had some knowledge of our earlier research on developing children's collaborative talk and reasoning (as described in Dawes, Mercer, and Wegerif 2004; Mercer and Littleton 2007).

## Data collection

The main data gathered consisted of the following:

(1) Video recordings, focusing mainly on the teacher, of sequences of three lessons.
(2) Video/audio recordings of one group of pupils working together during lessons (at least one group in each class).
(3) Pupils' written work related to the recorded lessons (along with teachers' assessments), if available.
(4) Any other assessment data (such as end of unit tests), if available.
(5) Recordings of interviews with teachers and six pupils in each class.
(6) Recordings of video-stimulated interview sessions with teachers.

Approximately 120 hours of classroom talk (video and audio of group work) and 20 hours of interviews with teachers and pupils were recorded, and all relevant data was transcribed.

## Data analysis

Our analysis was mainly concerned with identifying processes of interaction, within and across the related series of lessons, using the methodology called sociocultural discourse analysis (Mercer 2005, 2008). This methodology highlights the historical, contextualised and purposeful nature of classroom talk and involves both qualitative and quantitative methods of discourse analysis. The qualitative analysis consisted of a detailed examination of video and transcript data, using the software *AtlasTi*. Case studies were compiled, which included contextual notes about the schools, curricula and the contents of the series of lessons overall, including the use of information and communication technology (ICT), apparatus and any other equipment.

## The case studies

This paper draws only on data gathered in the classrooms of two teachers located in two different primary schools, which we call Havenhill and Beckstones. We have selected this data because these teachers differed in their use of talk in ways which highlight the kind of variation we observed across the sample of 12 teachers as a whole. Both taught in similar urban locations, one teaching a mixed class of years 5 and 6 (ages 9–11) and the other year 7 (ages 11–12: this English region was unusual in including year 7 children within the primary rather than secondary section). Both schools served populations with a mixed socio-economic background, mostly children from lower socio-economic environments. For each teacher, we have chosen illustrative extracts from the beginning of the second of the series of three lessons we have recorded. The names of all participants have been changed to preserve anonymity.

In terms of some crude measures, the interactions in the selected lessons in both Havenhill and Beckstones (and the others recorded in the classrooms of these teachers) were quite similar. In whole-class sessions, both teachers contributed about the same proportion of the talk (88% of the words spoken in Beckstones, 85% in Havenhill). Most of the talk in whole-class discussions consisted of initiation-response-follow-up/feedback (IRF) exchanges (Sinclair and Coulthard 1975), and most of these were of the conventional nature whereby a teacher asked a closed question and evaluated the brief response provided by the student. Both teachers arranged for children to spend some time talking about the curriculum topic in pairs or small groups. But, as we will see, more detailed qualitative analysis of the dialogue revealed some differences which, while more subtle, have educational significance.

### *Case study 1. Havenhill year 7: acids and alkalis*

The teacher told us that the topic 'acids and alkalis' was 'almost new' for the pupils; there had been a previous lesson (prior to our recordings) in which the teacher had 'set up' the topic and provided little new scientific content. That lesson was related to nutrition, with some consideration of the role of acids in food for causing indigestion. In the first recorded lesson some 'learning intentions' (to use the common National Curriculum term) were set out by the teacher and shared with the pupils, which are as follows:

(1) To discover how acids and alkali are used in everyday situations.

(2) To select and note appropriate information about uses and effects of acids and alkali.
(3) To understand that neutral solutions can be made by adding acids to alkali.

However, these science education goals were supplemented by another 'talk' agenda, in which the teacher was trying to encourage the children to use talk more effectively for learning, both in whole-class sessions and while they worked together in groups. This involved the teacher talking with the class about how they should work together and agreeing with them some 'talk rules' which they would follow while working in groups. The data being used by us here comes from the second recorded lesson of the series.

As is usual in English primary schools, the teacher opened the second lesson of the series with a whole-class discussion. We joined the beginning of that discussion in Sequence 1 as the teacher is eliciting from children their views about how they should work together in groups during science enquiry.

(*Note: In all transcripts, T = teacher; P = pupil, or names provided if known; unclear words are in brackets.*)

*Sequence 1: lesson 2, initial whole-class discussion, Havenhill*

| | |
|---|---|
| T: | So what are our talk rules? What, talk, uh, rules should we have? Paul? |
| PAUL: | When someone else is talking you don't call out? |
| T: | Right, good boy. Adira, something else? You can put your hands down. |
| ADIRA: | You have to co-operate. |
| T: | You all have to co-operate, so it's a group responsibility for completing the task. It's not up to one person, it is a group responsibility. What about if you can't make your mind up? If two people, if things aren't quite going, going as they should be? |
| | (*Various pupils raising their hands*) |
| P: | Write down both ideas. |
| T: | Write down both ideas, if that's part of the [problem]. And if you've got a real problem? |
| P: | You could vote. |
| T: | You could vote, good way of sorting it out. |
| | (*Various pupils raising their hands*) |
| T: | You still might want to write down, this is the majority. Anything else we could do, Adam? |
| ADAM: | Explain why you think your answer is right. |
| T: | Right explain, take your time to – don't just say, well I think this – |

ADAM:    Why.

T:    Which is a word you guys often use. And if the worst come to the worst, I'm going to be working this afternoon with a little group of people that were absent for part of last week's lesson, so I shall be focused over there, but if you do need me, you could always come and speak to me if you have to. Jayden? What were you going to say?

P:    Um you could um also decide like, one person says that um, if two people, if there's more than two people answers, then you could choose like um. Other people could vote if their answer is – they could work out why their answer won't work.

T:    Yes if you suddenly work out that your answer doesn't work, it doesn't mean to say that you have to stick to what you suggested, it can actually be complimentary enough to say to other people – hang on a minute, oh, now I see what you're talking about. So you need to listen to each other, that is just as important.
*(Teacher addresses researchers who are video-recording)*
Have you decided where you are [going to be]? *(She turns to the class)*
Right then. Acids and not feeling too great, so you guys really need to tune into what your colleagues are saying, because this is what, part of what they were discovering last week. What did we what did we discover Nick about not feeling great and acids last week?

NICK:    Um that you can you either dilute it, or neutralise.

T:    Oh now we're, we can dilute it or neutralise it, I'm glad you got those two words in. But where is this acid that's, that's not making us feel too great? Burning on the end of my fingers? Nope, where is this acid?
*(Teacher walking around the classroom, pupils raising their hands)*

T:    Oh let's have a think? Um I think we'll ask the lovely Heather.

HEATHER:    Um I think it's probably inside um your tummy or inside your body.

T:    Yes inside your tummy, because do you remember when we first started acids and alkalis? We were looking at some of the foods that were acidic. Can you think of any of the foods that were acidic?

P:    Lemons?

T:    Lemons, good boy, so lemons are acidic, what else did we think of?

P:    Citric acid.

T:    There was citric acid, what did you think of *(inaudible)*?

P:    Tomatoes.

T:        Tomatoes, so well done. So there were foods that were acidic. And what was there in our stomach, what was in our stomach that we needed to help break down these foods? Put your hand down sweetheart. Adam?
          (*Teacher walking around the classroom, pupils raising their hands*)

ADAM:     Acid.

T:        Acids, so we've got acids that we eat, and acids in our stomach, mm and what's that doing to our acid levels? Katie, is it going up or down?

KATIE:    Up.

T:        It's going up and we discovered, last week one of the things we discovered was that acids and alkalis are used in everyday situations, to try and balance things out again. And which, we introduced two new words last week. Ben, we introduced neutralise – to neutralise and to dilute. (*Teacher pointing to the words written up on the wall*)

*Comment:* Sequence 1 is essentially a series of IRF exchanges, in which the teacher checks pupils' initial knowledge on matters relevant to the lesson. We can see that both agendas – the 'talk' one and the 'scientific' one – figure in this extract. The teacher begins by invoking a set of 'ground rules', which relate to her talk agenda. These ground rules were also displayed in the class, and she often referred to them at the start of lessons. The shift from one agenda to the other is made very clearly, after the teacher interacts briefly with the researchers. We have called such shifts (in either topic or communicative approach) 'turning points' in classroom dialogue (Scott and Ametller 2007).

After this turning point, the dialogue focuses on the link between everyday understanding of a phenomenon (indigestion) and the scientific 'story' – that acids can be neutralised by adding a similar strength alkali. The teacher makes a link between past and present experience, and between everyday and scientific knowledge, by asking Heather whether she 'remembers when we first started acids and alkalis' and further asks her to 'think of any of the foods that were acidic'. Overall, our analysis indicated that the Havenhill teacher regularly offered pupils information about how activities were temporally organised, with links between past and future activities explained briefly but logically. In relation to her 'dialogic' agenda, she repeatedly highlighted the functional aspects of talk, as it was used in the class, by referring back to the established ground rules and how the children were expected to behave in forthcoming group activities. In relation to the science agenda, she regularly related newly introduced ideas to the children's everyday knowledge, such as linking 'acids' to indigestion.

During interviews with the children after the lessons, they also referred to their everyday knowledge, while at the same time using the new terms like 'alkaline' and 'neutralisation'. The teacher also regularly asked children to recall what they already knew about scientific procedures, in preparation for forthcoming activities.


### Case study 2. Beckstones year 6: rocks and soils

The Beckstones data also come from the second lesson of the recorded series. In the previous lesson, the class had looked at rock samples. The teacher opened Lesson 2 with a whole-class session. Just before the lesson began, she had written on the whiteboard:

> 'LI: To understand the structure of soil.
> SC: Can you identify the soil type in Beckstones & describe how this may affect us?'
> (*NB. LI = Learning intention and SC = Success criteria*)


### Sequence 2: lesson 2, Beckstones

| | |
|---|---|
| T: | Right. Don't talk. |
| | (*Teacher is at her desk preparing to start the lesson. She drops some papers*) |
| T: | Can you pick it up Skye and Gemma? That will be so helpful, instead of just sitting there and going 'Yes right'. |
| | (*Pupils help the teacher pick up paper from the floor*) |
| T: | There's enough for each person, on the table. |
| | (*Teacher gives a pupil papers to hand out*) |
| T: | Can you just (*inaudible*). Whose mess is all that? Get it into a neat pile, and two, there should be, Hailey, a box of compasses in the bottom cupboard, can you get them out for me please? Right this table, Faye's table can we straighten up and move down a bit? This table can go to the right a bit. |
| | (*All pupils are helping set up the classroom*) |
| T: | I can see one pen on the floor, a pencil on the floor, and there's a chair that's got no home. Nick what's happening (*inaudible*) in front of you? Right that table, would you like to go and get your jars of soil please? And just put them in the tray. |
| P: | Miss Johnson do you see compasses? |
| | (*Pupils go to get their equipment and the preparation continues*) |
| T: | Excuse me? What does that say? It's a compass. Right. Right are we sorted? |
| | (*All pupils are returning to their desks*) |
| T: | (*To researcher*) Um thank you. (*Teacher takes lapel microphone and puts it on*) |
| T: | Ok, right. Books away please, let's have a look at you today. Simon we're going to be doing lots of talking today, but we |

need to be talking about the right things. Everything away. Come on it's a nice sunny day, and we've got stuff to do. OK. You're there so Marc and David can give you a nudge, when you need to focus. Sit next to Hailey please Becky. Alright now, today we're moving on a little bit from rocks. We did some work last week and we talked about rocks, and we're moving now onto soil. And if you remember, um, you were asked over the last weekend to collect some soil, and to do a little bit of your own investigation. Well today we're going to sort of bring that into our lesson, and we're actually going to look at soil; um it's very important. It supports habitats, it also; well let's face it, it supports our ecosystem, it supports our world. And if we need to today, to sort of just have a little think about what soil is, and what purpose it has; I think personally, personally I think it's quite an important one, but let's find out. So today we're going to understand, the intention is to understand the structure of soil. What goes in it, what makes it? And by the end of today, I am hoping, and you're going to be hoping, that you can actually identify the soil type, that we have in Beckstones. Where we are, where most of us or many of us live. And also, be aware of how that actually affects us, because believe it or not soil does affect us every day, all the time. Now I'm going to start off with a question, what is the purpose of soil? Ok, I just want you to think about that first; what is the purpose of soil? I'm going to give you about [a] 10 or 15 second[s] to think; for you to think about what the purpose of soil is. What does it do and why is it here? How does it affect you, how does it affect me or us? Who does it affect, who doesn't it affect? OK, we've started off with a bit of thinking to get us into the mode of soil. OK, with your person next to you, and you might have a, a new person next to you, that you're going to talk to today. I'd like you to think about the following points; where do we find it? What does it look like? Is it all the same? And what's it used for? I'd like you to think about those three questions. Have a moment with your, your talk partner, and then see what the talk partner opposite you or next to you thinks? So the question was; what does it look like? What's it used for? Is it always the same? OK, and where do we find it? Let's go.

*(All pupils start to talk to each other at the same time. Teacher is talking to one pair of pupils at one table. After two minutes 10 seconds the teacher raises her hand to call the class together again)*

T:   Just a really quick feedback now, I've had quite an interesting conversation with Becky and Hailey. Um where do we find it? When do you come into contact with soil, Dominic?

DOMINIC:      Um you can find it under trees, near around the trees and, around bushes and everything.

T:            All right, commonly known as perhaps in the garden, or perhaps outside a garden, perhaps, you know, all around us. Uh, is it all the same colour?

CLASS:        No.

T:            What colours do you know of, for soil?
              (*Several pupils raise their hands*)

T:            Bridget?

BRIDGET:      Um, sandy soil, I was just about to say that sometimes that can get washed away, so it needs trees to keep it.

T:            Yes, you're jumping ahead a little bit; I'm asking actually what colour you get soil in? All right, hold that thought because we'll probably need that information a little bit later. OK? Georgina? Uh Georgina?

GEORGINA:     Um, you can get black soil, like kind of, like compost in the garden.

T:            Right have you been to a place where you've seen black or very dark brown soil?

GEORGINA:     Yes.

T:            Where?

GEORGINA:     Um my garden.

*Comment:* Initially the teacher is mainly concerned with organisation and order in the classroom rather than the curriculum. After some exchanges with pupils about such matters, she talks in an authoritative/non-interactive mode. During this she sets up a discussion activity amongst the pupils involving 11 questions about soil. After a very short time of group discussion (during which she talks with one group – dialogue not included here), she calls the class back to attention and engages them in a series of IRF exchanges about where soil is found – a relatively simple issue for year 6 children. She revises a child's answer 'around trees and bushes' to the more general 'inside and outside gardens – all around us'. She then asks another simple question about colour, rejecting a more sophisticated suggestion 'sandy soil' and asking a pupil to 'hold that thought' about the function of trees for preventing erosion until later in the lesson, when it will apparently be more relevant. This was the only reference made by the teacher in that lesson to the future trajectory of children's study of this topic. However, our analysis showed that Bridget's comment was not revisited later in the lesson: the topic of erosion did not figure again at all. The teacher then reasserts her question about the colour of the soil.

## Results and discussion

As illustrated by the commentaries on the examples above, following is our analysis.

- Both teachers referred to the temporal organisation of events, both within and across lessons.
- Both teachers used questions to encourage children's active involvement in lessons. That is, they both regularly generated some interactive/authoritative dialogue (as defined by Mortimer and Scott 2003).
- In both the classes, the dynamic progress of the talk in the whole-class sessions depended heavily on teacher-generated IRF exchanges. This is not, in itself, a critical comment on their practice, as IRF exchanges can be used very effectively to sustain dialogue, and for a variety of pedagogic purposes (as discussed by Mercer 1995; Wells 1999). Initiating questions can be used to provoke pupils' imagination, to explore their wider relevant experience and to get them to explain their reasoning. However, in these two classrooms almost all of the initiations were used in the 'traditional' way, to check the state of pupils' understanding of the topic being studied.
- Both teachers provided opportunities for children to talk together in pairs or groups in the normal course of a lesson as would be expected within a dialogic teaching approach. However, only the Havenhill teacher allowed such discussion to continue for more than one or two minutes.
- Neither teacher generated the sort of whole-class discussion which Mortimer and Scott (2003) call 'dialogic/interactive', wherein pupils take extended turns, and the teacher picks up ideas pupils have offered in those turns and then uses them to build new directions for the discussion. This kind of discussion has been identified as an important aspect of dialogic teaching by Alexander (2000).
- In their own 'authoritative' presentations, both teachers sometimes made connections between everyday experience and scientific explanations. But only the Havenhill teacher made pedagogic use of this, by regularly relating the everyday phenomena that had been discussed to new scientific knowledge as the class moved from everyday accounts of phenomena to more scientific ones.
- Both teachers elicited pupils' existing ideas about the topics under discussion, but neither picked up what was offered by pupils and used it to make connections between the various ideas and contrasts with the scientific perspective on the topic (a positive feature of dialogic science teaching identified by Scott, Mortimer, and Aguiar (2006) which they call *interanimation*). Moreover, the Beckstones teacher invariably left little space for pupils' contributions based on their wider experience, and avoided any extended discussion on them. Issues raised by pupils were never 'built in' to the content of the lesson as it developed.
- The Havenhill teacher more often used discursive strategies that gave the dialogue a cumulative, temporally cohesive quality, such that it might be expected to help pupils perceive a meaningful trajectory through their classroom activities.

- The Havenhill teacher made quite explicit the trajectory of learning for the relevant science topic across activities and lessons, and set out clearly an agenda for learning, as identified by Alexander (2000) as a feature of dialogic teaching. In contrast, the Beckstones teacher offered little in the way of helping pupils see that their activities were cumulative and purposeful.

- The Havenhill teacher made the use of dialogue itself a matter for consideration with the class, and explicitly focused on the quality of the talk of the pupils in their groups (again identified as a feature of dialogic teaching by Alexander 2008a). She reported that before the recorded lessons, she had spent time developing the awareness and skills of the children in ways of talking and working together effectively, and she regularly referred back to that common experience of setting up group-based activities in the recorded lessons. She also regularly emphasised the value of talk for learning. The Beckstones teacher did not report such preparatory activity, or refer to it in the recorded lessons. There was little evidence from her lessons that she wished pupils to value talk as a tool for learning, or that she felt that they needed to become more aware of how to use it. Although she required the children to talk together at certain points, any comments about their talk were concerned with classroom order and control rather than with its use as a tool for learning (which is consistent with the responses of the teachers interviewed by Fisher and Larkin (2008)).

Despite some superficial similarities in the organisation of talk in the two classrooms that have figured in this paper, it can be seen that there were some interesting and important differences. The practice of the Havenhill teacher embodied a much higher regard for the value of talk as a tool for learning, and of the need to develop children's awareness and skills in using it. She showed greater awareness of her role as a model for using talk for learning and of the value of balancing group work with whole-class activity. Less tangibly, the ethos of her classroom seemed more encouraging for the expression of children's ideas, which then informed further discussion. In Alexander's (2008b) terms, her teaching was much more 'dialogic'. The effects of this seemed apparent in the more committed and enthusiastic participation of children in her class.

Nevertheless, although both these teachers generated some features of dialogic teaching in their practice, others were absent or rare. Much of the whole-class talk in both classrooms matched the conventional characteristics of classroom talk observed in schools in many countries over recent decades (as described, for example, in Edwards and Westgate 1994; Mercer 1995). Observations in the project as a whole, across the 12 primary and secondary teachers, showed that the extent to which dialogue was effectively exploited as a pedagogic tool varied considerably. Only two teachers came close to representing Alexander's 'dialogic teaching' (one of whom was the Havenhill teacher), and only three teachers regularly engaged pupils in extended discussions of the type Mortimer and Scott (2003) call 'dialogic-interactive'. There are several possible reasons for this. It is widely acknowledged that the pressure English primary teachers are under to 'get through' the prescribed National Curriculum militates against a more adventurous, open-ended approach to classroom dialogue (Smith et al. 2004). Fisher and Larkin's (2008) survey suggests that teachers continue to be more concerned with keeping talk polite and orderly than with exploiting its learning potential.

Alexander (2008b) suggests that the continued dominance of the 'basics' of reading, writing and numeracy within the English education system diverts away teachers' attention from talk. This is in contrast to the way talk is accorded value in the classrooms of France, Russia and some other European countries. Our own view (supported by other researchers, e.g. Hardman 2008) is that the results of years of research about classroom talk have had relatively little impact on the content of the initial and in-service training of teachers in the United Kingdom. Most teachers do not have a high level of understanding of how talk 'works' as the main tool of their trade, and very few have been taught specific strategies for using it to the best effect. Our interviews and other discussions with the teachers in our project – who were self-selected on the basis of their interest in dialogue – indicated that even they were relatively unaware of the patterns and functions of teacher–pupil talk in their classrooms. Yet our experience of providing initial training and professional development courses for teachers suggests that they are very receptive to information and guidance on such matters. It would seem that this is an aspect of initial teacher training and professional development which, in England at least, would merit a significant investment.

## Developing pedagogic activities: talking points

One test of applied educational research, such as the one we have described, is whether the results can be used to offer relevant advice to teachers about how to develop their practice. We have described elsewhere activities which teachers can use to help develop their pupils' awareness and skill in the use of talk for collaborative, group-based problem-solving (Dawes, Mercer, and Wegerif 2004). In this project, we have tried to devise pedagogic activities which will help teachers to instigate and develop useful whole-class dialogue between them and their students. We provide here an example of one activity, *Talking Points*, which combines both of those aims and, as we know (from observations and informal feedback from teachers), has been found useful.

*Talking Points* (Dawes 2008a, 2008b) employs a simple resource for stimulating speaking, listening, thinking and learning. The 'talking points' are basically a list of statements which may be factually accurate, contentious or downright wrong. They provide a focus for discussion, by offering a range of ideas about a topic which the children can consider together. Assessing the truth of these statements stimulates children's thinking; and making explicit their knowledge and experiences to justify their beliefs enables children to compare their understandings. As we will show, a teacher can also learn about children's current levels of understanding from the outcomes of those discussions and decide on useful points for subsequent whole-class talk, further exploration, activity, demonstration or research. Once they are familiar with this technique, teachers can readily generate their own talking points or teach children how to do so.

We can demonstrate the value of this kind of activity in practice by using Sequence 3 given below, recorded in a year 5 English primary school class. After a brief introductory session, the children were given a group-based activity in which the group of three students discussed a set of talking points about the solar system and tried to decide whether they were true or false. The transcript consists of three sections: an extract from the small-group discussion; an extract from the whole-class 'feedback' session that followed; and then part of a whole-class 'demonstration' that concluded the lesson.

### Sequence 3: year 5, talking points

| | |
|---|---|
| VIOLA: | OK (*reads*) 'The moon changes shape because it is in the shadow of the earth'. |
| FRANNIE: | No, that's not true because there's the clouds that cover the moon. |
| VIOLA: | No, it isn't . . . Yes . . . |
| GABRIELLE: | Yes. |
| VIOLA: | Because in the day we think, oh the moon's gone, it hasn't gone, it's just the clouds that |
| FRANNIE: | Have covered it. |
| GABRIELLE: | Yes, that's why I, like, every time, well on Sunday I went out and it was like five in the morning right, and the moon was still out so that's fine 'cos it was still dark, right? |
| VIOLA: | Yes. |
| GABRIELLE: | So when we went out it was like five, four, four o'clock, something like that, like at that time there wouldn't be the moon out would there, but I saw half the moon out and I said, I said to my Mum's friend, I said 'Look Tony, there's the moon already out', and he said 'Oh yes'. Because in the morning when we came, there was the clouds. |
| T: | OK everybody, finish up the one you're talking about. |
| VIOLA: | So what do we think? |

GABRIELLE:     I think it's false.
FRANNIE:       False.
(*We now move into the following whole-class 'feedback' session*)
T:             Keighley, would you read out number nine for us?
KEIGHLEY:      (*reads*) 'The moon changes shape because it is in the shadow of the earth'.
T:             Right, now what does your group think about that?
KEIGHLEY:      True.
T:             What, um, why do you think that?
KEIGHLEY:      Hm, because it's when earth is dark then, hm, we're not quite sure but we think it was true.
T:             Right, people with hands up – (*to K*) who would you want to contribute?
KEIGHLEY:      Um, Sadie?
SADIE:         I think it's false because when the sun moves round the earth, it shines on the moon, which projects down to the earth.
T:             (*nods*) do you want to choose somebody else? That sounds good.
SADIE:         Matthew
MATTHEW:       Well, we weren't actually sure 'cos we were (thinking) the actual moon changes which it never does, or, if it is our point of view from earth, which it puts us in the shadow.
T:             That's a good point, isn't it, it doesn't actually change, it looks as if it changes shape to us, that's a really good point.

We move now to the last part of the lesson. The teacher has a large photo of a half moon on the interactive whiteboard. She also has on a table a lamp (sun), a globe (earth) and a tennis ball (moon).

T:             Can anybody describe to me why we can only see one side of the moon from earth? Gabrielle?
GABRIELLE:     (*inaudible; nobody else offers a response*)
T:             OK, we can only see one side of the moon from earth because the moon is going round the earth, Ok, and it keeps the same side of itself to the earth all the time like that. This little dot here (*indicating dot on the tennis ball*) look, that's one of those craters on the moon. If we're in the UK here, we can only see this dot here, and we can't see anything on *this* side at all because it doesn't turn round, it keeps that dot (*orbits the moon round the earth*) – we have to colour it so that we will be able to see. Ok, let's see why the moon actually changes shape. It takes about a month, 27, 28 days for the earth, for the moon to go round the earth.
               A moonth, that's what a month means. Yes 27.3 if we're going to be precise.

|         |                                                                  |
|---------|------------------------------------------------------------------|
|         | OK?                                                              |
| CHILD:  | A mownth.                                                         |
| T:      | A moonth, that's why it's called a month. Here we are, somebody was saying they thought it might have ice, doesn't have any water, no atmosphere and no water. It's just rock. OK. This phrase, 'the phases of the moon', we use to mean the way the moon *appears* to, as Matthew pointed out, change shape. The way the moon appears to change shape. You can see here we've got this half moon effect, you see here? (*indicates whiteboard*) |
| ALL:    | Yes.                                                             |
| T:      | But there's something making a shadow on the moon here, let's look what that is. Because that's what we need to find out before we finish today. Carlie, are you with me? |
| KEIGHLEY: | I brought in a book in which it shows all the different stages of the moon. |
| T:      | Right, OK, that'll be helpful. We'll look at it in a book 'cos I think to see pictures really helps doesn't it? OK, let's just see if we can work it out now. (*Teacher positions the ball, the 'earth' and the lamp in a line, with the earth in the middle; the 'moon' is, however, lifted so that the lamp shines on it.*) Here's the earth, here's the sun, here's the moon. Right. How much of the moon do you think we can see from earth? |
| CHILDREN: | Half (*which is wrong; this would be a full moon*). |
| T:      | Think! The *moon*; this is the sun, our source of light, it's really shining off into space, we're facing the moon, here we are (*the UK is facing away from the sun*) we're facing the moon, how much of that moon can we see? |
| CHILDREN: | Half/a third maybe?                                             |
| T:      | Right.                                                           |
| WALTER: | We can't see these sides, or the back.                          |
| T:      | We can't see any of this (*indicating the back of the 'moon'*). |
| WALTER: | So we can only see about a third (*children still do not understand*). |
| T:      | Right look, if the sun's shining from here there is nothing between the sun and the moon, so from here on earth what we can see is a circle, a big shiny full moon. Right? That's a full moon, we can see the whole caboodle, if we're here on earth and the sun's over there. However, have a look now, what happens now. If I put the moon here (*between the sun and the earth*) here's the sun, is there any light from the sun falling on this moon that we would be able to see from earth? |
| CHILDREN: | No.                                                             |
| T:      | What would we see if the moon is in that position?             |

CHILDREN:   Nothing.

T:   Yes, it would be totally dark. We get a completely black effect because we can't see it, we can only see it if there is light falling on it, and all the light is falling on this side and we're not over there, we're over here. Yes?

TOM:   If it's like that, the reason we can't see anything really because it's so dark around it.

T:   Yes it's dark, yes, the light needs to land on it for us, it can't shine on itself. So that's when it's the darkest bit of the moon, we can't see it (*returns 'moon' to first position*). That's a full moon, over here relative to the earth (*moves moon to second position*) and that's when it's dark. However, wait a minute let's get this right. If we come half way around (*moves the moon so that the lamp and ball are at a right angle with the earth at the vertex*), the sun's shining on this bit, but not on this bit, what would we see then?

CHILDREN:   Half/half moon.

T:   It would look like that (*points at picture of half moon on whiteboard*).

CHILDREN:   Yes/Ooh.

T:   Yes, the sun's shining on that bit, but not on this bit, we'd see a half moon. So that means that the moon is putting a shadow on itself, it's not the earth throwing a shadow on it, or a planet throwing a shadow on it, it's in its own shadow if you like. The shadowy bit is just not lit up by the sun. And from earth we can only see about half of it, while the other half of it is this side. And this is how it works (*moves the moon round the earth*) dark, half moon, full moon, half moon, and that's what happens. With those little crescents in between. Viola? (*Viola has her hand up*)

VIOLA:   I've learned something now.

T:   Yes (*laughs*) I'm a bit worried about what. Go on then.

VIOLA:   I didn't know that, I know that you can't see the other half, but I don't know how to explain it (*laughs*)

T:   Maybe, you need to give it a chance for it to sink in and think about it, it's quite hard to understand, I find it hard to understand.

*Comment:* In the first part of this sequence, we see three children discussing a 'talking point', drawing on whatever relevant experience and knowledge they can find to judge its veracity. We can see that they do not understand why the moon 'changes shape'. Nevertheless, the group activity focuses their attention on this topic and their relevant collective knowledge, in a way that would not be so easy in a teacher-led discussion. Moreover, we can see that they all participate and listen to each others' contributions. The quality of the talk in this group, and in most other groups in the classroom, reflects the teacher's successful pursuit of a 'talk agenda' in her lessons (as described for the Havenhill teacher above).

In the middle section, we see the teacher engaging with the pupils in talk which has some 'dialogic' features (in the sense that this term is used by both Alexander (2008a) and Scott, Mortimer, and Aguiar (2006)). In relation to Alexander's use of the term we can see that students are given opportunities and encouragement to question, state points of view and comment on ideas and issues which arise during lessons; the teacher's questions are designed to provoke thoughtful answers ('Why do you think that?'). The children's answers provoke further questions and form building blocks for further dialogue. In Scott, Mortimer, and Aguiar's (2006) terms, the talk is *interactive/dialogic* because the teacher engages the children in a series of questions, but these provide an opportunity for children to express their ideas. Moreover, the teacher does not make a critical assessment of these ideas as right or wrong, but rather takes account of them and allows the dialogue to continue. By using this interactive/dialogic approach, the teacher learns about the children's current understanding of the topic of the lesson and is able to use this information in developing the theme of the lesson.

In the final part of the sequence, the talk has a different pattern. Scanning over the sequence as a whole, it is quickly apparent that in the final part the teacher's talk takes up a much greater proportion of the dialogue. She uses these longer turns to explain to the children (with the use of models) how the solar system generates the moon's phases. She again questions the children, but this time the questions are used for different purposes – to check that the children are following her explanation, and to carry out some 'spot checks' on whether they have understood its implications and so on. Twice it seems that the children evidently have not understood, so the explanation and demonstration continue, with the questions simplified to focus on key points and to reinforce correct responses. The dialogue here can be described as *interactive/authoritative*. It is used to provide children with information about the solar system, which is absolutely necessary for their understanding of how it works, and a model-based spoken presentation of this kind is the most effective way of doing so. We might note at the end of the sequence that Viola, one of the students in the earlier group discussion extract, comments 'I've learned something now'. We cannot be sure, but it seems likely that the group discussion had 'primed' her to be receptive to the teacher's demonstration and explanation in a way that would not have happened if the teacher had begun the lesson with the authoritative demonstration. In describing and evaluating the talk in this lesson, then, we can see that it is the quality of the dialogue as whole that matters, and important is the way it is temporally organised as a means for establishing and maintaining a collective consciousness. It is the complementary variety of the talk that makes this 'dialogic teaching'. The *Talking Points* type of activity offers a way to help a teacher pursue such a dialogic pedagogy.

## Conclusion

Our research leads us to believe that initial teacher training and professional development should include more specific tuition in the effective use of talk for learning. We have found that even teachers who express an interest in dialogic teaching may need reassurance that this is, indeed, an effective way to help children's learning and understanding of science; and that their students need to develop an awareness of the nature and importance of their own participation in classroom talk. Our research supports the view that better motivation and engagement are found amongst children whose views are sought and valued through dialogue. Finally, we suggest that teachers can be helped to develop a more dialogic pedagogy through the use of certain techniques like *Talking Points*, which can be incorporated into the fabric of a lesson and used with children who know that their ideas and voices will be listened to with respect.

## Acknowledgements

This paper is based on a project entitled 'Dialogic teaching in science classrooms' carried out in 2005–2007 by Phil Scott and Jaume Ametller of the University of Leeds, Neil Mercer and Judith Kleine Staarman of the University of Cambridge, and Lyn Dawes of the University of Northampton. The research was funded by the Economic and Social Research Council (RES-000-23-0939). The members of the research team gratefully acknowledge that funding and the co-operative involvement of teachers in Calderdale and Milton Keynes.

## References

Alexander, R. 2000. *Culture and pedagogy: International comparisons in primary education.* Oxford: Blackwell.
Alexander, R. 2008a. *Towards dialogic teaching: Rethinking classroom talk.* 4th ed. York, UK: Dialogos.
Alexander, R. 2008b. Culture, dialogue and learning: Notes on an emerging pedagogy. In *Exploring talk in schools*, ed. N. Mercer and S. Hodgkinson. London: Sage.
Dawes, L. 2008a. *The essential speaking and listening: Talk for learning at key stage 2.* London: Routledge.
Dawes, L. 2008b. Encouraging students' contribution to dialogue during science. *School Science Review* 90, no. 331, 101–107.
Dawes, L., N. Mercer, and R. Wegerif. 2004. *Thinking together: A programme of activities for developing speaking, listening, and thinking skills.* 2nd ed. Birmingham, UK: Imaginative Minds.

Driver, R., P. Newton, and J. Osborne. 2000. Establishing the norms of scientific argumentation in classrooms. *Science Education* 84, no. 3, 287–312.

Edwards, A.D., and D.P.G. Westgate. 1994. *Investigating classroom talk.* 2nd ed. London: The Falmer Press.

Fisher, R., and S. Larkin. 2008. Pedagogy or ideological struggle? An examination of pupils and teachers' expectations for talk in the classroom. *Language and Education* 22, no. 1, 1–16.

Galton, M. 2007. *Learning and teaching in the primary classroom.* London: Sage.

Hardman, F. 2008. Teachers' use of feedback in whole-class and group-based talk. In *Exploring talk in schools,* ed. N. Mercer and S. Hodgkinson. London: Sage.

Kelly, G.J., C. Brown, and T. Crawford. 2000. Experiments, contingencies and curriculum: Providing opportunities for learning through improvisation in science teaching. *Science Education* 84, no. 5, 624–657.

Lemke, J.L. 1990. *Talking science: Language, learning and values.* Norwood, MA: Ablex Publishing Company.

Mercer, N. 1995. *The guided construction of knowledge: Talk amongst teachers and learners.* Clevedon, UK: Multilingual Matters.

Mercer, N. 2005. Sociocultural discourse analysis: Analysing classroom talk as a social mode of thinking. *Journal of Applied Linguistics* 1, no. 2, 137–168.

Mercer, N. 2008. The seeds of time: Why classroom dialogue needs a temporal analysis. *Journal of the Learning Sciences* 17, no. 1, 33–59.

Mercer, N., L. Dawes, R. Wegerif, and C. Sams. 2004. Reasoning as a scientist: Ways of helping children to use language to learn science. *British Educational Research Journal* 30, no. 3, 359–377.

Mercer, N., and K. Littleton. 2007. *Dialogue and the development of children's thinking: A sociocultural approach.* London: Routledge.

Mortimer, E.F., and P.H. Scott. 2003. *Meaning making in secondary science classrooms.* Maidenhead, UK: Open University Press.

Ogborn, J., G. Kress, I. Martins, and K. McGillicuddy. 1996. *Explaining science in the classroom.* Buckingham, UK: Open University Press.

Scott, P., and J. Ametller. 2007. Teaching science in a meaningful way: Striking a balance between 'opening up' and 'closing down' classroom talk. *School Science Review* 88, no. 324, 77–83.

Scott, P., E. Mortimer, and O. Aguiar. 2006. The tension between authoritative and dialogic discourse: A fundamental characteristic of meaning making interactions in high school science lessons. *Science Education* 90, no. 4, 605–631.

Sinclair, J., and R. Coulthard. 1975. *Towards an analysis of discourse: The English used by teachers and learners.* London: OUP.

Smith, F., F. Hardman, K. Wall, and M. Mroz. 2004. Interactive whole-class teaching in the national literacy and numeracy strategies. *British Educational Research Journal* 30, no. 3, 395–411.

Wells, G. 1999. *Dialogic inquiry: Toward a sociocultural practice and theory of education.* Cambridge: Cambridge University Press.

*The use of digital technology for supporting talk in classrooms has been one of my interests since the time of the Spoken Language and New Technology project in the early 1990s (as described in Chapter 3). A new opportunity arose in the first years of the new century with the government-sponsored introduction of interactive whiteboards into the classrooms of almost all English primary schools in the early years of the twenty-first century. As has commonly been the case with IT, this new technology was introduced with wild claims that it would 'transform pedagogy' for the better, without there having been any research on if or how it could actually do so. With the aim of rectifying this situation, I began a new phase of this research with Karen Littleton, Julia Gillen, Judith Kleine Staarman and Alison Twiner at the Open University; and when I moved to Cambridge, it continued with my new colleagues Sara Hennessy and Paul Warwick, as described in this chapter.*

# 12 Using interactive whiteboards to orchestrate classroom dialogue

*Mercer, N., Hennessy, S. & Warwick, P. (2010). Using interactive whiteboards to orchestrate classroom dialogue.* Technology, Pedagogy and Education *(Taylor and Francis), 19, 2, 195–209.*

## Abstract

This paper focuses on the use of interactive whiteboards (IWBs) as a tool for encouraging and supporting classroom dialogue. Our concern here is with the promotion of 'dialogic' communication between teachers and students, which is now widely recognised as educationally valuable. In this study we investigated how teachers could use the *technical interactivity* of the IWB to support *dialogic interactivity*. The design of the study was predicated upon a partnership between the authors and three UK (primary, middle school and secondary) teachers of 8- to 14-year-olds; examples of practice reported here derive mainly from secondary history. Outcomes include illustrative examples of teachers' effective strategies for using the IWB for orchestrating dialogue. Implications for teachers' initial training and professional development are considered.

## Introduction

This paper reports research on how the interactive whiteboard (IWB) can be used to support and enhance classroom learning through 'dialogic' teaching. The study took place in the context of almost total saturation of UK schools with IWBs. It builds upon our previous work on the critical role of the teacher in purposefully exploiting digital tools to support subject learning. This approach differs from that of most other research into educational technology, which typically highlights the potential of the tools for 'transforming' learning. In this paper, our particular focus is on how teachers can exploit the technical interactivity of the IWB to support dialogic interactivity. We have asked: *How can teachers using a 'dialogic' approach to teaching exploit the multimodality and interactivity of the IWB to support student learning?*

As we will explain, drawing on the work of Alexander (2004) and others, we characterise a dialogic pedagogy as one that actively builds on learners' contributions, engages both teachers and students in generating and critically evaluating ideas, and encourages explicit reasoning and the joint construction of knowledge. In our study, the three participating teachers first engaged with us in discussions about dialogic teaching that were informed by previous research and which aimed for practical outcomes. The teachers then developed classroom activities using the IWB during whole class teaching and any associated group work.

## Background: classroom use of interactive digital technologies

The introduction and promotion of educational technology through government initiatives in the UK has generally been 'technology-led', rather than being more appropriately 'educationally-led' (Dawes, 2001), with the result that little attempt has been made in such programmes to link technology use to the needs of teachers and students, or to what research has shown are effective ways of teaching and learning. Programmes for training teachers to use new technologies have also suffered from what Lankshear (1997) described as 'applied technocratic rationality' – a view that technology has an independent integrity and a power that can be unleashed through learning certain basic skills. In sum, research, policy and training initiatives have often tended to ignore the vital need to relate the use of new forms of technology to what is known about effective pedagogy.

In the UK, there has been substantial government investment and policy-makers' interest in IWBs in education and an exponential increase in their numbers in UK schools (sixfold between 2002 and 2005: Kitchen, Mackenzie, Butt, & Finch, 2006) before the implications for teaching and learning were even investigated (e.g. Smith, Higgins, Wall, & Miller, 2005). Nevertheless, teachers and learners are enthusiastically adopting this powerful tool, which seems ideally suited to supporting interactive whole class teaching. In practice, however, it seems in many cases to be associated with superficial collaboration, motivation and participation at the expense of uptake questioning (Higgins et al., 2005) and student talk and reflection (Gillen, Kleine Staarman, Littleton, Mercer, & Twiner, 2007; Smith, Hardman, & Higgins, 2006). Government-funded research shows that pressure to 'get through' curriculum content means that IWB use may decrease thinking time and opportunity for learner input, resulting in teacher-only operation (Moss et al., 2007). In our earlier studies of IWB use in secondary science, students' physical manipulation of objects was desired by teachers but constrained by systemic school and subject cultures, curricular and assessment frameworks (Hennessy, Deaney, Ruthven, & Winterbottom, 2007). Nevertheless the large-scale SWEEP study of primary teachers (Somekh et al., 2007) indicated that IWB use became embedded after a period of 2 years, and new or improved pedagogical practices then began to emerge. Around a quarter of teachers reported more interactive lessons with greater active pupil involvement, made possible by the functionality of the board.

## The technical interactivity of the IWB

Interactive whiteboard systems comprise a computer linked to a data projector and a large touch-sensitive electronic board displaying the projected image; they allow direct input via finger or stylus so that objects can be easily moved around the board or transformed by teacher or students. 'Flipchart' software provided with the board or obtained separately provides a variety of functions, including those which replicate non-digital technologies such as flipcharts, dry-wipe boards, overhead projectors, slide projectors and video-players, and others which have not previously been possible on a large, vertical display. These comprise '*technical interactivity*' (Smith et al., 2005), and as Beauchamp and Parkinson (2005), Miller, Glover, and Averis (2005) and others have noted, these functions include:

- drag and drop (objects on the board can be matched or moved around);
- hide and reveal (objects placed over others can be removed or 'rubber' reveals hidden text);
- highlighting (transparent colour can be placed over writing or other objects);
- spotlighting (view restricted to circular area of screen);
- animation (objects can be rotated, enlarged and set to move along a specified path);
- annotation of objects displayed (textual or graphical);
- tickertape (text moves continuously across screen);
- indefinite storage and quick retrieval of material, 'flipcharts' and annotations;
- feedback (when a particular object is touched, a visual or aural response is generated);
- automatic handwriting recognition and text formatting features.

## The dialogic interactivity of the IWB

By distinguishing between 'technical' and 'dialogic' interactivity, we intend to highlight the distinction between what a piece of technology can do, and what it can be used to achieve educationally. The IWB offers teachers and students a ready facility for finding, entering, modifying and saving text and other items relevant to their task in hand. It is 'interactive' in the sense that it responds easily and quickly to the user's commands. Our interest, however, has been in if and how this facility can be used to support the dynamics of educational dialogue – and whether it offers special advantages over alternative 'tools' for doing so. This interest has been shaped and informed by research that takes a sociocultural perspective on education, as we will explain.

### Dialogic teaching and a sociocultural perspective on the use of ICT in the classroom

A sociocultural perspective highlights the significance of mediating tools (or 'mediating artefacts') and technologies in the social processes of learning (Säljö, 1999; Wertsch, Tulvoiste, & Hagstrom, 1993). This perspective emphasises the role of language as the prime cultural tool, while also in more recent years offering valuable insights into the use of computer-based technology (for example, Crook, 2007; Dawes, Mercer, & Wegerif, 2004). This perspective has formed the main basis for the development of a 'dialogic' pedagogy: an approach in which the teacher strives for the active involvement of students in the process of knowledge construction through the use of talk and other means of communication (Alexander, 2004). In recent years, other researchers have also made persuasive and influential arguments for the importance of the quality of teacher-student dialogue in the development of children's understanding of science and other curriculum subjects (Lemke, 1990; Mortimer & Scott, 2003; Wells & Bell, 2008). Interventional, school-based studies have provided supportive empirical findings (for example, the research in Mexican schools reported by Rojas-Drummond & Mercer, 2004; and the UK-based research reported by Mercer & Littleton, 2007). The work of Brown and Palincsar, carried out in the 1980s and explicitly linked to Vygotskian theory, was a significant early contribution in this respect (e.g. Brown & Palincsar, 1989). Their *Reciprocal Teaching* approach involved the use of specific dialogic strategies by both teachers and children in primary/ elementary school. One of its aims was to encourage more critical and elaborated contributions from pupils, who made impressive gains in reading comprehension. More recently, Kim, Anderson, Nguyen-Jahiel, and Archodidou (2007) have shown that the similar kind of teacher-led dialogue they call *Collaborative Reasoning* leads to improvements in reading comprehension and the quality of written argument for secondary/high school students.

The dialogic approach to teaching involves orchestrating classroom talk and activity so that teachers and learners are actively commenting and building on each other's ideas, together posing questions and co-constructing interpretations (Alexander, 2004). Preconditions for dialogue include open-ended tasks and higher order questioning, and a supportive classroom ethos for exploring and sharing ideas. Recent incarnations of national examinations and policy strategies in the UK have moved increasingly towards an emphasis on classroom discussion of controversial topics and development of dialogue skills in some subjects. Yet a conflicting policy and school inspection emphasis on rapid lesson pace (disregarding the desired pace of learning) and soliciting correct answers, coupled with many teachers' and policymakers' lack of understanding of dialogic pedagogy, means that dialogic teaching is not commonly observed: 'In many classrooms most of the dialogue appears to occur more by accident than in a deliberate, conscious manner' (Smardon & Bewley, 2007, p. 2).

Research has suggested that multimodal technologies such as the IWB can contribute to the creation of a 'dialogic space' (Wegerif, 2007), wherein educationally valuable dialogue and teacher-guided learning can take place (Gillen et al., 2007). To understand if and how it can do so, we need to consider not the potential functionalities of the IWB, but its actual uses in classroom contexts and teacher perceptions of those uses. The main question that this paper addresses is thus: *If teachers are consciously aiming to enact a dialogic, interactive pedagogy, how can/do they use the technical interactivity of the IWB to do so?* Our particular focus in this study is with archetypal use of the IWB in whole class teaching. Elsewhere, we have explored the use of the IWB by collaborative pupil groups during lessons: Warwick, Mercer, Kershner, and Kleine Staarman (2010, in press).

## Research participants, methodological approach and research strategy

Our study involved three teachers who use an IWB as an integral part of their everyday practice. Participants were selected on the basis of having an observably dialogic pedagogical approach to teaching. They included a Deputy Head Teacher who worked with primary children (aged 10–11) and who focused on Personal, Social and Health Education; a Head of English who focused on crime story writing with middle school children (aged 12–13); and a Head of Humanities who worked with secondary children (aged 13–14) on World War 1. In this article we draw particularly on the latter case.

The teachers participated in a series of workshops on dialogic teaching, before going on to design and trial IWB-supported lessons. (They had a total of 6 days each of funded release time from teaching to enable them to participate.) Collaborative video analysis and discussion of 'critical episodes' (see Phase 3) then enabled an examination of how IWB use supported classroom dialogue. Our methodology is summarised below (and described in more detail by Hennessy, Warwick, & Mercer, 2011).

### Phases and methods of research

*Phase 1:* Teachers were observed and video-recorded teaching a topic over two lessons each, to familiarise the team with their current practice and to pilot our recording procedures. They all participated in three one-day workshops, in which video data from the six pilot lessons, along with footage of other teachers using IWBs during an earlier research project ('T-MEDIA': Hennessy & Deaney, 2009), were used as a stimulus for discussion. The teachers and researchers evaluated illustrated approaches and assessed their applicability to the teachers' own contexts, discussing ways of further exploiting the IWB technology to enhance their approaches. The nature of productive classroom dialogue and ways to encourage it were also discussed. Teachers were encouraged to keep unstructured diaries of their reflections on pilot lessons and workshop experiences. Other resources included professional development activities generated through a series of 'Thinking Together' projects (conducted with other teachers) as reported by Dawes, Mercer, and Wegerif (2004) and Mercer and Littleton (2007: see http://thinkingtogether.educ.cam.ac.uk/). These activities help teachers to engage children in classroom dialogue. Copies of Alexander's (2004) pamphlet on Dialogic Teaching, a chapter on forms and functions of teacher-student dialogue (from Mortimer & Scott, 2003) and a short article on questioning strategies (Cardellichio & Field, 1997) were distributed too.

*Phase 2:* A sequence of three lessons was video-recorded in each classroom. The teachers kept diaries of their pre- and post-lesson reflections and planning. They were interviewed once about their plans (using a semi-structured schedule) and twice again after lessons about using the IWB to support dialogue and how successful their actions had been (two post-lesson interviews increased the database without being overly demanding). Flipchart files and captured annotations, lesson plans, worksheets, digital photographs and copies of pupil work provided valuable additional data.

*Phase 3:* Copies of the videos were distributed, and the whole team reconvened for a fourth half-day workshop to review our experiences, to share teacher-selected video clips and to use these in defining criteria for identifying 'critical episodes' of the phenomena of interest (9–10 per case), as follows. Selected episodes (a) collectively illustrated a range of IWB uses and (b) included dialogue that was perceived to be stimulated by well-selected resources that were engaging and/or meaningful to learners; linked with any level of IWB use but including some pupil ownership of the board; arising from opportunities for focused, cumulative, open-ended discussion in whole class, pairs, or groups; moving forward students' learning.

Discussion of critical episodes chosen and commented upon independently by teachers and researchers, along with diaries and interview transcripts, was then carried out by one researcher with each teacher. They exchanged their thoughts and selections, then met for 3–5 hours to compare and reconcile them, reviewing video-recorded episodes or screen shots as needed. Analytic commentary, interspersed with direct quotes about the episodes from the post-lesson interviews, and the outcomes of the negotiations were incorporated into a set of review notes for each case (drawing on the meeting transcript). These described the part played by the technology and the teacher in each chosen episode, the underlying rationale and effectiveness of the pedagogical approach in terms of quality of dialogue, and the level of student participation.

The process enabled us to identify what the data in each case revealed about the integration of IWB use for supporting substantive teacher-student and student-student dialogue. The teachers' pedagogical approaches were thereby evaluated with reference to our criteria for dialogic teaching (as defined above). This phase culminated in a final agreed set of critical episodes from each classroom, a rationale for their selection, and some conclusions about dialogic pedagogy in the context of IWB use.

*Phase 4:* A final (fifth) half-day workshop focused on the expected impact of participation within the schools and the perceived obstacles to adoption of a dialogic approach and to IWB use by novices (as reported by Hennessy et al., 2010, in press; and Warwick, Hennessy, & Mercer, 2010, submitted).

*Phase 5:* Finally, the research team conducted a cross-case analysis comparing and contrasting approaches to exploiting the IWB to support a dialogic approach in the three very different settings. We trawled teacher diaries, interviews, workshop and review meeting transcripts, and accreditation reports using HyperResearch™ 2.6, a software tool for qualitative data analysis, coding material pertaining to teacher strategies for using the IWB. We also revisited videos of critical episodes and annotated the transcripts with comments on dialogue quality and teacher strategies in order to identify how shared understandings and new interpretations were being progressively created through the dialogue, and to examine what sorts of connections were made during interactions within and across critical episodes. A series of screen shots and photographs of IWB artefacts in the making were also prepared for interpreting the rich and complex classroom interactions that took place.

## Findings

The data reported here derive mainly from our critical episode and transcript analyses; space does not permit embellishing the account with interview, meeting and accreditation report extracts, but these are evident in a paper focusing on the research collaboration (Hennessy et al., 2011). In Phase 1, teacher workshops and pilot video recording received an enthusiastic response from all of the teachers, yielding a range of thoughtful diary reflections such as the following typical comments:

> Sense of teachers and researchers with a common purpose. . . . Particularly important is that while the IWB is a key tool, it has to serve learning purposes.
>
> (Lloyd)

> The first workshop day has enabled me to really start thinking in depth about my own practice and the powerful impact a more structured approach to 'talk' in the classroom could have. . . . Alexander [2004] – the idea of dialogic teaching being cumulative, with children and teachers building on each other's ideas, really stood out for me, as it is the one which I feel I currently address the least. . . . [I]n order to move

forward, I need to look now at . . . using questioning more effectively to enable cumulative talk to take place more regularly.

(Caroline)

All of the teachers took up the opportunity for university accreditation (a Certificate of Educational Enquiry) through writing a report of their experiences, and one has gone on to Masters study. An important outcome from this preparatory work with the teachers was to operationalise dialogic teaching with the IWB. That is, one aim of the discussions was to identify the kinds of dialogic strategies that the IWB could help the teachers carry out. During this discussion, we agreed that dialogue *should make reasoning explicit* and *support the cumulative co-construction of knowledge and understanding*. We also agreed that a teacher might use the IWB to carry out any of the following pedagogical intentions:

- Scaffold learning;
- Support the temporal development of learning;
- Involve pupils in co-constructing knowledge;
- Encourage evaluation and synthesis;
- Develop a learning community;
- Develop pupil-pupil dialogue;
- Support provisionality of students' evolving ideas;
- Guide lesson flow;
- Develop pupil questioning.

The group's conception of dialogue (as a way of creating collective meaning) widened to include the use of non-verbal dialogue at the IWB – including sharing understandings or creating new digital artefacts through annotation, drawing, manipulation, linking, sorting etc. (often in conjunction with talk) – and non-verbal dialogue away from the IWB including, for example, producing diagrams, drawings or ordered elements, and manipulating/annotating paper replicas of IWB images. The role of mediating artefacts in making emerging thinking explicit and supporting the progression of dialogue over time is explored in more detail by Hennessy (2011).

## Case study: using the IWB to teach history

Because of space limitations, our choice in this paper is between giving three or so small examples of different teachers using the IWB during a lesson, or showing in more detail how one teacher used it during a series of lessons. We have chosen to do the latter, because we accept Alexander's (2004) view that one important aspect of dialogic teaching is its cumulative nature. That is, dialogue should be used to help students develop a learning trajectory, or pursue a 'learning journey' over time. We have therefore taken examples from a series of three lessons about World War 1 that were recorded in one history teacher's classroom with students aged 12–13.

If I ever get sent to the front with a regiment, I shall shed tears of joy. I do envy Chris going off so soon, but I think this dog will have his day soon too.

We expect to be moved to the front at any moment. The men apparently will be in the trenches alternate 24 hours, changing with a fresh lot of men during the night. I am behind HQ, probably a dug out where I sit and wait for the wounded to be brought to me. I am told that doctors are not allowed in the trenches. I am told that the feeding at the front is splendid and there is a Daily Mail for every 10 men.

Our men have had a terrible experience of 24 hours in trenches, drenched through and in some places knee deep in mud and water. To see them come out, line up and march off is almost terrible. They don't look like strong young men. They are muddied to the eyes. Their coats are plastered with mud and weigh an awful lot with the water that has soaked in. Their backs are bent and they stagger and totter along with the weight of their packs. Their faces are white and haggard and their faces glare out from mud. They look like wounded, sick, wild things. Many, too many who are quite beat are told they must walk it. Then comes the nightmare of a march of 2 to 4 miles which they do in a trance.

*Figure 12.1* Henry's annotations.

## Example 1: whole class discussion of a non-fiction text

The first example comes from the first lesson. The title the teacher gave this lesson was 'What can poetry tell us about the Western Front?' but he used further, non-fiction texts and other resources to explore this theme, presenting them on the IWB. He first put up an extract from an army doctor's notes, and asked one of the students to come up and annotate it. The student did so, as shown in Figure 12.1.

### Transcript 1: the doctor's account

T:      Right, look on the board here, this is what a doctor wrote in 1914 at the start of the war. What are the significant things about what he wrote here? What significant things, somebody come up and underline something off the front row, Henry could you come and do it for me? Come and underline something that's significant about what he's written here.
        *(Henry walks up to IWB, presses pen tool on IWB and begins to underline without talking)*

T:      Yep, and what else?
        *(Henry continues underlining)*

T:      Very good, who can explain why Henry has underlined those things? Robert.

ROBERT:   It showed that at the beginning of the war people thought it was a good thing.

T:   Excellent, brilliant it was a good thing, people thought at the start of the war. Alex would you agree with that?

ALEX:   Yes.

T:   Is there anything that Alex you might underline that Henry hasn't?

ALEX:   Umm.

T:   OK Henry, just explain why you've underlined that. I completely agree with you, thanks Alex that's great, thanks Robert.

HENRY:   Well because this the first part is talking about how you might get sent to the front of the front line of the war which would probably be to do with the trenches.

T:   Yep.

HENRY:   And he thinks it's like a good thing, like an honour and so he'd be really, he thinks he'd be really happy if he was sent there. He's envying his friend, the soldier who's gone off as well and hopes he will as well.

## Comment

The IWB offers the facility for teacher and students to share and discuss ideas on texts in a whole class setting – and the teacher uses this quite effectively here to stimulate some whole class dialogue about both the target text and Henry's underlined parts of it. In relation to the earlier list of pedagogical intentions that a teacher could pursue with the IWB, it can be seen here to be used to 'scaffold' the pupils' learning, because it enabled the teacher to provide a material support for the development of their ideas. It also helped the teacher involve the pupils actively in co-constructing knowledge and understanding. Of course, this could have been achieved without an IWB – for example by the teacher pinning up a large copy of the text on the wall for Henry to annotate. It is hardly ever the case that the IWB provides a completely unique kind of opportunity which could not have been achieved using other technology. Moreover, this use of the IWB is hardly innovative. But we argue that one should not judge teachers' uses of the IWB by how 'whizzy' they are; we should judge them by how well they harness the technology to serve effective pedagogical strategies – those that stimulate and move on student thinking. The ease with which this kind of technological interactivity can be achieved using the IWB means that it may encourage teachers to set up such opportunities for dialogue when they would not otherwise feel they had the time to do so. A key advantage is that the student's annotations can much more easily be modified, stored or revisited than if a paper copy was involved. The IWB in this way supported the provisionality of the students' developing understanding.

Regarding the quality of the dialogue – we see here some interaction between teacher and students which, in Mortimer and Scott's (2003) terms, is more 'dialogic' than 'authoritative'. It is certainly the case that the dialogue adheres to the usual Initiation-Response-Feedback (IRF) pattern of classroom talk, but the teacher uses his questions to elicit a variety of students' views. And although he provides positive feedback on their responses ('Excellent, brilliant'), he does not define their answers as 'right/wrong' as would be the case in the more archetypal, 'authoritative/interactive' dialogue. Moreover, the students take turns which are longer than the typical responses of students to teachers' questions. In these ways, the transcribed passage has some characteristics of dialogic teaching (Alexander, 2004). In this example, we can see how the technical interactivity is being used successfully to enable dialogic interactivity.

### Example 2: pair and whole class discussion of a poem

Later in the same lesson, the teacher put up on the IWB a poem about life in the WWI trenches by Wilfred Owen, 'Dulce et Decorum est', which he had introduced in Lesson 1. It is a graphic account of the deprivations of war, as when Owen recounts:

> Men marched asleep. Many had lost their boots
> But limped on, bloodshod. All went lame, all blind.
> (Stallworthy, 1983)

The teacher was able to use the multimodality of the IWB to show some relevant photographs, downloaded from a web source, such as that shown in Figure 12.2.

The teacher then used the 'cover and reveal' facility of the IWB to highlight just the first two lines of the poem. He asked the students to discuss these two lines with a partner: 'Ask your partner what they think is interesting and ask them why'. The teacher interacted with some of the pairs while they did so. A whole class discussion then followed, in which the teacher attempted to elicit from the pairs what they had discussed, as in the following extract. Each pair of students had a small (non-digital) whiteboard on which they could record their responses.

### Transcript 2: identifying interesting words

T:                      Tell me, key words that you think there. I tell you what I'm going to change that, interesting words that you think there are. Just write on your whiteboard one interesting word and why you think it's interesting. (*Class working silently*)

| | |
|---|---|
| T: | Right see what your partner thinks. Ask your partner what they think is interesting and ask them why. Go. (*Class discuss in pairs*) |
| STUDENTS IN ONE PAIR: | ...knock-kneed...he a really nice... (*whispering*). |
| T: | (*to a pair of students*) Right Ricky what have you got? Knock-kneed. Imagine, explain that for me, what's it mean to you, conjure up an image of it. |
| RICKY: | (*inaudible answer*). |
| OTHER STUDENT: | ...that's a bit scarier than that. |
| T: | A bit like what Joe and Daniel, yeah I do it like that and these are in like that. OK. (*To whole class*) Right, somebody, something interesting then please about the poem. What do we think about the poem. |
| RICKY: | Knock-kneed. |
| T: | Ah, Ricky, me and Ricky have just been saying knock-kneed is an interesting one. I think Joe and Daniel, for me am I right, they've seen that because they emphasised that quite a bit in their dramatisation. What's it mean to you? |
| JOE/DANIEL: | They say that their knees have been worn out quite a lot, they're old and they're bruised or broken. (*This discussion continued for several minutes*) |

*Figure 12.2* One of the photographs displayed by the teacher.

## Comment

Here we can see that the teacher used the 'cover/reveal' facility of the IWB to focus students' close attention on to part of the poem – thus scaffolding their learning about it by reducing the complexity of the task. He then used this resource to develop pupil-pupil dialogue (as in the list above) by allowing them time and 'dialogic space' (Wegerif, 2007) in pairs to think about and share their joint responses and feed them back to the rest of the class. Throughout this discussion, several took turns in the dialogue that were quite extended (though they still did not match the typical length of turn taken by the teacher), resembling the kinds of student contributions seen as valuable by advocates of 'dialogic' pedagogies (Alexander, 2004; Kim et al., 2007).

### Example 3: imagining the experience

The above discussion of the poem and pictures were followed up in the third lesson of the series, in which the teacher led a discussion of the question 'Is it possible for us to imagine the experience of trench warfare?' (written up on the IWB). The teacher initially played the class an audio recording of the sounds of trench warfare, and also played a (silent) film on the IWB. Part of this discussion (edited for brevity) is transcribed below.

### Transcript 3: imagining trench warfare

RICKY:     It's like when you imagine winning the lottery . . . it wouldn't necessarily be like what you think.

ROBERT:   You can imagine what it would look like, but you can't imagine what it would feel like or how you would be feeling.

OWEN:     Yes, because on the DVDs or on the films and the poems and stuff, it explains and you can see what it looks like, in wasteland, and you're both in trenches, but you wouldn't know what it was like to go ages without food or water.

RICKY:     That's partially true, but you wouldn't know what it would be like to be shot by a bullet or be bombed or something. You wouldn't see what it looked like either.

FELIX:     Every single person's experience with it would be different. Everybody's got different feelings towards the war, and you wouldn't know what anyone would have felt like, even if we were there, you would only know what you felt like.

T:        Yes, can we ever achieve a common understanding of anything?

The teacher used the IWB to sum up the main points of the discussion, as shown in Figure 12.3.

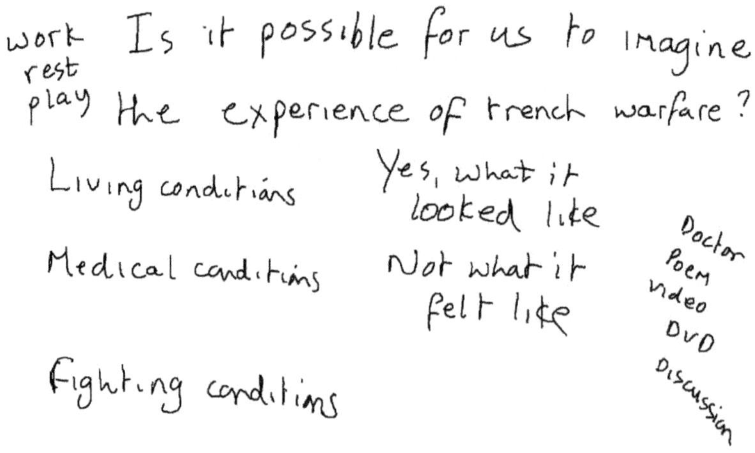

*Figure 12.3* The teacher's summary of the main points raised in the discussion.

*Comment*

As the extract in Transcript 3 shows, the teacher successfully elicited some relevant and interesting views on the question offered to the students. The discussion was certainly 'dialogic', in Mortimer and Scott's (*op.cit.*) sense, because students offer a range of reasoned views – and it is also 'interactive' as those views are debated and synthesised by the students. The teacher took a non-evaluative, commenting role. The IWB is at this point being used simply to record the outcomes of the class discussion, which could be done as easily with non-electronic technology. But the more salient point is that this same technology acted as a 'digital hub', enabling the teacher to easily show a wide range of digital resources presented in different modalities – poems, a historical diary, photographs, audio and visual tracks of a film played separately. These functioned as pivotal stimuli for the subsequent discussion, and to allow students to annotate texts, while he led classroom discussions about them. With reference to the earlier list of teaching 'intentions', the teacher used the IWB to guide lesson flow and encourage evaluation and synthesis. By basing the discussion and group activity throughout the series of three lessons on this flexible yet coherent (and annotatable) set of resources, he could also be seen to support the temporal development of learning and develop a learning community (which, according to Alexander, 2004, is one of the key aspects of dialogic teaching).

## Discussion

By conceptualising the use of the IWB within a framework of dialogic teaching, the teachers in our project have been encouraged to look for effective ways of exploiting its interactive and multimodal features to support their pedagogical aims. As a result, both the teachers and researchers considered the functionalities of the IWB from a pedagogical perspective (rather than, say, attempting to use all the functionalities because they are available). With this in mind, let us re-consider our central research question: *How can teachers using a 'dialogic' approach to teaching exploit the multimodality and interactivity of the IWB to support student learning?* For reasons of space, we have only shown a few illustrative examples from practice. But our analysis shows that these were typical in the sense that a wide range of visual (including video), auditory and text-based functions was used by the three teachers and their pupils as stimuli for reasoning. Moreover, in each case teachers encouraged students to test provisional ideas. Individual and collective thinking were embodied within a series of evolving digital representations that were purposefully manipulated, reformulated, annotated, saved and/or revisited so that meanings were created cumulatively over time through sustained, responsive dialogue. The extent to which the dialogues promoted were educationally effective (or at least could be judged to be so, from our perspective) varied, of course.

Further teacher strategies observed in all three cases included engaging all students vicariously in IWB activity and intertwining this with other kinds of activity. These strategies resonate with findings from Cutrim Schmid's (2010) longitudinal study of a language teacher developing competency in designing more open IWB-based materials, managing interactions mediated by the IWB and rationing IWB use. While we acknowledge that our teachers had already developed a dialogic pedagogy, we know from other studies (e.g. Warwick et al., 2011) that adopting a dialogic approach is demanding for teachers, in terms of both lesson preparation and the interactive demands on them during the lesson. In the early stages of its adoption, at least, it seems to require a degree of awareness on the part of the teacher that is almost certainly not commonplace. It is not easy for teachers to transcend the conventional patterns of classroom interaction, even if their aim is to do so. However, it can be expected that, over time, the relevant strategies will become less self-conscious and more a natural part of classroom interaction.

It is clear from our study that the IWB allows a flexibility in the marshalling of resources that enables teachers to create interesting multimodal stimuli for whole class dialogue much more easily than do other technologies. However, it is the (evolving) pedagogy that determines the nature of IWB use – it seems that a tool such as the IWB can present new possibilities for a teacher, but it is as the servant of pedagogy and not its master. It is through the orchestration of the perceived affordances of the IWB that such dialogic intentions of teachers can be fulfilled. The same function of an IWB may be used to support dialogic or more traditional didactic strategies. However, those teachers with dialogic intentions strive to employ a variety of IWB functions to enhance the quality of pupils' learning experience. Thus the effective use of the IWB as an educational tool is not inherent in the hardware, software or even the materials it displays. It is predicated upon the teacher's practical understanding of how to engage students and to help them learn. Any training that teachers – especially pre-service teachers – receive in the use of such technology needs to take this into account.

The outcomes of this study thus form a basis for wider professional development, and we are currently working with the teacher participants to share with others the lesson materials and video footage illustrative of supporting dialogic teaching with the IWB. The framework for describing pedagogical strategies that we co-constructed during our analyses should also prove useful. Collectively these resources might serve to stimulate discussion, development and trialling of dialogic approaches by pre-service teachers or colleagues working in other settings. They are freely available via our website at http://dialogueiwb.educ.cam.ac.uk/.

## Acknowledgements

We are very grateful to the teachers and students who willingly participated in the study. The work was funded mainly by the UK Economic and Social Research Council (ref. RES063270081) as part of a Research Fellowship programme of work carried out in 2007–09 by Sara Hennessy. A research development grant from the Faculty of Education funded the research assistance helpfully provided by Silvia Stetco-Belknap. We also appreciate the efficient secretarial assistance and data processing undertaken by Bryony Horsley-Heather. Finally, we wish to acknowledge the helpful comments by three peer reviewers on an earlier draft of this article.

## References

Alexander, R. J. (2004). *Towards dialogic teaching: Rethinking classroom talk*. Cambridge: Dialogos UK Ltd.

Beauchamp, G., & Parkinson, J. (2005). Beyond the 'wow' factor: Developing interactivity with the interactive whiteboard. *School Science Review*, 86(316), 97–103.

Brown, A. L., & Palincsar, A. S. (1989). Guided, co-operative learning and individual knowledge acquisition. In L. B. Resnick (ed.), *Knowing, learning and instruction* (pp. 393–451). Hillsdale, NJ: Lawrence Erlbaum.

Cardellichio, T., & Field, W. (1997). Seven strategies that encourage neural branching. *Educational Leadership*, 54(6), 33–36.

Crook, C. K. (2007). Learning science and learning technology: A place for cultural psychology. *British Journal of Educational Psychology Monograph Series*, II(5), 1–17.

Dawes, L. (2001). What stops teachers using new technology? In M. Leask (Ed.), *Issues in teaching using ICT* (pp. 61–79). London: Routledge.

Dawes, L., Mercer, N., & Wegerif, R. (2004). *Thinking together: A programme of activities for developing speaking, listening and thinking skills for children aged 8–11*. Birmingham: Imaginative Minds.

Gillen, J., Kleine Staarman, J., Littleton, K., Mercer, N., & Twiner, A. (2007). A 'learning revolution'? Investigating pedagogic practice around interactive whiteboards in British primary schools. *Learning, Media and Technology, 32*(3), 243–256.

Hennessy, S. (2011). The role of digital artefacts on the IWB in mediating dialogic teaching and learning. *Journal of Computer Assisted Learning, 27*(6), 463–489.

Hennessy, S., & Deaney, R. (2009). 'Intermediate theory' building: Integrating multiple teacher and researcher perspectives through in-depth video analysis of pedagogic strategies. *Teachers College Record, 111*(7), 1753–1795.

Hennessy, S., Deaney, R., Ruthven, K., & Winterbottom, M. (2007). Pedagogical strategies for using the interactive whiteboard to foster learner participation in school science. *Learning, Media and Technology, 32*(3), 283–301.

Hennessy, S., Warwick, P., & Mercer, N. (2011). A dialogic inquiry approach to working with teachers in developing classroom dialogue. *Teachers College Record, 113*(9), 1906–1959.

Higgins, S., Falzon, C., Hall, I., Moseley, D., Smith, F., Smith, H., et al. (2005). *Embedding ICT in the literacy and numeracy strategies*. Final Report. Newcastle, UK: Centre for Learning and Teaching, School of Education, Communication and Language Sciences, University of Newcastle upon Tyne.

Kim, I., Anderson, R. C., Nguyen-Jahiel, K., & Archodidou, A. (2007). Discourse patterns during children's collaborative online discussions. *Journal of the Learning Sciences, 16*(3), 333–370.

Kitchen, S., Mackenzie, H., Butt, S., & Finch, S. (2006). *Evaluation of curriculum online report of the third survey of schools*. London: National Centre for Social Research.

Lankshear, C. (1997). *Changing literacies*. Philadelphia: Open University Press.

Lemke, J. (1990). *Talking science: Language, learning and values*. Norwood, NJ: Ablex.

Mercer, N., & Littleton, K. (2007). *Dialogue and the development of children's thinking*. London: Routledge.

Miller, D., Glover, D., & Averis, D. (2005, 14–17 September 2005). *Developing pedagogic skills for the use of the interactive whiteboard in mathematics*. Paper presented at the BERA 2005, University of Glamorgan.

Mortimer, E. F., & Scott, P. H. (2003). *Meaning making in secondary science classrooms*. Milton Keynes: Open University Press.

Moss, G., Jewitt, C., Levacic, R., Armstrong, V., Cardini, A., Castle, F., et al. (2007). *The interactive whiteboards, pedagogy and pupil performance evaluation: An evaluation of the Schools Whiteboard Expansion (SWE) Project: London Challenge* (No. RR816). London: DfES.

Rojas-Drummond, S., & Mercer, N. (2004). Scaffolding the development of effective collaboration and learning. *International Journal of Educational Research, 39*(2), 99–111.

Säljö, R. (1999). Learning as the use of tools: A sociocultural perspective on the human-technology link. In K. Littleton & P. Light (Eds.), *Learning with computers: Analysing productive interaction* (pp. 144–161). London: Routledge.

Schmid, C. (2010). Developing competencies for using the interactive whiteboard to implement communicative language teaching in the English as a Foreign Language classroom. *Technology, Pedagogy and Education, 19*(2), 159–172.

Smardon, D., & Bewley, S. (2007). *What students say about their learning: How can this improve learning?* Paper presented at the British Educational Research Association Annual Conference.

Smith, H. J., Higgins, S., Wall, K., & Miller, J. (2005). Interactive whiteboards: Boon or bandwagon? A critical review of the literature. *Journal of Computer Assisted Learning, 21*(2), 91–101.

Smith, F., Hardman, F., & Higgins, S. (2006). The impact of interactive whiteboards on teacher-pupil interaction in the national literacy and numeracy strategies. *British Educational Research Journal, 32*(3), 443–457.

Somekh, B., Haldane, M., Jones, K., Lewin, C., Steadman, S., Scrimshaw, P., et al. (2007). *Evaluation of the Primary Schools Whiteboard Expansion Project (SWEEP): Report to the Department for Education and Skills.* London: Becta.

Stallworthy, J. (1983). *The complete poems and fragments of Wilfred Owen.* London: Chatto and Windus.

Warwick, P., Hennessy, S., & Mercer, N. (2011). Promoting teacher and school development through co-enquiry: Developing interactive whiteboard use in a 'dialogic classroom'. *Teachers and Teaching: Theory and Practice, 17*(3), 303–324.

Warwick, P., Mercer, N., Kershner, R., & Kleine Staarman, J. (2010). In the mind and in the technology: The vicarious presence of the teacher in pupils' learning of science in collaborative group activity at the interactive whiteboard. *Computers and Education, 55*(1), 350–362.

Wegerif, R. (2007). *Dialogic, education and technology: Expanding the space of learning.* New York, NY: Springer.

Wells, G., & Bell, T. (2008). Exploratory talk and guided inquiry. In N. Mercer & S. Hodgkinson (Eds.), *Exploring talk in school.* London: Sage.

Wertsch, J. V., Tulvoiste, P., & Hagstrom, F. (1993). A sociocultural approach to agency. In E. A. Forman, N. Minick & C. A. Stone (Eds.), *Contexts for learning: Sociocultural dynamics in children's development* (pp. 336–356). New York, NY: Oxford University Press.

*This chapter uses the theoretical framework of neo-Vygotskian sociocultural theory to try to bring together ideas I had encountered in different strands of psychology – evolutionary, developmental and educational – as well as some ideas from other fields such as linguistics and educational research. I had noticed that evolutionary psychology seemed to be focused on the human capacity for individual competition rather than on collaboration, which I felt was inappropriate and unjustified. I also felt that available evidence cast doubt on a conception of language (as offered by Steven Pinker and others) as something rather separate from the rest of human cognition. My aim was to offer a perspective on human development, communication and learning which recognised the essentially social, collaborative nature of our species.*

# 13 The social brain, language, and goal-directed collective thinking

## A social conception of cognition and its implications for understanding how we think, teach, and learn

*Mercer, N. (2013). The social brain, language, and goal-directed collective thinking: a social conception of cognition and its implications for understanding how we think, teach, and learn.* Educational Psychologist *(Routledge),* 48, 3, 148–168.

## Abstract

In recent years, researchers in evolutionary psychology and anthropology have proposed that the distinctive nature of human cognition is the product of our evolution as social beings; we are born with "social brains" that enable us to manage complex social relationships in ways other animals cannot. I suggest that the concept of the social brain is potentially useful for understanding the dynamic, iterative relationship between individual and collective thinking, and the role of language in mediating that relationship. However, I argue that its current conceptualization is too narrow and individualistic; the concept should be redefined to take account of the distinctive human capacity for thinking collectively. I suggest that Vygotskian sociocultural theory offers a framework for this reconceptualization, which would then enable us to achieve a better understanding of the relationship between "intermental" (collective) activity and "intramental" (individual) intellectual activity and development. I use this theoretical base to propose three explanations for the observed effects of collaborative learning on individual learning and development.

In 2010 the United Kingdom's Royal Society of Arts (RSA) organized a seminar entitled *The Social Brain and the Curriculum*, which brought together researchers from evolutionary psychology, neuroscience, computer-related studies, and educational research to share their views on this matter. One of the key issues that emerged was "The brain's sociality: The brain's constant orientation to others and the creation of meaning through brains interacting, rather than through the operation of individual internal cognition" (RSA, 2010, p. 2). In that seminar, the neuroscientist Frith took an evolutionary psychology stance to argue that the human brain is designed to enable people to adjust sensitively to one another's perspectives and emotions, so as to enable cooperative activity from which a whole community can benefit (see Wolpert & Frith, 2004). As a contributor to the seminar series, I was heartened to discover that neuroscientists and evolutionary psychologists were interested in social aspects of cognition and in addressing educationally relevant questions. However, the series did not allow any opportunity for the development of these ideas. For example, there were implications for how we could integrate different fields of study, and for how such a unified approach might address educational issues. One of my motivations for writing this article is to try to take these issues further.

The concept of the "social brain" was introduced by the evolutionary anthropologist Dunbar (1998) and has since generated some interesting and imaginative discussion about the relationship between individual mental capacities and social interaction. It represents the view that human intelligence has an intrinsically social quality, in that evolution has equipped us with brains that enable us to operate effectively in complex social networks. By linking cortical functioning, individual thinking, and social interaction, it seems to me that this concept could usefully bring together research in neuroscience, evolutionary psychology, developmental psychology, social psychology, and educational psychology, as well as connecting with other fields such as sociolinguistics and linguistic philosophy. However, I argue that if it is to fulfill that role, the social brain concept needs further development, because the social nature of human cognition has not been properly recognized in its development so far. The main focus of interest in the social brain has been on how individuals cope with the informational and emotional complexity of social life, so as to maximize the achievement of their personal goals. The concept has been strongly linked to evolutionary theory, but only through a narrow focus on the survival value for an individual of being able to understand the behavior and motives of others. No account has been taken of the potential survival value of a cognitive capacity for collaboration. Yet one reason why people engage socially, which can also be linked to human evolutionary success, is so that they can think collectively in order to pursue common goals. I suggest that our brains are "social" in that they have been designed, through evolution, to enable us to reason together and get things done.

Our evolved capacity for collective thinking also enables each new generation to benefit from the past experience of their community, which has given our species survival advantages over competitors. It is widely recognized by psychologists working in developmental and educational fields of inquiry that children learn to make sense of society and their environment by being engaged in dialogue by their carers, drawn into collective activities, and guided in ways of reasoning about experience. The potential capabilities of each child's social brain are developed through social interaction. However, this recognition does not seem to have permeated discussions of the social brain within cognitive and evolutionary psychology. The crucial role of language in such processes has also not yet been properly accommodated within those discussions. I propose a way that an evolutionary account of human origins can be linked to our understanding of the psychological mechanisms that underpin these aspects of human life, and in particular to the social and cognitive processes involved in education. To do so, a theoretical framework is needed for dealing with the relationship between collective thinking and the development of individual cognition – between the "intermental" and the "intramental" – and I suggest this could best be achieved by taking a sociocultural perspective based upon Vygotsky's work (Vygotsky, 1962, 1978). On this basis, I offer three possible explanations of how intermental activity might influence intramental development and then relate these to findings from several fields of research. A broader conception of the social brain emerges from this discussion, which has implications for future research in education and other fields, as I explain toward the end of the article. But first I consider how the concept of the social brain has emerged from research in evolutionary studies and neuroscience.

## Evolutionary psychology, neuroscience, and the social brain

Researchers within the relatively new field of evolutionary psychology have striven to explain how the ways we think have shaped, and been shaped by, the struggle of our ancestors to survive and eventually become the dominant species. In early stages of its development, evolutionary psychology invoked a strongly individualistic notion of human cognition, explaining the origins and nature of human thinking in terms of the selective advantage individuals would gain over other individuals through thinking and behaving in certain ways, which would give them and their offspring a competitive advantage over others. The focus thus tended to be on competition between humans, with the success of the species as a whole being explained through the proportionally greater survival of the offspring of more successful individuals. Thus Miller (1999) argued that young men produce more "displays" of art, music, and other cultural products than women or older men because they are most highly motivated to compete for mates. At its crudest, as sometimes represented in the press or in media discussions, this approach might seem to be based on doubtful, analogical comparisons between the ways males of other species aggressively compete and the social behavior of men in modern society; but this would do a great disservice to the scholarly work in this field. However, evolutionary psychology has had a strong association with the kind of evolutionary account offered in Dawkins's (1976) book *The Selfish Gene*, whereby altruistic and collaborative behavior is expected to be limited to closely related individuals and interaction with nonrelatives is perceived as basically competitive. Thus one evolutionary psychologist writes, "It is not unreasonable to hypothesise that humans have evolved xenophobic fears of strangers and outgroup members" (Buss, 2001, p. 966). There have been philosophical criticisms of such highly individualistic, competitive applications of Darwinism (e.g., Midgley, 2010), and recently within evolutionary psychology (and the closely related field of evolutionary anthropology) a recognition of the intrinsically complex nature of human social life, and the cognitive demands this makes of people, has begun to influence accounts of how and why the human brain has evolved in the way that it has. As I explain, some evolutionary scholars have begun to describe the distinctive nature of human cognition in terms of our ability to operate within complex social relationships. This links with other fields of psychological investigation, and not only with social psychology. For example, researchers in neuroscience claim to have identified features of neural function which show that we are sensitive, sometimes unconsciously, to very subtle "social signals" that enable us to respond to the intentional actions of others. This evidence has been used by some evolutionary psychologists (and anthropologists) to support their claims that the design of the human brain supports an inherently social function.

Dunbar (1998), a leading scholar in the field of evolutionary psychology/anthropology, has been prominent in setting out the case for the brain's "prosociality." He commented that the conventional wisdom over the past 160 years in cognitive psychology and neuroscience has been that the prime function of the human brain is to enable individuals to process factual information about the world as effectively as possible. The unstated implication has been that the evolutionary struggle for survival would favor individuals with the best sensory, information-processing, and memorizing abilities. It is only relatively recently that it has been suggested that the nature and size of the human brain might also reflect the survival advantages of a more subtle kind of mental capacity, that of being able to make sense of complex social relationships. This has led evolutionary psychologists to propose that our brains have evolved to be able to perform specific "cognitive feats such as calculating the status trajectories of oneself and others in the group, and modeling the consequences of the injury or death of a kin member" (Buss, 2001, p. 968). New fields of research have since been defined ("social neuroscience" and even more specifically "developmental social cognitive neuroscience"; see Zelazo, Chandler, & Crone, 2009) to pursue this perspective. There has been a particular interest in how we notice and respond to the subtle social signals of people we interact with, even if we are not consciously aware of doing so. Research has identified "mirror neurons," which become active not only when a primate carries out an action but also when they observe a community member carrying out the same action. Most studies have involved monkeys, but recently neuroscientists have reported identifying the activity of mirror neurons in humans (Mukamel, Ekstrom, Kaplan, Iacoboni, & Fried, 2010). However, this "mirror" activity apparently arises only with the observation of *intentional* actions. It had already been well established by social psychologists that when people interact, they tend to reflect each other's gestures and postures (e.g., Chartrand & Bargh, 1999), and so this seems to offer a neural correlate for such findings. Commenting on the significance of this, Frith and Singer (2008) said, "Through the automatic activation of mirror systems when observing the movements of others, we tend to become aligned with them in terms of goals and actions" (p. 3875).

However, doubts have been expressed about the evolutionary account of the origins of mirror neurons in humans, for example by the psychologist Heyes (2010). She pointed to the lack of evidence that the human brain has single neurons that are biologically programmed to discharge when an action is performed or observed, and argued that rather than being "hard-wired" to respond in that way, the evidence reflects the effects of our associative learning, as we correlate the experiences of performing and observing the same actions. She cited studies which show that experience modifies mirror responses (so that, e.g., pianists respond more to observations of piano-playing finger movements than nonpianists), supporting that view. But whereas Heyes is unconvinced that hard-wired mirror neurons should be given a major role in the evolutionary development of the social brain, she conceded that her associative learning explanation of their origins is still compatible with mirror neurons having social-cognitive functions, which include understanding and predicting the actions of others, and language processing.

Even if mirror neurons are not hard-wired, it seems that our brains have been evolutionarily designed for living in a complex society. As Grist (2009) explained,

> We become aware of others because our brains can apply "theory of mind" – this is the cognitive endeavor of attributing thoughts to others. Part of theory of mind consists in thinking about what other people are thinking about other people – "what does Jane think about Tom's behavior towards Pablo, given that Pablo is upset about his father's illness?" This is a very complicated kind of cognition and is, as far as we know, unique to humans. The social brain hypothesis in evolutionary anthropology contends that human brains have evolved to be as big as they are so that we can think about and manage our relationships with other people.
>
> (p. 44)

The claims made by Grist and by Frith and Singer can be related not only to the well-established concept of theory of mind (Premack & Woodruff, 1978) but also to that of social cognition (as discussed, e.g., by Fiedler & Bless, 2001). The basic claim made by evolutionary anthropologists and psychologists is that advanced skills in social cognition – the ability to infer emotion and interpret social behavior – would be differentially selected for among our early ancestors. A species that possessed such skills would be more able to organize larger and more complex social groups. Individuals with the most developed skills within a community would have advantages in achieving their goals (including reproductive goals) because they could make sense of such social complexity (Dunbar, 1998) to help them compete with rivals (Buss, 2001) and so ensure that more of their offspring survived.

These discussions of social cognition by evolutionary psychologists represent a significant shift in perspective from the individual to the social. But they still tend to focus only on individual cognition and competition, rather than joint intellectual activity and collaboration. They also tend to describe the relevant skills as just being "there," inherent in the natural capabilities of the individual brain. From the perspective of an educational researcher, this seems simplistic and even inaccurate. Theory of mind can be considered a distinctive capacity within the broader notion of metacognition, in that it involves making assessments not only of one's own state of knowledge, intentions, and so on, but also of those of other people. Research in educational and developmental psychology suggests that, like other metacognitive and social skills, theory of mind develops through practice and guidance as children become involved in dialogues with other people, as I describe in a later section.

## Individual and collective thinking

Making a link with evolutionary psychology, the linguistic philosophers Mercier and Sperber (2011) proposed that the human capacity for reasoning should primarily be understood as a competitive social mechanism, whereby we each strive to persuade others to comply with our preferred courses of action. Although this is interesting and plausible, it shares the weakness of the evolutionary psychology accounts just discussed by explaining human survival only in terms of individual people negotiating the social world and pursuing their own agendas. This may provide part of the explanation for the origins and nature of the cognitive capacity of our species, but it fails to acknowledge one of the most important functions of our social-cognitive capabilities, which is that we are able to engage together in goal-orientated, knowledge-building, and problem-solving activities. We do not only use reasoning as an individual weapon to resist other people's agendas; we also use it in dialogues to find the best possible solutions to the problems we jointly encounter. Frith and Singer (2008) hinted at this when they said, "When joint action requires cooperation, shared representations of task requirements and goals are very important in order to achieve better performance. Such sharing is referred to as *common knowledge*" (p. 3876).

The creation of "common knowledge" is an interactive, complex, discursive process, as educational research has shown (Edwards & Mercer, 1987/2012), and there is more to collective thinking than sharing knowledge. Theory of mind capabilities allow us not only to assess others' emotional states or try to exert a social influence on them: They also enable us to make assessments about what knowledge we have in common with another person, and judge their levels of understanding or skill in relation to particular topics or tasks. In ways that are just not possible for other species, we use interactions to continually refine our judgments of the relative states of knowledge and understanding of other people (Jeong & Chi, 2007). Both assessments of what others think and know and metacognitive reflections on our own thought processes are involved. These allow us to jointly activate the practical cycles of planning, acting, reflecting, and replanning by which we solve problems, share knowledge, and construct new joint understandings. Such mental capacity distinguishes us from other primates, as Tomasello (2008) explained:

> The great apes – chimpanzees, bonobos, gorillas and orangutans – communicate almost exclusively for the purpose of getting others to do what they want. Human infants, in addition, gesture and talk in order to share information with others – they want to be helpful. The free sharing of information also creates the possibility of pedagogy – in which adults impart information by telling and showing, and children trust and use this information with confidence. Our nearest primate relatives do not teach and learn in this manner.
>
> (p. 1)

One does not have to be convinced that "telling and showing" is a uniquely human behavior to accept that our species has developed it to unique levels of sophistication. Through becoming sensitive to the limits of one another's levels of understanding, we are especially able to engage effectively in interactions whereby one person helps another to learn. We differ from our primate relatives by having what Hermann, Call, Hernandez-Lloreda, Hare, and Tomasello (2007) called "cultural intelligence," by which they mean the ability to make sense of a complex, shifting social world and operate as a fully functioning member of it. Their comparative study found that young children (1 year old) "far outstripped" chimpanzees and orangutans on tests of social cognition. But we have evolved the ability to do more than just make sense of a complex society and interact successfully within it. To an extent that is impossible for other primates, we are able to not merely interact but to "interthink" (Littleton & Mercer, 2013; Mercer, 2000). Through the use of language and other modes of representation, we can link our individual minds to create a powerful problem-solving tool. It is likely to be this, rather than individualized competition, that has ensured the dominance of our species. As an emergent species, our ancestors would compete well with other species because they could use language and other modes of representation to define common problems and plan in advance how to deal with them. They could also reflectively discuss the success or otherwise of those actions and plan again accordingly. By creating abstract representations of experience together, they could use them to explore the past and the future. Older members of a community could induct each new generation into their complex society's way of getting things done and share with them the insights of past collective thinking. Their children would learn ways of using language for representing the physical world and for reasoning about it. Collective intellectual activity thus would come to have a significant influence on the development of individual cognition. This perspective on the relationship between the social and the individual may seem obvious to educational and developmental psychologists, but it has not yet figured in discussions of the concept of the social brain.

Why has there been so little recognition of the importance, or even the existence, of collective thinking in evolutionary psychology? It may be because cognitive psychology has generally upheld the commonsense view that thinking just goes on in individuals' heads, and topics such as problem solving, learning, and remembering have been studied accordingly. It is one of the most prestigious fields of psychological inquiry, and so it may simply be that this perspective has been carried over into evolutionary psychology. The study of collective thinking, which includes how people solve problems in groups or how one person helps another to learn, has been pursued quite separately by developmental, educational, and discursive psychologists (see, e.g., Cazden, 2001; Howe, 2010; Mercer & Littleton, 2007; Middleton & Edwards, 1990). Studies of how people think alone and how they think together have never been united. I suggest that this division is an obstacle to developing a proper understanding of how humans think. Cognitive achievements and activities do not, of course, take place only in social settings, and I offer no arguments against the study of individual learning, remembering, or problem solving. But unless researchers recognize how the inherently social nature of our species shapes our cognition and its development, and the fact that we frequently learn, reason, and solve problems collectively, the accounts they generate will misrepresent how people actually think and learn in real life.

## The cognitive functions of language

Dunbar (1998) argued for the crucial role of language in the operation of the social brain as follows:

> For humans, one important aspect of [theory of mind] concerns its relevance to language, a communication medium that crucially depends on understanding interlocutors' mental states or intentions. The kinds of metaphorical uses of language that characterize not only our rather telegraphic everyday exchanges (in which "you know what I mean?" is a common terminal clause) but also lies at the very heart of the metaphorical features of language.
>
> (p. 189)

This is in accord with my own argument even if, once again, the focus is on the assessment of emotions and intentions, rather than on the collective representation of experience and the joint pursuit of solutions to problems.

It could well be, as some have argued (Levinson, 2006), that our evolving capacity for reading the intentions of others underpinned the emergence of language; but this does not explain the significance of language as both a cognitive and cultural tool. Language is the prime means at our disposal for making a dynamic assessment of shared understanding and developing it, and so has a central, integrated position in enabling human cognition to be both individual and social:

> By participating in the conversations that accompany and grow out of the everyday activities in which he or she is involved together with other members of the culture, the child learns to use the semiotic tool of language, which enables him or her to "connect" with other people; at the same time, and by virtue of the mediating role that conversation plays in these activities, the child simultaneously "assimilates the experience of humankind," as this is encoded in the semantic system of that culture's language.
>
> (Wells, 1999, pp. 19–20)

There is more to this than humans using language to share information accurately, as some cognitive/evolutionary psychologists have claimed, such as Pinker (1994), when he said, "Simply by making noises with our mouths we can reliably cause precise new combinations of ideas to arise in each other's minds" (p. 15). Indeed we can pass on information to each other, and it is vital to human life that we do so. But as a generalization, Pinker's claim is patently false, as any teacher who has instructed a class of children on what to do will know when they all begin to do rather different things. Language's power as a tool for creative, collective thinking partly lies in the possibility that listeners may each interpret a speaker's words in rather different ways. Scholars are still interpreting the words of orators, philosophers, playwrights, and poets, hundreds of years after those words were expressed, and offering new insights into the human condition as a result. As Vygotsky's contemporary and compatriot, the literary scholar Bakhtin (1981), put it – or rather, as I interpret what he wrote – the words we hear or read do not simply activate a mental dictionary, they generate dialogic responses in our own minds as we use our existing knowledge to make sense of them. Vygotsky (1962) himself argued that language is both a cultural tool and a psychological tool, linking the "intermental" and the "intramental" in a reciprocal relationship, and so is inextricably bound up with the development and application of more advanced forms of reasoning. Thus Vass and Littleton (2010) suggested that "interpsychological thinking is a prerequisite for intrapsychological thinking: it is through speech and action with others that we learn to reason and gain individual consciousness" (p. 107).

The view that language is thoroughly integrated with other important nonlinguistic aspects of thinking is, of course, at odds with some influential views on language and cognition, notably of those who remain committed to a view of language as a discrete cognitive "module" or capacity (e.g., Pinker, 1994, 2007). But emerging findings from neuroscience support the more integrated view, as they suggest that mental abilities associated with some nonlinguistic skills, such as the appreciation of rhythmic patterns and structures in music, are also involved in language abilities. Thus Goswami (2009, p. 182), who has studied both linguistic and musical aspects of cognition, cited research (Abrams, Nicol, Zecker, & Kraus, 2008) on children's cortical responses to speech, which has shown that neural tracking of the "speech envelope" (the rhythmic, syllabic sequence of speech sounds) is accurately monitored by the right, not the left, hemisphere. Reviewing evidence from neuro-imaging research, Patel (2003) argued that syntactic features shared by music and language are processed by the same parts of the brain, and therefore that neuroscientists should no longer focus on language "in isolation."

We might also consider here research on bilingualism for what it tells us about the relationship between language and general cognitive functioning. Up to the middle of the 20th century, reviews of research tended to conclude that growing up bilingually causes some cognitive deficits, through some kind of "overloading" of cognitive capacities (Darcy, 1963; Macnamara, 1966). In contrast, more recent research has shown that there are general cognitive benefits from growing up bilingual (Diaz, 1983; Grosjean, 2010). For example, it seems that bilingual children perform better in nonverbal problem-solving tasks, which depend on selective attention or inhibitory control, as these controlling abilities have been enhanced through exercising linguistic choices between different languages (Bialystok & Feng, 2010). This advantage seems to continue throughout the bilingual's lifespan. The current view seems to be that bilingualism may offer both cognitive benefits and disadvantages. This is apparently also supported by evidence from neuro-imaging research (Bialystok et al., 2005). Bialystok and Feng (2010) offered this summary: "The picture emerging from these studies is a complex portrait of interactions between bilingualism and skill acquisition in which there are sometimes benefits for bilingual children, sometimes deficits, and sometimes no consequence at all" (p. 121). It is not of great significance to us here as to whether the effects of bilingualism on nonverbal reasoning are positive or negative: The key point is that this research indicates that language skills are integrated with nonverbal reasoning skills, and that language experience is linked to the development of those skills. As one bilingualism scholar wrote, "Language attributes are not separated in the cognitive system, but transfer readily and are interactive" (Baker, 2006, pp. 168–169). Evidence thus increasingly supports the view that language is involved with both specific and non-specific aspects of brain function, and so is a fully integrated component of human cognition. If we want to understand the functioning of the social brain, in the broader sense of the term, and its development through childhood, I therefore suggest we need to recognize the crucial role that language plays in enabling us to think collectively and individually.

## The role of language in development and learning

In recent years, one major influence on classroom research has been the emergence of a sociocultural theory of education and cognitive development derived from Vygotsky's work (as described, e.g., by Daniels, 2001, 2008; it is also known as cultural-historical activity theory: van Oers, Elbers, van der Veer, & Wardekker, 2008). Its basic premise is that human intelligence is essentially social and cultural, and that the relationship between social activity and individual thinking underpins cognitive development. As Vygotsky (1978) put it, "Human learning presupposes a specific social nature and a process by which children grow into the intellectual life of those around them" (p. 88). This has inspired empirical examinations of how social interaction influences individual learning, problem solving, and representations of knowledge. One leading sociocultural psychologist suggests that "all too often the focus of sociocultural research has been on *intermental* (social, interactional) processes *per se*, to the neglect of explanations of how these intermental processes forge the *intramental* processes that sit at the heart of cognitive development" (Rojas-Drummond, 2009, p. 241). My own view is that interest in intramental processes has tended to dominate; but in any case this theory's potential for making the link between social processes and individual thinking is there to be exploited. Sociocultural theory provides a theoretical basis for the primacy of language as a cultural and cognitive – and hence educational – tool. A model of the social brain in which language is a fully integrated component is compatible with two Vygotskian claims that (a) the development of individual psychological (intramental) functions is commonly preceded by involvement in related social (intermental) activity, and the acquisition of language has a transformative effect on the nature of an individual's thinking. Sociocultural theory does not, as some of its critics have claimed, suggest that "everything that can be thought can be thought in language, and everything that can be represented, can be represented in language" (Jewitt, 2008, p. 7). There is no need to make any such extreme claims to justify a special focus on language, as I hope to show.

Empirically, it has been known for some time that the quality of children's language experience in the early years is a good predictor of their subsequent educational achievement (Hart & Risley, 1995; Wells, 1986, 2009). A good explanation for this involves children's induction into ways of using language for explaining and reasoning. Education is popularly understood as the transmission and acquisition of facts and skills, but educational success requires the ability to justify opinions, analyses, solutions, and conclusions. Although arguments can sometimes be presented through other communicative modes (such as the use of mathematical notation, and by physical demonstration in science or music), language is essentially involved in all academic subjects. Moreover, achieving competence in specific subjects requires the use of specialized discourses, or genres, of subject communities; and those genres are not mere jargon, but cultural tools designed for pursuing collective scholarship and inquiry (Christie & Martin, 1997; Kress, 1987; Swales, 1990). The linguist Martin (1993) described them as rule-governed, goal-orientated social processes embodied in language. They represent ways that individual thinking is made accountable to the normative rules of collective activity within specific communities of thinkers; and fluency in the appropriate genres is a requisite for full admission to those communities. Thus the educational researcher Pea (1993) argued, "*Expertise* is defined dynamically through continuing participation in the discourse of a community, not primarily through the possession of a set of problem-solving skills and conceptual structures" (p. 271). As Lemke (1990) famously put it, science education should enable students to become fluent speakers of science. The same principle applies in a great many nonacademic knowledge domains (Barton, 2009; Goodman, 1996; Lave & Wenger, 1991). Even if one is concerned with the development of understanding the content of a field of knowledge, rather than the manner in which it is expressed, language has a crucial role. In the debate about key factors in enabling students' conceptual change in science education, Treagust and Duit (2008a), leading researchers in that field, have agreed with classroom researchers such as Wells (2008) that dialogue is commonly the "dynamic motor" for such change. Their own examples of transcribed dialogue (Treagust & Duit, 2008b) illustrate this well.

A sociocultural explanation of the role of language in individual and collective cognition can be based upon Vygotsky's proposed link between the intramental and the intermental. It begins with children learning and using the functional forms of language they hear around them. They practice these forms in "pretend play," acting out social roles such as "teacher" and "pupil" (Elbers, 1994). They "ventriloquate" the ways they hear adults making sense of the world as they try to make sense of the world themselves (Maybin, 2006). Those social modes of communication offer templates for individual sense making. If learning to participate in a subject like science involves learning to "speak" it, then learning to think like a scientist must involve some internalization of the subject discourse as a tool for reasoning about the relevant phenomena. Thus the genres of various discourse communities provide resources for organizing the process of individual thinking. One strength of Vygotsky's model, not always well appreciated, is that he envisaged the intermental-intramental relationship as enabling a kind of spiral intellectual development: Members of a new generation gain cultural understanding from their elders through the forms and content of dialogue, which then empowers them to make new, original insights, which are then shared and so enrich the culture of the community. It is through using the resources of specialized language genres that subjects, disciplines, trades, and other fields of human endeavor can persist and grow, within and across generations. In evolutionary terms, the emergent capacity to refine the tool of language into a diversified toolkit would offer adaptive advantages in dealing with changing environmental circumstances.

Understanding the role of language in children's intellectual develop-ment requires an analysis of how the intermental-intramental relationship is embodied in social interaction. The process whereby an expert guides a novice toward new understanding and competence is one of the basic, key features of human society; it is a manifestation of the powers of the social brain. It depends on the establishment and maintenance of an intersubjectiv-ity that, at least in formal educational settings, is normally mediated through language. Instructing a learner, or providing useful feedback on their efforts, is very difficult without some kind of spoken or written dialogue. It is inter-esting and useful to highlight the multimodality of classroom education, by which gestures, nonlinguistic symbols, images, artifacts, and physical settings can also shape learning processes (e.g., Jewitt, Kress, Ogborn, & Tsartsarelis, 2004), but such analysis should not obscure the prime, central role of language.

Educational research on collaborative learning has mainly been motivated by an interest in if, and how, group-based learning activities help the learning and conceptual development of individual children (see, e.g., Howe, 2010; Slavin, 2009). I pursue that interest in the next section. But that is not the only reason for studying collaborative learning. We should recognize the importance of children learning to be good collaborative problem solvers. Understanding the role of language is vital for analyzing more symmetri-cal, collaborative types of learning and problem solving. In almost all joint problem-solving tasks it is impossible to collaborate properly without talk-ing with a partner (or using the written "talk" of electronic communica-tions). As the eminent classroom researcher Barnes (2010) put it,

> It is worth considering what is implied when, after someone has asked you to make a decision, you reply, "I'd like to talk it over first." It's not that you expect that the talk will give you new information. It's rather that you know from experience that the matter in question can often appear quite differently as a result of talking it through. The situation and its priorities and implications can take a different shape, a different meaning. You may see connections that were not immediately apparent, or realise that some of the options might have results that need to be con-sidered. In that case, the talking is contributing to your understanding by reshaping what you already in a sense "know." This provides a use-ful model for the function of talk in learning, in that some kinds of talk contribute to understanding without necessarily adding new material.
>
> (p. 7)

## The intermental and the intramental: explaining the effects of collective reasoning on individual reasoning

The distinctive quality of the social brain that has enabled the success of our species is, I have suggested, the capacity to link the intermental and the intramental. We have evolved to become able not only to make sense of complex social relations as individuals, but also to design and use those relations to create cognitive capability that transcends individual limitations. Moreover, we use collective cognition to enable the cognitive development of each new generation. This is the essence of the Vygotskian claim that social activity shapes psychological development. But the nature of that influence, regarding how elements of collective, social thinking affect subsequent individual thinking, has never been made clear (in Vygotsky's work or that of any other sociocultural theorist). This is a potentially very complex matter, and so for the sake of clarity I choose to approach it in the following way. First, I consider a specific aspect of cognitive development: the development of children's reasoning. Second, I consider how one kind of collective thinking, collaborative problem solving in the classroom, might stimulate the development of an individual child's reasoning capabilities. As I explain later, there is evidence that such joint activity can indeed, under certain conditions, have stimulating, beneficial effects – but for the moment, I am concerned only with elucidating the hypothetical mechanisms for any such effects. I propose that there are three possible explanations, which might be called *appropriation*, *co-construction*, and *transformation*. I believe they are worth considering in some detail, because, although they are not mutually exclusive, they represent a series of relatively stronger theoretical claims about how language-based collaborative learning and problem solving might shape individual learning and development.

1   *Appropriation:* Children could learn successful problem-solving strategies and explanatory accounts from each other during joint activity. Through talking, they can share relevant knowledge effectively as they carry out a task, and explain their strategies to each other. They could thus acquire new, useful information and successful strategies for solving problems from each other and go on to apply them in any subsequent individual situation. This represents a relatively weak claim for the influence of joint activity on the development of individual thinking, because it merely identifies other people's explanations and demonstrations of knowledge and cognitive strategies as important resources for individual learning. Language plays an important role here, but only in so much as it is a medium for transmitting information with a fair degree of accuracy from one mind to another.

2   *Co-construction:* By using talk to coordinate their mental efforts, children could not only share ideas but also argue productively about them, to jointly construct new, robust, generalizable strategies together for completing a task that are better than any of them would have devised alone. Their improved group performance would reflect what has been called the "assembly bonus effect," whereby the performance of a group is better than that of its best member (Laughlin, Hatch, Silver, & Boh, 2006). Similarly, Woolley, Chabrsi, Pentland, Hashmi, and Malone (2010) invoked the notion of "collective intelligence" when reporting a

study showing that the success of group endeavors is not strongly correlated with the average intelligence of group members but is correlated with the average social sensitivity of members and the equality in distribution of their conversational turn-taking. Individuals could then go on to use the new, effective strategies and solutions that the group had generated when faced with similar problems alone. This represents a stronger claim for the influence of social (intermental) activity on individual (intramental) learning and development because it locates the genesis of (at least some) effective cognitive strategies, understanding of problems and the generation of solutions in the dynamics of the "dialogic space" (Wegerif, 2007) of collaborative activity and not just in individual heads. Individuals in a group could also gain new levels of understanding through co-construction, through any explanations provided by their peers. "Co-construction" would also explain findings such as those of Smith et al. (2009), who reported that peer discussion among undergraduates enhanced their understanding of scientific concepts even when none of the individual participants initially had the requisite knowledge.

3  *Transformation:* The experience of group discussion could transform the nature of subsequent individual reasoning. If the norms of discussion required reasoning to be made explicit, and claims to be justified, the argumentation involved in collaborative problem solving might promote children's metacognitive, critical awareness of how they reasoned. Engaging in rational debate could also stimulate their theory of mind capacities, as they became more aware of the possibility of different points of view, of how these might be set against their own assumptions, and of any contradictions generated. This would encourage a "reflective stance" and develop a capacity for intramental "dialogue" (Muller-Mirza & Perret-Clermont, 2009). This would help them to become more able to assess possible problem-solving strategies in a critical way, and to monitor and regulate their own problem solving when subsequently doing a task on their own. A child's thinking would thus be transformed, through intermental activity, so that they began to reason intramentally in a more "dialogic" way.

All three explanations are compatible with current versions of sociocultural theory. All three acknowledge, in different ways, the case for the special significance of language use in the development of reasoning. They all invoke the capacities of the social brain for sharing information, assessing common knowledge, and planning goal-directed activity – and for enabling useful knowledge and cognitive skills to be taken up among members of a community. As they are not mutually exclusive, all three explanations might be invoked to account for the effects of collaborative learning on individual learning and achievement. But although the "appropriation" explanation is quite prosaic, the "co-construction" and "transformation" explanations are not. "Co-construction" implies the exercise of some collective intelligence, which can achieve more than individuals can alone and which depends upon the quality of interaction. The "transformation" explanation is the most intriguing, because it embodies Vygotsky's claims about the transformative effects of social experience on psychological development, and of the key role of language in shaping individual cognition. It is also in accord with philosophical arguments offered by Wegerif (2010) and others that higher forms of human reasoning are essentially dialogic, meaning that the skilled thinker is able to take and consider different, even conflicting, viewpoints and debate them internally. It also could be related to the claims discussed earlier that reasoning functions best when set in argumentative contexts (Mercier & Sperber, 2011). But it links argumentation with the success of collective endeavor and with individual cognitive development, in a way which purely competitive, individualized accounts of the functions of reasoning, like Mercier and Sperber's, cannot.

We might also consider if, and how, such explanations might relate to less socially symmetrical educational processes, such as when an adult helps a child, individually or as a member of a class, to learn or gain new understanding. The simplest explanation is again one of appropriation, whereby the adult simply shares relevant information with the child, provides instruction, or demonstrates a strategy that the child acquires and uses. There would normally be no expectation here that the adult would gain a better understanding of the phenomenon under consideration, or would improve their level of skill in performing a task. But the process might nevertheless involve some form of co-construction, whereby the adult and the child generated a new, shared conception of the task in hand or the topic being studied. The adult might gain new insights into the learning task through becoming aware of the limits of understanding and misunderstandings of the child, whereas the child's understanding would converge on that of the adult. The interaction might also generate a new, clearer, and more explicit representation of the relevant knowledge, which was then shared by both teacher and learner. (It is a common experience for a teacher to find that teaching a topic to a learner who is struggling reveals the limits of their own understanding of it.) The child and adult would use language and other modes to establish intersubjectivity (in the sense used by Wertsch, 1979) and pursue the kind of goal-orientated, progressive, interactive process known as "scaffolded" learning (Bruner, 1983). Subsequently, the child could start to use a mental representation of the adult-led, scaffolded interaction in which they had been involved as a way of self-regulating their future individual activity. Their thinking would be transformed as a result. As I go on to show, this explanation has links with accounts of the development of children's ability to self-regulate their learning offered by developmental psychologists and educational researchers.

## Dialogue and the development of self-regulation and metacognition

Wertsch's (1979) seminal article on social interaction and higher mental processes made an important contribution by illustrating and explaining how the social regulation inherent in adult-child dialogues provides a model for the self-regulation of individual cognition. His transcribed examples of parent-child interaction provided the kind of empirical illustration that was lacking in Vygotsky's original account. Moreover, Wertsch went beyond the exposition of Vygotsky's ideas by offering an original model of four levels of interaction between an adult "teacher" and a child working together on a task, based on the quality of intersubjectivity attained by the participants. He showed how, at the fourth, most advanced level, a child began to use speech for self-regulation, which was similar in form and function to the speech used earlier by the adult when scaffolding the child's activities. He therefore provided evidence, underpinned by sociocultural theory, for how external regulation provides the resources for developing self-regulation. We know now that this process is not confined to preschool development. Children as old as 9 or 10 can be observed coregulating their group activity in class by invoking the earlier, authoritative instructions of the teacher (Warwick, Mercer, Kershner, & Kleine Staarman, 2010). Regarding individual development, research indicates that children's ability to regulate, monitor, and reflect upon their problem solving correlates strongly with their success as learners and problem solvers (Veenman & Spaans, 2005; Whitebread & Pino-Pasternak, 2010). On the basis of meta-analyses of such research, some have claimed that the emergence of self-regulation is the main determinant of effective learning (Swanson, Hoskyn, & Lee, 1999; Wang, Haertel, & Walberg, 1990). The effects of dialogic experience on the development of the ability to self-regulate could thus be a crucial, transformative feature of cognitive development.

It has been widely observed that young children quite naturally talk aloud as they play alone, using language to regulate their solitary activities. Such "egocentric speech," as Piaget (1926) first described it, is normally no longer used when we grow older; not only because its use would be seen as a mark of eccentricity, but (if we follow Vygotsky rather than Piaget) because it has become internalized as the "silent speech" or "inner speech" of more mature cognition. The "transformation" explanation of the effects of dialogue on reasoning invokes a similar process to this process, whereby collective reasoning amongst peers, or scaffolded learning with an adult, acts as a template for the self-regulating mechanism of "inner speech," which is used in individual reasoning. As Clark (1998) put it,

> When the child, confronted by a tricky challenge, is "talked through" the problem by a more experienced agent, the child can often succeed at tasks which would otherwise prove impossible (think of learning to tie your shoelaces). Later on, when the adult is absent, the child can conduct a similar dialogue, but this time with herself.
>
> (p. 66)

Researchers have explored the ways that parents vary in how they use language to scaffold learning activities (e.g., Fidalgo & Pereira, 2005). Some have noted how parents of young children often use elaborative questions to guide discussions about shared experiences – and that such discussions seem to enhance children's abilities to recall those events (Reese, Haden, & Fivush, 1993). Observing how mothers and children (aged 30–42 months) discussed events they had previously experienced, Rudek and Haden (2005) noted that

> the "system" for talking about mental states seems . . . to be surprisingly well developed just as children enter a period in which there is marked changed in their understanding of mind. . . . The use of mental terms . . . during reminiscing may help to focus children's attention on mental processes such as thinking, believing, and knowing and encourage thought about memory and what it takes to remember.
>
> (pp. 543–544)

Reviews of research on the development of metacognitive and self-regulatory abilities by Dignath, Buettner, and Langfeldt (2008); Hattie, Biggs, and Purdie (1996); and Whitebread and Pino-Pasternak (2010) conclude that such abilities can be significantly improved through adult guidance, which inevitably involves dialogue. Typically, those interventions that obtained significant improvements have involved making metacognitive and learning strategies explicit to children and encouraging them to reflect and talk about their learning. Several pedagogical techniques have been used to do so. Whitebread and Pino-Pasternak summarized the main types as follows:

- "Co-operative group work" (Forman & Cazden, 1985): A range of techniques involving children in collaborative activities that oblige them to articulate their own understandings, evaluate their own performance, and be reflective about their own learning.
- "Self-explanations" (Siegler, 2002): An instructional practice that requires children to give "how" and "why" explanations about, for example, scientific phenomena or the events in a story and then asks children to give explanations of their own and an adult's reasoning.
- "Self-assessment" (Black & Wiliam, 1998): A range of pedagogical ideas involving children's self-assessment of their own learning, including, for example, children making their own choices about the level of difficulty of tasks to be undertaken and selecting their best work for reflective portfolios.
- "Debriefing" (Leat & Lin, 2003): A range of techniques for reflecting upon an activity or piece of learning including "encouraging pupils to ask questions," "making pupils explain themselves," and "communicating the purpose of lessons" (Whitebread & Pino-Pasternak, 2010, p. 686).

Psychologists committed to an individualistic account of learning might see the success of these techniques as no more than evidence of effective instruction; in other words, they might feel it necessary only to invoke the appropriation explanation for children's learning to self-regulate. Techniques like "self-explanation" and "self-assessment" sound as if they are just things an individual does alone. But that would ignore the essentially interactive quality of those techniques, which involve conversations between experimenters/teachers and children which make demands on children's communicative and theory of mind capabilities. For example, a leading researcher on the educational value of self-explanations describes what is involved as follows:

> The particular form of self-explanation that we have examined involves asking children to explain the reasoning of another person. In particular, children are presented with a problem, they advance an answer, they are given feedback concerning the correct answer, and then the experimenter asks them, "How do you think I knew that?"
>
> (Siegler, 2002, pp. 38–39)

Siegler then went on to describe the effects on learning of this interactive, dialogic technique: "The results indicated that, as hypothesised, encouraging children to explain the reasoning underlying the experimenter's answer resulted in their learning more than feedback alone or feedback in combination with requests to explain their own reasoning" (Siegler, 2002, p. 40). Spoken dialogue has a crucial function in the practice of the other techniques too, with references by the researchers involved to children being encouraged to ask questions, give explanations, explain themselves to another person, and so on. One of the researchers responsible for the development of the self-assessment techniques included in the previous list has commented,

> The core activity of assessment for learning is the involvement of learners in formative dialogue, with their teachers, and with one another. Only through such activity can they become actively engaged in their own learning, and so acquire the confidence and skill needed to become effective learners.
>
> (Black, 2009, p. 5)

Researchers into seemingly individual activities such as metacognition and self-regulation increasingly recognize that cognitive processes can be embedded in social interaction, and that collective metacognitive activity enables individual metacognition. Terms like "socially shared metacognition" (Iiskala, Vauras, Lehtinen, & Salonen, 2010) and "socially mediated metacognition" (Larkin, 2009) have been used by researchers to describe people reflecting together about problem-solving strategies and the outcomes of actions. Groups are described as using reasoned discussion to "coregulate" their activities (Volet, Summers, & Thurman, 2009).

Moreover, research on metacognition and self-regulation provides some indirect support for the most radical, "transformation" explanation of how spoken dialogue can enable cognitive development. It seems that researchers consider the development of the individual ability to self-regulate a transformation in the quality of a child's thinking – a step change in the way they are able to learn and solve problems. Their research also supports the view that dialogue, of the right kind, enables this transformation. The important role of spoken language in that developmental process, though not always explicitly acknowledged in research on self-regulation, is also apparent. As I go on to explain, this provides us with a useful perspective for understanding the results of research on collaborative learning.

## Educating the social brain: collaborative learning and cognitive development

Research on collaborative learning and problem solving has been an active field since the middle of the last century. Interventional methods have commonly been used to try to improve social relations or communications among students and see if this improves the quality of collaborative learning, and hence learning outcomes. Most research has involved children, but some studies have been carried out with adults. As previously mentioned, most of that research has also been concerned with the effects of collaborative learning on individual learning and development, rather than on the development of collaborative problem-solving skills. It has been found, for example, that experience of group-based reasoning activities improves subsequent individual performance of reasoning on a task (e.g., Augustinova, 2008). School-based studies have provided convincing evidence for the educational value of collaborative learning. Roseth, Johnson, and Johnson's (2008) meta-analytic review of 148 studies involving students aged 11 to 15 concluded that cooperative learning has positive effects on academic achievement, with Slavin's (2009) review drawing similar conclusions.

We also know that some particular features of the talk between collaborating partners are associated with good individual learning outcomes. Howe (2009, 2010) described a series of related studies on collaborative learning in science education. For example, in pairs, 8-year-olds were asked to predict whether an empty metal box, or a solid rubber ring, would float in a tank of water. Having talked about this and agreed on a prediction, they would then test this with real objects. The children were pre- and posttested (immediately after the task, and after a substantial delay of some weeks) on their understanding of the relevant phenomena. It was found that significantly better results on delayed posttests of learning and understanding were obtained when groups of children (a) were asked to seek agreement on their predictions before testing them (even if they did not achieve agreement) and (b) worked in a group in which contrasting opinions were expressed. Moreover, it did not seem to matter whether agreement was actually reached, or if contrasting views were reconciled. What was important was that "seeking agreement" and "contrasting opinions" were features of the discussions. In explaining these results, Howe suggested that (a) having to seek agreement encourages children to pursue their discussions in more depth and to more certain conclusions and (b) unresolved contradiction between ideas during conversation particularly primes children's metacognition – with the result that they subsequently reflect more on what they think about the phenomenon, and on the significance of their observations. This is in accord with the results of some studies involving adult participants, which found that the generation of debate was a requirement for group activities to lead to improved performance on reasoning tasks: see, for example, Schulz-Hardt, Brodbeck, Mojzisch, Kerschreiter, and Frey (2006).

Other research has suggested that for dialogue in problem-solving groups to be productive (in terms of assisting problem solving, learning, and the development of understanding), it should have the characteristics of what my colleagues and I have called Exploratory Talk (a term originally used by Barnes, 1976; see also Barnes, 2008). Exploratory Talk is dialogue in which

> partners engage critically but constructively with each other's ideas. Statements and suggestions are offered for joint consideration. These may be challenged and counter-challenged, but challenges are justified and alternative hypotheses are offered. Partners all actively participate, and opinions are sought and considered before decisions are jointly made.
>
> (Mercer & Littleton, 2007, p. 59)

It represents language being used not just to distribute information among people (cf. Pinker, 1994) but being employed as a *social mode of reasoning*. Others have used the terms "transactive dialogue" (Berkowitz, Gibbs, & Broughton, 1980) and "accountable talk" (Keefer, Zeitz, & Resnick, 2000; Michaels & O'Connor, 2002) to describe similar ways of using talk effectively for collective reasoning. As Howe (2010) commented, research on collaborative learning does "not merely confirm that . . . transactive dialogue, exploratory talk, or whatever can precipitate growth; it also shows that these forms of social interaction are so powerful that they can sustain cognitive activity over many weeks" (p. 80).

The value of collaborative, group-based activity in the classroom has been clearly demonstrated, in relation to the study of various curriculum subjects (see also Mercer & Sams, 2006; Sfard, 2001; Slavin, Groff, & Lake, 2009). But research on classroom-based group work embodies a paradox: It has shown the value of collaborative learning, but it has also shown that much of the group activity which goes on in classrooms has little educational value. The relevant research was mainly carried out some time ago (e.g., Bennett & Cass, 1989; Wegerif & Scrimshaw, 1997), but no evidence has been offered more recently to suggest that the situation has improved significantly. Moreover, a recent meta-analysis of collaborative learning approaches for developing reading skills concludes that not all discussion approaches are created equal, nor are they equally powerful at increasing students' high-level comprehension of text. It is one thing to get students to talk to each other during literacy instruction but quite another to ensure that such engagement translates into significant learning.

(Murphy, Wilkinson, Soter, Hennessy, & Alexander, 2009, p. 761)

This paradox can be resolved, fortunately, by distinguishing between what normally happens and what could, or should, happen. The ability to think collectively may be an important and defining characteristic of our species, but that does not mean that children are born knowing how to do it well. To make the most of collaborative learning activities, it is necessary for partners to use their social brains and the cultural and psychological tool of spoken language to best effect. Some educational research has studied the effects of training children in the use of language as a tool for collective reasoning, as I go on to describe in the next section. That research will also provide a useful basis for further consideration of the three explanations (appropriation, co-construction, and transformation) of how *inter*mental activity can assist *intra*mental development.

## Integrating teacher-student talk with collaborative learning

A study of teachers in Mexican classrooms (Rojas-Drummond, Mercer, & Dabrowski, 2001) found that those whose students achieved the best learning outcomes (as represented by assessments of their progress in mathematics and literacy) not only avoided the dominance of closed questions but also organized more interchanges of ideas and mutual support amongst pupils and generally encouraged pupils to take a more active, vocal role in classroom events than the less effective teachers. That is, they enacted a sociocultural, "dialogic" model of education, even though they did not necessarily describe it as such. More large-scale studies are needed to test the value of a dialogic pedagogy (Reznitskaya & Gregory, 2013). But overall, the available evidence supports those researchers who have argued for a more dialogic classroom pedagogy in which students have opportunities to express their understandings and misunderstanding, think aloud, ask questions, and explore ideas without being immediately evaluated as "wrong" or "right" by the teacher (Alexander, 2001, 2008; Dawes, 2008; Mercer, 1995; Nystrand, 1997; Skidmore, 2006; Scott, 2008; Wells, 1999, 2009). It seems, therefore, that classroom education should provide opportunities for students to think collectively, co-constructing knowledge and understanding and solving problems collectively. But if group work is to be productive, teachers also need to scaffold the development of students' intramental capabilities. As the science education researcher Black (2009) commented,

> By listening carefully to what others say, by giving emphasis to reasoned understanding rather than to formulaic answers, and by trying to help

the class to arrive at consensus in a shared understanding rather than by imposing a conclusion arbitrarily, a teacher can make whole-class dialogue a model for pupils' group discussions. In both contexts, pupils are experiencing engagement in reasoned discourse.

(p. 4)

Black's comments are supported by empirical research. In their review of mathematics teaching, Walshaw and Anthony (2008) concluded that "classroom work is made more enriching when discussion involves the co-construction of mathematical knowledge through the respectful exchange of ideas" (p. 543). Webb, Nemer, and Ing (2006) reported that differences between teachers in the extent to which they asked students to elaborate their problem-solving strategies corresponded strongly to the extent to which students did so during group discussions. Their general conclusion is that one of the main influences on children's talk in groups is the kind of talk that their teacher uses in interactions with them; but that teachers may not often model effective discussion in whole-class sessions. Yet children may not have many opportunities to learn how to conduct reasoned discussions in their out-of-school lives, or may not realize that they should engage in them when given collaborative tasks in the classroom. If their teachers do not raise their awareness of how they might talk and work together, or provide them with models and guidance, they are unlikely to develop the relevant skills for collective thinking and apply them appropriately. It is not so surprising, then, that in peer group discussions the talk is often off-topic, unproductively disputational, and inequitable. Children may all have inherited the capabilities of the social brain, but like most human capabilities they require exercise and training.

Some interventional research has studied the effects of teachers guiding students in "collaborative reasoning." For example, Reznitskaya et al.'s (2001) study involved students aged 10 to 11 years, constituting three classes that participated in teacher-led collaborative reasoning discussions of literary texts for a period of 5 weeks. These students and students from three comparable classrooms, who had not engaged in collaborative reasoning, were asked to write persuasive essays. The essays of the intervention class students were found to contain a significantly greater number of relevant arguments, counterarguments, rebuttals, formal argument devices, and uses of text information. Through analyzing the talk during such interventions, in which a teacher modeled and guided discussions of that kind about literary texts, Chinn, Anderson, and Waggoner (2001) concluded,

Four cognitive processes integral to good thinking and greater learning were found more frequently in Collaborative Reasoning discussions than in Recitations [i.e. those based on the traditional "closed question" type of interaction]. In comparison with students in Recitations, students in Collaborative Reasoning discussions (a) made many more elaborations, (b) made many more predictions, (c) provided evidence at a rate nearly 10 times higher than in Recitations, and (d) were much more likely to articulate alternative perspectives.

(p. 398)

A rather different illustration of how whole-class and group work activities can be integrated is provided by research involving a revision method called *prescriptive tutoring* (Soong & Mercer, 2011). Its aim was to reveal secondary school students' misconceptions and misunderstandings in physics by getting them to solve physics problems with a partner in their class. However, the partners collaborated only through computer-mediated communication, and their dialogue was saved as text. Before they began to work together online, the students were encouraged by their teacher to agree on a set of "ground rules" for making their discussions suitably rational, explicit, and equitable. (The rationale for this is explained in more detail next, in relation to the Thinking Together research.) These ground rules stated that the students would agree to

- share their ideas and listen to each other;
- consider what their partner(s) has written or drawn;
- respect each other's opinions;
- give reasons for their ideas;
- express their ideas and workings neatly and clearly;
- in the case of disagreement, ask "why?" or provide reasons for their disagreement;
- only work on solving the problems (e.g., no web-surfing);
- try to concur on a solution, prior to asking the teacher to check their answer.

By agreement with the students, their teacher was allowed to read their online dialogues and use them as a basis for subsequent whole-class discussions. Implemented and evaluated in a public secondary school in Singapore, the results of prescriptive tutoring showed that students in the experimental group significantly outperformed students in a matched control group on postintervention tests of understanding of physics concepts.

Some researchers have tried to ensure that collaborative learning is more effective by encouraging teachers to use whole-class sessions to guide and model children's use of language for reasoning. The Thinking Together intervention studies carried out by myself and colleagues have so far involved more than 700 children, aged 6 to 14. These studies have been described in detail elsewhere (e.g., Mercer & Littleton, 2007), so I summarize here only those aspects relevant to my argument. Essentially, each class agrees to follow a set of "ground rules" for talking together in groups, which early studies showed help to generate more Exploratory Talk. Students are then expected to apply these rules during all curriculum-related group work, and the teacher uses whole-class sessions to model Exploratory Talk and encourage children's meta-awareness of the ways they use language for reasoning (Dawes, 2012).

Compared with control classes following their normal course of study, results have shown that children who follow the Thinking Together intervention program begin to use much more Exploratory Talk and pursue group activities more cooperatively. One study with children aged 9 and 10 found that they also gained significantly higher scores in national, curriculum-based tests of science and mathematics (Mercer, Dawes, Wegerif, & Sams, 2004). Moreover – and crucially for the case I am making here – the children in the interventional classes became significantly better at reasoning, as assessed by the Raven's Progressive Matrices test (Raven, Court, & Raven, 1995) both collectively and alone. Before the intervention, children in both control and experimental classes were given the Raven's test twice: once in groups and once (using a different version of the test) on their own, in that order. After the intervention, they all again did the test in groups and as individuals. The intervention children obtained better group *and* individual scores on the postintervention collaborative application of the test than the control children (although the intervention children had no more opportunities to practice the Raven's problems than the control children). It seems that they had learned not only how to "interthink" more effectively but also how to reason better on their own. These results have been replicated in Mexican schools (Rojas-Drummond & Mercer, 2004).

These results can be related to the three explanations of how intermental activity influences intramental learning and development I offered earlier. I consider each in turn, regarding how they might explain the greater success of the children in the experimental groups in the postintervention, group-based, and individual Raven's tests.

### Appropriation

The relative success of the experimental children in the postintervention group-based Raven's test must depend on those children applying better problem-solving strategies than those in control classes. It is unlikely that more individual children in the experimental classes came along with effective strategies already in place than those in the control classes, so greater success in the *group* test would depend on the experimental children being better than control children at sharing and making use of any effective strategies that individual members already knew, or devised on the spot, in this one session. An appropriate explanation of the relatively greater success of the experimental children in the *individual* tests would thus depend on a significant number of them having learned better strategies from each other in that one group session.

## Co-construction

The greater success of the experimental children in the postintervention group test could result from individual children in the experimental groups being more able than control class children to combine and apply their relevant knowledge and insights to the task, and so construct effective new strategies for solving the Raven's problems than they would have done alone. On the basis of their training and practice in Exploratory Talk, they would do this through a process of reasoned argumentation, whereby any suggestions made by group members would be critically evaluated and any resultant successful strategies constructed would be learned and subsequently applied by individual members when working alone. Their relative success as individuals thus would depend crucially on them being more able than children in the control classes to construct new strategies in the one postintervention group session and then use them in the individual session.

We can see a group of children engaging in the kind of co-constructive approach to solving a Raven's problem that would accord with this explanation in Sequence 1, which comes from an experimental class in a study carried out in Mexican schools. As the sequence begins, the children (aged 12) are trying to decide which one of a possible set of patterns would logically complete an unfinished sequence of patterns made up of features that the children refer to as dots, crosses, and stars.

*Sequence 1: Georgina, Luis, and Mauro doing Raven's test item E5*

| | |
|---|---|
| GEORGINA: | Here they remove the dots and this, this cross (*points at a drawing*) |
| MAURO: | No but wait, it does not fit |
| LUIS: | No, wait |
| MAURO: | No |
| GEORGINA: | Let's look at the sequence. Here it is like this, they remove the cross and the dots. Here they are not there any more, here (*points*) |
| LUIS: | And here they remove only the dots |
| GEORGINA: | Yes, the dots. And this part, only the star |
| MAURO: | It would be this one, look at it (*points*) |
| LUIS: | Which they have removed |
| MAURO: | It would be this one, because, look, it goes like this (*points*) |
| GEORGINA: | But how, if it doesn't have dots? |
| LUIS: | It doesn't have dots. Just the cross would remain |
| GEORGINA: | Yeah, because they have been removed! |
| | (*Georgina writes down option number 1 on the answer sheet, which is correct*) |
| | (Adapted from Rojas-Drummond & Mercer, 2004, p. 109) |

Some aspects of their reasoning may not be clear to a reader, because they sometimes (and appropriately enough) rely on pointing to a pattern to support their arguments; but the discussion nevertheless has many features of Exploratory Talk with its challenges, reasoned justifications, and equitable distribution of conversational turns. Together, they construct and employ a mental scenario in which the originators of the test have differentially "removed" certain features from specific patterns in the series, leading to the logical inevitability of one of the possible solutions being correct. From reading the sequence, it would be difficult to attribute the group's success to the contributions of any one member.

### Transformation

Their teachers' modeling of Exploratory Talk and establishment of "ground rules" for discussion would enable the experimental children to solve problems more effectively in the group tests, because they would use that experience of external regulation to coregulate their activities. This would make them more effective at sharing knowledge and co-constructing an explanation, as previously suggested. But that external regulation, and their practice in using Exploratory Talk as a group, would also act as a template for self-regulation and reasoning when they tackled problems alone in the *individual* tests. That is, Exploratory Talk would act as a template for carrying out the "inner dialogue" of individual reasoning. In the postintervention individual sessions, the relative success of the experimental children would thus not necessarily depend on their retention and employment of useful strategies co-constructed in the group session. It could also be assisted by their enhanced ability to reason "dialogically" about *any* problems they were given. They would engage in any new problem-solving task in a more metacognitive, self-regulatory way. This would make it more likely that they achieved correct solutions, as they would be more able to generate and apply good strategies for themselves and not only recall them from the previous group session.

According to the "transformation" explanation, then, the success of the Thinking Together intervention would depend on it having enabled children to not only become more able to have reasoned discussions with peers but also become more able to have a "reasoned discussion" on their own. This represents a very strong claim for the effects of social activity on individual cognition, because it explains the development of a sophisticated, educated manner of individual thinking through the internalization of collective reasoning. The cognition of a normally developing child would not only be "social" because the human brain has inherent sensitivities to the signaled intentions and emotions of others (as argued by evolutionary psychologists), but because it embodies a way of thinking that takes account of the possibility of multiple, varied perspectives and explanations which need to be compared and evaluated. We might note here that, in research discussed earlier, Howe (2009) found that the incidence of unresolved contradictions or disagreements during children's collaborative problem-solving science tasks had a positive correlation with scores on *delayed* posttests of children's scientific understanding but not on *immediate* posttests. Those findings suggest that even if the co-construction of a satisfactory explanation is not achieved during collaboration, the kind of intermental activity which takes place during Exploratory Talk may stimulate subsequent intramental "dialogue," which enables the individual to achieve a new level of understanding.

Are there reasons for believing that the "transformation" explanation applies to the results of the Thinking Together interventions: that the intervention children's "monological" reasoning became more "dialogic" through some kind of internalization of their Exploratory Talk? There are, though only to a limited extent. We have evidence that intervention class children went on to deal more successfully as individuals than control class children with new types of reasoning problems and provided better written arguments to support their arguments in English assessments (Mercer & Littleton, 2007, Chapter 6). "Transformation" would also account for intervention children's subsequently improved performances when dealing with new mathematics, science, and English assignments involving reasoning which they had not practiced with their peers – they could apply to them an improved general reasoning skill that involved thinking dialogically. There is also some anecdotal evidence from teachers participating in the Thinking Together research that they observed that children were able to reason more effectively (in speech and writing) about new topics after the intervention. However, the Thinking Together studies preceded the formulation of the three explanations of effect, and so were not designed to discriminate between them. Perhaps, as sociocultural researcher Futoshi Hiruma (personal communication, May 12, 2008) suggested, in any new studies children from intervention and control classes should be asked to "think aloud" as they deal individually with new types of problem-solving tasks, to test the hypothesis that the intervention children would offer more explicitly reasoned protocols that were related to the structure and content of the classroom dialogues in which they had been involved. This might be combined with Howe's (2009) methodology of immediate and delayed posttests of children's understanding after collaborative work – which could include their developing understanding of how they use talk for thinking together and/or how they reason alone. The use of sociocultural discourse analysis (Mercer, 2008, 2009), with its methods for tracking the temporal trajectory of talk through time, and hence the appropriation by children of linguistic items and structures from their earlier experiences, would be appropriate here. This would tell us more about if, and how, dialogue can transform the quality of individual reasoning.

A related possible line of inquiry would build stronger links between research on dialogue and that on the development of metacognition and self-regulation. My colleagues[1] and I have already designed and tested an intervention program on that basis, for use by Year 1 teachers with their classes. Essentially, it requires teachers to use the Thinking Together approach to raise children's awareness and skills in working and talking together, and then engage them in a series of collaborative problem-solving tasks that require collective reasoning. This program has so far been tested in a pilot study (the Children Articulating Thinking [ChAT] Project) involving six primary school teachers and their classes. The main hypothesis has been that developing the children's use of language as a tool for social, joint regulation in problem solving will stimulate the development of their individual self-regulation and metacognitive abilities – and that this will be demonstrated through comparisons with children in control classes when they subsequently attempt individual tasks. The results (unpublished as yet) are encouraging, with children in intervention classes becoming better at discussing problems together and coregulating their activity. They improved significantly more than control classes on measures of conceptual understanding, quality of reasoning, and metacognition on a music task. They were also able to explain their reasoning to a researcher more explicitly when doing both a music-related and a science-related task (concerned with floating and sinking). We have also tested for any improvements in children's performance on a problem-solving task where they had to assemble a model railway track to a given template (adapted from Karmiloff-Smith, 1979), but results of that are not yet available. A larger study, involving a modified intervention program, is being planned.

## Does collaboration help to solve problems?

I have offered evidence in support of the value of collective intellectual activity for the development of children's reasoning. But my argument early in this article for the evolutionary importance of the emergence of a capacity for thinking collectively also requires evidence to show that, at least in some situations, collective thinking is more productive and effective than solitary thinking. One source is from studies of pairs and teams of adults working together. These range from quasi-experimental studies (as reviewed in Nemeth, 1995; Paulus, Dzindolet, & Kohn, 2012) to more ethnographic accounts (Miell & Littleton, 2008) and biographical case studies (John-Steiner, 2000). I mentioned earlier the assembly bonus effect, discovered by some researchers, whereby the performance of a group is better than that of its best member (Laughlin et al., 2006); and that although the success of group endeavors does not correlate strongly with the average intelligence of group members, it is correlated with the average social sensitivity of members and the equality in distribution of their conversational turn-taking (Woolley et al., 2010). Biographical case studies strongly encourage the view that some of the most significant and creative human achievements can be explained only through the joint activity of more than one talented individual, with conversational interaction between collaborators being seen as important. Psychological research on creativity has correspondingly begun to widen its focus from understanding the talents of gifted individuals to include studies of how people are collectively creative. Several studies take a sociocultural theoretical perspective, in which culturally framed ways of communicating and the use of cultural tools are considered important (Miell & Littleton, 2004; Paulus & Nijstad, 2003; Sawyer, 2012; Sawyer & DeZutter, 2009). In a meta-review of research on "orchestrating creativity," Ha¨ma¨la¨inen and Va¨ha¨santane (2011) noted that within recent studies of collaborative creativity, "the different roles of group members, including mutual explaining and shared knowledge construction, have been seen to enable new creative processes and outputs" (p. 172). Some researchers have begun to offer "co-construction" explanations of creativity, even sometimes using that term (Rojas-Drummond, Mazon, Fernandez, & Wegerif, 2006).

However, reviewing experimental studies into group-based work activity, one team of experienced researchers has commented, "We do not know of a study that has clearly demonstrated . . . enhanced performance of teamwork relative to working as individuals" (Paulus et al., 2012, p. 348). Some research has highlighted the flaws in collective thinking processes, as when "groupthink" leads to unjustifiable consensus (Janis, 1982). Surprisingly, too, there seem to have been few detailed studies of how the use of talk in noneducational working groups leads to effective creative and outcomes (though see Edwards & Middleton, 1986; Middup, Coughlan, & Johnson, 2010; Miell & Littleton, 2008). Nevertheless, extrapolating from the available evidence to connect with my theme here, it is possible to draw some conclusions. The most reasonable answer to the question, "Do people solve problems more effectively when working together than alone?" is "In the right circumstances, yes." It depends to some extent on the nature of the task, and on the quality of the interactions within a group. As in studies of collaborative learning in educational settings, working teams have been found to achieve better solutions than individuals, and sometimes very significantly so, but only if they communicate effectively. For example, "groupthink" can be avoided by following ground rules that encourage reasonable dissent (Nemeth, 1995). Relevant research supports the view that the success of working teams depends on members using, when appropriate, a mode of interaction which resembles Exploratory Talk (Littleton & Mercer, 2013). Yet, as in the classroom, problem-solving discussions in the workplace are often not of this kind. As mentioned earlier, in evolutionary anthropology and psychology it tends to be assumed that the skills of social cognition are "hard-wired" and ready to use. But, like educational research, research in this field encourages the view that although people inherit a distinctively human capacity for thinking socially and collectively, these skills need to be developed and practiced.

# Conclusions

In this article, I have suggested that the concept of the social brain could help to integrate research in evolutionary psychology, developmental psychology, social psychology, educational psychology, and other fields such as linguistics and philosophy, generating a better account of the distinctive nature of human cognition. The origin of the concept lies in evolutionary studies of human behavior, and that lively field of inquiry offers a fresh perspective that should not be ignored in more established fields of psychological and educational research. But I suggest that we should question its evolutionary account of our origins, which is predicated principally upon competition between individuals. I have argued instead that our evolution has equipped us with the distinctive human capability for engaging in goal-orientated collective thinking, so that we are able to achieve more together than we each could do alone. I have therefore proposed that the concept of the social brain should be developed beyond its initial definition, which is concerned with how humans interpret and negotiate complex social relations to pursue their individualistic needs. The sociality of the brain does not just enable each of us to cope with the complexity of society and pursue our own agendas, it also enables us to solve problems together and to create and develop knowledge at the cultural level. Although collective intellectual activity is not always more creative and productive than individual efforts, research has shown that it has the kinds of distinctive functions and benefits which support my argument.

Research in several fields provides additional support for an expanded conception of the social brain, as I have shown. The special human capacity for "theory of mind" allows us to appreciate that we each may have different perspectives and concerns, and motivates us to assess and monitor one another's states of understanding and common knowledge. This provides a basis for educating each new generation, as intermental activity allows more experienced members of a community to have a formative influence on the intramental development of less experienced members. I have used findings from several lines of inquiry to argue that the process of reasoning collectively, which has been crucial for the success of our species, provides a template for the development of individual reasoning. The distinctive nature of the social brain, then, is encapsulated in the relationship between the intermental and the intramental, the social and the psychological. Language, which has evolved in conjunction with the social brain, has a special role in mediating that relationship, through its integration with cognition generally and its use as both a cultural/social and psychological tool (or, rather, toolkit). I have offered three explanations of the effects of collaborative learning and dialogue on the development of children's reasoning – *appropriation*, *co-construction*, and *transformation*. They stand as potentially complementary, rather than as alternative, explanations. Individualistic accounts of reasoning and its development are inadequate in comparison because they struggle to explain both the "assembly bonus effects" of collective intellectual activity and the ways that educated modes of individual thinking embody essential features of reasoned dialogue.

Through creating links between evolutionary, social, developmental, and educational psychology, the expanded concept of the social brain could strengthen a sociocultural account of human learning and cognitive development and might also help neuroscience research and educational research become better integrated. The direct relevance and value of the findings of neuroscience for improving educational practice and theory have been recognized to be limited so far, even by those involved (Goswami, 2007). Most neuroscience research has been aimed at explaining brain function, not addressing educational concerns (Willingham, 2009). Moreover, when educational issues have been addressed by neuroscientists there has been a narrow focus on how research might serve the perceived needs of practitioners, and how to make the findings of neuroscience intelligible to teachers, rather than how neuroscientists could collaborate with psychologists of education or other researchers in investigating educational research questions (Mason, 2009). For example, if neuroscience could begin to identify the ways in which language functions are related to, or integrated with, more general processes of learning or problem solving, it might help explain why children's early language experience can so profoundly affect the course of their intellectual and academic development. Could neuroscientists also contribute to our understanding of such processes by studying how brains operate in conjunction: for example, how spoken dialogue is reflected in the brain functioning of partners? Or could they investigate whether the exercise of "theory of mind" capacities, the establishment of common knowledge, and the formulation of joint plans of action involve "mirrored" neural activity in the brains of partners engaged in joint problem solving? More adventurously, we might hope for studies that investigate ways that the brain activity of teachers and students, or collaborating learners, is correlated during joint activity. By combining the methods of neuroscience with those of discourse analysis, we might even seek the correlates of Exploratory Talk. And if neuroscience research provided more evidence that language use is indeed a wholly integrated aspect of brain function, this might encourage more educational and psychological researchers to investigate the role of language in learning and conceptual development, and specifically in the development of metacognition and self-regulation.

A reviewer of this article in draft suggested that it would be better directed at an audience of evolutionary psychologists and neuroscientists, rather than psychologists of education who commonly take a sociocultural perspective and so do not need to be persuaded of its value or of the need to study processes of collaborative learning. But the focus of most research on collaborative learning has been on the effects of joint intellectual activity on individual learning and development, rather than on understanding and improving collaborative problem solving in its own right. This suggests that researchers in that field may be, ironically, trapped in a similar kind of individualistic perspective to those in evolutionary and cognitive psychology. The ability to think collectively in the pursuit of common goals is just as important today as it was in our evolutionary past. If that ability can be developed and enhanced, as research strongly suggests, educational research and practice should be concerned with its development per se, and not only with collaboration as a pedagogical device for individual tuition. We commonly hear today of the need for "good team players" – and that does not just mean being amiable colleagues. It is in the interests of society that children are taught how to become effective interthinkers.

The explanatory framework I have used, sociocultural theory, does not avoid or deny recognition of the role of the individual in "making sense" but examines that role in the context of processes of collective thinking activity and the creation of socially shared knowledge. In an earlier issue of this journal, Säljö (2009) suggested that "the point of a theory does not lie in its correspondence with the world (which would be the realist perspective) but rather in its explanatory power in relation to a set of issues" (p. 204). My interest in the social brain and collective thinking has a strong practical dimension. I want to know why some teachers are better than others at helping their students achieve higher levels of attainment, how levels of attainment are related to features of children's social and communicative experience, and why and how group work promotes learning. I also want to know how best to educate children as "interthinkers." Research has shown that the potential of the social brain is often being squandered in classroom education, because it is not being used, or educated, effectively. We know that collaborative learning benefits individual learning, but only under certain conditions. We are now able to identify the pedagogical strategies that can maximize the educational impact of classroom interactions and to develop children's skills in reasoning collectively. We need to ensure that children gain the most benefit from collaborative learning, and enable them to take part productively in the collective thinking activities of the wider world. More educational benefit would be likely to come from this than from the pursuit of such popular "neuromyths" as "learning styles," "right/left laterality," and "whole-brain learning" (as discussed by Goswami, 2007). In summary, then, I hope that I have provided good reasons for psychologists of education to adopt, adapt, and develop the concept of the social brain. In doing so, and making links with colleagues in other branches of psychology, the outcome might be a better and more useful understanding of the distinctive nature and origins of human cognition.

## Acknowledgments

Thanks to Clark Chinn, Lyn Dawes, Usha Goswami, Christine Howe, Karen Littleton, Bert van Oers, Deborah Pino-Pasternak, David Whitebread, and three anonymous reviewers for very constructive comments on drafts of this article.

## Note

1 David Whitebread, Deborah Pino-Pasternak, Christine Howe, Jane Warwick, Penny Coltman, and Usha Goswami.

## References

Abrams, D. A., Nicol, T., Zecker, S., & Kraus, N. (2008). Right hemisphere auditory cortex is dominant for coding syllable patterns in speech. *Journal of Neuroscience*, *28*, 3958–3965. doi:10.1523/JNEUROSCI.0187-08.2008

Alexander, R. J. (2001). *Culture and pedagogy: International comparisons in primary education* (pp. 391–528). Oxford, UK: Blackwell.

Alexander, R. J. (2008). Culture, dialogue and learning: Notes on an emerging pedagogy. In N. Mercer & S. Hodgkinson (Eds.), *Exploring talk in schools* (pp. 91–114). London, UK: Sage.

Augustinova, M. (2008). Falsification cueing in collective reasoning: Example of the Wason selection task. *European Journal of Social Psychology*, *38*, 770–785. doi:10.1002/ejsp.532

Baker, C. (2006). *Foundations of bilingual education and bilingualism*. Clevedon, UK: Multilingual Matters.

Bakhtin, M. (1981). *The dialogic imagination*. Austin, TX: University of Texas Press.

Barnes, D. (1976). *From communication to curriculum*. Harmondsworth, UK: Penguin.

Barnes, D. (2008). Exploratory talk for learning. In N. Mercer & S. Hodgkinson (Eds.), *Exploring talk in school* (pp. 1–16). London, UK: Sage.

Barnes, D. (2010). Why talk is important. *English Teaching: Practice and Critique*, *9*, 7–10.

Barton, D. (2009). Understanding textual practices in a changing world. In M. Baynham & M. Prinsloo (Eds.), *The future of literacy studies* (pp. 38–53). Basingstoke, UK: Palgrave Macmillan.

Bennett, N., & Cass, A. (1989). The effects of group composition on group interactive processes and pupil understanding. *British Educational Research Journal*, *15*, 119–132. doi:10.1080/0141192890150102

Berkowitz, M., Gibbs, J., & Broughton, J. (1980). The relation of moral judgement stage disparity to developmental effects of peer dialogues. *Merrill-Palmer Quarterly*, *26*, 341–357.

Bialystok, E., Craik, F., Grady, C., Chau, W., Ishii, R., Gunji, A., & Pantev, C. (2005). Effect of bilingualism on cognitive control in the Simon task: Evidence from MEG. *NeuroImage*, *24*, 40–49. doi:10.1016/ j.neuroimage.2004.09.044

Bialystok, E., & Feng, X. (2010). Language proficiency and its implications for monolingual and bilingual children. In A. Durgunoglu & C. Goldenberg (Eds.), *Dual language learners: The development and assessment of oral and written language* (pp. 121–138). New York, NY: Guilford.

Black, P. (2009). Looking again at formative assessment. *Learning and Teaching Update*, *30*, 3–5.

Black, P., & Wiliam, D. (1998). *Inside the black box: Raising standards through classroom assessment.* London, UK: Kings College School of Education.

Bruner, J. S. (1983). *Child's talk: Learning to use language.* Oxford, UK: Oxford University Press.

Buss, D. (2001). Human nature and culture: An evolutionary psychology perspective. *Journal of Personality, 69,* 955–978. doi:10.1177/ 026565908500100113

Cazden, C. (2001). *Classroom discourse: The language of teaching and learning* (2nd ed.). New York, NY: Heinemann.

Chartrand, T. L., & Bargh, J. A. (1999). The chameleon effect: The perception–behavior link and social interaction. *Journal of Personality and Social Psychology, 76,* 893–910. doi:10.1037//0022-3514.76. 6.893

Chinn, C., Anderson, R., & Waggoner, M. (2001). Patterns of discourse in two kinds of literature discussion. *Reading Research Quarterly, 36,* 378–411. doi:10.1598/ RRQ.36.4.3

Christie, F., & Martin, J. (1997). *Genre and institutions: Social processes in the workplace and school.* London, UK: Cassell.

Clark, A. (1998). Magic words: How language augments human computation. In P. Carruthers & J. Boucher (Eds.), *Language and thought: Interdisciplinary themes* (pp. 162–183). Cambridge, UK: Cambridge University Press.

Daniels, H. (2001). *Vygotsky and pedagogy.* London, UK: Routledge/Falmer.

Daniels, H. (2008). *Vygotsky and research.* Abingdon, UK: Routledge.

Darcy, N. (1963). Bilingualism and the measurement of intelligence: Review of a decade of research. *Journal of Genetic Psychology, 103,* 259–282. doi:10.1080/0 0221325.1963.10532521

Dawes, L. (2008). Encouraging students' contribution to dialogue during science. *School Science Review, 90,* 101–107.

Dawes, L. (2012). *Talking points: Discussion activities in the primary classroom.* London, UK: David Fulton.

Dawkins, R. (1976). *The selfish gene.* Oxford, UK: Oxford University Press.

Diaz, R. (1983). Thought and two languages: The impact of bilingualism on cognitive development. *Review of Research in Education, 10,* 23–54. doi:10.2307/1167134

Dignath, G., Buettner, G., & Langfeldt, H.-P. (2008). How can primary school students learn self-regulated learning strategies most effectively? A meta-analysis on self-regulation training programmes. *Educational Research Review, 3,* 101–129.

Dunbar, R. (1998). The social brain hypothesis. *Evolutionary Anthropology, 6,* 178–189.

Edwards, D., & Mercer, N. (2012). *Common knowledge: The development of understanding in the classroom.* London, UK: Methuen/Routledge. (Original work published 1987)

Edwards, D., & Middleton, D. (1986). Joint remembering: Constructing an account of shared experience through conversational discourse. *Discourse Processes, 9,* 423–459. doi:10.1080/01638538609544651

Elbers, E. (1994). Sociogenesis and children's pretend play: A variation on Vygotskian themes. In W. de Graaf & R. Maier (Eds.), *Sociogenesis re-examined* (pp. 58–72). New York, NY: Springer. doi:10.1007/ 978-1-4612-2654-3-13

Fidalgo, Z., & Pereira, F. (2005). Sociocultural differences and the adjustment of mothers' speech to their children' cognitive and language comprehension skills. *Learning and Instruction, 15,* 1–21.

Fiedler, K., & Bless, H. (2001). Social cognition. In M. Hewstone & W. Stroebe (Eds.), *Introduction to social psychology* (pp. 123–146). London, UK: Sage.

Forman, E. A., & Cazden, C. B. (1985). Exploring Vygotskian perspectives in education: The cognitive value of peer interaction. In J. V. Wertsch (Ed.), *Culture, communication and cognition: Vygotskian perspectives* (pp. 323–347). Cambridge, UK: Cambridge University Press.

Frith, C., & Singer, T. (2008). The role of social cognition in decision making. *Philosophical Transactions of the Royal Society, 363*, 3875–3886. doi:10.1098/rstb.2008.0156

Goodman, S. (1996). Market forces speak English. In S. Goodman & D. Graddol (Eds.), *Redesigning English: New texts, new identities* (pp. 141–163). London, UK: Routledge.

Goswami, U. (2007). Neuroscience and education: From research to practice. *Nature Review Neuroscience, 7*, 406–413. doi:10.1038/nrn1907

Goswami, U. (2009). Mind, brain, and literacy-biomarkers as usable knowledge for education. *Mind, Brain, and Education, 3*, 176–184. doi:10.1111/j.1751-228X.2009.01068.x

Grist, M. (2009). *Changing the subject: How new ways of thinking about human behavior might change politics, policy and practice*. London, UK: Royal Society of Arts. Retrieved from www.thersa.org/ data/assets/pdf file/0020/250625/Nov28th-2009ChangingThe-Subject Pamphlet.pdf

Grosjean, F. (2010). *Bilingual: Life and reality*. Cambridge, MA: Harvard University Press.

Ha¨ma¨la¨inen, R., & Va¨ha¨santare, K. (2011). Theoretical and pedagogical perspectives on orchestrating creativity and collaborative learning. *Educational Research Review, 6*, 169–184. doi:10.1016/j.edurev.2011.08.001

Hart, B., & Risley, T. R. (1995). *Meaningful differences in the everyday experience of young American children*. New York, NY: Brookes.

Hattie, J. A., Biggs, J., & Purdie, N. (1996). Effects of learning skills interventions on student learning: A meta-analysis. *Review of Educational Research, 66*, 99–136. doi:10.2307/1170605

Hermann, E., Call, J., Hernandez-Lloreda, M. V., Hare, B., & Tomasello, M. (2007). Humans have evolved specialized skills of social cognition: The cultural intelligence hypothesis. *Science, 317*, 1360. doi:10.1126/science.1146282

Heyes, C. M. (2010). Where do mirror neurons come from? *Neuroscience and Biobehavioural Reviews, 34*, 575–583. doi:10.1016/j.neubiorev.2009.11.007

Howe, C. (2009). Collaborative group work in middle childhood: Joint construction, unresolved contradiction and the growth of knowledge. *Human Development, 52*, 215–219.

Howe, C. (2010). *Peer groups and children's development*. Oxford, UK: Wiley-Blackwell. doi:10.1002/9781444318098

Iiskala, T., Vauras, M., Lehtinen, E., & Salonen, P. (2011). Socially shared metacognition of dyads of pupils in collaborative mathematical problem-solving processes. *Learning and Instruction, 21*, 379–393. doi:10.1016/j.learninstruc.2010.05.002

Janis, I. (1982). *Groupthink: Psychological studies of policy decisions and fiascoes*. New York, NY: Houghton Mifflin.

Jeong, H., & Chi, M. (2007). Knowledge convergence and collaborative learning. *Instructional Science, 35*, 287–315. doi:10.1007/ s11251-006-9008-z

Jewitt, C. (2008). *Technology, literacy, learning: A multimodality approach*. London, UK: Routledge.

Jewitt, C., Kress, G., Ogborn, J., & Tsartsarelis, C. (2004). Exploring learning through visual, actional and linguistic communication: The multi-modal environment of science classroom. *Educational Review, 53*, 6–16. doi:10.1080/00131910120033600

John-Steiner, V. (2000). *Creative collaboration*. New York, NY: Oxford University Press.

Karmiloff-Smith, A. (1979). Problem solving construction and representation of closed railway circuits. *Archives of Psychology, 47*, 37–59.

Keefer, M., Zeitz, C., & Resnick, L. (2000). Judging the quality of peer-led student dialogues. *Cognition and Instruction, 18*, 53–81. doi:10.1207/S1532690XCI180103

Kress, G. (1987). Genre in a social theory of language. In I. Reid (Ed.), *The place of genre in learning* (pp. 33–43). Geelong, Australia: Deakin University Press. doi:10.1111/j.1754-8845.1992.tb01061.x

Larkin, S. (2009). Socially mediated metacognition and learning to write. *Thinking Skills and Creativity, 4*, 149–159. doi:10.1016/j.tsc.2009.09.003

Laughlin, P. R., Hatch, E. C., Silver, J. S., & Boh, L. (2006). Groups perform better than the best individuals on letters-to-numbers problems: Effects of group size. *Journal of Personality and Social Psychology, 90*, 644–651. doi:10.1037/0022-3514.90.4.644

Lave, J., & Wenger, E. (1991). *Situated learning: Legitimate peripheral participation*. Cambridge, UK: Cambridge University Press. doi:10.1017/CBO9780511815355

Leat, D., & Lin, M. (2003). Developing a pedagogy of metacognition and transfer: Some signposts for the generation and use of knowledge and the creation of research partnerships. *British Educational Research Journal, 29*, 383–416. doi:10.1080/014 11920301853

Lemke, J. L. (1990). *Talking science: Language, learning and values*. Norwood, MA: Ablex.

Levinson, S. C. (2006). On the human "interaction engine". In N. J. Enfield, & S. C. Levinson (Eds.), *Roots of human sociality: Culture, cognition and interaction* (pp. 39–69). Oxford, UK: Berg.

Littleton, K., & Mercer, N. (2013). *Interthinking: Putting talk to work*. Abingdon, UK: Routledge.

Macnamara, J. (1966). *Bilingualism and primary education*. Edinburgh, UK: Edinburgh University Press.

Martin, J. (1993). Genre and literacy: Modeling context in educational linguistics. *Annual Review of Applied Linguistics, 13*, 141–172. doi:10.1017/ S0267190500 002440

Mason, L. (2009). Bridging neuroscience and education: A two-way path is possible. *Cortex, 45*, 548–549. doi:10.1016/j.cortex.2008.06.003

Maybin, J. (2006). *Children's voices: Talk, knowledge and identity*. Basingstoke, UK: Palgrave Macmillan.

Mercer, N. (1995). *The guided construction of knowledge: Talk amongst teachers and learners*. Clevedon, UK: Multilingual Matters.

Mercer, N. (2000). *Words and minds: How we use language to think together*. London, UK: Routledge. doi:10.4324/9780203464984

Mercer, N. (2008). The seeds of time: Why classroom dialogue needs a temporal analysis. *Journal of the Learning Sciences, 17*, 33–59. doi:10.1080/10508400701793182

Mercer, N. (2009). The analysis of classroom talk: Methods and methodologies. *British Journal of Educational Psychology, 80*, 1–14. doi:10.1348/000709909X479853

Mercer, N., Dawes, R., Wegerif, R., & Sams, C. (2004). Reasoning as a scientist: Ways of helping children to use language to learn science. *British Educational Research Journal, 30*, 367–385. doi:10.1080/01411920410001689689

Mercer, N., & Littleton, K. (2007). *Dialogue and the development of children's thinking*. London, UK: Routledge

Mercer, N., & Sams, C. (2006). Teaching children how to use language to solve maths problems. *Language and Education, 20,* 507–527. doi:10.2167/le678.0

Mercier, H., & Sperber, D. (2011). Why do humans reason? Arguments for an argumentative theory. *Behavioral and Brain Sciences, 34,* 57–74. doi:10.1017/S0140525X10000968

Michaels, S., & O'Connor, M. C. (2002). *Accountable talk: Classroom conversation that works*. Pittsburgh, PA: University of Pittsburgh.

Middleton, D., & Edwards, D. (Eds.). (1990). *Collective remembering*. London, UK: Sage.

Middup, C., Coughlan, T., & Johnson, P. (2010). How creative groups structure tasks through negotiating resources. In M. Lewkowicz, P. Hassanaly, M. Rohde, & V. Wulf (Eds.), *Proceedings of COOP 2010: Computer supported cooperative work* (pp. 203–221). London, UK: Springer-Verlag. doi:10.1007/978-1-84996-211-7 12

Midgley, M. (2010). *The solitary self: Darwin and the selfish gene*. London, UK: Acumen. doi:10.1017/UPO9781844654833

Miell, D., & Littleton, K. (2004). *Collaborative creativity: Contemporary perspectives*. London, UK: Free Association Books.

Miell, D., & Littleton, K. (2008). Musical collaboration outside school: Processes of negotiation in band rehearsals. *International Journal of Educational Research, 47,* 41–49. doi:10.1016/j.ijer.2007.11.006

Miller, G. F. (1999). Sexual selection for cultural displays. In R. Dunbar, C. Knight, & C. Power (Eds.), *The evolution of culture* (pp. 71–91). Edinburgh, UK: Edinburgh University Press.

Mukamel, R., Ekstrom, A., Kaplan, J., Iacoboni, M., & Fried, I. (2010). Single-neuron responses in humans during execution and observation of actions. *Current Biology, 20,* 750–756. doi:10.1016/j.cub.2010.02. 045

Muller-Mirza, N., & Perret-Clermont, A-N. (2009). *Argumentation and education*. New York, NY: Springer. doi:10.1007/978-0-387-98125-3

Murphy, P., Wilkinson, I., Soter, A., Hennessy, M., & Alexander, J. (2009). Examining the effects of classroom discussion on students' comprehension of text: A meta-analysis. *Journal of Educational Psychology, 101,* 740–764.

Nemeth, C. J. (1995). Dissent as driving cognition, attitudes, and judgments. *Social Cognition, 13,* 273–291. doi:10.1521/soco.1995.13.3.273

Nystrand, M. (1997). *Opening dialogue: Understanding the dynamics of language and learning in the English classroom*. New York, NY: Teachers College Press.

Patel, A. D. (2003). Language, music, syntax and the brain. *Nature Neuroscience, 6,* 674–681.

Paulus, P. B., Dzindolet, M., & Kohn, N. (2012). Collaborative creativity-group creativity and team innovation. In M. Mumford (Ed.), *The handbook of organizational creativity* (pp. 327–358). London, UK: Academic. doi:10.1016/B978-0-12-374714-3.00014-8

Paulus, P. B., & Nijstad, B. A. (2003). *Group creativity: Innovation through collaboration*. New York, NY: University Press.

Pea, R. (1993). Learning scientific concepts through material and social activities: Conversational analysis meets conceptual change. *Educational Psychologist, 28,* 265–277. doi:10.1207/s15326985ep2803 6

Piaget, J. (1926). *The language and thought of the child*. New York, NY: Harcourt Brace Jovanovich.

Pinker, S. (1994). *The language instinct*. London, UK: Penguin.

Pinker, S. (2007). *The stuff of thought: Language as a window into human nature.* London, UK: Penguin.

Premack, D., & Woodruff, G. (1978). Does the chimpanzee have a theory of mind? *Behavioral and Brain Sciences, 1,* 515–526. doi:10.1017/S0140525X00076512

Raven, J., Court, J., & Raven, J. C. (1995). *Manual for Raven's progressive matrices and vocabulary scales.* Oxford, UK: Oxford Psychologists Press.

Reese, E., Haden, C. A., & Fivush, R. (1993). Mother–child conversations about the past: Relationships of style and memory over time. *Cognitive Development, 8,* 403–430. doi:10.1016/S0885-2014(05)80002-4

Reznitskaya, A., Anderson, R., McNurlen, B., Nguyen-Jahiel, K., Archodidou, A., & Kim, S. (2001). Influence of oral discussion on written argument. *Discourse Processes, 32,* 155–175. doi:11207/S15326950DP3202&304

Reznitskaya, A., & Gregory, M. (2013). Student thought and classroom language: Examining the mechanisms of change in dialogic teaching. *Educational Psychologist, 48,* 114–133. doi:10.1080/00461520.2013.7758958

Rojas-Drummond, S. (2009). Rethinking the role of peer collaboration in enhancing cognitive growth. *Human Development, 52,* 240–245.

Rojas-Drummond, S., Mazon, N., Fernandez, M., & Wegerif, R. (2006). Explicit reasoning, creativity and co-construction in primary school children's collaborative activities. *Thinking Skills and Creativity, 1,* 84–94. doi:10.1016/j.tsc.2006.06.001

Rojas-Drummond, S., & Mercer, N. (2004). Scaffolding the development of effective collaboration and learning, *International Journal of Educational Research, 39,* 99–111. doi:10.1016/S0883-0355(03)00075-2

Rojas-Drummond, S., Mercer, N., & Dabrowski, E. (2001). Teaching-learning strategies and the development of problem solving in Mexican classrooms. *European Journal of Psychology and Education, 16,* 179–196.

Roseth, C., Johnson, D., & Johnson, R. (2008). Promoting early adolescents' achievement and peer relationships: The effects of cooperative, competitive and individualistic goal structures. *Psychological Bulletin, 134,* 223–246. doi:10.1037/0033-2909.134.2.223

Royal Society of Arts. (2010). *Royal Society of Arts education seminars: Curriculum and the social brain.* Retrieved from www.thersa.org/projects/education/education-seminars-2010/curriculum-and-the-social-brain

Rudek, D., & Haden, C. (2005). Mothers' and preschoolers' mental state language during reminiscing over time. *Merrill-Palmer Quarterly, 51,* 523–549. doi:10.1037/0033-2909.134.2.223

Sa"ljo", R. (2009). Learning, theories of learning, and units of analysis in research. *Educational Psychologist, 44,* 202–208. doi:10.1080/ 00461520903029030

Sawyer, R. K. (2012). *Explaining creativity: The science of human innovation* (2nd ed.). New York, NY: Oxford University Press.

Sawyer, R. K., & DeZutter, S. (2009). Distributed creativity: How collective creations emerge from collaboration. *Journal of Aesthetics, Creativity, and the Arts, 3,* 81–92. doi:10.1037/a0013282

Schulz-Hardt, S., Brodbeck, F. C., Mojzisch, A., Kerschreiter, R., & Frey, D. (2006). Group decision making in hidden profile situations: Dissent as a facilitator for decision quality. *Journal of Personality and Social Psychology, 91,* 1080–1093. doi:10.1037/0022-3514.91.6.1080

Scott, P. (2008). Talking a way to understanding in science classrooms. In N. Mercer & S. Hodgkinson (Eds.), *Exploring talk in school* (pp. 17–36). London, UK: Sage.

Sfard, A. (2001). Symbolizing mathematical reality into being: How mathematical discourse and mathematical objects create each other. In P. Cobb, K. E. Yackel, &

K. McClain (Eds.), *Symbolizing and communicating: Perspectives on mathematical discourse, tools, and instructional design* (pp. 37–98). Mahwah, NJ: Erlbaum.

Siegler, R. S. (2002). Microgenetic studies of self-explanation. In N. Granott & J. Parziole (Eds.), *Microdevelopment: Transition processes in development and learning.* Cambridge, UK: Cambridge University Press. doi:10.1017/CBO9780511489709.002

Skidmore, D. (2006). Pedagogy and dialogue. *Cambridge Journal of Education, 36,* 503–514. doi:10.1080/03057640601048407

Slavin, R. E. (2009). Cooperative learning. In G. McCulloch & D. Crook (Eds.), *International encyclopaedia of education* (pp. 161–178). Abington, UK: Routledge.

Slavin, R. E., Groff, C., & Lake, C. (2009). Effective programs in middle and high school mathematics: A best-evidence synthesis. *Review of Educational Research, 79,* 839–911. doi:10.3102/0034654308330968

Smith, M. K., Wood, W., Adams, W., Wieman, C., Knight, J., Guild, N., & Su, T. (2009). Why peer discussion improves student performance on in-class concept questions. *Science, 323,* 122–124. doi:10.1126/science.1165919

Soong, B., & Mercer, N. (2011). Improving students' revision of physics concepts through ICT-based co-construction and prescriptive tutoring. *International Journal of Science Education, 33,* 1055–1078. doi:10.1080/09500693.2010.489586

Swales, A. (1990). *Genre analysis: English in academic and research settings.* Cambridge, UK: Cambridge University Press.

Swanson, H. L., Hoskyn, M., & Lee, C. (1999). *Intervention for students with learning disabilities: A meta-analysis of treatment outcomes.* New York, NY: Guilford.

Tomasello, M. (2008, May 25). How are humans unique? *The New York Times Magazine.* Retrieved from www.nytimes.com/

Treagust, D., & Duit, R. (2008a). Compatibility between cultural studies and conceptual change in science education: There is more to acknowledge than to fight straw men! *Cultural Studies of Science Education, 3,* 387–395. doi:10.1007/s11422-008-9096-y

Treagust, D., & Duit, R. (2008b). Conceptual change: A discussion of theoretical, methodological and practical challenges for science education. *Cultural Studies of Science Education, 3,* 297–328. doi:10.1007/s11422-008-9090-4

van Oers, B., Elbers, E., van der Veer, R., & Wardekker, W. (Eds.). (2008). *The transformation of learning: Advances in cultural-historical activity theory.* Cambridge, UK: Cambridge University Press.

Vass, E., & Littleton, K. (2010). Peer collaboration and learning in the classroom. In K. Littleton, C. Wood, & J. Kleine Staarman (Eds.), *International handbook of psychology in education* (pp. 105–136). Leeds, UK: Emerald.

Veenman, M. V. J., & Spaans, M. A. (2005). Relation between intellectual and metacognitive skills: Age and task differences. *Learning and Individual Differences, 15,* 159–176. doi:10.1016/j.lindif.2004.12.001

Volet, S., Summers, M., & Thurman, J. (2009). High-level co-regulation in collaborative learning: How does it emerge and how is it sustained? *Learning and Instruction, 19,* 128–143. doi:10.1016/j.learninstruc.2008.03.001

Vygotsky, L. S. (1962). *Thought and language.* Cambridge, MA: MIT Press.

Vygotsky, L. S. (1978). *Mind in society: The development of higher psychological processes.* Cambridge, MA: Harvard University Press.

Walshaw, M., & Anthony, G. (2008). The teacher's role in classroom discourse: A review of recent research into mathematics classrooms. *Review of Educational Research, 78,* 516–551. doi:10.3102/0034654308320292

Wang, M. C., Haertel, G. D., & Walberg, H. J. (1990). What influences learning? A content analysis of review literature. *Journal of Educational Research*, *84*, 30–43.

Warwick, P., Mercer, N., Kershner, R., & Kleine Staarman, J. (2010). In the mind and in the technology: The vicarious presence of the teacher in pupil's learning. *Computers and Education*, *55*, 350–362. doi:10.1016/j.compedu.2010.02.001

Webb, N., Nemer, K., & Ing, M. (2006). Small-group reflections: Parallels between teacher discourse and student behavior in peer-directed groups. *Journal of the Learning Sciences*, *15*, 63–119. doi:10.1207/s15327809jls15018

Wegerif, R. (2007). *Dialogic education and technology: Expanding the space of learning*. New York, NY: Springer.

Wegerif, R. (2010). *Mindexpanding: Teaching for thinking and creativity in primary education*. Maidenhead, UK: Open University Press/McGraw Hill.

Wegerif, R., & Scrimshaw, P. (Eds.). (1997). *Computers and talk in the primary classroom*. Clevedon, UK: Multilingual Matters.

Wells, G. (1986). *The meaning makers: Children learning language and using language to learn*. London, UK: Hodder & Stoughton.

Wells, G. (1999). *Dialogic inquiry: Toward a sociocultural practice and theory of education*. Cambridge, UK: Cambridge University Press. doi:10.1017/CBO9780511605895

Wells, G. (2008). Learning to use scientific concepts. *Cultural Studies of Science Education*, *3*, 329–350. doi:10.1007/s11422-008-9100-6

Wells, G. (2009). *The meaning makers: Learning to talk and learning to learn* (2nd ed.). Bristol, UK: Multilingual Matters.

Wertsch, J. V. (1979). From social interaction to higher psychological processes: A clarification and application of Vygotsky's theory. *Human Development*, *22*, 1–22. doi:10.1159/000272425

Whitebread, D., & Pino-Pasternak, D. (2010). Metacognition, self-regulation & meta-knowing. In K. Littleton, C. Wood, & J. Kleine Staarman (Eds.), *International handbook of psychology in education* (pp. 615–713). Leeds, UK: Emerald.

Willingham, D. (2009). Three problems in the marriage of science and education. *Cortex*, *45*, 544–545.

Wolpert, D., & Frith, C. (2004). *The neuroscience of social interactions: Decoding, influencing, and imitating the actions of others*. Oxford, UK: Oxford University Press.

Woolley, A., Chabrsi, C., Pentland, A., Hashmi, N., & Malone, T. (2010). Evidence for a collective intelligence factor in the performance of human groups. *Science*, *330*, 686–688. doi:10.1126/science.1193147

Zelazo, P., Chandler, M., & Crone, E. (Eds.). (2009). *Developmental social cognitive neuroscience*. New York, NY: Psychology Press. doi:10.1111/j.1750-8606.2012.00241.x

*In 2010, my Cambridge colleague David Whitebread and I had an idea for a conference that would bring together researchers from two strands of psychological research: one concerned with cognitive development in early childhood and the other with teaching and learning in schools. Representing these two strands ourselves, we realized that both were strongly influenced by Vygotskian sociocultural theory, but had developed quite separately, and sometimes used different ways of describing the same phenomena. It seemed to us that both strands would benefit if we shared what we knew and developed a common framework for understanding children's cognitive development and educational progress. We were successful in gaining a grant from the British Psychological Society to fund this conference, and very pleased when we were able to recruit an impressive international cast of researchers to take part. One outcome was the monograph in the 'Current Trends' series of the* British Journal of Educational Psychology, *in which this chapter first appeared.*

# 14 Classroom talk and the development of self-regulation and metacognition

*Mercer, N. (2013). Classroom talk and the development of self-regulation and metacognition. In D. Whitebread, N. Mercer, C. Howe & A. Tolmie (eds), Self-Regulation and Dialogue in Primary Classrooms. BJEP Monograph Series II, 10, 1–24 (Leicester: British Psychological Society).*

## Abstract

### Background

The development of young children's ability to organize their learning and problem-solving activities (self-regulation) and to reflect on their intellectual efforts (metacognition) have been major topics of research in recent years. In that same period, much attention has been given to the functions of classroom talk for mediating learning and collective problem solving. Despite both these lines of enquiry being inspired by the work of Vygotsky, they have typically involved different groups of researchers, amongst whom there has been relatively little joint activity; and no common conceptual framework has been created for bringing them together.

### Aims

The main aim of this paper is to bring together two lines of research – on the development of self-regulation and on classroom talk – and identify shared points of reference which could be helpful for developing a common theoretical framework and coordinated lines of enquiry.

### Methods

Three concepts are discussed which have been central in relevant research, namely 'dialogue', 'metacognition' and 'self-regulation'. To these are added the concepts of 'co-regulation' and 'exploratory talk'. Research from both lines of enquiry is then discussed in relation to these concepts. The resources of Vygotskian sociocultural theory and relevant empirical evidence are then used to propose a synthesis of the two lines of research, so as to bring the key concepts and the research they inform into one sociocultural account of how children learn and develop cognitively.

## Conclusions

It is concluded that research in both lines of enquiry would benefit from being integrated, and that it is possible to develop a common conceptual framework and agreement on the definitions of key concepts. It is proposed that future research on the development of self-regulation should take more precise account of the crucial role of language in mediating such development; and that future research on language and learning in school should attend more to the processes by which external regulation shapes the development of co-regulation and self-regulation. Finally, it is suggested that the integration of the two lines of enquiry could make a significant contribution towards fulfilling Vygotsky's aim of explaining the dynamic relationship between intermental and intramental activity and understanding its role in learning and cognitive development.

## Introduction

In recent decades, there has been much research interest in the development of children's 'self-regulation', meaning their ability to organize and take control of their own learning. The focus in such research has mainly been on individuals, though the ways pairs or groups of children learn to regulate their activity has also been given attention. That research has commonly included a concern with the development of metacognition – children's ability to think about their thinking. The same period has also been a busy one for the study of language and learning in the classroom, with a focus on both teacher-student interaction and the collaborative activity of children in groups. Although research on self-regulation has tended to focus on children aged 4–7 and that on classroom talk on children older than 6, some studies within both lines of research have involved children of similar ages. Both lines of enquiry have been pursued by psychological researchers with some allegiance to Vygotsky (1999). However, researchers within these lines of enquiry have had little contact or mutual influence. The development of self-regulation and metacognition has not been given much direct attention in research on classroom talk; and interactional talk has rarely been subject to rigorous analysis in research on self-regulation and metacognition. And despite researchers in both groups acknowledging the influence of Vygotsky and the sociocultural theory that has been built upon his work, different explanatory frameworks and conceptual vocabularies have been employed. The result is that we currently lack a clear, unified account of how the use of spoken language is involved in the development of self-regulation and metacognition.

The conference which generated the monograph in which this article originally appeared was conceived as a response to the current situation, with its main aims being to consider the contributions made by these two lines of enquiry to our understanding of learning processes and classroom practice in primary schools, to explore commonalities between the two literatures, to consider theoretical implications and to outline future plans for a more integrated research agenda. The organizers argued that bringing together these two lines of investigation could provide new and valuable insights into children's cognitive development and into educational processes, and so represent an innovative step forward in explaining the relationship between the use of spoken dialogue and the development of young children's thinking, learning and communication skills. It could also generate better practical guidance for the professional development of teachers and inform educational policy. These aims and hopes have all shaped the contents of this paper.

I begin by discussing some key concepts that are associated with the two lines of research under consideration. I then summarize some findings from both lines of enquiry, and discuss how they might be integrated. Because a Vygotskian, sociocultural perspective on cognitive development, learning and education has underpinned, or at least informed, most research within both lines of enquiry, I use this to try to provide the basis for a common theoretical framework. Finally, I consider the potential value of achieving a synthesis, and how this might inform the design and aims of future research.

## Defining terms and explaining concepts

Three key concepts, which figure in the papers within this monograph, are *self-regulation, metacognition* and *dialogue*. These terms are currently not part of a common research vocabulary for discussing learning and cognitive development; the use of them tends to reflect researchers' involvement with one or other of the two lines of enquiry identified above. I suggest that establishing a shared understanding of the meaning of these terms, and of the concepts they represent, would be helpful for developing a more comprehensive theoretical account of children's learning and cognitive development and so enable the integration of research efforts. I will consider each of them in turn, along with two more: *co-regulation* and *exploratory talk*.

(i)  *Self-regulation.* The ability to 'self-regulate' is normally taken to mean a person being able to control their thoughts and actions to achieve personal goals and respond to environmental demands as they arise (Perry, 2013). Webb, Franke, and Turrou (2013) cite Hadwin's (2008) definition of effective self-regulators as 'those who set goals and make plans for their learning, monitor their progress toward their goals, and revise their strategies for reaching their goals as necessary'. It seems to me that, for the development of a common conceptual framework, this is probably the least problematic or contentious of the three key concepts: the main issue will be how to relate it to the functions of talk in classrooms.

(ii)    The terms *co-regulation* and *shared regulation* are also used in the research literature, to refer to ways that children are involved in the management of their own and partners' activity within a group. Volet, Summer and Thurman use 'co-regulation' in this way as a subcategory of 'social regulation', while noting that other researchers (Hickey, 2003; McCaslin, 2004) have used it 'to refer to the process by which social environments support or scaffold individual participation and learning' (Volet, Summer, & Thurman, 2009, p. 129). Volet et al. also note that the term 'shared regulation' has been used to refer to the 'constant monitoring and regulation of joint activity, which cannot be reduced to mere individual activity' (Vauras, Iiskala, Kajamies, Kinnunen, & Lehtinen, 2003, p. 35). In their discussion of computer-supported collaborative learning, Järvellä and Hadwin (2013) make a strong distinction between co-regulation and shared regulation. They propose that the former should be used to refer to individual group members guiding or constraining the activities of other members, while the latter should be used when group members jointly construct and maintain shared regulatory processes. While their discussion of these terms is insightful and useful, I am not convinced by it, or by the brief illustrative examples of transcribed talk that they provide, that these two kinds of social regulatory activity can be reliably distinguished; and so I propose for now to use the term 'co-regulation' to cover both. But a very important idea is involved here, which is very relevant to both the lines of enquiry being considered in this paper; how two or more people coordinate and combine their intellectual resources effectively to get something done. My suggestion is that 'co-regulation' is the best term to use, because it captures well the meaning of regulation which 'cannot be reduced to mere individual activity'. It can be argued that the regulation of group-based activity could be conceptualized as the simultaneous occurrence of 'self-regulation' and 'other-regulation' (Howe, pers. comm.); but I would suggest that to do so provides only an individualistic account of a process which involves thinking collectively. A distinctive feature of human psychology, grounded in our evolutionary history, is that we are able to use language and other modes of communication to solve problems together. We are born with 'social brains' which enable us not only to interact but to 'interthink' (Mercer, 2013). This means that the development of the skills involved in thinking collectively cannot be understood as two separate items, children's self-regulation of their own actions and their regulation of other children's activity. By taking this perspective on children's monitoring and regulation of their joint learning activity we can also make useful links with children's use of talk during collaborative learning, as I will go on to explain.

(iii)   *Metacognition*. In the research literature on the development of self-regulation, I have found it hard to find a clear distinction being made between self-regulation and metacognition. The relevant meaning of the 'meta' prefix in the latter term would seem to be 'of a higher or second order kind' (according to *The Concise Oxford Dictionary*, which uses 'metalanguage' as the lexical illustration of this meaning). The University of London's Psychology and Society (2012) website defines metacognition as 'the understanding and awareness of one's own mental or cognitive processes', and this seems to me an appropriate 'plain English' definition.

The emergence of metacognition has been accorded some importance in research on children's learning. Winne (2001, p. 169) describes 'metacognitive monitoring' as 'the key to self-regulating one's learning'. Higgins (2013) links the two concepts throughout, for example by saying that 'metacognition and self-regulation are key dimensions for supporting learning'. Perry (2013) also links the two closely, as in saying that 'self-regulated learners exercise metacognition'. However, I find this linkage problematic. A person can be highly metacognitive without being effectively self-regulatory (as with someone who is paralysed by reflective indecision). Likewise, someone driving a car can be very effectively self-regulatory without exercising any reflective awareness. It is also unclear to me, from the research literature, whether being metacognitive is meant to involve a self-conscious, reflective consideration of one's own thought processes. The idea of someone not being conscious of being metacognitive seems to me an oxymoron, but I am open to persuasion that some 'higher order' cognitive mechanisms for reflecting upon one's thoughts and behaviour might operate outside conscious control. How we infer their existence is another matter. I suggest we need a clearer specification of this term.

Regarding the relationship between metacognition and co-regulation, we might note this comment by one researcher involved in this field of study: 'Metacognitive theory was developed to explain the operation of individual minds, and has not yet been fully explicated as a group-level phenomenon' (Hogan, 1999, p. 1103). That comment would still seem to apply in more recent times (see for example Veenman, Van Hout-Wolters, & Afflerbach, 2006). Of course, one can argue that metacognition must refer to internal mental processes which are therefore, by definition, operating in the minds of individuals (Whitebread, pers. comm.). But the kind of evidence offered for metacognitive activity is commonly of people responding reflectively to specific questions about their thoughts, and so is a joint product of the discursive processes of collective thinking involved in interviews (Potter & Wetherell, 1994). The internal mental processes involved cannot easily be separated from the features of the interactive context in which they are generated, so again to limit the phenomenon to an individualistic conceptualization seems questionable.

(iv)   *Dialogue*. This is an everyday word which has taken on a special meaning within research on classroom talk. But even amongst that community of researchers, it has been used in different ways. It can be used in quite a literal sense, to mean talk between two or more people (e.g. Alexander, 2006; Scott, 2008), or more metaphorically to refer to a process of sharing and co-constructing ideas which transcends particular conversations and which may even only involve one person's consideration of another's words in their absence (e.g. Lefstein, 2010; Wegerif, 2010). In discussing the educational functions of talk, Lefstein says that 'dialogue entails a back-and-forth movement, between my own and the Other's horizons . . .' (Lefstein, op. cit., p. 175) but adds that '. . . dialogue is not about method or form of interaction, but is most fundamentally an epistemological position' (op. cit., p. 176). Some researchers, while focusing concretely on the use of talk, have nevertheless argued for a broad, 'inclusive' definition of dialogue to mean any classroom conversation in which two or more people contribute (Littleton & Howe, 2010). Others place a more 'restrictive' definition on the term, defining dialogue as talk in which the views of all participants are actively shared and considered. This distinguishes it from classroom talk which is dominated by the authoritative ideas of a teacher, and in which students take only relatively passive roles (Alexander, 2006; Scott, 2008). For the study of communication in the classroom, I favour this more restrictive definition, as we already have the more general terms 'discourse', 'talk', 'conversation' and 'interaction'; and I also favour the literal rather than metaphorical use of the term, by which two or more people have to be actively involved in communicating. (I am not convinced that through reading I can ever really have a dialogue with Vygotsky, however much I would love to do so: c.f. Wegerif, 2010). On such a literal basis, Alexander (2008) describes classroom dialogue as 'achieving common understanding through structured, cumulative questioning and discussion which guide and prompt, reduce choices, minimize risk and error, and expedite the "handover" of concepts and principles' (p. 103). Scott says 'in dialogic talk there is always the attempt to acknowledge the views of others, and through dialogic talk the teacher attends to the students' points of view as well as to the school science view' (Scott, 2008, p. 20). Wells (1999) uses the term 'dialogic inquiry' and Alexander uses the term 'dialogic teaching' to refer to approaches to classroom education in which (amongst other things) a teacher ensures that such active, two-way exchanges of ideas and joint knowledge building are given some priority.

(v)   *Exploratory talk* is a term first coined by Barnes (1976) to distinguish the use of talk in the classroom for thinking, in contrast to 'presentational talk' in which a speaker offers an audience a prepared speech of some kind. In the way it has been used more recently (e.g.

Dawes, Mercer, & Fisher, 1992; Harris & Ratcliffe, 2005; Mercer, 2000), it essentially means a dialogue (in the restrictive sense defined above) in which members of a group share all relevant information and engage critically but constructively with each other's ideas. They all actively participate, ask each other questions and take each other's responses into account in seeking agreement for joint decisions. To an observer, their collective reasoning is 'visible' in the talk. Some features of exploratory talk, notably the seeking of agreement, have been specifically shown to be associated with positive learning outcomes in science education (Howe et al., 2007). It is a form of classroom dialogue based on principles of equality and the joint pursuit of a common goal. Resnick and colleagues (Michaels & O'Connor, 2002; Resnick, 1999; Wolf, Crosson, & Resnick, 2006) have independently identified such dialogue and named it *accountable talk*. The occurrence of exploratory/accountable talk depends on interlocutors agreeing, explicitly or implicitly, to adhere to a set of interactional norms or 'ground rules' for generating such an equitable, reasoned discussion (Edwards & Mercer, 1987/2012). In other words, when a group of children engage in exploratory talk, they are co-regulating their collective thinking or problem-solving activity, using the cultural and cognitive tool of spoken language. If they invoke the 'ground rules' during their discussion – for example, to complain that one participant's voice is not being heard – they are also demonstrating a metacognitive awareness of their language use and co-regulating their collective learning strategies.

## Findings from the two lines of enquiry

In order to establish what empirical and theoretical resources are available for relating the study of self-regulation and metacognition to the study of classroom talk, I will next consider some relevant findings from each of the two main lines of enquiry.

### Research on metacognition and self-regulation

Research has shown that individual differences in both metacognitive and self-regulatory abilities predict learning achievement, independent of IQ (Higgins, 2013; Perry, 2013; Wang, Haertel, & Walberg, 1990; Whitebread & Pino-Pasternak, 2010). However, for the reasons explained earlier, it is not always easy to discern if metacognition, self-regulation or both are the focus of attention. Some research has focused on children's metacognition about specific knowledge domains, such as mathematics (Hegarty, Mayer, & Monk, 1995). Those researchers conclude that expert, successful problem solvers differ from novice, unsuccessful problem solvers in their ability to form a mental representation of the problems before engaging with the search for a solution. Expert problem solvers also maintain a reflective approach while carrying out their chosen heuristic strategy. It seems too that successful problem solvers can draw on a wider range of strategies for self-regulating their activity, when compared to less successful problem solvers (Pape & Wang, 2003).

Overall, the evidence suggests that specially designed interventions can develop metacognitive skills and help children learn self-regulatory strategies, which then impact positively upon their academic learning. A recent meta-analysis of intervention studies in primary/elementary schools reported quite large effect sizes (an average of 0.82 for metacognitive strategy use and 0.43 for academic performance: Dignath, Buettner, & Langfeldt, 2008). Typically, those interventions have involved aspects of both self-regulation and metacognition, for example by explicitly teaching children problem-solving strategies and encouraging them to reflect on the use of those strategies and consider how useful they were.

Regarding co-regulation, some school-based intervention studies have shown that if teachers encourage children to reflect on how they work together in a group, this can improve their ability to organize their joint activity – and have a positive impact on their individual academic attainment. A good example of such research is the *Social Pedagogic Research into Group-work* project (SPRinG) carried out in primary schools in the UK by Baines, Blatchford, and Chowne (2007; see also reviews of collaborative learning research by Slavin, 2009; Howe, 2010).

### Research on talk, reasoning and the regulation of group work

Although my focus in this paper is on talk in classrooms, it is relevant to note that research has shown that the amount and quality of pre-school children's conversations with parents or other carers in the home are good predictors of their eventual educational attainment (Goswami & Bryant, 2007; Hart & Risley, 1995; Wells, 2009). The quality of talk in a child's home is likely to be associated with other potentially influential non-verbal factors, and so should not be considered as a single causal influence; but nevertheless such research encourages the view that involvement in certain ways of using language for thinking and learning about experience can positively influence children's learning and cognitive development.

With older children, school-based interventional research has found that if teachers raise children's metacognitive awareness of how they use language when working in groups and encourage them to set appropriate 'ground rules' for discussions, this can raise attainment in several domains. For example, in one programme of research in which I have been involved, the *Thinking Together* series of interventional studies (reported in Mercer & Littleton, 2007), changes in the quality of talk in groups in primary classrooms were found to be associated with significantly improved attainment for the individual children involved, as measured by tests of reasoning, mathematics and science. In one typical study of this series, seven 'target' (interventional) classes of children aged 9–10 in primary schools were first of all guided by their teachers into using an agreed set of 'ground rules' when working together, in order to encourage their metacognitive awareness of how they interacted and their greater use of exploratory talk. They were then taught the usual mathematics and science curriculum for eight months, but using an approach which gave priority to group-based activity and whole-class dialogue in which teachers encouraged children to reflect critically on their use of talk. 109 children completed the programme. A further 121 children in 'control' classes completed the same mathematics curriculum without any change in teaching style. Both groups were given tests before and after, based on the Standard Assessment Tasks (SATs) which have been used throughout English state schools to assess children's attainment in their study of the National Curriculum at age 10–11. As reported in more detail in Mercer, Dawes, Wegerif, and Sams (2004) and Mercer and Littleton (2007), qualitative and quantitative assessments of children's discussions showed that children in target classes began to use much more exploratory talk. In doing so, they became more effective at co-regulating their collaborative activity (as judged by both researchers and their teachers) and achieved significantly better results in collective reasoning tasks. Significantly greater improvements in individual non-verbal reasoning, as assessed pre/post by the Raven's Progressive Matrices test (Raven, Court, & Raven, 1995), were found for children in the target classes. The pre/post SATs scores for mathematics and science also showed a significantly higher improvement for children in target classes.

These findings have been replicated internationally. A study by Wegerif, Perez, Rojas-Drummond, Mercer, and Velez (2005) in Mexico examined the impact of a similar intervention in state schools in Mexico City. While the target class children's Raven's test scores increased over the period of the intervention, the control children's actually decreased. This result confirms the link between the development of language skills for collective learning activity and the development of individual reasoning skills. Rojas-Drummond, Littleton, Hernandez, and Zuniga (2010) also report positive effects of the intervention on the processes and quality of Mexican children's writing. However, they also comment that this research has highlighted the ways that different types of collaborative task may tend to elicit different kinds of dialogue, with 'convergent' tasks (focused on finding one right answer) eliciting more exploratory talk than 'divergent' tasks (which have more open-ended outcomes). They suggest we need to avoid defining exploratory talk as the only educationally effective dialogue for co-regulating collaborative learning.

Reznitskaya et al.'s (2006) study in the USA involved 115 students aged 10–11 years, constituting three classes who participated in teacher-led 'collaborative reasoning' discussions for a period of five weeks (which essentially meant teachers shaping group dialogue so that it resembled exploratory talk, though that term was not used: see Chinn, Anderson, & Waggoner, 2001). These discussions involved students from three comparable classrooms who had not engaged in collaborative reasoning, and were asked to write persuasive essays. The essays of the intervention class students were found to contain a significantly greater number of relevant arguments, counter-arguments, rebuttals, formal argument devices and appropriate uses of text information.

Other research has focused on the quality of interactions between teachers and students in whole-class sessions. A systematic review of studies of teacher-student interaction in the teaching of mathematics in primary schools concluded that more 'dialogic' interaction was associated with improved learning outcomes (Kyriacou & Issitt, 2008); though a more recent and more general systematic review (of 158 studies of classroom talk) concludes that no clear answer can yet be given to the question of how teacher-student talk should be organized to be most beneficial to students' learning (Howe & Abedin, 2013). A tentative conclusion is that students benefit if teachers encourage discussion in both whole classes and groups, but only if certain conditions are met. These conditions would involve teachers raising their students' metacognitive awareness of how they use talk for learning, offering guidance and encouraging them to establish suitable 'ground rules' for co-regulating discussion. Teachers should also 'model' exploratory talk as an effective way of using language for reasoning, thus providing an external regulatory model for students' own co-regulation and eventual self-regulation. The conditions must also allow students sufficient time to practise their skills in suitable collaborative tasks.

### Research which combines elements of both lines of enquiry

As mentioned in the introduction to this paper, the two lines of enquiry of relevance here have generally been pursued by different groups of researchers. A partial exception is an interesting study by Hogan (1999), which was concerned with how students aged 13–14 studied science. It involved the design and implementation of a classroom intervention called *Thinking Aloud Together* (not to be confused with *Thinking Together*, as described earlier), which aimed to develop students' metacognitive regulation of their scientific reasoning by enhancing their metacognitive awareness of how they constructed knowledge together *and* improving their skills in reasoning collectively. Hogan uses the term 'collaborative reasoning', to describe what students were encouraged to do, but does not define it or provide detail about how it was encouraged. As defined by the researchers who introduced this term (Chinn et al., 2001; Reznitskaya et al., 2001) and as discussed in the previous section, it represents a form of interaction which has many of the characteristics of exploratory talk. No explicit training in the use of talk was involved, but students wrote lists of ways of behaving which they thought helped or undermined intellectual collaboration. They also wrote prompts (e.g. 'What do you mean by that?' 'Would you say more about that?' 'I think what I hear you saying is . . .') on cards to use to provoke one another's thinking. 163 students in an American middle school took part, randomly assigned to treatment and control conditions. Teachers enacted the intervention, and pre/post assessments of students were made with regard to both their metacognitive awareness of how they worked in groups and their ability to apply their existing knowledge to new science-based problems. Video-recordings of discussions by actors were used as part of a specially designed instrument, the Metacognitive Knowledge Assessment, to judge changes in their ability to 'metacognate' about collective reasoning. Their discussions in groups were also recorded, transcribed and analysed, qualitatively and quantitatively.

The results of this study were equivocal, in terms of encouraging research of this kind, as Hogan explains:

> In summary, students who received the intervention gained in metacognitive knowledge about collaborative reasoning and ability to articulate their collaborative reasoning processes in comparison to students in control classrooms. However, this enhanced metacognitive awareness did not translate into improved collaborative reasoning behaviors, nor, therefore, into deeper processing of ideas and information that would have been manifest as enhanced ability to apply conceptual knowledge.
>
> (Hogan, op. cit., p. 1095)

These results did not therefore support Hogan's initial hypothesis that students' enhanced metacognitive awareness would improve their group-based problem solving. In offering explanations for the limited effects of the intervention, Hogan noted that 'strong patterns in interpersonal dynamics and individual roles in groups that were evident from the start of the unit did not change as a result of the intervention' (Hogan, op. cit., p. 1099). Hogan also comments that the implementation of the intervention was limited by teachers' reluctance to make time available for reflective discussion, which could otherwise be used for more authoritative science instruction. This is of course a common experience for researchers – and one might note the conclusion of Dignath et al.'s (2008) meta-review of interventional studies of self-regulation and metacognition that stronger effects have been obtained when interventions are enacted by researchers than by teachers. For future research, Hogan makes the following proposal:

> The major adjustment would be enhancing the reflective aspects of the intervention, both reflections on group communication processes and reflections aimed at building students' metacognitive knowledge about the nature of their task. Metacognitive knowledge about the task was emphasized less in the original intervention than metacognitive knowledge about collaborative reasoning strategies, yet it seemed to be a key element in the performance of deep-processing groups.
>
> (Hogan, op. cit., p. 1104)

We might also note that in the *Thinking Aloud Together* intervention there was apparently (a) no direct focus on developing students' skills in using language for thinking (other than the use of 'prompts' by students mentioned above); (b) no establishment of an agreed set of common 'ground rules' for talking together; and (c) no expectation that teachers would 'model' effective ways of co-constructing knowledge in whole-class discussions. This absence of a focus on language use distinguishes Hogan's *Thinking Aloud Together* intervention from the *Thinking Together* research (Mercer & Littleton, 2007) discussed earlier. It was also absent from the *SPRinG* project (Baines et al., 2007, also mentioned earlier), which focused instead on children's developing meta-awareness of group processes, and reported smaller effects than *Thinking Together* on learning outcomes.

Interventional research on teaching 'thinking skills' to over 900 children aged 7–9 in the two ACTS (Activating Children's Thinking Skills) projects (Dewey & Bento, 2010; McGuinness, 2006) in England and Northern Ireland was expressly related to the concept of metacognition (though not the concept of self-regulation) and had a focus on classroom talk. Professional development sessions encouraged teachers to arrange their classrooms in ways that created opportunities for children's talk, to encourage children to think about their thinking and develop with children a vocabulary for talking about thinking. However, there does not appear to have been any explicit, precise focus on teaching children how to use talk for thinking collectively (as in the *Thinking Together* research, though that research is cited in ACTS publications), nor were collaborative learning activities built into the design. A quasi-experimental design involving over 900 children in the two projects allowed for comparisons between pupils in interventional and control schools on quantitative measures of self-perception ('myself as a learner') and general reasoning. Qualitative assessments were also made of pupils' views about thinking and learning in school, and teachers made assessments of perceived changes in pupils' behaviour and abilities. The intervention lasted two years. The results showed significantly greater improvements in reasoning for children in the intervention classes, though with quite small effect sizes. Qualitative results were very positive, with teachers noting that, for example, children became more 'keen to evaluate their own learning' (Dewey & Bento, op. cit., p. 338). Overall, then, the research discussed in this section provides some encouragement for the view that teacher-led interventions which focus on talk and metacognition can promote the development of children's abilities to co-regulate their collaborative learning and their use of effective cognitive, self-regulatory strategies for pursuing intellectual tasks alone.

## The educational context

How do the concerns and findings of the two lines of enquiry discussed above relate to educational policy and practice? Perry (2013) comments that educational policy makers have become more aware of the relationship between the ability to self-regulate and academic achievement. Internationally, there is growing interest in the role of schools in helping children to 'learn how to learn' (Black, McCormick, James, & Pedder, 2006; Higgins, 2013). Current interest in fostering 'independent learning' among young children is reflected by publications such as Featherstone and Bayley (2001) and Williams (2003), and by contemporary enthusiasm amongst teachers and education authorities for such approaches to classroom education as *Reggio Emilia* (Lewin-Benham, 2008)), *High/Scope* (Schweinhart, 2000) and *Building Learning Power* (Claxton, 2002), all of which are predicated on the principle of giving children more autonomy and control of their learning. Although direct links with empirical research are rarely made by proponents of those schemes, probably because the evidence base for them is not strong, their underlying principles can easily be related to the concept of 'self-regulated learning'.

However, there is no evidence that the development of self-regulation and/or metacognition is, in practice, given high priority by most teachers. It seems likely that ways of encouraging such development may not be a natural part of, or even compatible with, most teachers' normal practice. As mentioned earlier, Dignath et al. (2008) reported that relevant interventions attained higher effect sizes when conducted by researchers than when carried out by regular teachers. Hendy and Whitebread (2000) established that many early years teachers say that they wish to help young children develop as independent learners, but when interacting with children they overwhelmingly focus on 'managerial' issues of behaviour, rather than on learning processes. There is thus a need to consider how the use of effective teaching strategies for developing self-regulation can be related to what teachers expect to do, and feel they need to do, in their normal interactions with their pupils. This is likely to require some consideration of how they habitually talk with their pupils.

Policy makers' awareness of the potential importance of developing self-regulation, and of the role of talk in learning, still seems to be patchy and limited if the UK is taken as an example. It was encouraging that the government-sponsored Williams Review of mathematics teaching in the UK concluded that the teaching of mathematics 'must be truly interactive, in that children are given time to think, to talk (and be listened to) and to try out their own ideas and strategies' (Williams, 2008, p. 62). But in most educational policy documents and political rhetoric, the development of children's spoken language is usually treated as a marginal issue. The UK government has recently tried to eliminate the teaching of spoken English skills from the National Curriculum for English in primary schools, in which 'speaking and listening' has had a place since the introduction of a national curriculum in the 1980s. In the 2013 draft which was circulated for comment, the content focused only on reading and writing. Fortunately, opposition from researchers, teachers and others to these proposals seems to have had some effect and spoken language is being retained, albeit in a reduced form. But there is another possible reason for this change of heart. The government's new priorities were justified by a wish to improve British ratings in the international comparisons of educational attainment made by the OECD Programme for International Student Assessment (PISA), which have in the past focused only on literacy and numeracy. However, the OECD has announced that, from 2015, PISA will also include the assessment of 'Collaborative Problem Solving (CPS)', which it describes as 'a critical and necessary skill across educational settings and the workforce' (PISA, 2013, p. 1). Moreover, it states that students need to learn how to build shared understanding, handle disagreements and understand 'the type of collaboration and associated rules of engagement' involved (PISA, op. cit., p. 4).

It therefore seems that there is likely to be growing international interest in the role of schools for developing and assessing children's talk, metacognition and co-regulation skills. It can of course be argued that such skills are very hard to assess; but it can also be argued that it is only when a subject or skill is formally assessed that it is treated seriously by policy makers, teachers and students. And while it may be becoming more widely recognized that schools should be ensuring that all children learn to collaborate, there is still little awareness amongst policy makers and practitioners – and, I suspect, educational researchers – of the possibility that children need also to be helped to become effective users of spoken language because this can help develop their reasoning and learning. Moreover, a substantial body of research has shown that, within the UK at least, little of the talk which takes place between teachers and children could be described as 'dialogue' as I defined it earlier in this paper, nor could it be expected to help develop children's metacognition. For example, while Sylva, Melhuish, Sammons, Siraj-Blatchford, and Taggart (2004) identified 'sustained shared thinking' between teachers and children as a characteristic of the most effective practice in early years classrooms, it accounted for only a few percentage points of all the talk they observed, even in the most outstanding settings. Observing classrooms during the 'literacy hour' in English primary schools, Smith, Hardman, Wall, and Mroz (2004) drew similar conclusions, noting that very few teachers' questions sought to stimulate pupils' reasoning or reflections, and few teachers involved students in talk that might be considered dialogue (Fisher & Larkin, 2008). Research in other countries suggests that this is not a problem restricted to the UK (see for example Alexander, 2008; Webb, 2009).

## Theoretical resources

As mentioned early in this paper, the two relevant lines of enquiry – on the development of self-regulation and metacognition, and on learning through talk – have both been strongly influenced by the work which Vygotsky (1999) carried out in the early part of the twentieth century but which was only widely appreciated much later. To be more precise, researchers pursuing those lines of enquiry have adopted the sociocultural perspective on cognitive development and learning that has been constructed from Vygotsky's theoretical foundations since the last few decades of the twentieth century (Daniels, 2008; Wertsch, 1979). This is also sometimes called a 'cultural-historical' perspective (see van Oers & Dobber, 2013). It has some variants and is still in a state of development (see Daniels, op. cit.), but two essential features of it are very relevant here. Within sociocultural theory:

(a) *language is accorded an important role in learning and cognitive development.* Vygotsky (1999) argued that social interaction, using the prime tool of language, provides crucial 'intermental' experiences which shape children's individual, 'intramental' development. He also argued that the acquisition and use of language is inextricably bound up with the development of more advanced forms of reasoning. As Vass and Littleton interpret this, 'interpsychological thinking is a prerequisite for intrapsychological thinking: it is through speech and action with others that we learn to reason and gain individual consciousness' (2010, p. 107). Figure 14.1 is a basic representation of the process involved. Children are born into a social world, in which their interactions with others are mediated by language even before they fully understand it. As they learn language and engage with the people around them, they hear those people using language to make sense of the world. They therefore do not only commonly gain new experience in the company of other people; they are often offered a commentary on that experience as they do so. And children are normally active in their engagement with others; they put their own accounts of experience into talk, and ask questions about what they are experiencing. The ways they come to make sense of the world are thus shaped by the knowledge that they hear encoded in language, and by their own active use of language as a

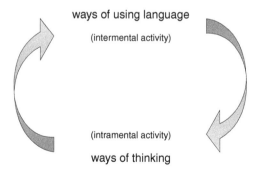

ways of using language

(intermental activity)

(intramental activity)

ways of thinking

*Figure 14.1* The Vygotskian relationship between social language use and cognitive development.

sense-making tool. Moreover, this is not a one-way process, but rather a continuing, temporal spiral or helical process; because as they develop, into adults, each new generation's contributions to the linguistic interactions of their community may contribute to the shared knowledge and practices of that community, including ways language is used within it. It is this kind of sociocultural theoretical narrative which has strongly informed research on classroom talk and its role in learning and cognitive development.

(b) *adults are accorded an important role in modelling and scaffolding children's self-regulated activity.* The nature of human childhood, in normal circumstances, is that one is born into a community which supports, constrains and guides the activity of its juveniles until they are capable of taking care of themselves, and familiar with the normative requirements of community life. One of the ways that they become capable of relatively independent existence is that they have to learn how to take over for themselves (from their adult carers) the responsibility for controlling, monitoring and reflectively assessing their behaviour. Vygotsky not only saw the adult as taking a very active, shaping role in that learning process, he also proposed that children's experiences of being regulated could provide a template for regulating their own behaviour. Thus he proposed that a child who is guided and instructed through a logical set of procedures for solving a certain kind of problem can 'internalize' those procedures as a way of solving such problems alone. That is, the child creates internal, psychological correlates for the external, social mechanisms which have regulated their behaviour in the earliest years. Figure 14.2 is a very basic representation of this intermental-intramental process, designed to give it the same helical form as the process shown in Figure 14.1.

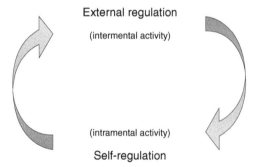

*Figure 14.2* The Vygotskian relationship between external, social regulation and the development of self-regulation.

Vygotsky also proposed that there were strong connections between (a) and (b). For example, he suggested that young children's commonly observed use of 'egocentric' speech for talking themselves through a problem was an echo of such external regulation, and that this illustrated the way language functions as both a cultural tool and a psychological tool. Children can be 'talked through' a strategy for solving a problem by an adult; they then become able to talk themselves through the same kind of problem; and even when they eventually do not need to talk aloud to think, they may nevertheless still be using language-based procedures for thinking. In a recent appraisal of Vygotsky's work Miller (2011, p. 370) puts it as follows, 'Not only can I instruct you and be instructed by you, but I can also instruct myself, and this function of inner speech is the basis for self-regulation.'

Although Vygotsky has provided the main resources for the development of sociocultural theory, we should also note the relevance and value of the concept of *socio-cognitive conflict*, which was derived by Perret-Clermont (1980) and others from the work of Piaget (1970). This can be incorporated into a sociocultural account of the influence of spoken language on conceptual change. In a recent discussion of the socio-cognitive processes involved in learning, with reference to research on children carrying out joint problem-solving activities, Tartas, Baucal and Perret-Clermont comment:

> It seems that being confronted with different answers from someone else creates a discrepancy between the learner's initial understanding and the necessity to grasp a new perspective; the learner then enters into a reflexive stance that may lead to the restructuring of his or her own thinking.
>
> (Tartas, Baucal, & Perret-Clermont, 2010, p. 67.)

Tartas et al. also comment that 'transactive discussions', whereby a participant's actions can be observed to respond to the spoken reasoning of a partner, have repeatedly been shown to promote cognitive growth – for example in studies reported by Azmitia and Montgomery (1993) and Howe and Tolmie (1998).

## Towards a synthesis

### Conceptual links

Some researchers have already made links between features of classroom talk and the development of self-regulation and metacognition. In their interventional research on improving students' self-regulation strategies for memorizing, Ornstein, Grammer, and Coffman (2010) found beneficial effects of teachers asking what they called 'metacognitive questions', meaning that a teacher requested children to describe a potentially suitable strategy, or provide a justification for a strategy they had used. In other words, metacognitive questioning encouraged students to explain their ideas clearly and provide reasons for their views, as is expected in exploratory talk. This then helped them to consolidate the most effective strategies for memorizing.

Mercer and Howe (2012) suggest that one hypothesis for future research might be that the value of talk for learning is enhanced if teachers and children not only employ it in certain 'dialogic' ways, but if they become metacognitively aware of its value. That is, not only the quality of talk is important for its educational impact, but also participants' awareness of why it is important to talk about learning and problem solving. Thus interventions which enhance meta-awareness of how talk can be used most effectively for joint reasoning and problem solving during group work would be expected to achieve stronger effects than those which merely aim to improve the quality of relations and interactions within group work. This would explain the variations between the results of the *SPRinG* and *Thinking Together* interventions, as discussed above. Raising children's metacognitive awareness of the potential educational value of talk, and of how they use it to regulate their joint activity, could therefore be important for enabling them to use language as a tool for regulating learning and problem solving, jointly and alone.

Starting more from the stance of research into self-regulation and metacognition, a potentially interesting line of enquiry might be to describe with more precision the ways that talk is used by adults to represent regulatory procedures, and if/how these ways of representation are 'appropriated' (to use the Vygotskian term) by children as they begin to self-regulate. Some methodological links might be made with research in the linguistic ethnography tradition, inspired partly by Vygotsky's contemporary Bakhtin (1981), on how children 'ventriloquate' ways of describing the social world that they hear being used by adults – and in so doing begin to express the shared values of their community as their own (Maybin, 2006; Lefstein, 2010).

### Classroom talk and the development of effective co-regulation

My aim in this section is to use a set of transcribed examples of classroom talk to illustrate how the analysis of classroom talk can be related to the development of children's metacognition and their ability to regulate their learning activities. The examples come from one of the *Thinking Together* projects described above. It was based in British primary schools, and aimed to develop children's abilities to talk and work together when studying science and mathematics. The three transcripts were all recorded with the same class of 10 year olds, over a period of one school term (around four months). Early in that term, the teacher had organized a reflective discussion with the whole class about how they normally worked together in groups, and how they might talk and work together more effectively. The children had shown some interesting and relevant metacognitive insights into their own behaviour.

Drawing upon these, the teacher then proposed three 'ground rules' for how they should work together, and wrote them on the board as follows:

(1) Members of groups should seek agreement before making decisions.
(2) Group members should ask each other for their ideas and opinions ("What do you think?").
(3) Group members should give reasons for their views, and be asked for them if appropriate ("Why do you think that?").

She then put these up on the classroom wall, and asked the members of the class to agree that they would follow those rules, with the response being apparent general agreement. Transcript 1 comes from a lesson a week after the one in which the 'ground rules' had been proposed. As it begins, the teacher is standing in front of the whole class. The children are about to begin a computer-based, collaborative mathematics activity (in groups of three).

### Transcript 1: introductory whole-class session, March 18

| | | |
|---|---|---|
| TEACHER: | Before you go on to the next step on the computer what do you need to make sure that the whole group has done? Oh! More hands up than that. Emma? | |
| EMMA: | Agreed. | |
| TEACHER: | Agreed. The whole group needs to agree. | *Teacher writes 'everybody agrees' on the board.* |
| | OK one of my speech bubbles. I wonder what kind of things we might hear each other saying during today's lesson? | *Teacher draws a speech bubble. Points to a child.* |
| AXEL: | What do you think? | |
| TEACHER: | What do you think? Anything else you might hear people saying as we have today's lesson? Kaye? | *Teacher writes 'What do you think?' in speech bubble.* |
| KAYE: | What is your idea? | *Teacher draws a speech bubble and writes in it 'What is your idea?'* |
| TEACHER: | Brilliant! What's your idea? Oh, Sydney? | |
| SYDNEY: | Why do you think that? | |
| TEACHER: | Excellent. Well done. Any other things we might hear people say? Rebecca? | *Teacher draws a speech bubble and writes 'Why do you think that?'* |
| REBECCA: | I'm not too sure on that idea. What do you think? | |

| TEACHER: | Brilliant. Well done. What do we need to remember in our groups? Kiera? | *Teacher draws a new speech bubble.* |
| KIERA: | That everybody gets a turn to talk | |
| TEACHER: | Everybody gets a turn to talk. | *Teacher points to Anna.* |

In Transcript 1 we see the teacher setting up a series of 'closed' questions to obtain the answers she seeks from her students. But although such questions have tended to be stigmatized as the essence of teacher-dominated discourse, we should not underestimate their pedagogic value if used appropriately, as Wells (1999) and others have convincingly argued. Transcript 1 would arguably represent such an appropriate use, because the teacher is checking that the members of the class are aware of the ground rules they have agreed to use, and ensuring that the rules are at the forefront of their minds when they begin the group work. The teacher is taking an external regulatory stance in order to guide the children's subsequent co-regulation of their own activity. Nevertheless, the discussion has some obvious 'dialogic' features, with children taking active and extended roles in the talk and the teacher giving attention to the variety of ideas expressed. In Alexander's words, as quoted earlier, it uses 'structured, cumulative questioning and discussion which guide and prompt, reduce choices, minimize risk and error, and expedite the "handover" of concepts and principles' (Alexander, 2008, p. 103). Through this discussion, the teacher creates for the children a cumulative, cohesive, temporal link between their previous classroom experiences (the lesson in which they established and agreed on ground rules), the present lesson and their future activity. On the basis of his extensive research in primary classrooms, Alexander has argued that creating such links is an important and positive quality of effective 'dialogic' teaching.

But are we able to see the external regulatory guidance provided by a teacher being transformed into co-regulatory behaviour by children when the teacher is no longer present? I believe the next two transcripts do so. They are from the collaborative activity of two groups of children in the same class. Transcript 2 was recorded 11 days after Transcript 1 and Transcript 3 was recorded just over two months after that. In both cases, three children are working at the computer on a task in which they have to select an appropriate number to enter in a calculation. Emboldened text relates to my subsequent comments.

*Transcript 2: group work, 29 March: Alan, Muj and Neeran*

| ALAN: | Four. **What do you think?** |
| MUJ: | Yes, four |
| NEERAN: | Is fifteen a multiple of four? No four fours are sixteen. |
| ALAN: | Yes it is. No. No. |
| MUJ: | No |
| ALAN: | Is nine? |

MUJ:      No
NEERAN:   **Why do you think that?**
ALAN:     Because it goes four, eight then twelve, so it misses nine out.

In Transcript 2, we see talk which illustrates the hazy boundary between the use of language for 'thinking out loud' as an individual and thinking collectively (as noted by Barnes, 1976, in his original conceptualization of exploratory talk). Neeran asks a question and then answers it herself. Alan likewise agrees and then contradicts himself. Alan also asks Muj 'What do you think?' and Neeran asks Alan 'Why do you think that?' These are literal reproductions of the model speech acts included in the class's 'ground rules' on the classroom wall and offered during the whole-class discussion of Transcript 1 by the children Axel and Sydney). We therefore can see children here appropriating rules for co-regulation, and for co-constructing knowledge (Hogan, op. cit.), which their teacher has offered to them. Alan also acts out the rules in another way, by giving a reason for his view. However, their appropriation is very literal, and a sceptical reader could claim that the children are doing little more than 'parroting' the teacher's words and those of the ground rules on the wall. Nevertheless, these are speech acts being performed in an appropriate and meaningful context, which achieve suitable pragmatic effects (eliciting suitable collaborative responses from partners and progressing the discussion). Let us next consider Transcript 3, recorded two months later with another group.

### Transcript 3: group work, 7 June: Sofia, Kirsty and Beau

SOFIA:    Five, seven and five equals twelve. So put five.
BEAU:     Do you agree?
KIRSTY:   Yes, and then we need to sort this out.
          *[and then a little later . . .]*
SOFIA:    I know, why don't we use the seven again?
KIRSTY:   What do we do now?
SOFIA:    What do you think we should do?
KIRSTY:   I don't know, it's too hard. I have never done this before.
BEAU:     I haven't done this before.
SOFIA:    What can we remember? A blank square. All I can remember is
          numbers. Eight add one is nine.

In Transcript 3 we can see children quite clearly using talk of an 'exploratory' kind to think collectively. They ask for each other's views, and provide frank answers to questions ('I don't know, it's too hard'). Again we see children using questions such as 'What do you think?' and 'Do you agree?' which can be traced directly back to the ground rules introduced by their teacher (by now several months earlier). But we also see them use other, semantically related but different expressions: 'What do we do now?' and 'What can we remember?' These cognate expressions suggest that this group have not followed the ground rules only in a mechanistic way, by simply parroting model speech acts offered by the teacher, but rather have 'internalized' the ground rules in principle. Their adherence to the ground rules is less literal than that of the children in Transcript 2. That is, it seems that they have used their metacognitive awareness of how talk can be used for learning, and the external regulatory system provided by their teacher, and learned how to apply these cultural/psychological tools in an appropriate, creative way to co-regulate their problem-solving activity. In relation to sociocultural theory, and the processes depicted in Figures 14.1 and 14.2, they have taken up ways of using language they have heard *and* ways of being regulated and transformed them into self-regulated ways of talking, thinking and acting collectively. When we also note that these children were amongst those who demonstrated statistically greater individual improvements in mathematics, science and reasoning, compared with those members of classes who had not had teacher guidance on co-regulating their discussions, the development of links between the two lines of research – on classroom talk and on self-regulation – becomes even more appealing.

## Conclusions

Despite sharing theoretical roots in Vygotskian sociocultural theory, researchers concerned with the development of children's metacognition and self-regulated learning and those concerned with the use of classroom talk for developing children's reasoning, understanding and problem-solving abilities have tended to work separately. Both lines of research have produced some encouraging findings; and both sets of results would seem to have useful implications for understanding how children learn and develop cognitively, and for classroom practice in the primary school. I have highlighted some links which can be made, and in the previous section I have shown some ways that concepts derived from one line can be useful in explaining the results of research in the other. There has not yet, however, been any major project which has truly integrated the key concepts, principles and methodologies of both lines of enquiry.

The conference which generated this monograph could not, in one event, succeed in integrating these two lines of research, but I believe that it enabled ideas from one line of enquiry to become more accessible to the other. A proper integration would require more joint consideration by the researchers involved of what each line had to offer methodologically, theoretically and empirically, and how these could strengthen future research. For example, the role of talk between adults and children, or amongst children, is rarely subject to rigorous analysis in research on metacognition and self-regulation. Instead, language tends to be treated as a transparent medium for intermental processes, which is not theoretically or methodologically justifiable. On the other hand, the development of self-regulated learning, or of children's ability to co-regulate their joint activity, has not usually been considered in such terms within research on classroom talk or on collabora-tive learning in school, even though it patently is one important aspect of what is being studied. The development of metacognition, similarly, is rarely an explicit theme in such research, despite an interest in children's awareness of how they talk and work together.

Bringing the two lines of research together theoretically should be assisted by their common allegiance to a Vygotskian account of learning and cogni-tive development. Essentially, what is required is a theoretical framework that combines my Figures 14.1 and 14.2. This would enable the functional role of language as a cultural and psychological tool to be given more atten-tion in studies of metacognition and self-regulation, in acknowledgement of the fact that knowledge and understanding are commonly co-constructed by more than one person. And for studies of classroom talk – at least those which have allegiance to sociocultural psychology – it would encourage more attention to be given to language's functions for enabling co-regulation, and for enabling metacognition. In these ways, we would begin to build a more complete theoretical model of the relationship between the intermental and the intramental, between collective thinking and individual cognition. This development would, however, depend on the establishment of shared defini-tions of concepts, and the use of a shared conceptual vocabulary.

One final point: my discussion has been framed in terms of bringing together two distinct lines of research; but I would argue that these two lines of enquiry are not necessarily dealing with distinct psychological and social processes. Rather, they represent different perspectives on the same processes. By bringing them together, we see that the intermental activity of explor-atory talk may promote the intramental activity of self-regulated learning; and engaging in exploratory talk requires the development of metacognition and skills in co-regulation. Vygotsky's own theorizations would encourage us to believe that we are dealing with one process whereby the 'ways with words' which children experience in the intermental dialogues of their com-munities can act as intramental templates for the reflective planning and regulation of their individual intellectual activities. If that is so, then seeking to distinguish between the effects of promoting productive dialogue and promoting self-regulation could be futile, and we would be better advised to design interventions which expressly and effectively recognize that they are inextricably intertwined in the ways that human cognition develops.

# References

Alexander, R. (2006). *Towards dialogic teaching: Rethinking classroom talk*. Cam-bridge: Dialogos.

Alexander, R. (2008). Culture, dialogue and learning: Notes on an emerging peda-gogy. In N. Mercer & S. Hodgkinson (Eds.), *Exploring talk in schools* (pp. 91–114). London: Sage.

Azmitia, M., & Montgomery, R. (1993). Friendship, transactive dialogues and the development of scientific reasoning. *Social Development, 2*, 202–221.

Bahktin, M. (1981). *The dialogic imagination*. Austin, TX: University of Texas Press.

Baines, E., Blatchford, P., & Chowne, A. (2007). Improving the effectiveness of collaborative group work in primary schools: Effects on Science attainment. *British Educational Research Journal, 33*, 663–680.

Barnes, D. (1976). *From communication to curriculum*. London: Penguin Books.

Black, P., McCormick, R., James, M., & Pedder, D. (2006). Learning how to learn and assessment for learning: A theoretical inquiry. *Research Papers in Education – Special Issue, 21*, 119–132.

Chinn, C., Anderson, R., & Waggoner, M. (2001). Patterns of discourse in two kinds of literature discussion. *Reading Research Quarterly, 36*, 378–411.

Claxton, G. (2002). *Building learning power: Helping young people become better learners*. Bristol: TLO.

Daniels, H. (2008). *Vygotsky and research*. Abingdon: Routledge.

Dawes, L., Mercer, N., & Fisher, E. (1992). The quality of talk at the computer. *Language and Learning*, October Issue, 22–25.

Dewey, J., & Bento, J. (2010). Activating children's thinking skills (ACTS): The effects of an infusion approach to teaching thinking in primary schools. *British Journal of Educational Psychology, 79*, 329–351.

Dignath, G., Buettner, G., & Langfeldt, H.-P. (2008). How can primary school students learn self-regulated learning strategies most effectively? A meta-analysis on self-regulation training programmes. *Educational Research Review, 3*, 101–129.

Edwards, D., & Mercer, N. (1987/2012). *Common knowledge: The development of understanding in the classroom*. London: Methuen/Routledge.

Featherstone, S., & Bailey, R. (2006). *Foundations for independence: Developing independent learning in the Foundation Stage* (2nd ed.). Lutterworth: Featherstone Education.

Fisher, R., & Larkin, S. (2008). Pedagogy or Ideological Struggle? An examination of pupils' and teachers' expectations for talk in the classroom. *Language and Education, 22*, 1–16.

Goswami, U., & Bryant, P. (2007). Children's cognitive development and learning. In *Research report 2/1a: The primary review*. Cambridge: University of Cambridge.

Hadwin, A. F. (2008). Self-regulated learning. In T. L. Good (Ed.), *21st century education: A reference handbook*. Thousand Oaks, CA: Sage. Harris, R., & Ratcliffe, M. (2005). Socio-scientific issues and the quality of exploratory talk: What can be learned from schools involved in a "collapsed day" project? *The Curriculum Journal, 16*, 439–453.

Hegarty, M., Mayer, R. E., & Monk, C. A. (1995). Comprehension of arithmetic word problems: A comparison of successful and unsuccessful problem solvers. *Journal of Educational Psychology, 87*(1), 18–32.

Hendy, L., & Whitebread, D. (2000). Interpretations of independent learning in the early years. *International Journal of Early Years Education, 8*, 243–252.

Hickey, D. T. (2003). Engaged participation versus marginal nonparticipation: A stridently sociocultural approach to achievement motivation. *The Elementary School Journal, 103*, 402–429.

Higgins, S. (2013). Self regulation and learning: Evidence from meta-analysis and from classrooms. In D. Whitebread, N. Mercer, C. Howe, & A. Tolmie (Eds.),

*Self-regulation and dialogue in primary classrooms. British Journal of Psychology 'Current Trends' Monograph Series* (pp. 111–126). Leicester: British Psychological Society.

Hogan, K. (1999). Thinking aloud together: A test of an intervention to foster students' collaborative scientific reasoning. *Journal of Research in Science Teaching*, 36, 1085–1109.

Howe, C. (2010). *Peer groups and children's development*. Oxford: Wiley-Blackwell.

Howe, C., & Abedin, M. (2013). Classroom dialogue: A systematic review across four decades of research. *Cambridge Journal of Education*, 43, 325–356.

Howe, C., & Mercer, N. (2007). Children's social development, peer interaction and classroom learning. In *The primary review: Research survey 2/1b*. Cambridge: University of Cambridge.

Howe, C., & Tolmie, A. (1998). Productive interaction in the context of computer-supported collaborative science. In K. Littleton & P. Light (Eds.), *Learning with computers: Analysing productive interaction* (pp. 24–45). London: Routledge.

Howe, C., Tolmie, A., Thurston, A., Topping, K., Christie, D., Livingston, K., . . . & Donaldson, C. (2007). Group work in elementary science: Towards organizational principles for supporting pupil learning. *Learning and Instruction*, 17, 549–563.

Järvellä, S., & Hadwin, A. (2013). New frontiers: Regulating learning in CSCL. *Educational Psychologist*, 48, 25–39.

Kyriacou, C., & Issitt, J. (2008). What characterizes effective teacher-pupil dialogue to promote conceptual understanding in mathematics lessons in England in Key Stages 2 and 3? *EPPI-Centre Report no. 1604R*. Social Science Research Unit: Institute of Education, University of London.

Lefstein, A. (2010). More helpful as problem than as solution: Some implications of situating dialogue in the classroom. In K. Littleton & C. Howe (Eds.), *Educational dialogues: Understanding and promoting productive interaction* (pp. 170–191). London: Routledge.

Lewin-Benham, A. (2008). *Powerful children: Understanding how to think and learn using the Reggio approach*. New York, NY: Teachers College Press.

Littleton, K., & Howe, C. (2010). Introduction. In K. Littleton & C. Howe (Eds.), *Educational dialogues: Understanding and promoting productive interaction* (pp. 1–7). London: Routledge.

Maybin, J. (2006). *Children's voices: Talk, knowledge and identity*. Basingstoke: Palgrave Macmillan.

McCaslin, M. (2004). Coregulation of opportunity, activity, and identity in student motivation. In D. McInerney & S. Van Etten (Eds.), *Big theories revisited* (Vol. 4, pp. 249–274). Greenwich, CT: Information Age.

McGuinness, C. (2006). *Building thinking skills in thinking classroom: ACTS (Activating Children's Thinking Skills) in Northern Ireland*. Teaching and Learning Research Briefing, 18. ESRC Teaching and Learning Research Programme. Retrieved from www.tlrp.org

Mercer, N. (2000). *Words and minds: How we use language to think together*. London: Routledge.

Mercer, N. (2013). The social brain, language, and goal-directed collective thinking: A social conception of cognition and its implications for understanding how we think, teach, and learn. *Educational Psychologist*, 48(3), 148–168.

Mercer, N., Dawes, R., Wegerif, R., & Sams, C. (2004). Reasoning as a scientist: Ways of helping children to use language to learn science. *British Educational Research Journal, 30*, 367–385.

Mercer, N., & Hodgkinson, S. (Eds.). (2008). *Exploring talk in school*. London: Sage.

Mercer, N., & Howe, C. (2012). Explaining the dialogic processes of teaching and learning: The value of sociocultural theory. *Learning, Culture and Social Interaction, 1*(1), 12–21.

Mercer, N., & Littleton, K. (2007). *Dialogue and the development of children's thinking: A socio-cultural approach*. London: Routledge.

Michaels, S., & O'Connor, M. C. (2002). *Accountable talk: Classroom conversation that works*, CD-ROM. University of Pittsburgh.

Miller, R. (2011). *Vygotsky in perspective*. Cambridge: Cambridge University Press.

Ornstein, P., Grammer, J., & Coffman, J. (2010). Teachers' "mnemonic style" and the development of skilled memory. In H. Salatas Walters & W. Schneider (Eds.), *Metacognition, strategy use, and instruction* (pp. 23–53). London: The Guilford Press.

Pape, S. J., & Wang, C. (2003). Middle school children's strategic behavior: Classification and relation to academic achievement and mathematical problem solving. *Instructional Science, 31*, 419–449.

Perret-Clermont, A. N. (1980). *Social interaction and cognitive development in children*. London: Academic Press.

Perry, N. (2013). Understanding classroom processes that support children's self-regulation of learning. In D. Whitebread, N. Mercer, C. Howe, & A. Tolmie (Eds.), *Self-regulation and dialogue in primary classrooms. British Journal of Educational Psychology Monograph Series II: Psychological Aspects of Education – Current Trends, No 10* (pp. 45–68). Leicester: British Psychological Society.

Piaget, J. (1970). *The science of education and the psychology of the child*. New York: Viking Press.

PISA. (2013). *PISA 2015: Draft collaborative problem solving framework*. Paris: Organisation for Economic Co-operation and Development (OECD).

Potter, J., & Wetherell, M. (1994). *Discourse and social psychology*. London: Sage.

Psychology and Society. (2012). University of London website. Retrieved October 22, 2012 from www.psychologyandsociety. com/metacognition.html

Raven, J., Court, J., & Raven, J. C. (1995). *Manual for Raven's progressive matrices and vocabulary scales*. Oxford: Oxford Psychologists Press.

Resnick, L. B. (1999). Making America smarter. *Education Week Century Series, 18*(40), 38–40.

Reznitskaya, A., Anderson, R., McNurlen, B., Nguyen-Jahiel, K., Archodidou, A., & Kim, S. (2006). Influence of oral discussion on written argument. *Discourse Processes, 32*, 155–175.

Rojas-Drummond, S., Littleton, K., Hernandez, F., & Zuniga, M. (2010). Dialogical interactions amongst peers in collaborative writing contexts. In K. Littleton & C. Howe (Eds.), *Educational dialogues: Understanding and promoting productive interaction* (pp. 128–148). London: Routledge.

Schweinhart, L. J. (2000). The High/Scope Perry preschool study: A case study in random assignment. *Evaluation and Research in Education, 14*, 136–147.

Scott, P. (2008). Talking a way to understanding in science classrooms. In N. Mercer, & S. Hodgkinson (Eds.), *Exploring talk in school* (pp. 17–36). London: Sage.

Slavin, R. E. (2009). *Cooperative learning: Theory, research, and practice.* Boston, MA: Allymand Bacon.

Smith, F., Hardman, F., Wall, K., & Mroz, M. (2004). Interactive whole class teaching in the National Literacy and Numeracy Strategies. *British Educational Research Journal, 30,* 395–411.

Sylva, K., Melhuish, E. C., Sammons, P., Siraj-Blatchford, I., & Taggart, B. (2004). The Effective Provision of Pre-School Education (EPPE) project. In *Technical Paper 12 – The Final Report: Effective Pre-School Education.* London: DfES/Institute of Education, University of London.

Tartas, V., Baucal, A., & Perret-Clermont, A.-N. (2010). Can you think with me? The social and cognitive conditions and the fruits of learning. In K. Littleton & C. Howe (Eds.), *Educational dialogues: Understanding and promoting productive interaction* (pp. 64–81). London: Routledge.

Vauras, M., Iiskala, T., Kajamies, A., Kinnunen, R., & Lehtinen, E. (2003). Shared-regulation and motivation of collaborating peers: A case analysis. *Psychologia: An International Journal of Psychology in the Orient, 46,* 19–37.

Volet, S., Summers, M., & Thurman, J. (2009). High-level co-regulation in collaborative learning: How does it emerge and how is it sustained? *Learning and Instruction, 19,* 128–143.

van Oers, B., & Dobber, M. (2013). Communication and regulation in a problem-oriented primary school curriculum. In D. Whitebread, N. Mercer, C. Howe, & A. Tolmie (Eds.), *Self-regulation and dialogue in primary classrooms* (pp. 93–110). *British Journal of Educational Psychology Monograph Series II: Psychological Aspects of Education – Current Trends,* No 10. Leicester: British Psychological Society.

Vygotsky, L. S. (1999). *The collected works of L. S. Vygotsky. Vol. VI: Scientific legacy* (R. W. Rieber, Ed.). New York, NY: Plenum Press.

Wang, M. C., Haertel, G. D., & Walberg, H. J. (1990). What influences learning? A content analysis of review literature. *Journal of Educational Research, 84,* 30–43.

Webb, N. (2009). The teacher's role in promoting collaborative dialogue in the classroom. *British Journal of Educational Psychology, 79,* 1–28.

Wegerif, R. (2010). *Mind expanding: Teaching for thinking and creativity in primary education.* Buckingham: Open University Press.

Wegerif, R., Perez, J., Rojas-Drummond, S., Mercer, N., & Velez, M. (2005). Thinking Together in the UK and Mexico: Transfer of an educational innovation. *Journal of Classroom Interaction, 40,* 40–48.

Wells, G. (1999). *Dialogic inquiry: Towards a sociocultural practice and theory of education.* Cambridge: Cambridge University Press.

Wells, G. (2009). *The meaning makers: Learning to talk and learning to learn* (2nd ed.). Bristol: Multilingual Matters.

Wertsch, J. V. (1979). From social interaction to higher psychological processes: A clarification and application of Vygotsky's theory. *Human Development, 22,* 1–22.

Whitebread, D., & Pino-Pasternak, D. (2010). Metacognition, self-Regulation & meta-knowing. In K. Littleton, C. Wood, & J. Kleine Staarman (Eds.), *International handbook of psychology in education* (pp. 615–713). Leeds: Emerald.

Williams, J. (2003). *Promoting independent learning in the primary classroom.* Buckingham: Open University Press.

Williams, P. (2008). *Independent review of mathematics teaching in early years settings and primary schools.* London: Department for Children, Schools and Families.

Winne, P. H. (2001). Self-regulated learning viewed from models of information processing. In B. J. Zimmerman & D. H. Schunk (Eds.), *Self-regulated learning and academic achievement: Theoretical perspectives* (2nd ed., pp. 153–189). Mahwah, NJ: Lawrence Erlbaum.

Wolf, M., Crosson, A., & Resnick, L. (2006). Accountable talk in reading comprehension instruction. *CSE Technical Report 670*. Learning and Research Development Center, University of Pittsburgh.

*This chapter comes from a book celebrating the career of the educational researcher John Furlong, whose pioneering work, along with that of Douglas Barnes, Courtney Cazden, Tony Edwards and Gordon Wells, led the study of classroom talk in the 1970s. In this chapter Lyn and I review the subsequent history of that field of study and draw both positive and negative conclusions. We conclude that, while much understanding has been gained, research evidence about the most productive forms of teacher–student interaction lacks the weight of large-scale studies. However, since we wrote this article, two substantial studies have just been completed, each involving more than 70 British primary teachers, and both have provided encouraging support for 'dialogic' teaching. I refer to those studies in the introduction to this book.*

# 15 The study of talk between teachers and students, from the 1970s until the 2010s

*Mercer, N. & Dawes, L. (2014). The study of talk between teachers and students, from the 1970s until the 2010s.* Oxford Review of Education *(Routledge), 40, 4, 430–445.*

## Abstract

The close study of classroom talk has been an active field of research since the 1970s, when John Furlong made his significant contribution. Focusing particularly on research into teacher–student interactions, we will review the development of this field from the 1970s until the present, considering what has been learned and the educational implications of the results. We also discuss the impact of the findings of this research on teacher education, educational policy and classroom practice.

## Introduction

In this paper, we review the development of research into talk in the classroom, from the 1970s to today, with a particular focus on the study of teacher–student interaction. When John Furlong's book with Tony Edwards, *The Language of Teaching* (Edwards & Furlong, 1978), was published, the close study of classroom talk was quite a recent development within educational research. As one of those authors commented some years later, in an influential methodological handbook on analysing classroom talk: 'To find verbatim transcripts of classroom talk before 1970 is difficult' (Edwards & Westgate, 1994, p. 1). There had already been some significant interest in specific features of classroom talk, such as teachers' use of questions, mainly using the quantitative survey method of 'systematic observation' which did not involve recording and transcribing talk. Instead, trained observers noted the incidence of target features as they sat in classrooms, observing interactions in real time (Amidon & Hunter, 1967; Flanders, 1970). Such research gave us memorable insights such as Flanders's 'two-thirds rule', which says: in a lesson someone is usually talking for about two-thirds of the time, and two-thirds of that talk is usually by the teacher. Using their quantitative findings, researchers could look for associations between the relative incidence of particular features and other educational variables, such as learning outcomes. That style of research into talk continued through the 1970s and beyond (for example, in the *Oracle Project* research: Galton, Hargreaves, Comber, Pell, & Wall, 1999; Galton, Simon, & Croll, 1980) and its value is shown by the fact that it is still employed today as one of several distinctive approaches to the study of classroom talk (Mercer, 2009). However, it is not suitable for examining how the structure and content of talk develops through lessons, or how specific participants contribute to the development of shared understanding. That requires a researcher having access to an audio (or, ideally, a video) recording of the lesson (or series of lessons) which can be transcribed and reviewed for careful consideration. With the increased availability of such technology, and drawing on methods developed by anthropologists and sociolinguists, it became common to employ a qualitative approach to analysing classroom talk, with selected extracts from transcripts being used to illustrate and support analytic claims in research publications.

During the 1970s and early 1980s, an interest in the social and cognitive functions of language in social interactions was growing generally amongst psychologists, sociologists, anthropologists and linguists. This initiated the emergence of a new kind of sociology, ethnomethodology, which focused on social interaction at the micro-level and generated a new and very distinctive approach to analysing talk: *conversation analysis* (Garfinkel, 1974). Though that approach was (and still is) used only very rarely in classroom research, the ethnomethodological concern with talk as social action had a wider influence on educational research. Vygotsky's work, with its emphasis on the importance of spoken dialogue for children's cognitive development, had also recently become more available through translation and interpretation (e.g. Vygotsky, 1962, 1978). His conception of the special relationship between language and thinking began to have a significant influence on educational research, and not just amongst psychologists (Britton, 1978). Moreover, around that time researchers from varied disciplinary backgrounds used empirical studies to claim that the nature and quality of children's involvement in spoken dialogue could have an important effect on their educational achievement and participation (Bernstein, 1975; Heath, 1983; Wells, 1978). And through the efforts of pioneers in the field, such as Barnes, Britton, and Rosen (1969) in the UK and Cazden (1972) and colleagues in the USA, the relevance of studying teacher–student talk for understanding how education happened in classrooms became more widely accepted by teachers and those working in teacher education. However, at that time the initial training of teachers did not typically involve awareness-raising about classroom talk, its importance for children's development, or how it might be employed most effectively.

## Understanding the form and functions of classroom talk

The new interdisciplinary interest in spoken language led to some semi-nal contributions to our understanding of the structure and functions of classroom talk. A good example is the identification of the most common, minimal unit of interactional exchange between a teacher and a student. This exchange unit was given the acronym IRF (Initiation-Response-Follow-up: often modified to Initiation-Response-Feedback by British educational researchers) by the British linguists Sinclair and Coulthard (1975) and IRE (Initiation-Response-Evaluation) by the American sociologist Mehan (1979). This building-block of the most conventional kind of classroom talk cannot easily be ignored by any observer of classroom life, once it has been noticed. As a vehicle for 'closed' questioning, it has been observed as a common feature of life in English primary classrooms even in recent times (Hardman, Smith, & Wall, 2003). An archetypal example is:

TEACHER: What is the capital of Peru? (*Initiation*)
STUDENT: Lima (*Response*)
TEACHER: Yes, well done (*Follow-up/Feedback/Evaluation*).

Sinclair and Coulthard were not motivated by a wish to improve classroom education: they used classroom talk as data for exploring the textual struc-ture of interactive, spoken language. They combined the 'exchange' unit with other units such as 'act' and 'event' to construct a hierarchical system for describing the structure of classroom talk, which revealed its specific, cohesive nature as a distinctive language genre. Mehan's more sociological interest in the IRE unit was focused on the social order of the classroom, including its power relations, and demonstrated how talk functioned to sus-tain that order. Edwards and Furlong's research took a similar sociological perspective. As the sociologist of education Banks (1978) commented at that time, research such as that by Mehan, and Edwards and Furlong, was pioneering the task of 'building bridges' between sociological understanding of society as a whole (the macro-level of social structure) and specific social events (the micro-structure).

But while gaining a heightened perception of the nature and structure of interactional talk might seem obviously useful for a social scientist, was it also useful for teachers? This was one of the issues that Edwards and Fur-long addressed in their book. They wrote '. . . can it be argued that teachers need to discover a situation which they cope with in every working day?' (p. 2) They claimed that it is indeed useful for teachers to gain some insight into the nature of classroom talk, and they explained why:

The justification for this claim does not come from assuming some ultimate reality which only the expert social scientist is equipped to pen-etrate. It arises from the extreme difficulty of seeing what is familiar and recurrent. If the immediacy and pace of classroom events make it essential for teachers to make most of their work a matter of routine, then what is routine may have to be 'forced out its usual semi-consciousness' if it to be reflected upon at all.

(Edwards & Furlong, 1978, p. 2)

We can see in that statement the seeds of the development through the 1980s of what has been called 'the reflective practice movement' in education (Ziechner, 1994). Though claims about the value of reflection for improving practice can be traced back to Dewey (1933), it became a much more explicit and widespread focus of interest. Edwards and Furlong's research, as described in their book, was also important for bridging the gap between teachers and researchers in another way – by involving teachers as participants in the research, rather than as objects of the attention of detached observers. Their example encouraged many of us to try to live up to the expectation that we should not do research *on* teachers, but *with* teachers.

The empirical study of teaching talk that Edwards and Furlong report in their book was carried out in a large comprehensive school in Manchester. One of its aims was, as they put it, 'to describe a kind of teaching of which very little is known' (p. 7): that which took place in mixed ability secondary school classes. They were able to show that, in many ways, talk in these classrooms corresponded to the common patterns of talk in classrooms everywhere. Moreover, they showed how one significant aspect of a teacher's role is to monitor and manage how talk happens in their classroom. They described how the lessons they observed tended to consist of 'stages with perhaps some sharply differing rules about the appropriate quantity, distribution and forms of talk, and teachers have to provide the relevant "stage directions"' (p. 21). The sociolinguist Stubbs (1983) had identified six categories of such directing comments made by teachers, which he called *metastatements*. Edwards and Furlong provided examples of each of these categories from their observational data, as shown in Table 15.1.

Throughout the chapters of the book, Edwards and Furlong also provide detailed illustrations and analyses of the kinds of talk they observed. Almost all of it represented a highly authoritative style of 'transmission teaching'. As they conclude in the final chapter, 'Differences in the surface style of individual teachers seem to leave unaltered a basic structure of centrally controlled interactions and centrally managed meanings' (p. 147). They did not criticise the teachers they had observed for doing this, but rather explained what they saw as a '. . . coping strategy – a way of working developed to reconcile the difficult problems of maintaining order, communicating information, and providing at least some degree of pupil autonomy' (p. 149). They explained how classroom talk enabled the social and intellectual life of classrooms to happen, but they did not propose alternative regimes of classroom interaction. Nevertheless, implicit in their text is the idea that, as an educational tool, talk was commonly not being used to its full potential, because its use

*Table 15.1* Types of metastatements made by teachers (from Edwards & Furlong, 1978, p. 21)

| | |
|---|---|
| (1) *Attracting attention* | 'Girls, it might be might be a nasty rumour, but I've been told you're doing nothing.' |
| (2) *Controlling the amount and distribution of talk* | 'You're making too much noise at this table, you should be working.' |
| (3) *Specifying the topic* | 'We're going to look at the people on a small island, how they solve the problems of shelter, food, clothing, law and order – you know, the problems we looked at before half term.' |
| (4) *Checking or confirming understanding* | Is there anyone who doesn't know how to work out a map now? Nobody? Well, that's great, we've done well this morning.' |
| (5) *Correcting and 'editing' what is said* | 'Why will the eagle go for that one? "Cos it can't fly.' 'Well, no, it can fly – that's not the reason.' "Cos it's white.' 'Yes, because it's white. Why will it go for it because it's white?' 'It can see it better.' 'That's right, in that environment the other one is better adapted, it's – what's the word?' 'Camouflaged.' |
| (6) *Summarising* | 'So from a story from long ago we've used that story to work out how people thought about themselves, how they lived.' |

was so constrained by the dominant cultural norms of school; and that the dominant patterns of classroom talk limited the extent to which pupils were able to actively construct their own knowledge and understanding. Thus they conclude the book by saying:

> Close attention to the interpretative schemes which teachers and pupils seem to be using to construct and assign meanings makes it possible to identify the extent to which different teaching strategies reflect and reproduce less hierarchical relationships, and less sharply differentiated boundaries between teachers' and pupils' knowledge.
>
> (p. 155)

## The influence of research on educational policy

By the mid-1980s, stimulated by the work described above, the study of classroom talk had gained wide interdisciplinary and international interest. Psychologists, sociolinguists and anthropologists, as well as sociologists and English specialists, had become involved (e.g. Edwards & Mercer, 1987/2012; Green & Wallat, 1981; Hargreaves, 1984; Mercer & Edwards,

1981; Spindler, 1982). The research had promoted a growing awareness amongst policy makers (at least in some countries) of the educational importance of the study of classroom talk. This had first been apparent in the Bullock Report (1975) commissioned by the Westminster government, which said:

> We need to begin examining the nature of the language experience in the dialogue between teacher and class. . . . By its very nature a lesson is a verbal encounter through which the teacher draws information from the class, elaborates and generalises it, and produces a synthesis. His [sic] skill is in selecting, improving and generally orchestrating the exchange.
>
> (p. 141)

Bullock's and other official endorsements of the value of enquiry into classroom talk (for example ILEA, 1984) encouraged teachers to appraise the ways they interacted with students. Whether intended or not, research on classroom talk had stimulated an initiative for change, with the expectation that encouraging different patterns of classroom interaction from those usually observed might enable new and better ways of teaching and learning to emerge.

In England, government interest in the educational value of talk in the classroom probably reached its highest level in the 1980s, as represented by the establishment in 1987 of the National Oracy Project (which included England and Wales) by the newly formed National Curriculum Council (Norman, 1992). It ran until the end of its dissemination phase in 1993. The six aims of the project included 'to enhance the role of speech in the learning processes 5–16 by encouraging active learning' and 'to enhance teachers' skills and practice'. The term 'oracy' had been coined by one of the British pioneers of the study of classroom talk, Wilkinson (1970), as the analogue of literacy and numeracy. The project brought together teachers, teacher educators, researchers and policy makers: pupils themselves took an active role. Its main aim was to raise awareness about talk and its educational value, and so change its status as the 'poor relation' of reading and writing in educational culture; but it also encouraged the celebration of children's talk, in all its diversity. It generated much enthusiasm and activity in schools. In our experience, those who were involved invariably recall it today in very positive terms.

However, the impact of the National Oracy Project on educational policy and practice was, to a considerable extent, undermined by the election of a Conservative government in 1992 with a 'back to basics' agenda for education. From that time, oracy again became the neglected sibling of literacy and numeracy. Regarding pedagogy, the emphasis was moved strongly away from encouraging variety in the dialogue between teachers and students, and back towards a more traditional, transmissional style of teaching (Cox, 1991). But research into classroom talk continued.

## The development of analytic frameworks

Building on the knowledge gained from the early studies of teacher–student talk, the initial insightful ideas of the 1970s were developed into more systematic analytic approaches and explanatory frameworks by later researchers (Edwards & Westgate, 1994). Such work continued through the 1990s, particularly from the perspective of linguistic ethnography (see for example Creese, 2008; Gee & Green, 1998).

Following the identification of the IRF/IRE exchange and its association with the interrogation of a student by a teacher, as illustrated in the archetypal example included earlier, it became common amongst educational researchers to criticise teachers for their extensive and habitual use of such exchanges. Because IRFs were so commonly used to ask students 'closed questions', to which the teacher knew the only permissibly correct answer, it tended to be assumed that this linguistic form had a necessary association with that function in a dialogue. This led to suggestions during the 1980s and 1990s that teachers should try to avoid setting up IRFs, and minimise their use of questions (Wood, 1992). However, further careful analysis, for example by Wells (1999), showed that it is necessary to distinguish between form and function when analysing teacher–student exchanges and evaluating questions in teacher–pupil dialogue. As Wells (1999) in particular demonstrated, the IRF structure need not be tied to the use of closed questions. While such questioning certainly can require a student to guess what answer is in the teacher's mind, that is merely one possible function of the interchange. Teachers' questions can also serve other purposes, some of which may be more useful for assisting children's learning and developing their use of language as a tool for reasoning. In addition to their obvious behaviour management function – checking who is attending – teachers' questions can:

encourage children to make explicit their thoughts, reasons and knowledge and share them with the class;

'model' useful ways of using language that children can appropriate for use themselves, in peer group discussions and other settings (such as asking for relevant information possessed only by others, or asking 'why' questions to elicit reasons);

provide opportunities for children to make longer contributions in which they express their current state of understanding, articulate ideas and reveal problems they are encountering.

(Mercer & Littleton, 2007, p. 36)

## The importance of context

One reason why the qualitative analysis of talk became more popular than quantitative coding approaches during the 1980s and 1990s was a wider appreciation of the ways that the *context* of any conversation can affect its meaning for interlocutors (Edwards & Westgate, 1994). This means recognising not only the relevance of the physical setting and any artefacts shared by a teacher and students, but also the *common knowledge* that has been generated through the history of talk and shared activity of a teacher and their class (Edwards & Mercer, 1987/2012). The nature and extent of the prior knowledge shared by a teacher and students at the time the question is asked can affect the meaning and function of a question very significantly. 'Why does the moon appear to change shape?' would have a different educational function if asked by a teacher on first meeting a new class than if asked of the class after several lessons about the solar system. The former could represent an attempt by the teacher to see what prior knowledge the students were bringing to a new topic, while the latter could represent an attempt to evaluate the effectiveness of teaching. Such research highlights the methodological importance of studying classroom education as a journey through time for those involved, rather than a discrete series of teaching and learning events (Mercer, 2008).

This kind of realisation stimulated the development of new research methods. For example, Nystrand and colleagues in the USA devised a method they call *event history analysis* to study the antecedents and consequences of teachers' and students' questions as 'moves' in the flow of classroom discourse (Nystrand, 1997; Nystrand, Wu, Gamorgan, Zeiser, & Long, 2003). One of their special interests has been in episodes of classroom dialogue in which students took an active and sustained part in discussing ideas (as opposed to the episodes in which teachers did most of the talking and students made only brief contributions – which they, like so many other researchers, had observed tended to be the norm). They called these periods of active discussion *dialogic spells*. Their analysis shows how teachers can increase the likelihood of such spells through the use of certain strategies. These include actively welcoming and soliciting students' ideas; following up students' responses in their own remarks; asking more 'open' questions; and deliberately refraining from responding to a student's contribution with an evaluative feedback comment (and perhaps encouraging another student to offer an evaluative follow-up instead).

## Dialogic teaching

The work by Nystrand and colleagues also represents the growth of interest since the beginning of the 21st century in *dialogic teaching* – a term introduced and elaborated by Alexander (2006), and emerging from his cross-cultural analysis of primary school classrooms in five countries: England, France, India, Russia and the USA (Alexander, 2001). Perhaps because the forms and structures of classroom talk had become well defined through research in the 1970s and 1980s, researchers began to use this descriptive understanding to focus on ways of maximising the positive effects of teacher–student interaction. The aim of research on dialogic teaching has been of this kind, aiming to identify, and promote, those forms of interaction which have the most beneficial educational outcomes. At its heart is the assertion that children's learning and intellectual development will be best assisted if, for at least some of the time they are in class, they are encouraged and enabled to take an active and proportionally significant role in classroom talk. That is, dialogic teaching is that in which both teachers and pupils make substantial and significant contributions and through which pupils' thinking on a given idea or theme is helped to move forward. Its specification is intended to highlight ways that teachers can encourage students to use spoken language to explore and extend their own understanding. Alexander suggests that dialogic teaching is represented by certain features of classroom interaction:

- questions are structured so as to provoke thoughtful answers [. . .];
- answers provoke further questions and are seen as the building blocks of dialogue rather than its terminal point;
- individual teacher–pupil and pupil–pupil exchanges are chained into coherent lines of enquiry rather than left stranded and disconnected . . .

(Alexander, 2006, p. 32)

Another major contribution to the study of dialogic teaching was made by the British researcher Scott, who with his Brazilian colleague Mortimer recorded and analysed lessons in secondary science classrooms (Mortimer & Scott, 2003). Mortimer and Scott classified interaction between a teacher and students along two dimensions: *interactive-non-interactive* and *authoritative-dialogic*. As shown in Table 15.2 (adapted from Scott & Asoko, 2006), this generates four types of 'communicative approach':

A   Interactive/dialogic: teacher and students consider a range of ideas.
B   Non-interactive/dialogic: teacher reviews different points of view.
C   Interactive/authoritative: teacher focuses on one specific point of view and leads students through a question-and-answer routine with the aim of establishing and consolidating that point of view.
D   Non-interactive/authoritative: teacher presents a specific point of view.

According to this analysis, a dialogic teaching approach involves the teacher asking students for their points of view and explicitly taking account

*Table 15.2* Communicative approaches (adapted from Scott & Asoko, 2006)

|  | *Interactive* | *Non-interactive* |
| --- | --- | --- |
| **Dialogic** | A<br>Interactive/dialogic | B<br>Non-interactive/dialogic |
| **Authoritative** | C<br>Interactive/authoritative | D<br>Non-interactive/authoritative |

of what is said, for example by asking for further elaboration or by asking students to compare their ideas. Any specific lesson or series of teaching sessions might include episodes of each of the four communicative approaches and be considered dialogic overall. Indeed episodes of authoritative talk and non-interactive review are essential if students are to be offered access to knowledge and information. There is no implication in this analysis that any one approach is better, in educational terms, than another: it is the strategic balance that is important. For students to learn effectively, there will be times when they should sit quietly and listen to an authoritative explanation; but they are likely to develop a deeper understanding of a topic if they also have opportunities to express their own ideas, hypothesise, hear the thoughts of their fellow students, argue, reason and gain feedback from their teacher when 'thinking aloud' through a line of reasoning (Dawes, 2004; Myhill, Jones, & Hopper, 2005).

## The current state of research

Now that around 40 years have passed since those first explorations into the nature and functions of teacher–student talk, we can ask: where are we now? The field is still one of interdisciplinary endeavour, in which a range of approaches and methodologies are in use (see for example Mercer & Hodgkinson, 2008). One important methodological development has been the creation of specialised software for enabling both the qualitative and quantitative analysis of talk. Most educational researchers will be familiar with software like *NVivo*, which is used for the systematic storing, coding and analysis of data from observational research (and not just that concerned with classroom talk). Some talk researchers have also taken up the use of software designed by, and for, linguists and lexicographers. Research in linguistics, in recent decades, has been revolutionised by the development of computerised methods for analysing large electronic databases of written texts, which can include transcriptions of talk. Software packages known as 'concordancers' enable any text file to be scanned easily for all instances of particular target words. Commonly used examples of such software are Monoconc, Wordsmith and Conc 1.71. An attractive feature of the analysis they enable is that words can be identified as separate lexical items and as parts of a continuous text. Not only can the relative frequency of occurrence of particular words be measured, and the speakers who used them be identified, but the analysis can also indicate which words tend to occur together, and so help reveal the way words gather meanings by 'the company they keep'. The results of such searches can be presented as tabular *concordances*. Once recorded talk has been transcribed into a word file, a researcher can move almost instantly between occurrences of particular words and the whole transcription. This enables particular words of special interest to be 'hunted' in the data, and their relative incidence and form of use in particular contexts to be compared. The basic data for this kind of analysis, throughout, remains the whole transcription. By integrating this method with other methods, the analysis can be both qualitative (targeting particular interactions or extended episodes) and quantitative (comparing the relative incidence of 'key words', or of types of interaction as might a systematic observer). Initial exploratory work on particular short texts (or text extracts) can be used to generate hypotheses, which can then be tested systematically on a large text or series of related texts. For example, a researcher may want to see if a technical term introduced by a teacher is taken up by students later in a lesson, perhaps in their group-based activity. By locating all instances of the term in the transcription file, the ways it is used by teachers and students can then be considered (see, for example, Monaghan, 1999; Wegerif & Mercer, 1997).

In terms of outcomes of all these years of endeavour, there is quite a high degree of consensus amongst researchers about the educational implications of the results of this activity. The results of many years of research strongly suggest that when teachers make regular use of certain dialogue strategies, students' participation in class and their educational outcomes are likely to benefit (e.g. Brown & Palincsar, 1989; Chinn, Anderson, & Waggoner, 2001; Mercer & Littleton, 2007). Rojas-Drummond and Mercer (2004), comparing groups of Mexican teachers whose students achieved good learning outcomes in mathematics and literacy with those who did not, found that the former used question-and-answer sequences not just to test knowledge, but also to guide the development of students' understanding; the less successful teachers relied on more traditional forms of questioning. In a systematic review of 15 studies of talk in mathematics classrooms, Kyriacou and Issitt (2008) found better learning outcomes were associated with teachers using questions not just to elicit right answers, but to seek reasons and explanations.

However, like many other areas of educational research, critics can point to the absence of many large-scale studies, and even fewer using randomised control designs, to support these educational implications. Howe and Abedin (2013) have carried out a systematic review of four decades of research into classroom dialogue, in which they review 225 studies published between 1972 and 2011, and covering the full range of compulsory schooling. The scope of their review was quite broad, in that they used a definition of dialogue which is more or less synonymous with 'conversation', meaning 'all verbal exchanges where one individual addresses another individual or individuals and at least one addressed individual replies' (Howe & Abedin, 2013, p. 325), though they only included studies published in English. There was no restriction on the methods used, so both quantitative studies based on coded observations and qualitative studies based on the close analysis of transcripts were eligible, with rough equivalence between the two. Interestingly, they note a large increase in the number of studies published after 2001, with proportionally many more from non-English speaking countries (though published in English) in the last decade. These increases may be due to the increased accessibility of research electronically and the growing expectation of researchers internationally that they should publish in English. However, such factors do not explain why the UK, rather than the USA, became the dominant contributor to such research in that period, despite some major contributors to the field being located in the USA (for example Bloome, Carter, Christian, Otto, & Shuart-Faris, 2005; Dixon & Green, 2005; Heath, 2012; Wells & Ball, 2008). The majority of the studies in their review focused on teacher–student interaction, though some were concerned with students working in groups without a teacher (which is not the focus of our discussion here). Some of the research had a very specific focus, so that, as they note, 'In general, research concerned with student gender, attainment and ethnicity has focused upon which students respond to teachers and what form of feedback they receive' (p. 330).

They conclude that 'One key message is that much more is known about how classroom dialogue is organized than about whether certain modes of organization are more beneficial than others' (p. 325). They also comment:

> Looking at the dates when the relevant studies were published, it is likely that much the same conclusion would have been reached about the basic patterns [of participation in classroom talk] had our review taken place 20 years earlier, and it is of course interesting to see that so little has changed. It is also re-assuring to find results replicated. However, given an essentially static situation over 40 years . . . arguably the characterization of dialogic patterns should not be accorded high priority when it comes to future research.
>
> (Howe & Abedin, 2013, p. 345)

They also note continuing tensions between the use of quantitative and qualitative methods in the study of classroom talk, and suggest that this is limiting the success of establishing with any certainty whether some types of teacher–student interaction – such as those which are more 'dialogic' – can be associated with improved levels of participation amongst students or with better learning outcomes. They suggest that future research might best involve the design of large-scale studies which use quantitative methods to determine whether patterns of talk which qualitative analysis has suggested have particular educational value are indeed significantly associated with positive outcomes, and to such an extent that teachers can reasonably be expected to change their practices. This should not be taken as an argument for the superiority of large-scale, quasi-experimental quantitative studies over more intensive, smaller-scale, qualitative investigations, or for the simplistic application of 'medical models' of applied research to studies of teaching and learning (Goldacre, 2013). Rather, it is a plea for the value of 'mixed method' research to be taken more systematically into account in this field of study: a plea which we would wholeheartedly echo.

# Conclusions

In summary, educational researchers now know significantly more about the forms and functions of classroom talk and its influence on pupils' learning. Although not yet supported by the kind of evidence from large-scale, randomised control style studies which have been advocated recently by critics of educational research, the results have nevertheless identified some ways that teachers can most productively interact with students, and some ways that the value of any such interactions is commonly squandered. What is known now shapes, though probably still only to a limited extent, the initial and continuing training provided for teachers. However, some politicians (and their media supporters), at least in England, seem either completely unaware that any of this research has ever taken place, or determined to dismiss its evidence and educational implications. Thus the current English Secretary of State for Education (Michael Gove) has dismissed any implications from educational research that teachers should interact with students in anything but the most traditional ways as merely 'progressive', left-wing ideology. In his own words: 'almost any activity which is not direct instruction has been lauded by the so-called progressives while direct instruction has been held up to criticism and ridicule' (Gove, 2013). Nevertheless, an awareness of the importance of the quality of classroom interaction seems to have grown amongst those who are in direct contact with students, and who are best positioned to note the transformative power of a talk-focused approach to teaching and learning – the teachers (see for example Coultas, 2006; Dawes, 2004). In our own experience, as judged by requests for professional development sessions and participants' responses to such sessions, interest amongst teachers in understanding and improving the quality of classroom talk is higher than it has ever been, not only in Britain but internationally.

# Notes on contributors

Neil Mercer is Professor of Education at the University of Cambridge, where he is also Vice-President of the college Hughes Hall. He is a psychologist with particular interests in the development of children's language and reasoning abilities, and the role of the teacher in that development. His research with Rupert Wegerif and Lyn Dawes generated the *Thinking Together* approach to classroom teaching, and he has worked extensively with teachers, researchers and educational policy makers on improving talk for learning in schools. His most recent books are *Exploring Talk in School* (with Steve Hodgkinson), *Dialogue and the Development of Children's Thinking* and *Interthinking: putting talk to work* (both with Karen Littleton).

Lyn Dawes taught secondary Science before re-training to become a primary teacher. Now an Education Consultant, Lyn taught science and education at The University of Bedford, The University of Northampton and the University of Cambridge on PGCE and BA(QTS) courses. She has a special interest in 'Talk for Learning' and regularly provides practical workshops for education professionals in schools around the UK. These workshops are based on the Thinking Together approach to teaching and learning. Her most recent books are *Talking Points – discussion activities in the primary classroom*; and *Talking Points for Shakespeare Plays*.

# References

Alexander, R. (2001). *Culture and pedagogy: International comparisons in primary education*. Oxford: Blackwell.

Alexander, R. (2006). *Towards dialogic teaching*. York: Dialogos.

Amidon, E., & Hunter, E. (1967). *Improving teaching: The analysis of classroom verbal interaction*. New York, NY: Holt, Rinehart & Winston.

Banks, O. (1978). *The sociology of education: A bibliography*. London: Frances Pinter.

Barnes, D., Britton, J., & Rosen, H. (1969). *Language, the learner and the school*. Harmondsworth: Penguin.

Bernstein, B. (1975). *Class, codes and action. Volume 3: Towards a theory of educational transmissions*. London: Routledge & Kegan Paul.

Bloome, D., Carter, S., Christian, B., Otto, S., & Shuart-Faris, N. (2005). *Discourse analysis and the study of classroom language and literacy events: A microethnographic approach*. Mahwah, NJ: Erlbaum.

Britton, J. (1978). Vygotsky's contribution to pedagogical theory. *English in Education, 21*, 22–26.

Brown, A. L., & Palincsar, A. S. (1989). Guided, co-operative learning and individual knowledge acquisition. In L. B. Resnick (Ed.), *Knowing, learning and instruction* (pp. 393–453). Hillsdale, NJ: Lawrence Erlbaum.

Bullock Report. (1975). *A language for life: Report of the Committee of Enquiry appointed by the Secretary of State for Education and Science under the chairmanship of Sir Alan Bullock FBA*. London: HMSO.

Cazden, C. (Ed.). (1972). *The functions of language in the classroom*. New York, NY: Teachers College Press, Columbia University.

Chinn, C., Anderson, R., & Waggoner, M. (2001). Patterns of discourse in two kinds of literature discussion. *Reading Research Quarterly, 36*, 378–411.

Coultas, V. (2006). *Talking and learning in challenging classrooms: Strategies for behaviour management and talk-based tasks*. London: Routledge.

Cox, B. (1991). *Cox on Cox: An English curriculum for the 1990s*. London: Hodder & Stoughton.

Creese, A. (2008). Linguistic ethnography. In K. A. King & N. H. Hornberger (Eds.), *Encyclopedia of language and education, 2nd edn, Volume 10: Research methods in language and education* (pp.f language and educ, NY: Springer.

Dawes, L. (2004). Talk and learning in classroom science. *International Journal of Science Education, 26*, 667–695.

Dewey, J. (1933). *How we think: A restatement of the relation of reflective thinking to the educative process* (revised ed.). Boston, MA: D. C. Heath.

Dixon, C., & Green, J. (2005). Studying the discursive construction of texts in classrooms through interactional ethnography. In R. Beach, J. L. Green, M. Kamil, &

T. Shanahan (Eds.), *Multidisciplinary perspectives on literacy research* (pp. 349–390). Cresshill, NJ: Hampton Press.

Edwards, A. D., & Furlong, V. J. (1978). *The language of teaching*. London: Heinemann.

Edwards, A. D., & Mercer, N. (1987/2012). *Common knowledge: The development of understanding in the classroom*. London: Methuen/Routledge.

Edwards, A. D., & Westgate, D. (1994). *Investigating classroom talk* (2nd ed.). London: Falmer Press.

Flanders, N. A. (1970). *Analysing teacher behavior*. Reading, MA: Addison-Wesley.

Galton, M., Hargreaves, L., Comber, C., Pell, T., & Wall, D. (1999). *Inside the primary classroom: 20 years on*. London: Routledge.

Galton, M., Simon, B., & Croll, P. (1980). *Inside the primary classroom (the ORACLE Project)*. London: Routledge & Kegan Paul.

Garfinkel, H. (1974). The origins of the term "ethnomethodology". In R. Turner (Ed.), *Ethno-methodology: Selected readings* (pp. 15–18). Harmondsworth: Penguin.

Gee, J. P., & Green, J. (1998). Discourse analysis, learning and social practice: A methodological study. *Review of Research in Education*, 23, 119–169.

Goldacre, B. (2013). *Building evidence into education*. Retrieved from http://media.education.gov.uk/assets/files/pdf/b/ben%20goldacre%20paper.pdf

Gove, M. (2013, 5 September). *Michael Gove speaks about the importance of teaching*. Speech. Retrieved from www.gov.uk/government/speeches/michael-gove-speaks-about-the-importance-of-teaching

Green, J., & Wallat, C. (Eds.). (1981). *Ethnography and language in educational settings*. Norwood, NJ: Ablex.

Hardman, F., Smith, F., & Wall, K. (2003). "Interactive whole class teaching" in the National Literacy Strategy. *Cambridge Journal of Education*, 33, 197–215.

Hargreaves, D. (1984). Teachers' questions: Open, closed and half-open. *Educational Research*, 26, 46–52.

Heath, S. B. (1983). *Ways with words: Language, life and work in communities and classrooms*. Cambridge: Cambridge University Press.

Heath, S. B. (2012). *Words at work and play: Three decades of family and community life*. Cambridge: Cambridge University Press.

Howe, C., & Abedin, M. (2013). Classroom dialogue: A systematic review across four decades of research. *Cambridge Journal of Education*, 43, 325–356.

ILEA. (1984). *Improving secondary schools* (Report of the Committee on the Curriculum and Organization of Secondary Schools). London: Inner London Education Authority.

Kyriacou, C., & Issitt, J. (2008). *What characterizes effective teacher–pupil dialogue to promote conceptual understanding in mathematics lessons in England in Key Stages 2 and 3?* (EPPI-Centre Report no. 1604R). London: Social Science Research Unit, Institute of Education.

Mehan, H. (1979). *Learning lessons: Social organization in the classroom*. Cambridge, MA: Harvard University Press.

Mercer, N. (2008). The seeds of time: Why classroom dialogue needs a temporal analysis. *Journal of the Learning Sciences*, 17, 33–59.

Mercer, N. (2009). The analysis of classroom talk: Methods and methodologies. *British Journal of Educational Psychology*, 80, 1–14.

Mercer, N., & Edwards, D. (1981). Ground rules for mutual understanding: A social psychological approach to classroom knowledge. In N. Mercer (Ed.), *Language in school and community* (pp. 30–46). London: Edward Arnold.

Mercer, N., & Hodgkinson, S. (Eds.). (2008). *Exploring talk in school*. London: Sage.

Mercer, N., & Littleton, K. (2007). *Dialogue and the development of children's thinking.* London: Routledge.

Monaghan, F. (1999). Judging a word by the company it keeps: The use of concordancing software to explore aspects of the mathematics register. *Language and Education, 13,* 59–70.

Mortimer, E. F., & Scott, P. H. (2003). *Meaning making in science classrooms.* Milton Keynes: Open University Press.

Myhill, D. A., Jones, S., & Hopper, R. (2005). *Talking, listening, learning: Effective talk in the primary classroom.* Milton Keynes: Open University Press.

Norman, K. (Ed.). (1992). *Thinking voices: The work of the National Oracy Project.* London: Hodder & Stoughton.

Nystrand, M. (1997). *Opening dialogue: Understanding the dynamics of language and learning in the English classroom.* New York, NY: Teachers College Press.

Nystrand, M., Wu, L., Gamorgan, A., Zeiser, S., & Long, D. (2003). Questions in time: Investigating the structure and dynamics of unfolding classroom discourse. *Discourse Processes, 35,* 135–198.

Rojas-Drummond, S., & Mercer, N. (2004). Scaffolding the development of effective collaboration and learning. *International Journal of Educational Research, 39,* 99–111.

Scott, P. H., & Asoko, H. (2006). Talk in science classrooms. In V. Wood-Robinson (Ed.), *ASE guide to secondary science education* (pp. 55–73). Hatfield: Association for Science Education (ASE).

Sinclair, J., & Coulthard, M. (1975). *Towards an analysis of discourse: The English used by teachers and pupils.* London: Oxford University Press.

Spindler, G. (1982). *Doing the ethnography of schooling: Educational anthropology in action.* New York, NY: Holt, Rinehart & Winston.

Stubbs, M. (1983). *Language, schools and classrooms.* London: Methuen.

Vygotsky, L. S. (1962). *Thought and language.* Cambridge, MA: MIT Press.

Wegerif, R., & Mercer, N. (1997). Using computer-based text analysis to integrate quantitative and qualitative methods in the investigation of collaborative learning. *Language and Education, 11,* 271–286.

Wells, G. (1978). Talking with children: The complementary roles of parents and teachers. *English in Education, 12,* 15–38.

Wells, G. (1999). *Dialogic inquiry: Toward a sociocultural practice and theory of education.* Cambridge: Cambridge University Press.

Wells, G., & Ball, T. (2008). Exploratory talk and dialogic inquiry. In N. Mercer & S. Hodgkinson (Eds.), *Exploring talk in schools* (pp. 167–184). London: Sage.

Wilkinson, A. (1970). The concept of oracy. *The English Journal, 59,* 71–77.

Wood, D. (1992). Teaching talk. In K. Norman (Ed.), *Thinking voices: The work of the National Oracy Project* (pp. 203–214). London: Hodder & Stoughton.

Ziechner, K. (1994). Research on teacher thinking and different views of reflective practice in teaching and teacher education. In I. Carlgren, G. Handal, & S. Vaage (Eds.), *Teachers' minds and actions: Research on teachers' thinking and practice* (pp. 9–27). London: Falmer Press.

*At both the Open University and the University of Cambridge I have been fortunate to have colleagues whose understanding of digital technology has enabled me to investigate its educational use in ways I could never have done alone. I mention some of those colleagues in the introduction to Chapter 12. This chapter sets out the historical trajectory of one strand of this research, and Sara, Paul and I draw some conclusions about its educational implications.*

# 16 Dialogue, thinking together and digital technology in the classroom

## Some educational implications of a continuing line of inquiry

*Mercer, N., Hennessy, S. & Warwick, P. (2017). Dialogue, thinking together and digital technology in the classroom: some educational implications of a continuing line of inquiry.* International Journal of Educational Research, *(Elsevier), http://dx.doi.org/10.1016/j.ijer.2017.08.007.*

## Abstract

This article describes a continuing programme of school-based applied research. The basis of this research, which originated in a project called 'Thinking Together', lies in the relationship between language and cognitive development postulated by sociocultural theory. The research has developed and tested methods for improving the quality of classroom interaction amongst teachers and students, looking for improved levels of collaboration, reasoning and academic attainment as the desirable outcomes. A key strand of this research concerns the use of digital technology for supporting classroom dialogue and students' emerging thinking over time. As we will explain, the outcomes of several research projects pursuing this line of inquiry have yielded positive results which have direct implications for classroom pedagogy and practice.

## 1. Introduction

This paper is founded on a line of applied educational research aimed at understanding and improving the quality of communication through spoken language in the classroom, and on developing children's use of language as a psychological and cultural tool for learning and problem solving. The origins of this 'Thinking Together' research have strong roots in educational traditions in the UK that go back to the 1960s (as described in Mercer & Dawes, 2014). The classroom pedagogy it developed involves promoting a type of talk considered to be effective for thinking and learning that was first described by Douglas Barnes in the 1970s and called 'Exploratory Talk' (Barnes, 1976, 2008; Mercer 1995, 2000). Within our own research we have defined Exploratory Talk as dialogue in which:

- everyone engages critically but constructively with each other's ideas;
- everyone offers the relevant information they have;

- everyone's ideas are treated as worthy of consideration;
- partners ask each other questions and answer them, ask for reasons and give them;
- members of the group try to reach agreement at each stage before progressing;
- to an observer of the group, reasoning is 'visible' in the talk.

(Littleton & Mercer, 2013, p. 16)

A very similar kind of productive dialogue is known as 'Accountable Talk' in the USA (Resnick, 1999; Wolf, Crosson, & Resnick, 2006).

Our work encompasses the mediating role of digital technologies in enabling and extending Exploratory Talk and the joint construction of knowledge in classrooms. It has developed in recent years to exploit a range of technology tools now commonly found in classrooms (primarily in the developed world). In particular, the research explores how classroom dialogue is supported by teachers and learners together creating and manipulating digital knowledge artefacts that constitute records of their collective activity (Hennessy, 2011). Ongoing work focuses on teachers' uses of technology to foster rich new, multimodal forms of classroom dialogue. This paper also outlines our approach to helping teachers to develop their own skills in using dialogue for teaching and learning, incorporating the use of digital tools and helping their students to become better at using talk to work collaboratively to learn and solve problems.

## 2. Thinking together

### 2.1. Principles of the Thinking Together approach

The Thinking Together approach is underpinned by an educational principle expounded by Vygotsky (1962, 1978); that an important way in which children learn to think individually is through first learning to reason with others. In Exploratory Talk participants pool ideas, opinions and information, and think aloud together to create new meanings, knowledge and understanding. Generating Exploratory Talk depends on the willingness of all participants to respect some basic behavioural norms, which we call 'ground rules' (Edwards & Mercer, 1987, 2013). Suitable ground rules for talk can be created and agreed by a teacher and class. They are then used when children talk and solve problems together. The aim is to ensure that children's repertoire includes the speech genre of Exploratory Talk (not, as some critics have mistakenly claimed, to devalue other habitual ways of talking; Lambirth, 2006; see Mercer & Littleton, 2007, Chapter 6 for more on this). As we will explain, collaborative learning (often, in contemporary classrooms, supported by digital technologies) is one context in which we have studied the use of Exploratory Talk. Each class can develop its own set of ground rules, but these are variations of the ground rules suggested by the developers of the approach. These are that:

- All relevant information is shared openly.
- Each group member should be actively encouraged to contribute to the discussion.
- Everyone should listen to others attentively.
- Each suggestion should be carefully considered.
- Group members are asked to provide reasons for ideas and opinions.
- Constructive challenges to ideas are accepted and a response is expected.
- Alternatives are discussed before a decision is taken.
- The group works together with the purpose of reaching agreement.
- The group, not the individual, takes responsibility for decisions made.

(Dawes, Mercer, & Wegerif, 2000)

For children, these rules can be expressed in simpler language. We suggest that group work in classrooms (and other settings) is often unproductive because participants are not using appropriate ground rules (Littleton & Mercer, 2013). Working closely with primary teachers, the original Thinking Together research team members (Dawes et al., 2000) produced a series of 'Talk Lessons' for teaching these ground rules and applying them within normal curriculum teaching and learning (Dawes, 2008; also see the programme website).[1] The Talk Lessons encourage teachers to model dialogue and create a 'community of enquiry' in their classrooms in which children are guided in their use of language as a tool for both individual reasoning and collaborative problem solving.

There have been several experimental implementations and evaluations of the Thinking Together approach in the UK. These are described in detail, with their outcomes, in several publications (Wegerif, Mercer, & Dawes, 1999; Mercer & Littleton, 2007; Mercer, 2000). In 1995, through the support of the British Council for a research link between a research team in the UK and a research team in the psychology faculty of UNAM in Mexico City, Thinking Together was also implemented as 'Learning Together' in Mexican state schools (Rojas-Drummond & Alatorre, 2004; Rojas-Drummond & Mercer, 2004).

## 2.2. The basis of the research in a sociocultural theory of education

From a sociocultural perspective, education and cognitive development are cultural processes; knowledge is not only possessed individually but also created by and shared amongst members of communities; and the ways that knowledge is created are shaped by cultural and historical factors. Support for this perspective comes from recent research which suggests that human intelligence is intrinsically social and communicative (Mercer, 2013). An important implication of a sociocultural perspective is that one is encouraged to look for causes of educational success, and failure, in the nature and quality of the social and communicative processes of education rather than simply in the intrinsic capability of individual students, the didactic presentational skills of individual teachers or the quality of the resources that have been used. This means that the quality of the spoken interactions between students and teachers, and amongst students, can be of crucial educational significance.

The foundations of sociocultural theory lie in the work of Vygotsky (1962, 1978), who argued that the acquisition and use of language transforms children's thinking. He described language as both a cultural tool (for the development and sharing of knowledge amongst members of a community or society) and a psychological tool (for structuring the processes and content of individual thought). He also proposed that there is a close relationship between these two kinds of use, which can be summed up in the claim that 'intermental' (social, interactional) activity forges some of the most important 'intramental' (individual, cognitive) capabilities, with children's involvement in joint activities generating new understandings and ways of thinking. This sociocultural theory not only links the social and the psychological in an account of cognitive development, but also provides a theoretical basis for the primacy of language as a cultural and cognitive – and hence educational – tool (Mercer & Howe, 2012).

This theoretical case for the prime role of language in cognitive development and learning has several strands. The first strand concerns the collective process of constructing knowledge (whether amongst students or between teacher and students). This process must, by its nature, involve induction into reasoned argument. Although the most obvious focus of education is on the teaching and learning of curriculum knowledge, it would be surprising to find many teachers who did not think that their students should be learning how to construct arguments to support any opinions, analyses, solutions or conclusions that they present. The aim here is of course not simply to justify one's own stance; Schwarz and Baker (2016, Chapter 5) point out that classroom learning through argumentation dialogue is concerned with changes in viewpoint. While arguments can sometimes be presented through other communicative modes (such as the use of mathematical notation, and by physical demonstration in science or music), language is essentially involved in all subjects. The situated learning which enables people to join communities of practice almost always has a linguistic dimension, even if this is not fully recognised in studies of such processes (Lave & Wenger, 1991).

## 2.3. The quality of talk and joint activity in classrooms

In its initial stages, our research was strongly influenced by classroom-based studies which suggested that group work was often unproductive because children often lacked a clear understanding of the purposes of group discussion activities and of how they might be carried out most effectively (for example, Galton & Williamson, 1992). One reason seemed to be that teachers rarely made their expectations for such activities explicit, perhaps assuming that this was self-evident to pupils (Edwards & Mercer, 1987, 2013). The need for teachers to provide some guidance became apparent. In one of the first systematic reviews of studies of group work in school, Galton and Williamson concluded: 'For successful collaboration to take place, pupils need to be taught how to collaborate so that they have a clear idea of what is expected of them' (Galton & Williamson, 1992, p. 43).

In our research we have worked with teachers to establish conditions which would maximise the educational value of group-based activities. Our investigations suggest that the following conditions are important:

(i)   all participants must need to talk to do the task, so their conversation is not merely an incidental accompaniment;
(ii)  activity should be designed to encourage co-operation, rather than competition, between partners.
(iii) partners should have a good, shared understanding of the point and purpose of the activity;
(iv)  partners should have some 'meta-awareness' of how talk can be used for sharing ideas and solving problems effectively.

## 3. Establishing a dialogic pedagogy in the classroom

Throughout this line of research, which stretches over more than 20 years, we have worked closely with teachers to implement the ideas described above and to evaluate them through a series of classroom-based projects aimed at establishing a dialogic teaching approach in classrooms. By 'dialogic pedagogy' and 'dialogic teaching' we essentially mean an approach to teaching that is predicated on the active, extended involvement of students as well as teachers in the spoken interaction of the classroom, so that teaching and learning becomes a collective endeavour in which knowledge and understanding are jointly constructed (rather than talk being used by teachers merely to transmit curriculum content and assess its acquisition by students). In defining dialogic pedagogy, we draw on the seminal work of other classroom researchers such as Brown and Palincsar (1989); Nystrand, Gamoran, Kachur, and Prendergast (1997); Wells (1999); Mortimer and Scott (2003); and Alexander (2008). In our view, this pedagogy not only requires a teacher to engage students in thoughtful teacher-led classroom discussions; it also requires students to engage in Exploratory Talk when they are working collaboratively in groups without a teacher. As students cannot be assumed, on the basis of their out-of-school experience, to be familiar with the kind of reasoned discussion represented by Exploratory Talk, part of implementing a dialogic pedagogy must involve ensuring that students know how to engage in that type of dialogue.

There has been some variation in how we have worked with teachers across specific projects, but in summary the procedure has been as follows. Researchers first engage in professional development sessions with teachers, in which the notions of Exploratory Talk and 'ground rules' are made explicit and discussed. Teachers then 'model' that kind of talk for students, and each class agrees their own 'customised' set of ground rules for how they will talk together in groups. The children then pursue the rest of the specially designed teacher-led programme over a period of no less than 10 weeks. Lessons have a consistent format, in which teacher-led sessions and group-based activities are integrated, and in which the content of activities is directly related to the study of curriculum subjects. Researchers make observations throughout this process, as well as taking pre- and post-involvement measures of children's capabilities in language use, reasoning and academic attainment. Central to our approach to working with teachers is making the theoretical underpinning of dialogic teaching explicit; it is not simply a case of imparting new techniques and rules, but of researchers working with teachers to jointly develop a deeper understanding of the teaching and learning process itself, as elaborated in the next section.

### 3.1. What is learned through dialogic teaching and learning?

Key researchers in the field (e.g. see the collections edited by Littleton & Howe, 2010; Mercer & Hodgkinson, 2008) converge on the view that the quality of educational dialogues is a key factor in academic attainment. Our own and others' research (reviewed by Mercer, 2008) indicates that dialogic teaching can increase children's capacity for dialogue and reflective thought as well as developing subject knowledge. A series of studies has shown that Exploratory Talk training stimulates the development of (individual and group) reasoning skills (Mercer, 2008; Wegerif et al., 1998; Wegerif et al., 1999) while also enabling attainment in science (Mercer, Dawes, Wegerif, & Sams, 2004) and mathematics (Mercer & Sams, 2006). Research carried out by our colleagues in Mexico has reported generalisable oracy and literacy gains through collaborative writing activities involving Exploratory Talk (Rojas-Drummond, Littleton, Hernandez, & Zuniga, 2010).

There has been some debate about whether being able to conduct effective dialogue is a valuable 'end in itself' and whether teaching dialogue skills might divert activity from teaching curriculum subjects. While it is certainly the case that teachers often feel under pressure of time to 'deliver the curriculum', we believe that there need be no conflict between curriculum learning and learning to think and learn together with others; they go hand in hand. As Phillipson and Wegerif (2016) put it:

> Being better at dialogue means learning how to ask better questions, how to listen better, hearing not only the words but also the implicit meanings, how to be open to new possibilities and new perspectives,

while of course learning how to think critically about new perspectives through comparing different points of view. More than all these specific skills . . . to be more dialogic means to be more open to learning.

(Phillipson & Wegerif, 2016, pp. 1–2)

This learning includes teachers as well as their students; teachers' understandings of the teacher-learner relationship itself may change as they begin to take a sociocultural perspective, use opportunities to generate more productive dialogue with their students, and provide students with guidance on how to think collectively. They can devise suitable activities to create spaces which open up dialogue (as described by Nystrand et al., 1997; Wegerif, 2010).

Having made the case above for language as a cultural tool for knowledge building and argumentation, we also need to consider the important role in learning played by other cultural tools prevalent in classrooms today, especially digital technologies. We have chosen two examples from our various studies in this area to illustrate the key role that technology use can play in supporting joint reasoning through the exploration and evaluation of different ideas.

### 3.2. Computer-based collaborative activity

We have created computer-based, literacy-related activities in which children can practise and develop their skills in talking and thinking together. One of the first was designed by a member of the original research team, Wegerif (see Wegerif, Mercer, & Dawes, 1998). It was a piece of software called 'Kate's Choice'. This offers children an interactive narrative with a moral education/citizenship focus, and which is designed to elicit Exploratory Talk. The narrative introduces a girl called Kate, whose best friend Robert tells her that he has stolen a box of chocolates from a shop. He says that they are for his mother who is in hospital. Robert begs Kate not to 'tell'. She agrees, but subsequent events make it difficult for her to decide whether this promise should be kept. At each stage, the children (working in groups of three) are asked to help Kate resolve her moral dilemma. One frame from Kate's Choice is shown as Figure 16.1. The phrase 'Talk together about what Kate should do' on the computer screen prompts the children to discuss the choices presented. For children who have been involved in the Thinking Together project, the words 'talk together' are expected to cue the use of the ground rules for Exploratory Talk established with their teacher.

The task stimulates talk about the conflict between personal morality (loyalty to a friend) and social morality (stealing is a crime), which children usually find engaging. At each of several stages in the narrative, the children are asked to consider the relevant information at their disposal, and the points of view of each of the characters involved, before coming to a decision and proposing what should happen next. So although the content is focused

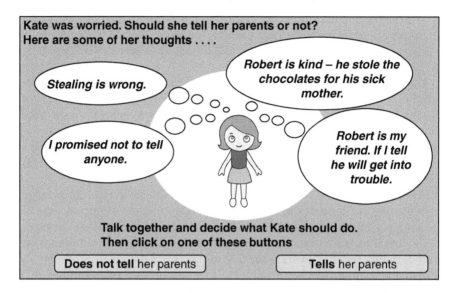

*Figure 16.1* The first decision point in Kate's Choice.

on citizenship issues, success in the task involves the effective use of various kinds of language skills. Taking a Vygotskian perspective, our hypothesis was if children participated in the task on the basis of appropriate 'ground rules' for talk, there would be good opportunities for them to practise these ways of talking and to develop their reasoning skills. The technology played a key role in structuring this activity, and it probably held their joint attention more effectively than would a shared written text. Also (unlike a human agent such as a teacher), the computer allowed the children whatever time they needed to generate a collective response to the questions raised at each decision point (Wegerif, Littleton, & Jones, 2003).

Our evaluation was not of the software in isolation, but rather as an element of the Thinking Together programme of activities. We wished to know whether this activity generated a productive, joint consideration of the narrative and the moral issues involved in it. We also wished to compare the way that children in the 'intervention' classes who had learned the 'ground rules' for Exploratory Talk carried out the activity compared with children in 'control' classes in similar schools (matched for aspects of social catchment) who were given the software without any special preparation for discussion. Mixed attainment and mixed gender groups of Year 5 children (age 10–11 years) in target and control classes were therefore observed and video recorded using Kate's Choice.

As first described in R. Wegerif et al. (1999), we were able to show that the talk of the target-class groups exhibited significantly more of the following features than did the talk of control groups. Children:

- asked each other task-focused questions;
- gave reasons for statements and challenges;
- considered more than one possible position before making a decision;
- elicited opinions from all in the group;
- reached agreement before acting.

In contrast, the talk of control groups showed more of the following features:

- the child controlling the mouse made unilateral decisions;
- the choice of the most dominant child was accepted without discussion;
- arbitrary decisions were made without debating the alternatives;
- children spent very little time at each decision point before moving on.

It seemed, therefore, that the Thinking Together programme had encouraged more effective use of language as a tool for comprehending a narrative text and reasoning about it – and that the Kate's Choice software provided a good framework for exercising those language skills. Target groups responded to the talk prompts provided by the software as an opportunity to engage with one another's ideas through Exploratory Talk. They also tended to spend much longer at each stage of the narrative as they considered the issues in more detail and made reasoned choices. The software was used by the children as a tool for thinking together, and not as a computer game in which speed of response is important.

Transcript 1 illustrates the talk of a group in an intervention class. It is taken from the first decision point encountered in the Kate's Choice narrative (Figure 16.1).

*Transcript 1: what do you think?*

GARY: Right we've got to talk about it. (*T looks at S*)
TRISH: What do you think? (*T points at G*)
SUE: What do you think?
GARY: I think even though he is her friend then um she shouldn't tell of him because um well she should tell of him um because was, was, if he's stealing it's not worth having a friend that steals is it?
TRISH: No.
SUE: Why do you think that?
TRISH: We said why.
I think that one as well do you? (*T points to the screen and looks at S*)
GARY: I think she should tell her parents. Do you? (*G looks at S*)
TRISH: I think I'm I think even though he is her friend because he's stealing she should still tell her parents and her parents might give her the money and she might be able to go to the shop and give them the money.

SUE:    I think um . . .
GARY:   . . . but then she's paying for the thing she stole so I think he should
get the money anyway. He should have his . . .
SUE:    I think that he should go and tell his mother.
GARY:   . . . own money Mum
TRISH:  Even though she has promised?
SUE:    Because he's well you shouldn't break a promise really should you?
GARY:   What's it worth having a friend if he's going to steal?
TRISH:  If he steals If you know he's stolen if she don't tell her parents then
he will be getting away with it (*T looking at S*)
GARY:   It's not worth having a friend that steals is it?
(*3 s pause*)
SUE:    OK then (*S puts hand on mouse*).
TRISH:  Ain't worth it is it?
SUE:    Tells her parents.
SUE:    (*clicks mouse*)
GARY:   Yeah go on.
(*Total time: 109 s*)

In this sequence, we can see the children exemplifying several key features of Exploratory Talk (as defined in the Introduction to this article). They all offer relevant information. They ask each other questions to elicit their views ('What do you think?') and request and offer reasons to support them ('Why do you think that?' 'I think even though he is her friend because he's stealing she should still tell her parents . . .'). They engage critically and constructively with each other's ideas. They appear to consider alternatives carefully before taking a shared decision. They can be seen to be implementing their agreed ground rules for talk. This is not perfect Exploratory Talk; few extra reasons are given in support of the initial position taken by Gary, and it is hard to tell if Sue is persuaded by the reasoning or merely acquiesces to the strength of the majority view. But certainly, to an observer, reasoning is visible in the talk.

## 4. Dialogue mediated by digital artefacts

As the research has proceeded, our theoretical perspective has been developed to foreground the role of artefacts in mediating dialogue (Hennessy, 2011). This is based on the notion that 'we think with and through artefacts' (Säljö, 1995, p. 91) that constitute mediational means (Wertsch, 1998) with particular affordances (Gibson, 1979) and constraints. In other words, they can facilitate or inhibit certain patterns of action. Using technology with a dialogic intention thus opens up new kinds of opportunities for learners and teachers publicly to share, explain, justify, critique and reformulate ideas – using language and other symbolic representations. Much of our work has centred on the use of the Interactive Whiteboard (IWB)[2] in whole class or group contexts (e.g. Gillen, Littleton, Twiner, Staarman, & Mercer, 2008; Hennessy, 2014; Mercer, Hennessy, & Warwick, 2010; Mercer, Warwick, Kershner, & Kleine Staarman, 2010). Our findings indicate that new dialogues can indeed centre and evolve around digital artefacts: provisional knowledge objects jointly created by teachers and learners. For example, in a study of primary school students working together on science tasks at the IWB (Warwick, Mercer, Kershner, & Staarman, 2010; Kershner, Mercer, Warwick, & Kleine Staarman, 2010), it became clear that the creation of a dialogic space for sharing ideas and co-constructing knowledge was possible with relatively simple uses of this complex technology.

In a class of students aged 8–9 (UK Year 4), the task set was to sort objects on the IWB into two categories – solid and liquid. The students used both the IWB and a set of physical objects to reason together about their choices, using the artefacts as 'referential anchors' (Arvaja, Häkkinen, & Kankaanranta, 2008, p. 270) for their discussions. The moveable nature of the objects on the screen meant that they could be provisionally placed as solids or liquids. As group assent was crucial to the final placing of an object (for example, wood in the solids category), this provisional placing enabled reasoning to be articulated without final commitment. Such provisional placing would have been less possible if, for example, they were gluing pictures of objects together on paper.

However, perhaps the most interesting event in this lesson, from a dialogic perspective, was when the teacher introduced air as an 'object' on the screen. The discussion in Transcript 2 ensued.

*Transcript 2: is air a liquid or a solid?*

S3: Air.
S2: Air? Air should go in liquids.
S3: Why, it's not a liquid?
S1: No it's solid.
S3: It's solid.
S2: No it's air, you can do that to it couldn't you?
S3: Yeah but you can't drink it or something like that, can you?
S1: I drank um air, in my water, you swallow air.
S3: You can't swim in it, can you?
S2: Yeah but it's like.
S1: You can swim with alcohol, but you can't swim with air. You can swim with air, you can, you can swim in air because in a swimming pool there's loads of air.
S2: The thing is air, it's like water yeah but, (*inaudible*) like you could. It's not like a brick, a solid, you couldn't; it's like, if you threw it against the floor (*inaudible*), you can't get it, could you? You can trap it, but then it just floats away.
S3: How you know it floats?

S1:    Um I think in between them.
S2:    Can't do that, you can't do that.
       (*Students place air in between solids and liquids on the IWB*)
S3:    Who votes it should be solid?
S2:    It's in between them.
S3:    Who votes it should be solid?
       (*Unable to hear students' conversation due to background noise*)
T:     Hello, where's that one gone? What's that one doing?
S3:    In between them two.
T:     It's between the two is it?
S1:    Yeah.
T:     Why?
S1:    Because (*inaudible*)
T:     It's not a solid or a liquid?
S3:    No.
T:     So you think it's a bit of a solid or a bit of a liquid? Or you think noth-
       ing like either?
S3:    Nothing like either.
T:     So should it go in the middle?
S2:    No.
T:     So you've decided it's nothing like either of them?
S2:    Yeah.

The dialogue shows many of the features of Exploratory Talk. The students asked each other task-focused questions (e.g. S3: 'why, it's not a solid?'), gave reasons for statements (e.g. S2: sequence ending in 'You can trap it, then it just floats away') and considered more than one possible position before making a decision (the discussion about positioning). They elicited opinions from all in the group and reached agreement, with the teacher's help, before acting. In this kind of situation, van de Sande and Greeno suggest that:

> Someone or something has to be positioned as a source of information for constructing an understanding that at least one of the participants lacks, and another participant (or other participants) need(s) to engage in an effort to understand the information that can be constructed by interpreting the source in a way that results in mutual understanding. We refer to the participant(s) whose positioning involves making this effort as the listener, and the individual(s) or other system that provides information as the source.
>
> (van de Sande & Greeno, 2012, p. 5)

In the dialogic space of interaction at the IWB, control of the screen object was crucial to the 'positional framing' of each student as listener or source. A screen shot (Figure 16.2) illustrates that 'command' of the screen object casts a student into the role of source, open to questions from the listeners.

*Figure 16.2* Students as source and listeners in the dialogic space at the IWB.

The example further illustrates how the technology served this process by helping to make different perspectives explicit to the group and the teacher, as the children in turn repositioned the digital objects. Indeed, it afforded a visual representation of the current state of the children's thinking, embodying the decision making, interpretations and progress made to date, such that the teacher was immediately able to question the group about their 'in-between' positioning of air.

Technologies such as a computer or IWB can additionally allow co-constructed artefacts (including annotations during a lesson on images or texts, or positioning of digital objects as above) to be saved, revisited, modified or repurposed at a later time. Thus, these artefacts render both learning histories and trajectories more visible, which can help dialogues progress over time. We have examples from other studies of where this affordance is productively exploited by a teacher – along with the visibility of the large IWB screen – to facilitate and chart the cumulative progress of whole class discussion, both within and across lessons (Hennessy, 2011). The teacher's role in purposefully linking talk with other modalities such as visual representations on an IWB is pivotal in supporting knowledge building (Gillen et al., 2008). In one study, for instance, we observed how a teacher engaged a secondary English class in annotating, highlighting and progressively transforming a poetry text and series of related images in real time during discussion – to explore a character's feelings, the significance of an evocative image for the poem's persona, and the ways in which the image and poem, plus other poems they had studied, were perceived to reflect today's society (Gillen et al., 2008).

How students are able to engage in such interaction, in semi-autonomous groups or as a whole class, while working with a digital mediating tool, is one of our central concerns. The first clue is usually the task. For example, in the work on solids and liquids illustrated above, though the task was not necessarily 'problem solving' in the manner characterised in some studies of the interaction between digital technologies and dialogue (e.g. Yoon, Ho, & Hedberg, 2005), it provided scope for reasoning and argumentation (Simon, Erduran, & Osborne, 2006; Simon, Johnson, Cavell, & Parsons, 2012). A crucial factor was that the teacher had a dialogic intention for the task, meaning that rather than considering the technology only as a tool for teaching science, he also used it as a tool for mediating dialogue (Coffin, Littleton, Whitelock, & Twiner, 2010; Jewitt, Moss, & Cardini, 2007; Twiner, Coffin, Littleton, & Whitelock, 2010).

Without developing a 'dialogic classroom', dialogic intentions for a task can fall very flat (Barron, 2003). Our research suggested a model (Figure 16.3) for productive interaction involving interactive technologies that foregrounds the teacher's role in constructing a dialogic ethos, modelling dialogic practices and encouraging student agency.

As Michaels and O'Connor (2012) also conclude, for this kind of activity to be productive, teachers need to encourage their students to:

- share, expand upon and develop their own thinking (by giving students time to think, providing opportunities for them to say more or encouraging them to re-phrase);
- listen carefully to the views of others (by asking other students to re-phrase or repeat the statements of others);
- deepen their own reasoning (by encouraging students to give reasons for their views, or provide a counter-example to the views of others);
- think with others (by asking whether students agree or disagree, whether they can add to what has been said or whether they can explain what someone else has said).

These procedures, central to the implementation of a Thinking Together approach in classrooms (Dawes, 2010), help to re-frame the classroom participation structures (Hennessy, Deaney, Ruthven, & Winterbottom, 2007; Rogoff, 1995), orienting students towards the dialogic in their group's work. The teacher in our example above not only generated appropriate

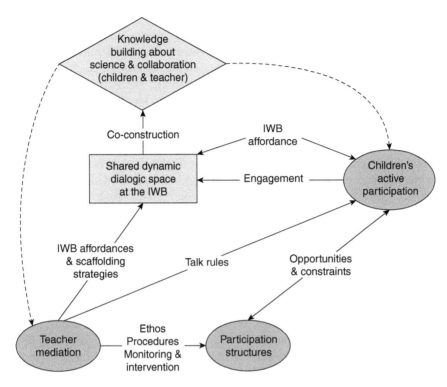

*Figure 16.3* Teacher mediation of student interaction with digital technology in a dialogic classroom space (from Warwick et al., 2010).

'ground rules' for discussion with his class, but also reminded them in each lesson of his expectations about how they should talk together; and he expected them to make joint assessments of how well they had collaborated.

## 5. Supporting teachers through targeted professional development for technology-mediated dialogue

The interactions in our examples above are not typical of group talk in schools; Exploratory Talk is a rare occurrence in classroom life, as is teaching of a very 'dialogic' kind, or the explicit teaching of talk skills. In their seminal review, Howe and Abedin (2013, p. 341) suggest that one reason why this is so is the tension a teacher may feel between allowing students' unfettered exploration of ideas and the need for them to learn the 'right answers', and so extended group discussion is not encouraged. Another reason may be that teachers of subjects other than language and literacy do not feel that teaching talk skills is within their remit. A third may be that researchers have not been effective in convincing teachers of the value of a

pedagogy which foregrounds ways of using language to construct knowledge and understanding.

The research literature reveals that targeted interventions with teachers
have inconsistent outcomes; top-down programmes that offer little practical
guidance and fail to develop a clear understanding of dialogic teaching inevitably do not shift traditional patterns of classroom interaction (e.g. Smith,
Hardman, Wall, & Mroz, 2004). In our own recent study, a baseline survey
indicated that only 19% of participating teachers initially demonstrated a
medium or strong understanding of dialogic teaching, even though some
had been involved in teacher professional development (TPD) sessions with
this focus (Hennessy, Dragovic, & Warwick, 2017). (Teachers who claimed
to understand the distinction between classroom talk and dialogue were
asked to describe what they meant by 'dialogue'; classification of 'strong'
understanding required explicit statements indicating that dialogue involves
building on others' responses and exploring different perspectives or ideas
rather than just 'discussion'.) It seems that new approaches to initial and
in-service teacher education need to be developed if more dialogic practices are ever to become widespread. And there is a further consideration. In
this technological age, the teacher's pedagogical stance and understanding
of how best to exploit the affordances of digital technologies are critical
in determining productive use of these tools in teaching and learning. Yet
TPD is often focused primarily on developing technology skills, and the
inadequacies of this focus are now well documented (e.g. Carlson & Gadio,
2002; Hennessy & London, 2013). Consequently, interactive use of even
ubiquitous technologies is uncommon; even 'dialogic' teachers may not use
technology effectively to support dialogue.

Our own approach to helping teachers use digital technology to mediate
dialogue is founded on the Thinking Together approach (introduced in Section 3), and more recently has drawn on models of effective TPD which have
been found to be effective. These encourage critical reflection, collaborative
learning with peers, observation and feedback; they are based on teacher
ownership and leadership; they include concrete, experiential workshop
tasks and iterative classroom trialling; and they focus on immediate teaching needs and support problem solving (Cordingley, Bell, Rundell, & Evans,
2003; Dudley, 2013; Twining, Raffaghelli, Albion, & Knezek, 2013; Wells,
2007, 2014). Such models offer fertile opportunities to encourage, extend
and structure professional dialogue, and to sustain TPD over time, enabling
teachers to embed practice (Cordingley et al., 2003; Hennessy & London,
2013). The starting point in the process depends on the elicitation of teachers' prior knowledge and experience of dialogic approaches and interactive
technology use; TPD needs to be adapted accordingly.

An important feature of our TPD programmes for technology contexts is
that they draw on research-based multimedia resources we have created to
stimulate discussion, reflection and inquiry. In particular, video footage of
teachers using technology interactively (from our previous projects) allows

viewers to experience and freely critique a wider range of practices, so that alternative pedagogical strategies can be compared and contrasted (Sherin, 2007). Workshops then involve teachers in designing and trialling new dialogic teaching approaches that in turn become the focus of peer discussion. We believe that it is important that teachers experience a dialogic approach to their own professional learning in workshops or through the use of support materials for school-based group study and action (Hennessy et al., 2017). As mentioned briefly above, our approach makes theory explicit to teachers and encourages them to consider its relationship to their own current practices. In some of our research, we have asked teachers to act as co-researchers with us, and to grapple with – and if necessary reformulate – the theory itself. The aim is to develop 'intermediate theory' (Hennessy, 2014): theory that bridges scholarly theory and practitioner knowledge related to a specific setting. Snow (2015, p. 461) likewise notes the virtues of studies where there is 'a commitment to the notion of two sources of knowledge (research and practice). Though the two sources might generate somewhat different types of knowledge, both types are judged to be of equal value and importance to improving educational outcomes.' In our studies, teachers review and comment on videos of their own lessons or those of their close colleagues, and the university researchers do the same, independently selecting 'critical episodes' and offering analytic commentary using our own professional lenses, and drawing on theory as appropriate. Ultimately, joint reflexive critique of the literature and insights emerging from the data by each small team of two to four 'co-researchers' culminates in democratically negotiated, enriched understandings of concepts from sociocultural theory, framed in accessible language to render them suitable for wider use and adaptation. A number of small studies of this kind are reported by Hennessy (2014).

One such research study involved collaborating with three teachers (who had already adopted dialogic practices) to agree on suitable definitions of dialogue and dialogic pedagogy, and develop new practices for supporting whole class dialogue through IWB use (Hennessy, Warwick, & Mercer, 2011). This culminated in a theoretically informed, practical model which was encapsulated in a published resource for school-based TPD (Hennessy, Warwick, Brown, Rawlins, & Neale, 2014), co-authored by the participating teachers. The book includes their own case stories and an intermediate theory tool for teachers' use in auditing their own practices. It is accompanied by open, online multimedia resources,[3] including a digital resource bank of annotated screen shots, video exemplars of dialogic classroom practice and IWB flipchart templates for creating activities. The materials are designed for use across phases (primary, middle and secondary schools) and subject areas. They are grounded in the Thinking Together approach and relevant sociocultural theory, and they also illustrate some powerful ways in which teaching can exploit digital technology to serve dialogic pedagogy and improve the quality and quantity of student participation.

In our most recent study we co-developed professional development workshops with teachers, which involved video-stimulated discussions of practices, use of the above-mentioned resource book and online resource bank, and testing the adapted and newly developed IWB-based teaching materials in lessons in between the workshops. Two workshops were conducted in each of five settings, involving a total of 80 teachers from 15 schools (Hennessy et al., 2017). Our research data derived from surveys, interviews, teachers' posters created during workshops, a portfolio of dialogic classroom practices mediated by the IWB (uploaded to the project website for other practitioners to use),[4] and follow-up lesson observations. This workshop model, with its close connection to daily classroom practice, proved successful – within only a few weeks – in helping teachers to develop their understandings of classroom dialogue and devise new approaches for supporting it. The research additionally confirmed the potential of the IWB as a powerful multimodal tool and teachers' capability for harnessing its distinctive affordances to create dialogic spaces. Teachers devised IWB-supported activities that built in opportunities for exploring and building on others' ideas, using the technology – and open-ended questioning – to develop new opportunities for individual and collective reasoning (Hennessy, 2011).

Teachers were keen to continue developing their practice in new directions after the research project had ended, including wider school development activities. The scope of the impact project was curtailed by limited funding, however, and actual sustainability over the long term is unknown. This is likewise the case with many other dialogic teaching TPD interventions; changes in practice are often observed, but whether these become embedded over the longer term is rarely investigated. Deep changes to practice are a long-term goal and often seem to require many hours/days of TPD (Osborne, 2015), even with teacher researchers engaged in a project.

This brings us to a key question regarding the translation of research into practice. Even if targeted interventions are found to be successful in improving educational practice, how can they be rolled out across a larger population of schools in a context of limited funding and consequent lack of sustained involvement from the initiators? Whilst noting that 'it is not just in relation to dialogic pedagogies that scalability issues are massive obstacles to the widespread implementation of good ideas', Howe and Mercer (2017, p. 90) point to a clear 'tension between promise and challenge' (Howe & Mercer, 2017, p. 83) that characterises a 'widening impact dilemma' facing many research-based initiatives on dialogic teaching and learning in schools. Whilst teachers are a profession open to change and innovation, both large- and small-scale contexts set a tone that determines their focus. Thus, in the UK, the downgrading of the importance of spoken language in a revision of subject requirements across the National Curriculum (DfE, 2013) was a clear indicator to school managements of where to, and where not to, focus their efforts in school development. Luckily, many individual school, school cluster and district managements are not led simply by prevailing (and transient) policy; and from our own work on the dialogic use of IWBs it seems clear that management support is crucial for sustaining innovation (Flitton & Warwick, 2012; Warwick, Hennessy, & Mercer, 2011). Such support includes buy-in from the school leadership team, especially the principal/head teacher; but it also means that dedicated time is found for pedagogy-focused teacher meetings to take place. In one study we were able to investigate the sustainability of an extensive multimedia TPD programme we developed ('OER4Schools')[5] to foster interactive teaching (including whole class and group dialogue) in primary schools in Zambia. Following the success of a peer-facilitated weekly workshop programme with 12 teachers in three grades over one school year, the management decided to roll out the programme to the whole school (35 teachers) as they hoped it would raise attainment levels. We revisited the school 18 months later, after the programme had been running independently of any input from the research team. Despite the many, complex challenges of this very low-resourced context, over half of the earlier participants were found to have maintained and developed their interactive teaching strategies and focus on pupil learning progress; recent joiners developed similarly. New peer facilitators had come on board. Traditional roles of teachers and pupils were shifting and a new classroom culture was emerging. One of the key facilitating factors identified was the national programme for statutory teacher group meetings scheduled outside lesson time, but within the working day (Haßler, Hennessy & Hofmann, 2018).

In thinking beyond the school setting, Snow (2015, p. 463) observes that 'time and effort need to be invested in nurturing relationships with districts and schools that are being buffeted by numerous demands and an accumulation of initiatives.' Support from school cluster, regional or district groups might be garnered through allying a focus on dialogue with systematic approaches to TPD. For example, recent work by Dudley and others (Dudley, 2013) has demonstrated how Lesson Study may provide a vehicle for teacher consideration of pedagogical change linked to pupil outcomes, and where this is embraced across schools it may be a powerful mechanism for change (Warwick, Vrikki, Vermunt, & Mercer, 2016). Again, Snow (2015, p. 463) refers to a colleague's powerful analogy in writing of 'the need to design not just the working end of the tool (the head of the hammer or clamp on the spanner) but also the handle – the end the user has to grasp in order to make use of the tool.' If the 'working end' is a dialogic classroom pedagogy, then the handle in this case is the range of enabling mechanisms; crucial to these are sustainable TPD structures and school management support. And we would further argue that linking digital technologies, as mediating tools, to a dialogic pedagogy strengthens the claims for contemporary relevance for dialogue research linked to TPD. The growing interest internationally in the development of '21st century skills'[6] in collaboration, communication and critical thinking provides a contemporary imperative to the work of researchers in dialogue.

## 6. Current research and future directions

A recent collaboration with our Mexican colleagues[7] produced the Cam-UNAM Scheme for Educational Dialogue Analysis (SEDA), and a specialised sub-scheme for teachers has since been developed by Hennessy and colleagues: Teacher-SEDA (T-SEDA). This tool supports teachers' systematic inquiry into dialogic practice in their own (or peers') classrooms; a resource pack contains tools and templates for observation and manageable coding of classroom interaction, a set of reliable dialogue categories with illustrative examples, guidelines for teachers to conduct cycles of reflective inquiry, and worked examples. It is currently being piloted by practitioners in several countries and we welcome the involvement of others.

There is growing evidence that dialogic teaching approaches can foster development of substantive curriculum knowledge. However, the evidence remains patchy and mainly small-scale, and such evidence is increasingly important to schools weighed down by accountability measures. Hence we are currently conducting an ESRC-funded study that explores the natural variation between primary school teachers in terms of how they and their students use spoken language (led by Christine Howe).[8] We are investigating whether teaching which is more 'dialogic' (determined through systematically coding lesson video recordings using an adapted version of SEDA) is related to children's learning gains on standardised tests in mathematics and English literacy, and also to scientific reasoning and general reasoning. The sample comprises 75 teachers, which allows us to conduct regression-style analyses to answer the question of whether classroom dialogue does in fact make a difference for subject learning. Many of the lessons employed technology, of course, so we will be able to explore its role in mediating dialogue using this wider dataset. If a relationship does emerge, our subsequent analyses of which dialogic moves are correlated with higher attainment should be of practical educational value.

The uses of digital technology that support a dialogic pedagogy need more exploration; research in this area is in its infancy, despite some encouraging results (e.g. Kerawalla, Petrou, & Scanlon, 2013). Many schools are now introducing tablets and other similar mobile devices to support teaching and learning; in our recent study participating schools which had invested in these devices were encouraged to apply new dialogic approaches to their use, and did so with considerable success. In the DiDiAC project,[9] led by one of the current authors (Warwick) in co-operation with Rasmussen and colleagues at the University of Oslo, the interactional relationship between spoken dialogue and a micro-blogging tool[10] is being investigated. This builds upon previous research on the editable, manipulable, provisional and temporal nature of screen objects – in this case texts – and the potentially transformative impact that their use may have on classroom dialogue and learning (Rasmussen & Hagen, 2015). The use of the micro-blogging tool is supported by web-based materials that link its use to classroom dialogue.

Overall, then, our research and that of others leads us to the following conclusions. It is clear that teachers can enable their students to develop their use of language as a cultural and psychological tool for reasoning and learning, though this rarely happens in schools today, in any country. While evidence from large-scale empirical projects is not yet available, the research evidence that does exist supports the view that this not only promotes the development of valuable communication skills, but also improves educational attainment in curriculum subjects. That evidence also encourages the view that this is best achieved through the use of a 'dialogic' pedagogy, which requires an awareness by both teachers and students of how language can best be used to enable collective thinking, learning and problem solving. Research indicates that digital technology can provide valuable support for the implementation of such a dialogic pedagogy; but the technology must be used with a dialogic intention, in the context of activities which are well designed to promote collective thinking. It is the pedagogy that is paramount, not the technology. Experience from interventional, school-based studies should also encourage researchers to maintain a realistic perspective regards the translation of research findings into changes in classroom practice. For any new procedures or practices regarding classroom talk or digital technology to be welcomed and adopted by teachers, evidence for the value of any innovations in helping teachers achieve their professional goals, and addressing problems they perceive as important, must be made clear – as must practical procedures for achieving a more interactive, dialogic climate in the classroom.

## Acknowledgements

We are most grateful to the teachers and the schools who participated in our studies over the years. The work was supported by the UK Economic and Social Research Council (ESRC) through a series of projects, including Interactive Whiteboards and Classroom Pedagogy (Mercer et al., 2004–2005, ref. RES-000-22-1269) Interactive Whiteboards and Collaborative Pupil Learning in Primary Science (Mercer, Warwick, & Kershner, 2007–2009, ref. RES-000-22-2556); IWBs and Dialogic Teaching, part of a Research Fellowship programme by Hennessy (2007–2010, ref. RES-063-27-0081) in conjunction with Mercer and Warwick; and a related ESRC Impact Acceleration Pilot Programme grant for the TPD impact study (Hennessy & Warwick, 2014: http://dialogueiwb.educ.cam.ac.uk/ evaluate/).

## Notes

1 thinkingtogether.educ.cam.ac.uk.
2 This particular technology is highly prevalent in UK classrooms and has now reached near saturation point.
3 http//tinyurl/OUPIWB.

4 http://dialogueiwb.educ.cam.ac.uk/evaluate/.
5 www.oer4schools.org.
6 See for example https://k12.thoughtfullearning.com/FAQ/what-are-21st-century-skills.
7 The three-year British Academy funded project (2013–2015) "A tool for ana-lysing dialogic interactions in classrooms" (http://tinyurl.com/BAdialogue) was conducted in partnership with the National Autonomous University of Mexico.
8 www.educ.cam.ac.uk/research/projects/classroomdialogue/.
9 www.educ.cam.ac.uk/research/projects/didiac/.
10 www.talkwall.net.

# References

Alexander, R. (2008). Culture, dialogue and learning: Notes on an emerging peda-gogy. In N. Mercer & S. Hodgkinson (Eds.), *Exploring talk in schools* (pp. 91–114). London: Sage.

Arvaja, M., Häkkinen, P., & Kankaanranta, M. (2008). Collaborative learning and computer-supported collaborative learning environments. In J. Voogt & G. Knezek (Eds.), *International handbook of information technology in primary and second-ary education* (pp. 267–279). Boston, MA: Springer.

Barnes, D. (1976). *From communication to curriculum*. Harmondsworth: Penguin Books.

Barnes, D. (2008). Exploratory talk for learning. In N. Mercer & S. Hodgkinson (Eds.), *Exploring talk in school* (pp. 1–15). London: Sage.

Barron, B. (2003). When smart groups fail. *Journal of the Learning Sciences, 12*(3), 307–359.

Brown, A. L., & Palincsar, A. S. (1989). Guided, co-operative learning and individual knowledge acquisition. In L. B. Resnick (Ed.), *Knowing, learning and instruction* (pp. 393–453). Hillsdale, NJ: Lawrence Erlbaum.

Carlson, S., & Gadio, C. T. (2002). Teacher professional development in the use of educational technology. In W. D. Haddad & A. Draxler (Eds.), *Technologies for education* (pp. 118–133). Paris and Washington, DC: UNESCO/AED.

Coffin, C., Littleton, K., Whitelock, D., & Twiner, A. (2010). Multimodality, orches-tration and participation in the context of classroom use of the interactive white-board: A discussion. *Technology, Pedagogy and Education, 19*(2), 211–223.

Cordingley, P., Bell, M., Rundell, B., & Evans, D. (2003). *The impact of collaborative CPD on classroom teaching and learning research evidence in education library. Evidence for policy and practice information and co-ordinating centre (EPPI-centre): Social science research unit, institute of education*. London: University of London.

Dawes, L. (2008). *The essential speaking and listening: Talk for learning at KS2*. London: Routledge.

Dawes, L. (2010). *Creating a speaking and listening classroom: Integrating talk for learning at key stage 2*. London: Routledge.

Dawes, L., Mercer, N., & Wegerif, R. (2000). *Thinking together: Activities for teach-ers and children at key stage 2*. Birmingham: Questions Publishing Co.

DfE. (2013). Department for Education. *English programmes of study: Key stage 1 and 2: National curriculum in England*. London: HMSO.

Dudley, P. (2013). Teacher learning in Lesson Study: What interaction-level dis-course analysis revealed about how teachers utilised imagination, tacit knowledge of teaching and fresh evidence of pupils learning, to develop practice knowledge and so enhance their pupils' learning. *Teaching and Teacher Education, 34*(1), 107–121.

Edwards, D., & Mercer, N. (1987). *Common knowledge: The development of understanding in the classroom*. London: Routledge.

Edwards, D., & Mercer, N. (2013). *Common knowledge: The development of understanding in the classroom*. London: Routledge 1987.

Flitton, L., & Warwick, P. (2012). From classroom analysis to whole-school professional development: Promoting talk as a tool for learning across school departments. *Professional Development in Education, 39*(1), 1–23.

Futuresource Consulting. (2015). *Interactive displays quarterly insight: State of the market report, quarter*. Dunstable, Bedfordshire: Futuresource.

Galton, M., & Williamson, J. (1992). *Group work in the primary classroom*. London: Routledge.

Gibson, J. J. (1979). *The ecological approach to visual perception*. Boston, MA: Houghton Mifflin.

Gillen, J., Littleton, K., Twiner, A., Staarman, J. K., & Mercer, N. (2008). Using the interactive whiteboard to resource continuity and support multimodal teaching in a primary science classroom. *Journal of Computer Assisted Learning, 24*(4), 348–358.

Haßler, B., Hennessy, S., & Hofmann, R. (2018). Sustaining and scaling up pedagogic innovation in sub-Saharan Africa: Grounded insights for teacher professional development. *Journal of Learning for Development, 5*(1), 21–38.

Hennessy, S. (2011). The role of digital artefacts on the interactive whiteboard in supporting classroom dialogue. *Journal of Computer Assisted Learning, 27*(6), 463–489.

Hennessy, S. (2014). *Bridging between research and practice: Supporting professional development through collaborative studies of classroom teaching with interactive whiteboard technology*. Rotterdam: Sense Publishers.

Hennessy, S., Deaney, R., Ruthven, K., & Winterbottom, M. (2007). Pedagogical strategies for using the interactive whiteboard to foster learner participation in school science. Learning, Media and Technology. *Special Issue on Interactive Whiteboards, 32*(3), 283–301 [Special issue].

Hennessy, S., Dragovic, T., & Warwick, P. (2017). *A research-informed, school-based professional development workshop programme to promote dialogic teaching with interactive technologies*. *Professional Development in Education*. Advance Online Publication http://doi.org/10.1080/19415257.2016.1258653

Hennessy, S., & London, L. (2013). *Learning from international experiences with interactive whiteboards: The role of professional development in integrating the technology*. OECD Education Working Papers No. 89. Paris: OECD Publishing. Retrieved from http://tinyurl.com/Oecdiwbs

Hennessy, S., Warwick, P., Brown, L., Rawlins, D., & Neale, C. (Eds.). (2014). *Developing interactive teaching and learning using the interactive whiteboard: A resource for teachers*. Maidenhead: Open University Press.

Hennessy, S., Warwick, P., & Mercer, N. (2011). A dialogic inquiry approach to working with teachers in developing classroom dialogue. *Teachers College Record, 113*(9), 1906–1959.

Howe, C., & Abedin, M. (2013). Classroom dialogue: A systematic review across four decades of research. *Cambridge Journal of Education, 43*(3), 325–356.

Howe, C., & Mercer, N. (2017). Commentary on the papers. *Language and Education, 31*(1), 83–92.

Jewitt, C., Moss, G., & Cardini, A. (2007). Pace, interactivity and multimodality in teacher design of texts for interactive whiteboards in the secondary school classroom. *Learning Media and Technology, 32*(3), 303–317.

Kerawalla, L., Petrou, M., & Scanlon, E. (2013). Talk factory: Supporting "exploratory talk" around an interactive whiteboard in primary school science plenaries. *Technology, Pedagogy and Education, 22*(1), 89–102.

Kershner, R., Mercer, N., Warwick, P., & Kleine Staarman, J. (2010). Can the interactive whiteboard support young children's collaborative communication and thinking in classroom science activities? *Computer-Supported Collaborative Learning, 5*(4), 359–383.

Lambirth, A. (2006). Challenging the laws of talk: Ground rules, social reproduction and the curriculum. *The Curriculum Journal, 17*(1), 59–71.

Lave, J., & Wenger, E. (1991). *Situated learning: Legitimate peripheral participation.* Cambridge: Cambridge University Press.

Littleton, K., & Howe, C. (Eds.). (2010). *Educational dialogues: Understanding and promoting productive interaction.* London: Routledge.

Littleton, K., & Mercer, N. (2013). *Interthinking: Putting talk to work.* Abingdon: Routledge.

Mercer, N. (1995). *The guided construction of knowledge: Talk amongst teachers and learners.* Clevedon: Multilingual Matters.

Mercer, N. (2000). *Words and minds: How we use language to think together.* London: Routledge.

Mercer, N. (2008). Talk and the development of reasoning and understanding. *Human Development, 51*(1), 90–100.

Mercer, N. (2013). The social brain, language, and goal-directed collective thinking: A social conception of cognition and its implications for understanding how we think, teach, and learn. *Educational Psychologist, 48*(3), 148–168.

Mercer, N., & Dawes, L. (2014). The study of talk between teachers and students, from the 1970s until the 2010s. *Oxford Review of Education, 40*(4), 430–445.

Mercer, N., Dawes, L., Wegerif, R., & Sams, C. (2004). Reasoning as a scientist: Ways of helping children to use language to learn science. *British Educational Research Journal, 30*(3), 367–385.

Mercer, N., Hennessy, S., & Warwick, P. (2010). Using interactive whiteboards to orchestrate classroom dialogue. *Technology, Pedagogy and Education, 19*(2), 195–209.

Mercer, N., & Hodgkinson, S. (Eds.). (2008). *Exploring talk in school.* London: Sage.

Mercer, N., & Howe, C. (2012). Explaining the dialogic processes of teaching and learning: The value of sociocultural theory. Learning. *Culture and Social Interaction, 1*(1), 12–21.

Mercer, N., & Littleton, K. (2007). *Dialogue and the development of children's thinking.* London: Routledge.

Mercer, N., & Sams, C. (2006). Teaching children how to use language to solve maths problems. *Language and Education, 20*(6), 507–527.

Mercer, N., Warwick, P., Kershner, R., & Kleine Staarman, J. (2010). Can the interactive whiteboard help to provide "dialogic space" for children's collaborative activity? *Language and Education, 24*(5), 367–384.

Michaels, S., & O'Connor, C. (2012). *Talk science primer.* Boston, MA: TERC.

Mortimer, E. F., & Scott, P. H. (2003). *Meaning making in science classrooms*. Milton Keynes: Open University Press.

Nystrand, M., Gamoran, A., Kachur, R., & Prendergast, C. (1997). *Opening dialogue: Understanding the dynamics of language and learning in the English classroom*. New York, NY and London: Teachers' College Press.

Osborne, J. (2015). The challenges of scale. In L. Resnick, C. S. C. Asterhan, & S. N. Clarke (Eds.), *Socializing intelligence through academic talk and dialogue* (pp. 403–414). Washington, DC: American Educational Research Association.

Phillipson, N., & Wegerif, R. (2016). *Dialogic education: Mastering core concepts through thinking together*. Abingdon: Routledge.

Rasmussen, I., & Hagen, Å. (2015). Facilitating students' individual and collective knowledge construction through microblogs. *International Journal of Educational Research*, *72*(1), 149–161.

Resnick, L. B. (1999). Making America smarter. *Education Week Century Series*, *18*(40), 38–40.

Rogoff, B. (1995). Observing sociocultural activity on three planes: Participatory appropriation, guided participation, and apprenticeship. In J. V. Wertsch, P. Del Rio, & A. Alvarez (Eds.), *Sociocultural studies of mind* (pp. 139–164). New York, NY: Cambridge University Press.

Rojas-Drummond, S., & Alatorre, J. (2004). The development of independent problem solving in pre-school children. In N. Mercer & C. Coll (Eds.), *Explorations in socio-cultural studies: Teaching, learning and Interaction* (Vol. 3, pp. 161–175). Madrid: Infancia Y. Aprendizaje.

Rojas-Drummond, S., Littleton, K., Hernandez, F., & Zuniga, M. (2010). Dialogical interactions amongst peers in collaborative writing contexts. In K. Littleton & C. Howe (Eds.), *Educational dialogues: Understanding and promoting productive interaction* (pp. 128–148). London: Routledge.

Rojas-Drummond, S., & Mercer, N. (2004). Scaffolding the development of effective collaboration and learning. *International Journal of Educational Research*, *39*(1–2), 99–111.

Säljö, R. (1995). Mental and physical artifacts in cognitive practices. In P. Reimann & H. Spada (Eds.), *Learning in humans and machines: Towards an interdisciplinary learning science* (pp. 83–96). Oxford: Pergamon.

Schwarz, B., & Baker, M. (2016). *Dialogue, argumentation and education: History, theory and practice*. New York, NY: Cambridge University Press.

Sherin, M. (2007). New perspectives on the role of video in teacher education. In J. Brophy (Ed.), *Advances in research on teaching* (Vol. 10, pp. 1–27). Bingley: Emerald.

Simon, S., Erduran, S., & Osborne, J. (2006). Learning to teach argumentation: Research and development in the science classroom. *International Journal of Science Education*, *28*(2–3), 235–260.

Simon, S., Johnson, S., Cavell, S., & Parsons, T. (2012). Promoting argumentation in primary science contexts: An analysis of students' interactions in formal and informal learning environments. *Journal of Computer Assisted Learning*, *28*(5), 440–453.

Smith, F., Hardman, F., Wall, K., & Mroz, M. (2004). Interactive whole class teaching in the National Literacy and Numeracy Strategies. *British Educational Research Journal*, *30*(3), 395–411.

Snow, C. E. (2015). Rigor and realism: Doing educational science in the real world. *Educational Researcher*, *44*(9), 460–466.

Twiner, A., Coffin, C., Littleton, K., & Whitelock, D. (2010). Multimodality, orchestration and participation in the context of classroom use of the interactive whiteboard: A discussion. *Technology, Pedagogy and Education, 19*(2), 211–223.

Twining, P., Raffaghelli, J., Albion, P., & Knezek, D. (2013). Moving education into the digital age: The contribution of teachers' professional development. *Journal of Computer Assisted Learning, 29*(5), 426–437.

van de Sande, C. C., & Greeno, J. G. (2012). Achieving alignment of perspectival framings in problem-Solving discourse. *Journal of the Learning Sciences, 21*(1), 1–44.

Vygotsky, L. S. (1962). *Thought and language.* Cambridge, MA: MIT Press.

Vygotsky, L. S. (1978). *Mind in society.* Cambridge, MA: Harvard University Press.

Warwick, P., Hennessy, S., & Mercer, N. (2011). Promoting teacher and school development through co-enquiry: Developing interactive whiteboard use in a "dialogic classroom". *Teachers and Teaching: Theory and Practice, 17*(3), 303–324.

Warwick, P., Mercer, N., Kershner, R., & Staarman, J. K. (2010). In the mind and in the technology: The vicarious presence of the teacher in pupil's learning of science in collaborative group activity at the interactive whiteboard. *Computers & Education, 55*(1), 350–362.

Warwick, P., Vrikki, M., Vermunt, J. D., Mercer, N., & Halem, N. van. (2016). Connecting observations of student and teacher learning: An examination of dialogic processes in Lesson Study discussions in mathematics. *Zdm, 48*(4), 555–569.

Wegerif, R. (2010). *Mind expanding: Teaching for thinking and creativity in primary education.* Buckingham: Open University Press/McGraw Hill.

Wegerif, R., Littleton, K., & Jones, A. (2003). Stand-alone computers supporting learning dialogues in primary classrooms. *International Journal of Educational Research, 39*(8), 851–860.

Wegerif, R., Mercer, N., & Dawes, L. (1998). Software design to support discussion in the primary classroom. *Journal of Computer Assisted Learning, 14*(2), 199–211.

Wegerif, R., Mercer, N., & Dawes, L. (1999). From social interaction to individual reasoning: An empirical investigation of a possible socio-cultural model of cognitive development. *Learning and Instruction, 9*(5), 493–516.

Wells, G. (1999). *Dialogic inquiry: Towards a sociocultural practice and theory of education.* Cambridge and New York, NY: Cambridge University Press.

Wells, J. G. (2007). Key design factors in durable instructional technology professional development. *Journal of Technology and Teacher Education, 15*(1), 101–118.

Wells, M. (2014). Elements of effective and sustainable professional learning. *Professional Development in Education, 40*(3), 488–504.

Wertsch, J. (1998). Mediated action. In W. Bechtel & G. Graham (Eds.), *A companion to cognitive science* (pp. 518–525). Oxford: Blackwell.

Wolf, M., Crosson, A., & Resnick, L. (2006). *Accountable talk in reading comprehension instruction (CSE technical report 670).* Los Angeles, CA: Center for the Study of Evaluation, National Center for Research on Evaluation Standards and Student Testing.

Yoon, F., Ho, J., & Hedberg, J. (2005). Teacher understandings of technology affordances and their impact on the design of engaging learning experiences. *Educational Media International, 42*(4), 297–316.

*As I mentioned in the introduction to this book, 'oracy' has had a difficult life as an educational concept since it was devised in the 1960s. The forward-thinking ideas of the seminal National Oracy Project in the UK in the 1980s were suppressed by 'back to basics' educational policies that focused on the teaching of phonics and numeracy. However, the importance of teaching all children spoken language skills has become more widely recognised in recent years, not least as an issue of social justice. At the time of writing, the concept of oracy is gaining political support and wider international recognition. It was at the beginning of this very welcome oracy revival that Ayesha Ahmed, Paul Warwick and I worked with members of the London-based* School 21 *and others to produce the Oracy Assessment Framework and Toolkit described in this chapter. Soon after we wrote it, we became founder members of the study centre* Oracy Cambridge *(https:// oracycambridge.org).*

# 17  An Oracy Assessment Toolkit

## Linking research and development in the assessment of students' spoken language skills at age 11–12

*Mercer, N., Warwick P., & Ahmed A. (2017). An oracy assessment toolkit: Linking research and development in the assessment of students' spoken language skills at age 11-12. Learning and Instruction (Elsevier), 48, 51–60.*

## Abstract

This article describes the development of a set of research-informed resources for assessing the spoken language skills (oracy) of students aged 11–12. The Cambridge Oracy Assessment Toolkit includes assessment tasks and procedures for use by teachers, together with a unique Skills Framework for identifying the range of skills involved in using talk in any specific social situation. As we explain, no comparable, 'teacher-friendly' instrument of this kind exists. Underpinning its development is the argument that teaching children how to use their first or main language effectively across a range of social contexts should be given higher priority in educational policy and school practice, and that the development of robust, practicable ways of assessing oracy will help to achieve that goal. We explain how the Toolkit has been developed and validated with children and teachers in English secondary schools, and discuss its strengths and limitations.

## 1. Introduction

If it is accepted that schools should be helping students to develop effective talk skills, then teachers need practical ways of monitoring and assessing the oracy skills of their students in a classroom setting. Useful schemes for assessing children's language development are available, but surprisingly no suitable assessment instruments seem to exist for children aged 11–12 (the start of secondary education in the UK and many other countries). Moreover, no clear skills framework exists for identifying the different aspects of spoken language use that young people need for the range of communication situations they will encounter. Such tools would help teachers to plan how to use classroom discourse to enable their students to become more metacognitively aware, and more skilled speakers and listeners.

## *1.1. The importance of spoken language education and assessment*

In recent years, researchers in developmental psychology, linguistics and education have emphasised the importance of talk for stimulating children's cognitive development, and its use as both a cognitive and social tool for learning and social engagement (see for example Van Oers, Elbers, van der Veer, & Wardekker, 2008; Whitebread, Mercer, Howe, & Tolmie, 2013). In doing so, they follow Vygotsky (1962), who gave the acquisition of language a crucial place in his model of cognitive development. As Vass and Littleton have put it, 'interpsychological thinking is a prerequisite for intrapsychological thinking: it is through speech and action with others that we learn to reason and gain individual consciousness' (Vass & Littleton, 2010, p. 107). Research in neuroscience and evolutionary psychology supports the view that language has evolved as an integrated component of human cognition, rather than as a separate and distinct capacity (Goswami, 2009; Mercer, 2008, 2013; cf. Pinker, 2007).

Like many capacities, language development is affected by the quality of experience. Our view is that oracy (like literacy) consists of a range of diverse skills, which may develop/be learned to different extents; and for many children only some skills may have been modelled and encouraged (by other people) in their out-of-school experience. By the time they reach secondary school, some children may have learned how to carry on informal conversations and to engage in lively banter with their peers, but not have developed the ability to speak confidently to a public audience or engage in a reasoned debate. Some may have developed much larger vocabularies than others. So, individual children's experience may generate very different oracy profiles. Such diversity may affect children's ability to participate in the language-based process of school education. Research has shown that the amount and quality of pre-school children's conversations in the home are good predictors of educational attainment in secondary school (Goswami & Bryant, 2007; Hart & Risley, 1995). A systematic review of research (Howe & Abedin, 2013) has found positive associations between student learning and the use of extended and cumulative responses in group interactions; and such responses often result from specific teaching about how to use talk effectively to engage in reasoned discussions (Dawes, 2008). Overall, this encourages the view that the extent to which schools give direct attention to oracy can influence students' learning and cognitive development through building their ability to use language effectively across a range of contexts. Further, it seems that the development of certain ways of using language can influence students' future social mobility; indeed, there are studies that are starting to show that there is a strong relation between oral communicative competence and social acceptance and status (van der Wilt, van Kruistum, van der Veen, & van Oers, 2015).

There is also growing recognition amongst those outside formal education of the importance of all young people learning to use talk effectively for social and democratic engagement, and in work-related activities. An expert report on skills for employability commissioned by the London Chamber of Commerce stated: 'Softer skills, such as team working and communication, are an important aspect of an individual's employability, and they will be in higher demand as we move towards a more knowledge-intensive economy.' (Wright, Brinkley, & Clayton, 2010, p. 8). This is why we believe that oracy needs to be assessed, and taught according to need. For many children, the only hope of developing a full repertoire of oracy skills is if oracy is given the same kind of attention in school that has traditionally been given to literacy.

The various issues discussed above persuaded us that the development of oracy deserves more attention in schools; and that giving it that attention would be assisted by the development of a valid, reliable but practical way for teachers to monitor and assess the spoken language skills of their students. In partnership with *School 21* (a school in London which has put oracy at the core of its curriculum)[1] we bid successfully to the Educational Endowment Foundation for funds to develop an 'Oracy Assessment Toolkit'. In summary, our motivation for developing the Toolkit was thus based on the following concerns:

(a)  the development of students' spoken language skills (oracy) is as important for their future lives as the development of their literacy and numeracy;
(b)  they need oracy skills to participate effectively in classroom life and in wider society;
(c)  like literacy and numeracy, oracy can be taught and assessed;
(d)  oracy is more likely to be recognised as an important part of the school curriculum if it can be assessed;
(e)  teachers need to assess the strengths and weaknesses of their students' spoken language skills if they are to provide suitable guidance and instruction, and they need to be able to assess the effects of their teaching on students' skills;
(f)  there are currently no 'teacher-friendly' tools available for assessing children's oracy at the age at which they commonly begin secondary school (which is normally 11 years old in the UK).

## 1.2. *Defining oracy*

Andrew Wilkinson introduced the term 'oracy' to refer to 'the ability to use the oral skills of speaking and listening' (Wilkinson, 1965, p. 13). It is our view that the introduction and use of a concept to describe children's overall ability to use spoken language is extremely valuable and justifiable, especially in relation to educational research, policy and practice. The same applies of course to the use of 'literacy' and 'numeracy': Wilkinson (1965) coined the term 'oracy' in order to try to give spoken language skills comparable status, and to help resist narrow, back-to-basics conceptions of school curricula which typically do not accord talk a similar status to reading and writing. Some researchers, policy makers and practitioners readily adopted

Wilkinson's term and definition, as in the UK's National Oracy Project (Norman, 1992). However, other terms such as 'communication skills' and 'speaking and listening' have tended to be used more widely in the English speaking world (DfES, 2003). Alexander has argued that such terms 'have become devalued by casual use' (Alexander, 2012, p. 2) and thus 'oracy' represents the best way to refer to 'children's capacity to use speech to express their thoughts and communicate with others, in education and in life' (Alexander, 2012, p. 10). Agreeing with those sentiments, in this paper 'oracy' is used to refer to the development of young people's skills in using their first language, or the official/educational language of their country, to communicate across a range of social settings.

### 1.3. Challenges in assessing oracy

The value of assessing oracy has been debated for many years (see Brooks, 1989). Howe (1991) described three main challenges for the assessment of oracy: the fact that spoken language is ephemeral; the restriction on the number of students that can be assessed at a time; and the context specificity of speech acts. He echoed Barnes' (1980) argument that to assess fairly we need a wide range of contexts in which to gather evidence. In such contexts, Cinamon and Elding (1998, p. 220) define progress as 'gaining increasing control over . . . language to a wider range of audiences, for a greater variety of purposes and in different settings'.

Teachers commonly feel less confident about what constitutes oracy skills in comparison with literacy skills. For example, Oliver, Haig, and Rochecouste (2005) interviewed Australian teachers in 13 secondary schools, concluding that they had a narrow concept of competence in oracy, mainly identifying it with the ability to make formal public presentations. Talk-based activities, such as group work, were considered to be 'peripheral to performance' (Oliver et al., 2005, p. 218). Overall, these teachers felt that they 'do not have the skills to assess oral language' (Oliver et al., 2005, p. 212).

An additional challenge in oracy assessment is that, in many situations, talk involves the integrated activities of two or more people; how can individual performance be isolated? For assessing talk in group tasks, Wilson et al. (2012) suggest that each individual's performance should be based on the aggregate of their performances over many groups and over multiple contexts, as well as using feedback from all group members about each individual's contribution. However, this would be impractical in 'normal' classroom settings. The PISA 2015 assessments (OECD, 2014) recognise the importance of skills in collaborative thinking, though the OECD has chosen to assess collaborative problem-solving skills individually, with a computer agent acting as the other group member. This avoids the problems of assessing an individual within a group, but removes the normal social features of a group of real students.

### 1.4. How has oracy been assessed?

Assessments of children's talk skills have commonly been concerned with competence in a specific speech genre, such as taking part in a debate, presenting a prepared monologue in public (Monroe, 2009) or engaging in collaborative problem solving (Mercer & Littleton, 2007; Rojas-Drummond, Littleton, Hernandez, & Zuniga, 2010). Such genre-based approaches only provide a limited picture of a child's overall competence. Moreover, our contact with school head-teachers and English specialists encouraged us to believe that they would ideally like to obtain a generic assessment in oracy for each child (comparisons with 'reading age' had been made in such discussions). Our aim was to enable this possibility (or a rather more finessed approach) by devising a set of specific, situational tasks to provide a profile of a child's oracy skills across a range of situations. The broad approach adopted was to first devise an over-arching oracy skills framework (see Section 2.2.1 and task examples below) and then to consider possible test tasks in the light of this framework. The framework could be applied to any suitable talk task so that the core oracy skills within it could be identified for assessment and so that a more holistic assessment could be arrived at across tasks.

Most importantly, this approach does not deny that different tasks, curriculum subject areas and genres have distinctive features in terms of the development of oracy skills, and that these can be highly specialised, applying only to a single genre for example. However, the generic skills-based framework developed and used within the project (Figure 17.1, below) has a very specific function. It provides an over-arching framework of *generic* skills – categorised as physical, linguistic, cognitive and social – from which relevant skills can be *selected* for assessment as relevant to a given task. So, 'building on the views of others' might be highly pertinent in an assessment of group talk, but not necessarily in public speaking; yet 'fluency and pace of speech' might pertain to a drama performance, a presentation and so on. The important thing is the selection of skills for assessment and their association with particular tasks, enabling the teacher to build a profile over time. Thus, we would not suggest that this framework is completely comprehensive for all language use in all contexts, curriculum areas or subjects. Nor do we suggest that the *whole* framework of skills is relevant to every context. However, we demonstrate how several assessments, used across time and in a range of contexts, can build a generic oracy profile for a student. Further, we demonstrate that this is only really possible if teachers have an overall framework of broad oracy skills as a template for their various assessments.

To consider previous assessments of oracy, one of the first attempts to make a holistic assessment of children's oracy was made in the UK by The Assessment of Performance Unit. Their survey (APU, 1988) monitored thousands of students aged 11 and 15, and included tasks designed to assess their oracy skills. Tasks included presentations and paired problem-solving

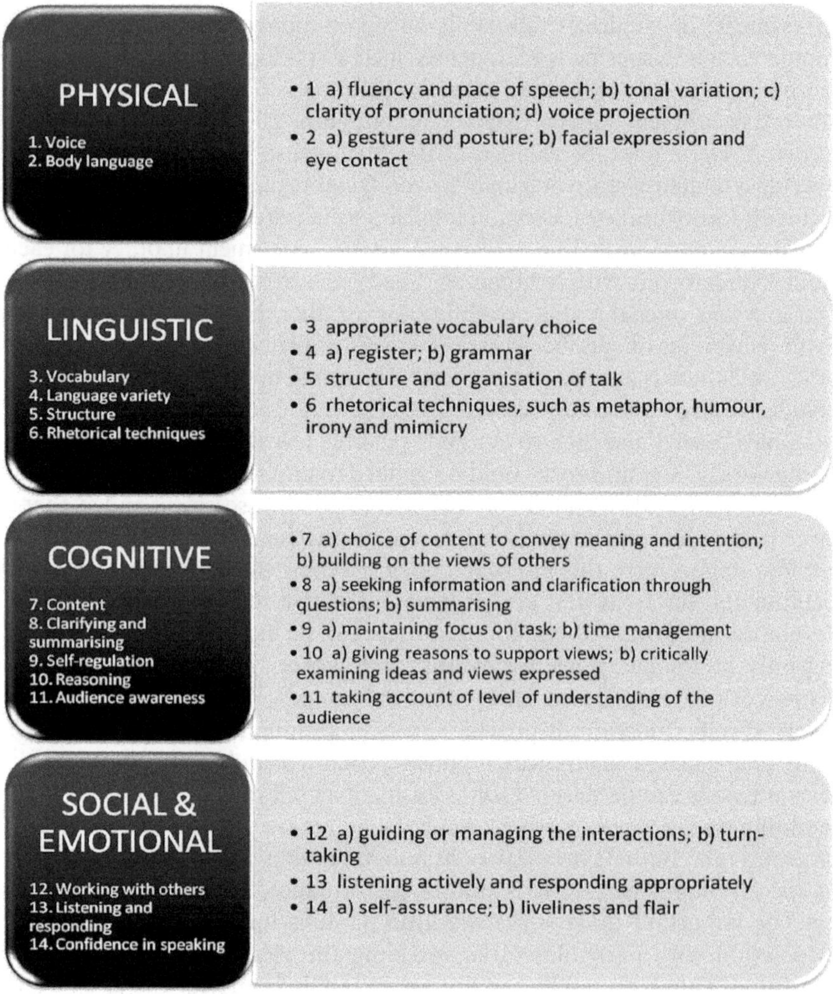

**PHYSICAL**

1. Voice
2. Body language

- 1 a) fluency and pace of speech; b) tonal variation; c) clarity of pronunciation; d) voice projection
- 2 a) gesture and posture; b) facial expression and eye contact

**LINGUISTIC**

3. Vocabulary
4. Language variety
5. Structure
6. Rhetorical techniques

- 3 appropriate vocabulary choice
- 4 a) register; b) grammar
- 5 structure and organisation of talk
- 6 rhetorical techniques, such as metaphor, humour, irony and mimicry

**COGNITIVE**

7. Content
8. Clarifying and summarising
9. Self-regulation
10. Reasoning
11. Audience awareness

- 7 a) choice of content to convey meaning and intention; b) building on the views of others
- 8 a) seeking information and clarification through questions; b) summarising
- 9 a) maintaining focus on task; b) time management
- 10 a) giving reasons to support views; b) critically examining ideas and views expressed
- 11 taking account of level of understanding of the audience

**SOCIAL & EMOTIONAL**

12. Working with others
13. Listening and responding
14. Confidence in speaking

- 12 a) guiding or managing the interactions; b) turn-taking
- 13 listening actively and responding appropriately
- 14 a) self-assurance; b) liveliness and flair

*Figure 17.1* Oracy skills framework.

activities. Students were assessed by trained assessors. Their main conclusions were that it is feasible to monitor speaking and listening performance on a national scale; that marker reliability was satisfactory; and that the assessment materials had communicative validity. They noted that 'almost all 11 year olds can modify their speaking strategies appropriately in accordance with the demands of different tasks and different audiences' (APU, 1988, p. 64). In a similar study in the Netherlands, the oracy skills of two hundred 10–12 year old students were measured by the research team (Van den Bergh, 1987). Six tasks were constructed and the study concluded that the assessment of oracy is feasible for this age group, with only 13% of the students failing or responding at a 'doubtful' level. Maybin (1988) criticised the APU's assessments because they were based on performances made outside normal contexts and were based on an individualistic, non-interactive model of language use. The problems of reducing a social phenomenon to a series of assessment tasks are made clear in Maybin's critique.

Recently, test developers have designed more interactive tasks. Latham (2005) created a Speaking and Listening Profile to help teachers to use the Speaking, Listening and Learning materials that supported the English National Curriculum; and diagnostic in-school assessment schemes for teachers in the UK have been devised by the Qualifications and Curriculum Development Agency (for example QCDA, 2010). These contained four assessment foci for speaking and listening (talking to others, talking with others, talking within role play and drama, and talking about talk) and four strands of relevant oracy skills (listening and responding; speaking and presenting; group discussion and interaction; drama, role play and performance). However, from summer 2014 a speaking and listening component will no longer count towards the final General Certificate of Secondary Education (GSCE) grade for examinations in English; this followed 'concerns about the effectiveness of the moderation of controlled assessment in the speaking and listening component' (Ofqual, 2013, p. 2).

Internationally, there is varied practice. For example, the Scottish Survey of Literacy includes an assessment of Listening and Talking using group discussion tasks at ages 8, 11 and 13. Oracy Australia (Education Department of Western Australia, 1997) offers oracy assessments for teachers to employ which focus on oral presentation, reading aloud, oral interpretation of literature and listening and responding. In the USA, the Common Core Standards for English Language Arts (CCSI, 2015), adopted by most states, provides a set of guidelines showing the expected standard for spoken language use at the end of each grade of schooling. However, none of these schemes include a framework which identifies the full range of skills required to meet the relevant assessment criteria.

## 2. The Cambridge oracy assessment project

### 2.1. Background to the project

As mentioned earlier, the Educational Endowment Foundation, a UK-based charity, funded researchers at the University of Cambridge to work with School 21 on a two year project aimed to develop a curriculum for teaching oracy and an 'Oracy Assessment Toolkit' for assessing students' levels of competence in oracy. The research team was to develop the toolkit for teachers to use with Year 7 students (age 11–12), enabling teachers' monitoring and assessment of student progress in oracy skills.

## 2.2. Method

The central aims of the research project were to create a Toolkit consisting of:

- an Oracy Skills Framework;
- a set of oracy assessment tasks;
- a rating scheme for assessing performance on the tasks and giving feed-back to students.

In order to develop the skills framework we proceeded by examining existing frameworks and testing schemes and consulting with relevant experts in focus group sessions. Our expert panel consisted of eight members with a variety of expertise (see Acknowledgements section for a list of names and affiliations).

In the development of the tasks we trialled initial tasks with Year 7 teachers and students near the start of the school year and end-of-year tasks later in the year with the same sets of teachers and students. The assessment rating schemes were trialled alongside the tasks. Throughout this trialling process we were revising our draft Skills Framework based on outcomes of the trials and further focus groups with our expert panel. Our consultative conference on Oracy Assessment in Cambridge, in which experts and practitioners were involved, also aided our development of the framework.

We also assisted School 21 staff in their aim of assessing the effects of their oracy-led curriculum by using the Toolkit to compare the performances of a sample of Year 7 children following the 'oracy-led' School 21 curriculum and a comparison school involved in the project (which we call MVC), which followed the usual National Curriculum (in which oracy is given relatively little attention).

The following sections address the key aspects of this process.

### 2.2.1. Developing the oracy skills framework

As described above, most previous approaches to assessing oracy have relied on performance criteria related to specific situations, such as public speaking or group work. We planned a more general framework that represented the range of skills which could be drawn upon in any situation, enabling teachers to build an 'oracy profile' for any student which would not be situation specific.

In iteratively constructing the Oracy Skills Framework, we were influenced by theoretical conceptions of language use such as Hymes' ethnography of communication (Hymes, 1977) and the systemic functional linguistics of Halliday and his associates (Halliday, 1978). Much of such discussion has been concerned with second language acquisition (e.g. Cummins, 1980; Housen, Kuiken, & Vedder, 2012; McNamara, 1997) but is relevant nevertheless. Building on earlier work by a range of applied linguists, Celce-Murcia,

Dornyei, and Thurrell (1995) offered what they called a 'pedagogically motivated model' of communicative competence designed for second language education which includes five components: (1) discourse competence; (2) linguistic competence; (3) actional competence; (4) sociocultural competence; and (5) strategic competence. While its breadth and subtlety are positive features, a disadvantage of that model, in our view, is that it seems to confuse the cognitive foundations of speech performance with observable features of talk and interaction. We wanted to create a framework that directed teachers' attention to what students actually said and did. In aiming to create a framework which would match not only expert understanding of the dimensions of competent language use, but also the concerns and perceptions of practitioners, we engaged in a series of consultations and discussions.

Discussions with our research partners in School 21 enabled sharing of professional and researcher expertise about what constitutes the effective use of spoken language and what might realistically be expected of 11 year olds in that respect when faced with the assessment tasks. Previously developed assessment tools for oracy were appraised. These included the APU assessments mentioned above and tools for assessing children's developing use of English as a second language. We reviewed debates about the importance of assessing complexity, accuracy and fluency (CAF: Housen & Kuiken, 2009) and tests such as IELTS (the International English Language Testing System) with its categories of fluency and coherence, lexical resource, grammar and pronunciation (IELTS, 2013). From these discussions and considerations the initial organising areas of the Skills Framework were devised.

Consultations were also undertaken with members of our expert group (see acknowledgements) – people of recognised stature in drama, English studies, sociolinguistics, applied linguistics and educational assessment. This group met three times during the development phase of the project (lasting approximately 14 months), and members were consulted individually and collectively by phone/email. We consulted teachers and gained the views of speech therapists, test developers and representatives of relevant organisations (including Cambridge Assessment, The Communication Trust (2013), The National Literacy Trust, The Scottish Qualifications Authority and the United Kingdom Literacy Association). Constructive criticism from such professionals enabled revision of both the framework and the assessment tasks. Reassuringly, however, the basic concept of a generalised skills framework for oracy and the chosen areas of the framework were supported by all.

Initially, the framework had eight main categories; but as a result of the iterative discussions with relevant experts as described above, this was reduced to four. The final version of the framework is presented in Figure 17.1. The four areas – physical; linguistic; cognitive; social and emotional – represent the different types of skill that are involved in the effective use of spoken language. The need to balance accuracy and complexity with clarity and practical usefulness means that the framework is presented in language unlikely to satisfy the rigorous criteria of an academic linguist. However, the intention was to create a framework comprehensible to, and useable by, classroom teachers.

The Skills Framework defines the conception of 'oracy' that forms the basis of the accompanying assessment tasks (used to elicit evidence of these skills) and the assessment rating schemes (used to evaluate this evidence). Each of the four skill areas contain a number of specific skills that are listed on the left hand side. These are then described in detail on the right hand side of the diagram. More details and a glossary of skills can be found at the project website.[2]

### 2.3. Task development

On arrival in secondary school, students will vary in their oracy skills, partly dependent on the extent to which their prior school and home experience has helped develop such skills. Tasks were therefore devised to allow teachers to make initial assessments together with a matched set of tasks for assessing progress at the end of students' first year. Validity was a major concern, and this meant ensuring that the tasks allowed the students to do 'what we want them to show us they can do' (Ahmed & Pollitt, 2011, p. 25). A set of Assessment for Learning (AfL) tasks were also devised which could be used throughout the year and adapted by the teacher to monitor development. The initial and end tasks were designed to sample a representative range of skills from the framework and, though there is some overlap in the skills assessed in each task, each one has a different emphasis. We were also concerned not to provide teachers with a large battery of tasks which it would seem impractical to achieve. That is, we aimed to generate a set of the minimum number of tasks which would best cover a wide range of skills. The tasks, and associated rating schemes, were trialled and refined against these criteria. Interviews were undertaken with both teachers and students, and adjustments were made to the final versions of tasks and assessment materials.

The first of the initial tasks devised was called 'Map', based on a task of the same name used by the Assessment of Performance Unit (APU, 1988). In this task, one student was given a map of a 'Treasure Island', and asked to plan a route from a port to a pirate's treasure hoard. However, they were told that this map was now out of date, and so they would need to consult a second student 'by phone' (in fact they sat back-to-back) who had an up-to-date version of the map. The task thus invoked such skills in our framework as 'seeking information and clarification through questions' and 'taking account of level of understanding of audience'. Whilst trials confirmed the value of this kind of task for assessing communication skills, this particular task proved problematic in its original form. There was some confusion amongst students carrying out the task about what 'real world' activity it was meant to simulate; and it did not encourage both students to take the role of explainer and questioner. Thus, an alternative paired instructional task, described below, was created for the end-of-year assessments.

The second initial task was a 'Talking Points' activity (Dawes, 2012). Talking Points are a set of somewhat controversial statements about a topic which students are asked to consider together and decide if, and why, they agree or disagree with the view expressed. This type of task has been found to be very effective for generating lively discussion (Dawes, Dore, Loxley, & Nichols, 2010; Mercer, Dawes, & Staarman, 2009). The aim of this task, which lasts 10 minutes, was to get the students to use skills in managing a discussion, giving and seeking views supported by reasons, building upon each other's ideas and working towards consensus.

The third initial task was a Presentation task in which the students had to give a 2-minute presentation to camera. They were given some preparation time with their teachers before the task; they were not allowed to use a script, but could bring a prompt card with them. Each student was allowed an unrecorded trial run and then they presented the 'real thing' to camera.

The three end-of-year tasks were designed to be parallel forms of the initial tasks, so that comparisons could be made between student performances. The skills involved in each task were the same for the initial and end-of-year versions, enabling teachers to make an assessment of the children's progress in oracy. To replace 'Map', a task based on Lego construction materials was created which allowed for assessment of the same skills. In this task, one student had a picture of a completed Lego model, while their partner had a box of Lego parts (which included not only those required for the model but also several others). They were asked to work together, sitting back-to-back, to enable the second student to build the model. Importantly, by switching roles, this new task enabled each student to take the role of both builder and guide.

As well as the three formal assessment tasks, five Assessment for Learning (AfL) tasks were devised for teachers to use in a whole class context. They focused on debate, drama, role play, group talk and presentation. Each can be adapted to suit a teacher's choice of content; teachers are provided with loose guidelines in which the talk objectives for the task are listed, followed by examples and assessment procedure guidelines. As well as teacher assessment, these tasks involve students' self and peer assessment (Clarke, 2001).

## 2.4. Rating scheme development

A three way rating scheme was developed for teachers to judge a student's performance on each skill for each task. This used a version of a mastery model in which students are judged as demonstrating each skill consistently, only some of the time or not at all. With such tasks, responses can be rated by making either holistic or analytic judgements. Holistic judgements involve giving the performance as a whole a single grade. Analytic judgements involve giving a series of grades for different aspects of the performance and then aggregating these, either with or without weightings. Harsch and Martin (2013) found no agreement amongst researchers on whether holistic or analytic methods yield more reliable and valid scores of students' writing; no comparable work has been done for oracy. In our scheme, assessors first make a rating based on a subset of skills from the Skills Framework, and then make an overall rating. This represents a combination of analytic and holistic approaches.

To ensure validity, focused marking criteria highlight the key skills involved in each task, as represented in the Skills Framework. Performance descriptors were based on observed characteristics of different levels of performance (Fulcher, Davidson, & Kemp, 2011; Greatorex, Johnson, & Frame, 2001). A panel of eight teachers from School 21 and MVC was set up. The research team led discussions with these teachers, aimed at bringing them to a common view of relevant skills; and we expected this to influence their judgement of students. Teachers were given an assessment sheet with a list of the relevant skills and a space to rate performance on each skill. They could rate a performance as Gold ('consistently demonstrates this skill'), Silver ('demonstrates this skill some of the time') or Bronze ('rarely or never demonstrates this skill yet'). During the development phase there were no exemplars for teachers to use to help them to judge the standard. As this was a research and development project, the devising of marking criteria – essentially what distinguishes a Gold performance from a Silver or Bronze – was central to the way in which the project was conceived. It was by engaging professionals in discussions around student responses to the tasks, and around the definition of oracy framework skills, that we were able to structure the video/descriptor items (accessed through our website) that form the guide materials for the Oracy Assessment Toolkit. As a result of this work, in the final version of the Toolkit there are exemplar videos of students performing at different levels, along with descriptors of the oracy skills seen in these exemplars. These help to benchmark the standard of performance on each of the tasks. During the trials it became apparent that some teachers wanted to use a more finegrained rating scheme and were using Bronze+, Silver+ and Gold+ to distinguish more levels of performance. We therefore added these finer levels of assessment to the assessment sheets used in the subsequent phase and went further in this refinement as the work with teachers progressed, as described below.

## 3. Trialling the tasks and assessment procedures

### 3.1. Schools and sample

Initial versions of the tasks were trialled in four schools. School 21, our primary partner in this project, mainly takes students from a multicultural population of low socio-economic status in London; and it has an 'oracy-led' curriculum. The other main school involved, MVC is a rural state comprehensive (i.e., non-selective) secondary school in eastern England that works to the National Curriculum, with a predominantly middle class intake. We also trialled early versions of the tasks in two triangulating schools, producing videos that were used with School 21 and MVC teachers to reduce the risk of bias in their observations. CWS is an urban state comprehensive secondary school in central England with a predominantly working class population of varied ethnic backgrounds; and CS is a comprehensive secondary school in a small market town in the north of England, serving a socially mixed but largely white indigenous population. Given that our aim was to create an assessment tool that could be used in any mainstream school, the natural variation amongst these four schools enabled us to test the assessment tasks and rating scheme on a suitably diverse population. Of these latter three, only CWS had previously been involved with the research team, through the provision of professional development sessions for its teachers on 'developing language for learning'.

Because of the geographical distances involved and the time-table of the project, it was only possible to include students (and teachers) from School 21 and MVC in the trialling of the final versions of the tasks. Students were selected from those whose parents had given permission for their involvement (only two students were excluded for such reasons). The researchers asked teachers to select a range of students who, on the basis of their initial impressions, represented a range of competence levels in spoken English.

In School 21 there were seven boys and five girls in the focus group, with reading ages ranging from 7.1 to 15+[3] and with a mean of 11.0. At MVC there were six boys and six girls in the focus group, with reading ages ranging from 8.6 to 14+ and with a mean of 12.0.

### 3.2. Procedures for developing the assessment toolkit

Sessions were video-recorded to enable the close analysis of students' performances, to facilitate discussion with teachers and others for standard-setting purposes and to provide exemplars on the Oracy Toolkit website. Two teachers in each school were asked to rate the performance of each student 'live' in response to a range of skills most pertinent to that task.

The development of the assessment criteria and scoring scheme also involved a review day with five teachers involved in the project. Videos of the performances of 16 students, from School 21, MVC and CS, were used as test materials. Using pairs of videos of students (selected by their teachers in terms of their availability and to provide some mixed gender pairings) carrying out each of the initial tasks, the teachers were asked to judge, for each of the tasks, which student was 'better' in terms of oracy. Allowing repeated viewing of videos when requested, new comparisons were then made between individual students. The same panel of teachers from School 21 and MVC was involved; and they ranked students from both schools. This meant that some teachers knew some of the students they were assessing, but not all. As mentioned earlier, through initial discussions with the research team we aimed to bring the teachers to a common view of relevant skills; and we expected this to influence their ranking of performances. During the ranking exercise the teachers could refer to the skills framework to focus their observations; however, they did not have any material that indicated levels of performance, as the purpose of the work at this point was to refine, through discussion, what characterised performances at different levels.

The five teachers (DS, LG, GV, SH and AS in Table 17.2) were asked to select the 'top two' students on each task; and then to make a paired comparison of these students (with video viewing again allowed if requested). This iterative process continued until an overall rank order of all the children for each task was decided. A different set of eight students was involved in each set of comparisons. There was a high level of consensus in the initial paired comparisons for each task, recorded as presented in the example Table 17.1 below.

The rank order of students by the teachers on this video review day matched the teachers' initial ratings for these performances for the Presentation task. For the Map task there is no contradiction in the rank order but most of these performances were rated 'Gold' overall so there was a lack of discrimination in this sample. However, the teachers were able to discriminate amongst the Gold performances when reaching an agreement on rank order. For the Talking Points task the rank order was less consistent with earlier ratings. The anomalies here were associated with the use of assessments from one of the project schools, where the teacher had not been trained in the use of the Assessment Toolkit and where a high number of Gold assessments had been made. Similar review days were carried out with the expert panel for the project and with a panel of five secondary school English teachers who were not involved in the project. At each, the participants rated students' responses, discussed both their ratings and the relevance of particular skills within the assessments, and commented on all aspects of the tasks.

Participating students (in all four schools) were interviewed in pairs or groups of three about their experiences of the tasks, using open questions

*Table 17.1* Presentation task initial pair scores (1 beats 0)

| Teacher | DS | LG | GV | SH | AS |
|---|---|---|---|---|---|
| Student 1 | 0 | 0 | 0 | 0 | 0 |
| Student 2 | 1 | 1 | 1 | 1 | 1 |
| Student 3 | 0 | 0 | 0 | 0 | 0 |
| Student 4 | 1 | 1 | 1 | 1 | 1 |
| Student 5 | 0 | 0 | 0 | 0 | 0 |
| Student 6 | 1 | 1 | 1 | 1 | 1 |
| Student 7 | 0 | 0 | 0 | 0 | 0 |
| Student 8 | 1 | 1 | 1 | 1 | 1 |

as a stimulus for discussion. Their views were sought on the tasks, focusing on the clarity of instructions, the level of difficulty and perceived value in assessing their oracy skills. In School 21 and MVC, after the three initial tasks had been trialled and again after the three end-of-year tasks had been trialled, the teachers were interviewed. The interviews and the review day discussions led to significant developments in the tasks for the final version of the Toolkit, most noticeably the replacement of the Map task by the Lego task. Typical comments here were:

> . . . The new map and the old map was hard because I didn't know. I thought that because it was a new map I hadn't thought that it was the same map but just new things on it, but it was different roads.
>
> (Student interview)

> they weren't really empathising with what their colleague could see. . . . I think the map task locked some of them out, actually. I think it was the least appealing to them and the one they found the hardest to do.
>
> (Teacher comment)

Although some of the students found the replacement Lego task hard, they found it more comprehensible and purposeful than the Map task.

> I found the Lego easier because someone was telling the other person where everything was. Then, with the map it wasn't very clear, because they weren't the same. So, it was quite hard to know where everything was.
>
> (Student interview)

And the teachers and experts agreed that the Lego task was an improvement:

> when we looked at the Lego task in comparison with the map task, they were able to [complete the] task very much better.
>
> (Teacher comment)

> The task is genuine; you're not pretending that you're sitting making a Lego model, you actually are making a Lego model and somebody else has got a picture of it.
>
> (Expert comment)

The expert panel felt that the Talking Points task allowed students to demonstrate the relevant skills identified, though they considered that some of the Talking Points about 'talk' were not controversial enough to provoke a lively debate and thus for students to demonstrate relevant skills. This was addressed in the end version of this task by involving the originator of the Talking Points activity format (Dawes, 2012) in a team session to devise new sets.

For the Presentation task, interview responses indicated that the students saw how useful the skills involved in this task would be. For example, one commented:

> I think it is because like when we get older we're going to have to like speak to people like face to face that we haven't met before and if you ... and in front of cameras like for a job interview we might be like that.
>
> (Student interview)

A general issue raised by both the experts and teachers was that of the clarity of the task instructions given to students and so these were modified accordingly. The interviews and video review days were a vital aspect of the work, allowing both theoretical and professional perspectives to be taken into account in the Toolkit design.

## 4. Results: assessing oracy with the Toolkit

### 4.1. Skills ratings on initial and end tasks

The initial tasks had been administered in School 21 and MVC in September, during the first part of the Autumn term. The end tasks were used in both schools in March/April. The final calibration of the assessment scheme involved teachers from School 21 and MVC. (Teachers from CS and CWS were invited, but attendance proved impossible.) Teachers used Bronze, Silver and Gold to make their ratings, and some also used Bronze+, Silver–, Silver+ and Gold–. For analysis the Bronze, Silver and Gold ratings were converted into numbers:

| | |
|---|---|
| Bronze | 1 |
| Bronze + | 2 |
| Silver – | 3 |
| Silver | 4 |
| Silver + | 5 |
| Gold – | 6 |
| Gold | 7 |

The teachers' mean overall task ratings for School 21 and MVC, the 'control' school, can be seen in Tables 17.2–17.4.

The differences between initial and end task means can be seen as a measure of progress. Limited progress can be seen in these ratings for School 21 in the individual presentation and group discussion tasks, but not in the paired instructional task. This may have been because of the discrepancies between the Map and the Lego tasks. (The only initial test scores available for comparison were of course based on the Map task.) The mean ratings for MVC show little progress. Teacher and expert discussions noted that the

*Table 17.2* Individual Presentation task mean ratings – teacher assessments

|                    | School 21 | MVC  |
| ------------------ | --------- | ---- |
| Initial task mean  | 3.64      | 4.46 |
| End task mean      | 4.11      | 4.23 |
| Difference in means| 0.47      | 0.23 |

*Table 17.3* Group Talking Points task mean ratings – teacher assessments

|                    | School 21 | MVC   |
| ------------------ | --------- | ----- |
| Initial task mean  | 4.20      | 4.50  |
| End task mean      | 5.00      | 4.02  |
| Difference in means| 0.80      | −0.48 |

*Table 17.4* Paired instructional task mean ratings – teacher assessments

|                    | School 21 | MVC  |
| ------------------ | --------- | ---- |
| Initial task mean  | 4.61      | 4.75 |
| End task mean      | 3.83      | 5.00 |
| Difference in means| −0.78     | 0.25 |

low progress measures may be explained by high initial task ratings by the teachers, who knew the students (albeit by only a few weeks of the school term) they were rating by the time of the initial assessments.

Due to the possible bias in the data caused by teachers knowing students (as noted above), the progress of School 21 and MVC students was also assessed using only researcher ratings. There is, of course, the potential for bias derived from the researcher knowledge of the data, but here it should be noted that the researchers were only familiar with the students through their task responses; they did not have the holistic view of the students that may have influenced the assessments from the teachers, who worked with the students regularly in their schools in a range of contexts.

The three researchers first rated students independently, and then through discussion sought a consensus score, as recorded in Tables 17.5–17.7. The small sample in each school prevents any differences being judged as statistically significant.

Researcher assessments for School 21 show clear progress in the oracy skills required for the Presentation task, with a difference of 1.64 between initial and final mean ratings. For MVC there is a very slight trend towards improvement but no real difference in the mean ratings.

In the Talking Points task for School 21, there is again an indication of progress in the oracy skills required, with a progress rating of 1.08. For

*Table 17.5* Individual Presentation task mean ratings – researcher assessments

|  | School 21 | MVC |
|---|---|---|
| Initial task mean | 2.91 | 3.90 |
| End task mean | 4.55 | 4.00 |
| Difference in means | 1.64 | 0.10 |

*Table 17.6* Group Talking Points task mean ratings – researcher assessments

|  | School 21 | MVC |
|---|---|---|
| Initial task mean | 4.17 | 2.33 |
| End task mean | 5.25 | 3.00 |
| Difference in means | 1.08 | 0.67 |

*Table 17.7* Paired instructional task mean ratings – researcher ratings

|  | School 21 | MVC |
|---|---|---|
| Initial task mean | 4.17 | 2.25 |
| End task mean | 4.75 | 2.50 |
| Difference in means | 0.58 | 0.25 |

MVC there is a trend in a positive direction but the progress rating is less than that for School 21.

In the instructional (Map/Lego) task, for School 21 there is again an indication of progress in the oracy skills required but the difference in means is very small at 0.58. For MVC there is again a slight trend in a positive direction.

The instructional task data in particular must be interpreted with caution since, as explained earlier, the replacement of Map with Lego means that differences in performance on this task may have been an artefact of these changes. However, it can be seen that School 21 students still achieved noticeably higher ratings than those in MVC on both initial and end tasks.

Overall, the ratings for the School 21 students were higher than those of the MVC students on two initial tasks and all three follow-up tasks. The higher initial scores for School 21 may be because of factors outside our control; by the time it was possible to administer the initial tasks (in October), the School 21 students had already begun studying the schools' distinctive 'oracy-led' curriculum, which provided training in both presentational and group interaction skills.

### 4.2. Comparative ratings and reliability

Video review sessions with researchers, project teachers, the project expert panel and a new panel of independent teachers were used to test the reliability of the rating scale. An established method for averaging correlations (Hatch & Lazaraton, 1991) was employed for calculating inter-rater reliability (IRR), as the more traditional Kappa statistic was unsuitable for our data given the small number of students and lack of variability within judges' ratings. The first step was to generate a Pearson correlation matrix and then calculate the average correlation after a Fisher Z transformation (to transform to a normal distribution and correct for the fact that these are ordinal data). The derived average of the transformed correlation coefficients, $r_{ab}$ was then substituted using the formula:

$$r_{tt} = \frac{n \cdot r_{ab}}{1 + (n-1)r_{ab}}$$

$r_{tt}$ = reliability of all the ratings
$n$ = number of raters
$r_{ab}$ = correlation between two raters (or average correlation if there are more than two).

The reliability of all the ratings $r_{tt}$ was then transformed back to a Pearson correlation.

Table 17.8 gives the IRR values for each of the three initial tasks and three end-of-year tasks for School 21 and MVC. The shared percentages of the variance are also given for each of the tasks. This is the portion of variance in the data that represents the shared consensus of the judges, with the rest of

*Table 17.8* IRR values for each of the three initial tasks and three end-of-year tasks for School 21 and MVC

| Task | IRR | Shared percentage of variance |
| --- | --- | --- |
| S21 Map | 0.69 | 48% |
| S21 Lego | 0.73 | 54% |
| S21 Pres1 | 0.28[a] | 8% |
| S21 Pres2 | 0.77 | 59% |
| S21 TP1 | 0.64 | 41% |
| S21 TP2 | 0.62 | 38% |
| MVC Map | Incomplete[b] | Incomplete |
| MVC Lego | 0.72 | 52% |
| MVC Pres1 | 0.88 | 77% |
| MVC Pres2 | 0.90 | 81% |
| MVC TP1 | Incomplete | Incomplete |
| MVC TP2 | 0.83 | 69% |

[a] This result is due to the lack of variability within one judge's ratings for this task, leading to an unreliable calculation of the correlation.
[b] The cells marked 'Incomplete' are where IRR could not be calculated due to missing data for each of the judges.

the variance being due to lack of perfect reliability in using the rating scales and inconsistencies in how they interpreted the students' performances.

To help ensure future reliability in the use of the Toolkit, a library of video exemplars has been provided on the project website to give teachers a benchmark standard of performance for each level. The examples have empirically derived level descriptors and should help teachers to rate their own students' performances in a reliable manner and give specific and informative feedback to the students on how well they demonstrate the various oracy skills in different contexts.

## 5. Discussion and conclusions

The Cambridge Oracy Assessment Project's main aim was to produce an Assessment Toolkit that combined research-based validity with a practical ease of use for teachers. Evaluations by our expert panels and feedback from participating teachers encourage us to believe that, to a reasonable extent, this aim has been achieved. Feedback from both teachers and students in the participating schools suggests that they perceived the tasks as valid tests of communicative skill – though several students commented that being video-recorded and observed by researchers made them more nervous and less fluent than they thought they would be in a more private situation. One can only hope that the use of the Toolkit in more normal school circumstances, as intended, would reduce this problem. In the final version of the assessment tasks, instructions have been made clearer; allowances have been made for the use of a finer grained scale with + and − as well as Bronze, Silver and Gold; and suggestions have been made in the Toolkit instructions about how to use assessments to design suitable teaching activities. We concede that the tasks might still be improved, given more time and resources; but they have been developed with due care and are now available for public scrutiny and use. The Oracy Assessment Framework has had a very positive response from experts and teachers, though we are very aware that it may lack subtlety and detail in the eyes of applied linguists.

In Section 1.3 we discussed the need for oracy assessments to take into account the social situation in which talk is used, and the risks of reducing an interactive social phenomenon to a series of set tasks. A criticism of the Toolkit might be that the presentation, group work and problem-solving activities are not 'real' in that they are set by researchers/teachers and do not naturally arise in the lives of the participating students. There is also the possibility that nervousness generated by a test situation disrupts a student's normal performance. However, similar criticisms can be made of formal tests of reading, numeracy, intelligence and so on. To the extent that the students recognise the importance of oracy skills (which interview data suggested our participating students did) and that tasks are clear and comprehensible in their procedures and criteria for success (which feedback suggests ours are), then one can expect that most will be motivated and able to perform to the best of their abilities. In other words, these issues can be dealt with just as effectively in relation to the assessment of oracy as they can for the assessment of other comparable skill sets.

One aspect of the overall project which we cannot deal properly with in this article is the evaluation of the innovative 'oracy-led' curriculum introduced by School 21. While small sample sizes must limit the confidence of claims, the higher scores of the School 21 students suggest that the development of students' spoken language skills is aided by their teachers (a) involving them in awareness-raising activities which encourage students' metacognition about ways of talking (as discussed in Mercer, 2013); (b) providing them with instruction on how to use talk effectively in different circumstances; and (c) embedding spoken language practice into the curriculum for all subjects (not just English, drama or modern languages). The higher skills scores were the major difference across the schools; but it was also interesting to note that our qualitative analyses of the video data showed that School 21 students: (i) took longer turns which allowed them to provide clearer explanations and reasons in group tasks (items 5, 7a and 10a in the Skills Framework, Figure 17.1); (ii) organised group tasks more effectively (items 12a and b); and, particularly in the presentation task, were (iii) more fluent and confident in their overall performance (items 1 and 14a). The value of an 'oracy-led' curriculum as used in School 21 has thus been supported by use of the Oracy Toolkit.

The outcomes of the project show that it is possible to provide teachers with (a) a framework for understanding the spoken language skills that their students will need to use talk effectively in the various social situations they find themselves in; (b) a set of tasks for assessing their students' oracy skills across a sample of such situations; and (c) a rating scheme which provides a valid and fairly reliable way of assessing individual students' levels of competence and the progress they make over time. Part of the motivation in developing the Toolkit was to raise the status of oracy as a crucial set of life skills on a par with those of literacy and numeracy. Once they leave school, most young people will find that skills in using spoken language will be required much more often than those of anything but the most basic skills of numeracy. By showing how spoken language skills can be monitored and assessed, and by identifying the skills that an 'oracy-led' curriculum can help to develop, we hope to help oracy achieve the place in school curricula for the 21st century that it deserves.

## Acknowledgements

We would like to acknowledge the positive collaborative efforts of our partners in this project, School 21; the support of our funders the Education Endowment Foundation; the project's independent evaluators Sheffield

Hallam University; the teachers and students in other schools that took part in this project – Melbourn Village College, Cambridgeshire (MVC), Cardinal Wiseman School and Language College, Coventry (CWS) and Cockermouth School, Cumbria (CS); and the project's expert advisory panel:

Alan Howe, Formerly of the National Strategies.
Greg Brooks, Professor of Education, University of Sheffield.
Janet White, JW English Consultancy Ltd.
Adrian Beard, Assessment and Qualifications Alliance.
Lyn Dawes, Educational Consultant.
Stephanie Merritt, Speech Therapist.
Lesley Hendy, Voice educator.
Evelina Galaczi, Cambridge English.

## Notes

1 School 21 is a 'free school', meaning that its founders have gained direct funding from the national government to establish a school which is not constrained by the National Curriculum for England and Wales. See http://school21.org.uk.
2 Please note that all elements of the Oracy Assessment Toolkit – which includes the glossary, all assessment tasks and the rating scheme sheets – are available at: www.educ.cam.ac.uk/research/projects/oracytoolkit/. As this is the case, they will not be included as appendices in this paper.
3 Reading ages above 14 are represented as whole years with a + sign in English schools.

## References

Ahmed, A., & Pollitt, A. (2011). Improving marking quality through a taxonomy of mark schemes. *Assessment in Education: Principles, Policy and Practice, 17,* 259–278.
Alexander, R. (2012). *Improving oracy and classroom talk in English schools: Achievements and challenges.* Retrieved October 15, 2013 from www.primaryreview.org.uk/downloads_/news/2012/02/2012_02_20DfE_oracy_Alexander.pdf
APU. (1988). Assessment of Performance Unit. *Language performance in schools: Review of APU language monitoring 1979–1983.* London: Her Majesty's Stationary Office.
Barnes, D. (1980). Situated speech strategies: Aspects of the monitoring of oracy. *Educational Review, 32,* 123–131.
Brooks, G. (1989). The value and purpose of oracy assessment. English *in Education, 23,* 87–93.
CCSI. (2015). Common core standards initiative. *English Arts Standards,* 23–24 and 49–50. Retrieved June 7, 2015 from www.corestandards.org/ELA-Literacy/
Celce-Murcia, M., Dornyei, Z., & Thurrell, S. (1995). Communicative competence: A pedagogically motivated model with content specifications. *Issues in Applied Linguistics, 6,* 5–35.
Cinamon, D., & Elding, S. (1998). Tracking talk. In J. Holderness & B. Lalljee (Eds.), *An introduction to Oracy: Frameworks for talk* (pp. 212–233). London: Cassell.
Clarke, S. (2001). *Unlocking formative assessment.* London: Hodder and Stoughton.
Communication Trust. (2013). *Speech, language and communication progression tools.* Retrieved April 10, 2014 from www.thecommunicationtrust.org.uk/

resources/resources/resources-for-practitioners/progression-tools-secondary/practitioners/universally-speaking/

Cummins, J. (1980). The cross-lingual dimensions of language proficiency: Implications for bilingual education and the optimal age issue. *TESOL Quarterly, 14,* 175–187.

Dawes, L. (2008). Encouraging students' contributions to dialogue during science. *School Science Review, 90,* 1–8.

Dawes, L. (2012). *Talking points: Discussion activities in the primary classroom.* London: David Fulton/Routledge.

Dawes, L., Dore, B., Loxley, P., & Nichols, L. (2010). A talk focus for promoting enjoyment and developing understanding in science. *English Teaching: Practice and Critique, 9,* 99–110.

DfES. (2003). *Speaking, listening, learning: Working with children in key stages 1 and 2.* London: Department for Education and Skills.

Education Department of Western Australia. (1997). *Oral language resource book.* Rigby: Heinemann.

Fulcher, G., Davidson, F., & Kemp, J. (2011). Effective rating scale development for speaking tests: Performance decision trees. *Language Testing, 28,* 5–29.

Goswami, U. (2009). Mind, brain, and literacy-biomarkers as usable knowledge for education. *Mind, Brain, and Education, 3,* 176–184.

Goswami, U., & Bryant, P. (2007). *Children's cognitive development and learning. Research report 2/1a: The primary review.* Cambridge: University of Cambridge.

Greatorex, J., Johnson, C., & Frame, K. (2001). Making the grade: Developing grade descriptors for accounting using a discriminator model of performance. *Westminster Studies in Education, 24,* 167–181.

Halliday, M. A. K. (1978). *Language as social semiotic.* London: Edward Arnold.

Harsch, C., & Martin, G. (2013). Comparing holistic and analytic scoring methods: Issues of validity and reliability. *Assessment in Education: Principles, Policy & Practice, 20,* 281–307.

Hart, B., & Risley, T. R. (1995). *Meaningful differences in the everyday experience of young American children.* New York, NY: Brookes.

Hatch, E., & Lazaraton, A. (1991). The *research manual: Design and statistics for applied linguistics.* New York, NY: Newbury House.

Housen, A., & Kuiken, F. (2009). Complexity, accuracy, and fluency in second language acquisition. *Applied Linguistics, 30,* 461–473.

Housen, A., Kuiken, F., & Vedder, I. (Eds.). (2012). *Dimensions of L2 performance and proficiency.* Amsterdam: John Benjamins.

Howe, A. (1991). *Making talk work: NATE papers in education.* London: National Association for the Teaching of English.

Howe, C., & Abedin, M. (2013). Classroom dialogue: A systematic review across four decades of research. *Cambridge Journal of Education, 43,* 325–356.

Hymes, D. (1977). *Foundations in sociolinguistics.* London: Tavistock.

IELTS. (2013). *Assessment criteria: Speaking.* Retrieved November 5, 2013 from www.ieltsessentials.com/pdf/BandcoreDescriptorsSpeaking.pdf

Latham, D. (2005). Speaking, listening and learning: A rationale for the speaking and listening profile. *English in Education, 39,* 60–74.

Maybin, J. (1988). A critical review of the DES assessment of performance Unit's oracy surveys. *English in Education, 22,* 3–18.

McNamara, T. (1997). "Interaction" in second language performance assessment: Whose performance? *Applied Linguistics, 18,* 446–466.

Mercer, N. (2008). Talk and the development of reasoning and understanding. *Human Development, 51*, 90–100.

Mercer, N. (2013). The social brain, language, and goal-directed collective thinking: A social conception of cognition and its implications for understanding how we think, teach and learn. *Educational Psychologist, 48*, 148–168.

Mercer, N., Dawes, L., & Staarman, J. K. (2009). Dialogic teaching in the primary science Classroom. *Language and Education, 23*, 353–369.

Mercer, N., & Littleton, K. (2007). *Dialogue and the development of children's thinking.* Abingdon: Routledge.

Monroe, S. (2009). *Discover your voice: Debating resources for Key Stage 2.* London: The English-Speaking Union Centre for Speech and Debate.

Norman, K. (Ed.). (1992). *Thinking voices: The work of the National Oracy Project.* London: Hodder & Stoughton.

Ofqual. (2013). *Analysis of responses to the consultation on the proposal to remove speaking and listening assessment from the GCSE English and GCSE English language grade.* Ofqual Report Number 13/5317. Retrieved January 7, 2014 from http://dera.ioe.ac.uk/17586/7/2013-08-29-analysis-of-responses-to-the-consultation-removal-of-speaking-and-listening.pdf

OECD (2014). *Education at a glance 2014: OECD indicators.* OECD Publishing. http://dx.doi.org/10.1787/eag-2014-en

Oliver, R., Haig, Y., & Rochecouste, J. (2005). Communicative competence in oral language assessment. *Language and Education, 19*, 212–222.

Pinker, S. (2007). *The stuff of thought: Language as a window into human nature.* London: Penguin.

QCDA. (2010). Qualifications and Curriculum Development Agency (*Introductory guidance for teachers (Active Shakespeare: Capturing evidence of learning).* https://dera.ioe.ac.uk//2606/

Rojas-Drummond, S., Littleton, K., Hernandez, F., & Zúniga, M. (2010). Dialogical interactions among peers in collaborative writing contexts. In K. Littleton & C. Howe (Eds.), *Educational dialogues: Understanding and promoting productive interaction* (pp. 128–148). Abingdon: Routledge.

Van den Bergh, H. (1987). *Large scale oracy assessment in The Netherlands.* Research and Technical Report 143. Amsterdam: SCO.

van der Wilt, F., van Kruistum, C., van der Veen, C., & van Oers, B. (2015). Gender differences in the relationship between oral communicative competence and peer rejection: An explorative study in early childhood education. *European Early Childhood Education Research Journal.* Published Online. http://doi.org/10.1080/1350293X.2015.1073507

Van Oers, B., Elbers, E., van der Veer, R., & Wardekker, W. (2008). The *transformation of learning: Advances in cultural-historical activity theory.* Cambridge: Cambridge University Press.

Vass, E., & Littleton, K. (2010). Peer collaboration and learning in the classroom. In K. Littleton, C. Wood, & J. K. Staarman (Eds.), *International handbook of psychology in education* (pp. 105–136). Leeds: Emerald.

Vygotsky, L. (1962). *Thought and language.* Cambridge, MA: MIT Press.

Whitebread, D., Mercer, N., Howe, C., & Tolmie, A. (2013). *Self-regulation and dialogue in primary classrooms.* British Journal of Educational Psychology Monograph Series II: Psychological Aspects of Education: Current Trends, 10. Leicester: British Psychological Society.

Wilkinson, A. (1965). *Spoken English*. Edgbaston, Birmingham: University of Birmingham.

Wilson, M., Neja, I., Scalise, K., Templin, J., Wiliam, D., & Torres Irribarra, D. (2012). Perspectives on methodological issues. In P. Griffin, B. McGraw, & E. Care (Eds.), *Assessment and teaching of 21st century skills* (pp. 67–141). New York, NY: Springer.

Wright, J., Brinkley, I., & Clayton, N. (2010). *Employability and skills in the UK: Redefining the debate*. London: The Work Foundation.

# Index

Note: numbers in italics indicate figures and numbers in bold indicate tables on the corresponding pages.